AGUECHEEK'S BEEF, BELCH'S HICCUP,

AND OTHER GASTRONOMIC

INTERJECTIONS

AGUECHEEK'S BEEF,

BELCH'S HICCUP,

and Other GASTRONOMIC

INTERJECTIONS

LITERATURE, CULTURE, AND FOOD
AMONG THE EARLY MODERNS

ROBERT APPELBAUM

THE UNIVERSITY OF CHICAGO PRESS
Chicago & London

ROBERT APPELBAUM
is Senior Lecturer in Renaissance Studies in the Department of English
and Creative Writing at Lancaster University. He is the author of
Literature and Utopian Politics in Seventeenth-Century England and
the co-editor of *Envisioning an English Empire: Jamestown and the
Making of a North Atlantic World.*

The University of Chicago Press, Chicago 60637
The University of Chicago Press, Ltd., London
© 2006 by The University of Chicago
All rights reserved. Published 2006
Printed in the United States of America

15 14 13 12 11 10 09 08 07 06   1 2 3 4 5

ISBN-13: 978-0-226-02126-3   (cloth)
ISBN-10: 0-226-02126-2   (cloth)

Library of Congress Cataloging-in-Publication Data

Appelbaum, Robert, 1952–
Aguecheek's beef, belch's hiccup, and other gastronomic interjections: literature,
culture, and food among the early moderns / Robert Appelbaum.
p. cm.
Includes bibliographical references and index.
ISBN 0-226-02126-2 (cloth: alk. paper)
1. Food in literature. 2. Food — Social aspects. I. Title.
PN56.F59A67 2006
809'.933559 — dc22
2006014543

For
Arthur H. Williamson,
historian, critic, Scot

Contents

Illustrations

Preface

EVERY NOW AND THEN, you will notice, a writer of the early modern period has something to say about food. It may be just to disclaim an unbecoming interest: I'm no glutton, the writer insists. Or the writer may be saying something about food in order to make a joke or to score a point against a political or religious enemy: a rival who's too fat or too thin, too ill-mannered or too extravagant or even a bit of each and altogether bizarre — "O monstrous!" says Shakespeare's Prince Hal about Falstaff. "But one half-penny-worth of bread to this intolerable deal of sack!" Or the writer may be objecting to an opponent who, whatever his real relation to food and drink may be, is in other things a hypocritical impostor, like a monk who feasts on butter and eggs and fine roasted sturgeon during what is supposed to be a fast day, and prides himself on his self-restraint; or an opponent who simply doesn't know what he is doing, like a presumably saintly matron who thinks that when she puts her tongue to the Communion wafer she is actually *eating God,* when she is really consuming (as far as the writer is concerned) an idol made of bread; or like a cranky Calvinist — for the allusions to food habits can work for any party on any side of the political and religious divides of the day — who thinks it is God's will that he should never enjoy himself and believes that eating and drinking have nothing to do with the body of the church and the salvation of the soul. The writer is really interested in something else — virtue, valor, personal advancement, amusement, faith, truth, doctrine, honor, or the humiliation of an opponent; the allusion serves an ulterior purpose. Yet the allusion is there. The allusions are all over the place in the sixteenth and seventeenth centuries. They speak of a reality, a form of material life, that is just below the surface, or perhaps not even just below but right there, at the same level as the polemics and the jokes. The food-oriented religious practices that the interjections allude to — the fish days, the ingestive sacraments, the ascetic self-restraint, or the rejection thereof in favor of divinely sanctioned pleasure — are not only vehicles for bemused or outraged putdowns; they are also commonly the object of concern. The writer interjects something about food in order to score a point regarding something else, yet the interjection is, finally, *about food too* — about what we do with it, what we want from it, what it means.

Meanwhile, writers may also be found to be saying something about food because of an overt interest in food itself, its cultivation, its preparation, its pleasures, its nutritional value, its ethnographic and cultural associations, its economic implications. The writer may have a mystical interest in food, imagining like the Neoplatonist Marsilio Ficino (1433–1499) that eating gold-colored substances may have a golden effect on the vital spirits within. The writer may well be an enthusiast — what some people dismissively call a glutton or what other, more worldly observers admiringly call a man or woman "of taste" — and wax poetic about salad herbs, mullet, or melon. The writer may be a doctor or an amateur healer, knowing as the old saw had it that "digestion is the root of life"; or he may be a hypochondriac, like the character in Molière, worried, as another saying had it, that "many dig their graves with their teeth." He may be a trader of goods — writers can be merchants too — a provisioner of ships, a dealer in sugar, rum, corn, or even slaves, hungry slaves, the state of whose souls might be ignored but whose bodies and productive power have to be fed and fed and fed. He or she may be a visitor to foreign lands, alarmed at how the Irish eat barbarously, without tables, taking crudely cooked meats "upon a bundle of grass," and then using "the same Grasse for napkins to wipe their hands" (according to the persnickety English traveler Fynes Moryson),[1] or how the French inexplicably delight in mushrooms and snails, the English dine on nothing but mutton and beef, and the Tupinamba Indians of Brazil organize their life around a ritual appetite for human flesh. Or again, the writer may just be a novelist — just! — pledged to that newfangled way of writing of the early moderns that Ian Watt long ago called "formal realism," concerned at all points with the minutiae of daily life and therefore with biscuits, raisins, and sausage, and the daily matter of experiencing and satisfying hunger. In *Simplicissimus,* a novel written in Germany in 1669, the eponymous hero, living through the violent displacements of the Thirty Years' War, goes through periods of starvation, extravagance, and back again several times: we follow him as he subsists in the woods on berries and water, as he works as a waiter to the rich and powerful, standing by while the latter feast on veal and mutton and then leave people like himself their scraps; we follow him as he leads a squadron of hard-up soldiers raiding the pantries of innocent tradespeople, filching sides of bacon, lest they starve to death, and even often enough as he himself acquires wealth and security and with a hearty appetite eats and eats and eats.

Food in the early modern period, it is clear, was not only a biological function, or an economic reality answering to a biological function, but also the object of a discourse. Or, better yet, it was the object of a multitude of discourses: stage plays, religious polemics, mystical tracts, cookbooks, medical texts, herbals, travelogues, novels, to name a few of the genres; primitivist legend, humoral physiology, Christian asceticism, utopian speculation, to name a few of the intellectual traditions or "discursive formations" entailed, as Michel Foucault once characterized them.[2] We can examine these discourses as evidence of something they represent—the real eating and drinking of early modern individuals, the real experience of hunger and desire, of pleasure and discomfort, of self-regulation and self-indulgence, of joy and guilt. And it is frequently to this "real" experience that our attention will be drawn in the pages that follow, as well any book aiming to discuss the "gastronomic" ought to do. Not a few recipes and descriptions of meals will be included in the pages to follow, which should provide ample material for the culinary imagination. But we can also examine these discourses in and of themselves: their forms, their material support, their propagation, their symbolic power. For it turns out that food in this period, as in any other—yet in its own way, in keeping with its own specific material conditions, assumptions, attitudes, and languages—bears a unique identity or set of identities. You will find that writers frequently allude to food not only because it is convenient to do so, but because they must; and that when they do so, they allude to a phenomenon as unique to themselves as mannerist painting or Tudor architecture or any other historically situated product of culture. The food itself is unique, made in unique ways or according to unique technologies, served and consumed by way of unique networks of behavior, sensation, and meaning. And the discourse that works with the food, taking food and food practices as its object, is unique, formulated according to historically and geographically specific conventions, and ascribing to food a unique set of objective identities.

It is to the character of these identities—complex and polysemic, at once material and symbolic, at once rigidly reproduced and malleably experienced, at once the outcomes of material practices and the subjects of language—that the present study is addressed.

For a proper introduction to the study, if I may be indulged, the reader should turn to chapter 1 of this volume, which begins with Shakespeare and the remarks about "beef" in *Twelfth Night* and about "baked meat" in *Hamlet,* but which includes a good deal of introductory material for the whole of the volume. There, again, I find a writer, and a writer's characters, saying something about food, making in effect an *interjection* about food. The interjection has a meaning; in fact it has many meanings. What are they? Why? What does the interjection tell us about the writer, the character, the writing, the culture? What does it tell us about food? About food and culture? About literature, food, and culture? In exploring the answers to these questions in this opening chapter, I discuss again how the identities of food in the period, even including the material arrangements made to put food on the table, were largely a product of the discourses — the intersecting genres and discursive formations — that expressed them. Demonstrating this I then elaborate two potentially contradictory ideas. On the one hand, even when engaged in by a single writer with a singular sensibility, the discourses entailed could operate at cross-purposes to one another. There is, for example, in the work of William Shakespeare, both a *comedy* of food and a *tragedy* of food, the one celebrative, the other mournful; the one hungry, as it were, the other nauseous; or, to put it another way, the one devoted to the joy of living, the other resigned to contempt for the foulness of the world. But even so, on the other hand, there is throughout this period — and indeed in most any period, and certainly within the otherwise contradictory work of a writer like Shakespeare — a phenomenon I refer to as *aesthetic community,* a convergence of networks of more or less voluntarily shared (and thereby symbolically asserted) sensations, feelings, and perceptions. Social regulations, economic conditions, and the commonalities of educated desire all go to encourage the formation of the aesthetic community of a culture. So again, on the one hand, looking at the identity of food in this period, one finds variety, divergence, competition, and contradiction; and, on the other, one finds community, structure, agency, regulation, and consent. What is wonderful about all this, really, is that the early moderns experienced food with great intensity and perspicuity. They wrote about it with an impressive awareness of the social, philosophical, and religious issues that eating and drinking in the human world can raise, not to mention a vivid alertness to the sensations of foodstuffs — their taste, their smell, their texture — and the digestive processes they demanded. Indeed, the science of the day dictated that even uneducated peoples would be preoccupied with how food made them feel, from the moment they first espied and scented the food product to the very end of digestion — which came not only in the movement of the bowels but also, according to that science, in perspiration and hair growth and intellectual activity and sensations of well-being and vigor, or of "obstruction" and lassitude, not to mention moods and dispositions: a "hot" temper, a coldly fear of water, a high-blooded sex drive. Food was a profound experience for the early moderns, even if it was also commonly suspected for its superficiality, for the temptations toward distraction and frivolousness that it placed before the individual. The experience of food reached as deep into the individual as the vitalities of the genitals, the brain, and the soul. It betokened the very inwardness of human life. The divine and original gift of consciousness was communicated through the

deep and inward experience people had with food; and so was the profane, original corruption — the constitutive pathology of human life — that sinful humanity brought upon itself.

The early modern period — beginning about 1450 with the invention of
print and the first stirrings of what is customarily called the Renaissance and
ending sometime in the early eighteenth century — constituted a unique chapter
in the history of food and food practices. It was the period when people stopped
eating with their hands and starting using forks, when diners stopped piling their
food on trenchers of bread from which the gravy was then unceremoniously
licked and started using plates of pewter, porcelain, and glass, from which gravy
could be taken by spoon or a forked piece of meat; it was a time when lords of
great estates stopped inviting armies of neighbors and retainers to eat dinner
together in the cavernous expanses of a great hall and started eating separately,
in private rooms, leaving their neighbors and their retainers to do likewise and
fend for themselves. In the early modern period, explorers and settlers brought
pigs, sheep, cows, chickens, and wheat to colonize the continents of North and
South America, and early traders brought back potatoes, tomatoes, squash,
beans, chocolate, maize, and turkey to load the tables of Europe. The ecologies
as well as the agricultural and trading practices of the Americas and Europe
underwent revolutionary change. The diet became more and more commodi-
fied, as well as varied; that is to say, it came to depend less on local products, locally harvested and prepared, than on far-fetched goods, many of them pre-
processed, which were bought and sold in the market by virtue of abstract
notions of quantity, quality, and price. Meanwhile, the role of the cook was transformed. The cook became a professional. Toward the end of the period, coffee-
houses, restaurants, and celebrity chefs and hosts appeared on the scene. Cookbooks became a serious business. And from the beginning of the early modern
era, so did diet books. The great humanist and scientific minds of the period, not
to mention a number of amateur hacks, were eager to bend their talents toward
explaining what people should eat, and when, and how. They had a scientific
guide to follow: the newly rediscovered works of Galen, the Greco-Roman physician of the second century A.D. They also had ideas of their own. The Florentine Ficino devised his own rules for the diet, the better to chase away the blues
and keep body and mind alight. So, a century later, did no less a figure than
Sir Francis Bacon (1561–1626), the guiding spirit of the scientific revolution. If
many early dietary writers cribbed from the ancients and did their best to hold
to received ideas about humors and temperaments and the magic properties of
"signatures," by the seventeenth century what was taken to be an independent,
experimental science of the diet held sway: some writers then began recom-

mending vegetarianism, others a fixed quantity of various foodstuffs measured out daily by weight, and some the cultivation of a civilized, epicurean "appetite," in contrast to the savage or rustic and unsatisfactory experience of "hunger."

The story of early modern food and food practices has often been identified with what Norbert Elias called the "civilizing process," and throughout the study to follow, a number of phenomena will be brought to light that confirm that characterization. Eating and drinking became more "civilized" in the course of the early modern period to the extent that it came to approximate the laws of sociality of the emerging modern nation-state and its "civil society": laws, for example, observed in public spaces like the modern restaurant, of polite indifference to others. But a number of phenomena will be brought to light that don't quite fit the "civilizing" model or that challenge its assumptions: for example, the contrast between high culture and low and between center and periphery that most developments of the model take for granted. Peasants had something like civility too, a civility of their own, even if they had no restaurants and no cities. But in any case, a story that is both similar to and different from the Eliasian narrative will enfold in the pages to follow—perhaps a more ambiguous narrative, and certainly one that will be concerned less with the nation-state and more with transnational, local, and especially hybrid food relations. It will also be less quick to take developments in the Île-de-France as a model of general historical process. England, Italy, the Low Countries, Germany, and the Americas will all be rifled for evidence in the story that is about to unfold as well as France. (I limit myself here so far as my competence as a historian and linguist and the constraints of time have limited my range.)

The story that unfolds is neither a good nor a bad one, in my view. It is a story neither of progress—even in Paris and Lyon—nor of degradation. It is simply the story of what happened. There were costs we can regret, like slavery and commodification and, in general, suffering (for the history of food in this period was often a history of suffering). There were achievements we can celebrate, like the invention of gastronomy or of "civilization" in its positive aspects. (It is of course equally possible to admire commodification and lament gastronomy, as the multinational food industry encourages us to do, and there have been strands of thought in the West that have even respected slavery while deploring "civilization.") But one way or the other, it is an interesting story, as well as, I hope the reader will agree, a story that matters, for if it is a story told about a remote era, it is also, inevitably, a story we tell about ourselves. I do not expect readers of this book to run out and try some of the recipes I include, although some may well end up doing so. I do hope that they will find occasions to think about the many meanings of food, the many languages it entails, and to consider both the imperatives and the perhaps insuperable difficulties involved (as I discuss in the conclusion to this book) in practicing an artful mindfulness with regard to one's food, in being, as Jean-Jacques Rousseau would put it, "philosophical" about it. This study will show, to put it in the simplest of terms, that food in the early modern period was many things, from an object of delight to an object of contempt, from a symbol of happy sociality to a token of selfish gluttony, from a commodity to be calculated in terms of its weight and bulk to a kind of medicine that, when taken in the right dosage, could all but guarantee a long and vigorous life. Thinking about food, examining the food practices of foreign peoples, experimenting with new forms of economic and therefore with gastronomic activity, early moderns encountered both the idea of an indescribable gustatory joy and the spectacle of the most reprehensible transgressions that humans — all humans, European and non-European alike — were capable of committing: the eating of "strange flesh," in contempt of profound taboos; the eating of the expressly forbidden, in contempt of obedience owed to God; the eating of other human beings, apparently in contempt of humanity itself. Most of this has nothing to do with us today, to be sure, at least not directly. But it is food for thought. And if then readers thinking about the foodways of the early moderns also begin to look at early modern literature and culture as a whole in a new light, all I can say is that such a beginning is what from the start I have really wanted to offer up to them: and bon appétit!

Acknowledgments

FINANCIAL SUPPORT for work on this volume came from a variety of sources, and I am deeply grateful to each of them: the Research Council of the University of Cincinnati, the National Endowment for the Humanities, the Folger Shakespeare Library, the Newberry Library, the Center for the Humanities at Wesleyan University, and the Faculty Research Fund of Lancaster University. Institutional support was also provided by the Department of English at the University of Michigan.

The libraries of the University of California, Berkeley, and the University of California, San Francisco, including the Bancroft Library at the former and the Rare Books Room of the latter, were where my research began. I then was fortunate to be able to take advantage of facilities at the Folger Shakespeare Library, the Newberry Library, the Huntington Library, the libraries of the University of California, San Diego, and the University of San Diego, the Beinecke Library at Yale University, the British Library, Special Collections at the Leeds University Library, and the historical collections of the Shakespeare Birthplace Trust in Stratford-upon-Avon.

Among the many people who helped me along the way, I have to point out in particular Terri Zucker, Valerie Traub, Rachana Sachdev, Karen Kupperman, John Wood Sweet, Pompa Banerjee, Eric Griffin, Peter Herman, Kate Narveson, Peter Hoyt, Jill Morawski, Maurice Slawinski, who helped me with my Italian, Michiel van Groesen, who helped me with things Dutch, and the staffs at the Folger Institute and the Center for the Humanities at Wesleyan. In addition, I must cite moral support from Nigel Smith and Andrew Hadfield and, in my own department at Lancaster, Alison Findlay, Hilary Hinds, and the redoubtable Richard Wilson.

There were audiences to which I presented some of this material and many people whose questions and comments helped me clarify and elaborate my work.

I should single out the audiences at Susquehanna University, the Society for Utopian Studies, the San Diego Shakespeare Society, Mira Costa College, California State University, San Marcos, the Group for Early Modern Cultural Studies at several locations, Wesleyan University, and the University of Neuchâtel.

Editors and readers at several journals where some of my ideas first appeared were instrumental in getting this study into shape: *Textual Practice, Textus,* the *Milton Quarterly,* and the *Journal of Early Modern Cultural Studies.*

Above all, I have to thank two scholars who are also experts in the field of early modern food studies who have been more generous toward me and my project than I had any right to expect, Ken Albala and Michael C. Schoenfeldt. The former read the entire manuscript, made many helpful suggestions, corrected a number of errors, and gave me much to think about on the whole, all in a spirit of exemplary liberality. Mike Schoenfeldt did all that too. And he was supportive of my labors since the very beginning, helping me raise funds, define projects, find places to work, think through issues, and reach into myself for the strength to persist. Thank you, Mike.

And Marion, *surtout.*

A Note on the Texts

I HAVE MODERNIZED spelling throughout. Whenever possible, I have used either the original first-edition text or a modern authoritative edition. But that has not always been possible. Where the translator of a foreign-language text is not cited, the translation — for better or worse — is my own.

Chapter One

AGUECHEEK'S BEEF,
HAMLET'S BAKED MEAT

I

"I AM A GREAT EATER OF BEEF," Sir Andrew Aguecheek says to his companion Sir Toby Belch, "and I believe that does great harm to my wit."[1] You might think the matter would end there. Sir Andrew has confessed something silly about himself, and the audience laughs. "I am a great eater of beef." If Sir Andrew is played in the usual way, the audience immediately registers the comic disparity: a great eater of beef; a thin, craven, and silly man. They register, too, the ridiculous disjunction implied by the inference. "I believe that does great harm to my wit." The idea is absurd. How can eating beef do harm to your "wit," your intelligence or mind? The inference doesn't follow; at best its very stupidity confirms the idea that Sir Andrew's intelligence is defective. But Sir Toby immediately responds, "No question." And then, turning the tables on the whole exchange, Sir Andrew disavows the sentiment: "An I thought that [i.e., that beef harms the wit]," he insists, "I'd forswear it." Well, what is it, then? Does Sir Andrew believe what he says? Does Sir Toby? Does beef affect the intelligence? How so? And what's so funny about this business, anyway?

In an earlier article, I once documented the trials and tribulations of scholars as they tried to make sense of the passage.[2] I mean scholars going as far back as the early eighteenth century. Almost all of them tried to explain the passage by begging the question. Given Sir Andrew's claims that beef eating harmed his wit, scholar after scholar glossed the line by saying, in effect, that during Shakespeare's day it was believed that beef eating harmed one's wits. But not one of se Polemone,& Adamantio. La cagion naturale n'asſegnarei coſì, che biſogna quella parte del capo per eſſer ben formata, che fuſſe leggiermente acciacata, acciò la cogitatiua fuſſe retta; mà eſſendo alta dimoſtra nell'intelletto alcun mancamento.

Capo piano.

L'altro eſtremo ſarà ſe fuſſe ſouerchiamente depreſſo in quel luogo. E però diſſe Alberto. Il capo humile, e quaſi piano è d'inſolenti giouani, e ſenza freno.

Della Fronte.   Cap. II.

QVella ſi dice faccia nell'huomo, che ſtà ſotto la caluaria parte della faccia è la fronte, che è locata ſotto il capello, terminata da gl'occhi, e dalle tempie, come Ariſtotele ne inſegna nel libro de gl'animali. Chiamaſi fronte, come diſſe Varrone, dal forame de gl'occhi, e porge molto giouamento nel conoſcere i coſtumi dell'animo. Plinio ragionando della fronte; ne dà ſegno di meſtitia, e d'allegrezza, clemenza, e ſeuerità. La fronte fù anticamente ſacrata alla vergogna, come ne moſtra il volgar prouerbio contro coloro, che hanno perduto ogni vergogna. S'han fregata la fronte, come ſe con la mano haueſſero nettato dalla fronte la vergogna. Sono alcuni ſcrittori che dalle linee, che ſi veggono ſegnate in lei, fanno vaticinij della lor vita, che ſi chiamano Metopoſcopi non che per quelle fuſſero ſforzati, come da neceſſità coſì eſſere; mà per vna certa inchinatione, & allettamento di ſangue, e di ſpirituali naturali.

In queſta tauoletta, che v'incontra, ci è dipinta la fronte grande dell'huomo, inſieme con la figura della fronte bouina, nella quale manifeſtamente ſi vede la ſcambieuole grandezza, e coſì nelle reſtanti tauolette ſi vedranno l'altre ſorti de fronti.

Fronte grande.

Quelli che ſono di gran fronte, ſono codatdi, e timidi, peche queſti ſegni, e queſti

---

Figure 1.1 Portrait of man and ox, from Giambattista della Porta's *De humana physiognomia* (1586). Reproduced by permission of Special Collections, Leeds University Library.

them was able to substantiate the claim. What they were able to find was something different: an idea going back at least as far as the great medical authority Galen (129–ca. 210 A.D.) and repeated in author after author from the Middle Ages to the time when *Twelfth Night* was written that beef, in the words of the sixteenth-century writer Thomas Elyot, "maketh gross blood, and engendreth melancholy."[3] That medical authorities equated beef eating with grossness and melancholy is very interesting information, if also, by our standards, somewhat peculiar. A foodstuff makes a "blood," possibly a "gross blood"; it is capable of affecting one's emotional health, causing "melancholy" among other things. How so? With information like this, we begin to confront the idea that among premodern peoples a different system from ours for understanding food, digestion, and the relation of food to health was prevalent. Food makes "blood"; "blood" affects emotional health; the wrong food causes a mood disorder. But the information about gross blood and melancholy says nothing about the effect of beef eating on intelligence, although scholars clearly tried to pretend that somehow it did: a problem made more difficult by the fact that premodern thinkers traditionally associated melancholy with intellectual ambition.[4]

Yet the cause is not lost. Had the scholars dug a bit harder, they might have discovered a book written by the Italian physician Gugliemo Grataroli (1516–1568), translated into English as *A Direction for the Health of Magistrates and Studentes* and published in 1574. "As for gross meats that are dry and hard as cow's Beef and such like," Grataroli writes in his advice to educated eaters, "I utterly disallow: because beside many other harms that it bringeth by reason of the hardness of it, and difficulty to be digested, this namely is one, that it inferreth harm to the reasonable part of man which is the mind."[5] To "infer" harm in Elizabethan English means to "bring" or "convey" it. "Cow's Beef," Grataroli insists, "and such like"—whatever else he is talking about here—are "gross," "dry," and "hard" and therefore "infer" problems, including, most importantly, a decline in mental capacity. So here is the basis of Sir Andrew's assertion: in the terms of traditional scholarship, the "source" of Sir Andrew's remark.

Even so, however, the question is far from settled. In his next utterance, Sir Andrew disavows the idea. "An I thought that, I'd forswear it." Why should anyone — Sir Andrew or Sir Toby or for that matter Shakespeare and his audience — believe that meats like beef harm the rational faculty? No other expert on the diet available to Shakespeare besides Grataroli was making such a claim or for that matter was using standard Galenic language to suggest a connection between food and intelligence. Beef is "gross"? Beef is "hard"? It is difficult to digest? "It inferreth harm to the reasonable part of man which is the mind"? How, the astute Elizabethan audience might be prompted to wonder, do the so-called authorities come up with these ideas?

There is counterevidence too. Whatever Gugliemo Grataroli thought, contemporary English writers as well as English custom dictated a more enthusiastic attitude toward beef consumption. "Beef is a good meat for an Englishman," the Montpellier-trained physician Andrew Boorde asserts.[6] Another physician, Thomas Cogan, makes an even stronger case, asserting the superiority of beef not only as nutrition but as a vehicle of prestige and national pride:

> Beef is of all flesh the most usual among English men. . . . I need not to show how plentiful it is throughout this land, before all other countries, and how necessary it is both by sea and for the victualing of ships, and by land for good housekeeping, insomuch that no man of honor, or worship, can be said to have good provision for hospitality, unless there be good store of beef in readiness. And how well it doth agree with the nature of Englishmen the common consent of all our nation doth sufficiently prove.[7]

English cookbooks of the time were in fact filled with recipes for beef: roasted, boiled, stewed, minced and baked in pies. A first-course menu in a cookbook published in 1594 stipulates the following order of dishes for a single service: "Pottage or stewed broth. Boiled meat or stewed meat. Chicken and Bacon. Powdered [salted] Beef. Pies, Beef, Pig, Roasted Beef, Roasted Veal, Custard."[8] So common was beef a part of the English diet that by the late sixteenth century the French were making fun of Englishmen, calling them "roastbeefs," and the satirist Thomas Nashe, concerned about the costs of overeating as well as the implications of carnality, was worried that the English should be known in the rest of the world as a people given to "bury" their "Spirits in Beef-pots."[9]

So Aguecheek's jest about beef, to the extent that it took a swipe at beef eating, was in fact taking a swipe at the habits of a good part of the play's audience. And it was taking swipes at them in a place where it was almost sure to hurt: their very Englishness, their very adoption of and identification with the singular practices of the southern half of the isle of Britain. When medical writers stipulated that beef was good to eat, they qualified the remark to say that it was good to eat for English people *because* they were English. They often argued that either habit or climate or local breeding practices changed the relationship of beef to digestion among the English. Even if beef caused "gross blood," according to the classic medical writers of the Mediterranean, whom the English generally took as their authorities, custom had habituated the English stomach to it, and so

Figure 1.2 *Grace Before the Meal,* by Anthonius Claessins (1581). The portrait is Dutch, not English, and the fittings of the room are somewhat different from what one would expect in Tudor England at the time, but this pious Protestant family well represents the curious mingling of religious and familial sentiment with lusty beef-eating sensuality that any prosperous northern European household would have been proud to be remembered for. That's one fine prime rib of beef occupying the center of the table. Reproduced by permission of the Shakespeare Birthplace Trust.

rendered beef less harmful or even beneficial. Custom is "of such force in man's body both in sickness and in health, that it countervaileth nature itself," Elyot avers; "in meat and drink every man feeleth in himself, that whereunto he hath been of long time accustomed, though it be not so good as other, yet doth it less harm than that whereunto he is not used."[10] And if custom alone didn't do the job, then the fact that England was a relatively cold country made English stomachs "hotter" or more "choleric" and therefore well-suited to such an otherwise "cold" and "gross" meat like beef. "The situation of our region, lying near to the north," writes William Harrison, "doth cause the heat of our stomachs to be of somewhat greater force; therefore our bodies do crave a little more ample nourishment than the inhabitants of the hotter regions are accustomed withal."[11] Moreover, English cattle were raised differently than other cattle; indeed, they were raised specifically for eating, with leisurely grazing, so that they were more tender and fat. Thus, Cogan adds that "all these authors, (in mine opinion) have erred in that they make the beef of all countries alike. For had they eaten of the beef of England, or if they had dwelt in this our climate, which through cold-ness . . . doth fortify digestions, and therefore requires stronger nourishment, I suppose they would have judged otherwise. . . ."[12]

Long-term regional differences in attitudes toward meat eating over and above the claims of medical science are a part of the story here. In the Italy of an authority like Grataroli (himself a religious refugee in Basel at the time he wrote *A Direction* but still recognizably Italian in many of his views), people had for centuries, even millennia, taken a Roman pride in subscribing to a relatively light diet, short of melancholic, lethargy-inducing red meat, but heavy on grains, wine, oil, vegetables, fish, and fowl. "Good thrifty men," Nashe says of Italians (and Spaniards along with them), "they draw out a dinner with salads. . . ."[13] They drew it out with bread as well. Another English traveler, Fynes Moryson, "pass-ing through Italy so famous for temperance," was somewhat aghast that al-though "we might have a Pullet and some flesh prepared for us, eating it with a moderate proportion of bread, the Italians at the same time, with a Charger full of herbs for a salad, and with roots, and like meats [i.e., foods] of small price, would each of them eat two or three penny-worth of bread."[14] Although the Ital-ian upper classes, like those in the rest of Europe at the time, seem to have ac-counted meat eating prestigious and indulged in it somewhat ostentatiously, by northern European standards even wealthy Italians were sparing in their diet as far as red-meat consumption was concerned. They clearly preferred lighter meats and a diet higher in complex carbohydrates and vegetables; along with their poorer country people, with the exception of certain regions like Tuscany, they generally eschewed eating "gross," "hard," and disease-inducing beef alto-gether.[15] Veal was a little different. Veal, as the Italian Bartolomeo Platina puts it, "is more safely eaten because it is almost of medium nourishment, and so the tables of the nobility seek it frequently, with no harm."[16] But beef was seldom indulged in. Oxen were raised and used as pack animals in Italy, not as livestock. "Great Herds of cattle are brought into Italy out of Hungary," Moryson ob-serves, "and from divers Countries of the Alps, but the Hungarian Oxen growing lean with driving far, and finding in Italy no Pastures wherein they may be fat-tened, this makes Italians basely to esteem of Beef."[17] In the most popular Italian cookbook of the sixteenth century, *Epulario,* though directions for preparing pork, veal, fish, and fowl are included (not to mention such vegetarian dishes as *macheroni Romaneschi*), there is thus not a single recipe for beef at all.[18] But it wasn't just agricultural exigencies or a preference for what we now call "the Mediterranean diet" that prevented Italians from consuming beef. Cicero and Varro both noted with respect an ancient taboo against beef eating, which persisted to their own day since killing and eating such "partners" in life as oxen would be inhumane.[19] That taboo clearly made itself felt both in agricultural practices and in psychosomatic responses to beef prevalent among Italians. The heat in Italy, "which persists for almost nine months of the year," the Italian writer Giacomo Castelvetro writes somewhat apologetically to English readers in a book discussing Italian food practices, "has the effect of making meat seem quite repellent, especially beef, which in such a temperature one can hardly bear to look at, let alone eat."[20] The taboo had made beef into an object of disgust. Though early modern people could not have known this, the Italians' mental disgust was reinforced auto-somatically, since beef requires a special enzyme to be digested, and sometimes individuals temporarily lose the ability to produce that enzyme if they go without eating beef for a while. The English had indeed become "hotter" with respect to beef, so far as their digestive systems were accustomed to producing the necessary enzymes. Conversely, Italians were "cold" to beef in part because they had trouble digesting it. Beef gave them stomachaches. "Gross meats that are dry and hard as cow's Beef and such like," as Grataroli puts it, again, "I utterly disallow: because beside many other harms that it bringeth by reason of the hardness of it, and difficulty to be digested. . . ." Whatever science a writer like Grataroli might have brought to bear on his analysis, much of what he wrote clearly stemmed from experience. Italians would not eat beef. They had no beef to eat. And they could not eat beef; it was too hard for them to digest.

But: "I am a great eater of beef and I think it does harm to my wit, yet if I really believed that I would forswear it." Well, what is it? The Italians had plenty of reasons for believing bad things about beef. "Beef is of a cool and dry nature," Platina had asserted, "being very hard both to cook and to digest. It offers gross, disturbed, and melancholic nourishment. It drives a person toward quartan fever, eczema, and scaly skin disease. . . ."[21] And no less an authority than Marsilio Ficino was at the same time stressing that "food badly digested dulls the sharpness of the mind with many dense vapors and such humors."[22] Yet English people, by contrast, had come to be adapted to beef consumption, with no evident ill effects; and their preferences had come to be reinforced by a vast social, economic, and cultural apparatus, which in their case extended from the prestige value of the "hospitality" associated with it to the long tradition of agricultural and economic practices that made it readily available. (It is not rarity alone that elevates the social value of a foodstuff; in many cases availability is actually more important.) The English took pride in their beef eating, often associating it with virility and strength as well as virtuous liberality and hence with the special valor of the English way of life.[23] "Bull's beef"—a rare treat—was thought to be especially effective in imparting masculine vigor and aggression. It was proverbial that a person with threatening anger in his countenance was someone who looked "as big as he had eaten bull beef"; the idea is related to our current word "bully," meaning a threatening ruffian.[24] And when writers like Harrison explain the difference between English stomachs and those of ancient Mediterranean authorities, they are clearly, with male pride, accounting English stomachs to be stronger than others, and to that extent more virile. Scholars like Grataroli, still subscribing to the ancient Mediterranean model, could thus say what they wanted. The people of England would keep their own counsel.

So Sir Andrew Aguecheek is expressing the following, in effect: "If I really thought that beef harmed the mind, I'd forswear it. I know what your authorities of Italy are saying. It makes me feel a little shabby sometimes. However, I do what I please. In doing what I please I assert, well, my virility. Do I not?" The thread continues in this and subsequent scenes. Food is a choice of personal style, the play emphasizes, and personal style is an indicator of sophistication and manliness. Sophistication is never far from Aguecheek's mind, partly because he has so little of it and partly because sophistication could detract from the qualities of manliness that are also seldom far from his mind. "Art thou good at these kickshawses, knight?" Sir Toby asks, as they continue their patter. And the word "kickshawses" refers primarily to food, from the "quelque choses" or side dishes of French cuisine; it refers only secondarily to conduct. "As any man in Illyria," Sir Andrew says. "Faith, I can cut a caper." He means he can do the dance, although Sir Toby immediately thinks of the pickled condiment, good with mutton. "And I think I have the back-trick simply as strong as any man in Illyria," he adds. He means another dance, although the "back-trick" may have other meanings.[25] And his leg, "'tis strong." It all adds up, doesn't it? On the one hand, I am a man; I am as good as any man; I am a gallant. On the other hand, my gallantry and indeed my manliness are evinced through my talent as a dancer and evoked metaphorically and perhaps directly caused by what I eat and drink—capers, mutton, "kickshawses," and above all beef. After all, as Sir Toby interjects, "were we not born under Taurus?" Ah yes, the bull. Our insecurities aside, we don't just eat the stuff, though that would be enough to the extent that "life consists of eating and drinking."[26] We were positively born under the sign of it. Appearances to the contrary, we are natural-born bullies. No question.

II

Food can make us laugh. Our need for food and the devices we muster to satisfy the need are instances of that "automatism" of the human organism whose representation, according to the philosopher Henri Bergson, is the foundation of laughter.[27] Aguecheek's original audience probably laughed, and even today audiences generally laugh (outbreaks of "mad cow disease" aside), because in drawing a causal connection between food consumption and personal identity, Aguecheek's jest reduces mental life to the level of objects, which obey objective mechanical laws. The remark entails a Bergsonian objectification of oxen (reducing these live, cooperative, and personable creatures to the status of meat, an impersonal item of consumption), for the sake of a Bergsonian objectification of hunger. It is only (if the word "only" is fair here) an added comic charm that the remark also puts into play a variety of disparities and potentially of anxieties (about England's relation to the cultural authority of the Mediterranean writers, or about virility and consumption) that makes it obey the rules of laughter explained in Freud's *Jokes and Their Relation to the Unconscious*. The confidence of the jest is indicative of underlying insecurities. "I am a great eater of beef. . . ." What does such a remark, for example, say about our impulses and anxieties with regard to "greatness." A "great eater"? Some are born great, as the play later suggests in its most famous lines, some are made great, and some have greatness thrust upon them. And isn't great eating — in a nation where beef eating is a sign of prosperity, liberality, and prowess — at once an expression of the impulse toward greatness and a travesty of the very notion of greatness, a travesty already embodied in the craven, silly character of the aristocratic, British-nominated Sir Andrew? (Although he seems to be an English gentleman, his name is actually Scottish. So we perhaps also have a case of a spindly Scotsman trying to act the part of a burly beef-eating Englishman: which only accentuates the joke all the more.) The comedy is dense, invoking a dense sort of laughter. Anxieties about masculinity, national identity, consumption, cultural authority, and the very object-ness of our Bergsonian object-ness underscore the Freudian significance of the audience's identification with and distance from the silly little man. But food then isn't only funny; the very humor that may be found in it is based on more serious matters.

It even entails what may be called a "hermeneutics of everything" effect. This discussion of the meaning of Aguecheek's beef could be carried on indefinitely, and it could be carried on indefinitely because the subject of food ultimately requires us to think about everything that is human, everything that is meaningful, everything that is subject to interpretation. Food is a phenomenon that exists at the border of the symbolic and the material. Indeed, although the materiality of life — the basis of human life in the human need for physical *things* — would seem to predominate in our relation with food, in our relation to food, materiality, in fact, is endlessly consumed by the world of symbols.[28] Let us be as specific about this as we can. The association of beef with virility, with national pride, with rivalry between northern European and southern

European customs, with hospitality, with good nourishment, with a requirement of the palate and a place of honor in a feast, and, more negatively, from an Italian point of view, with melancholy and gross blood, with sluggishness and stupidity, with overeating—all of this has little to do with the specific physical properties of eaters and things eaten. It has to do mainly with cultural appropriations of physicality.

When we examine what a culture eats and, along with that, what it says and thinks about what it eats, we find that nearly everything it does or says or thinks about food has been absorbed into a body of symbolic articulations. The reason for this is partly to be found in the nature of language and discourse, which symbolically consume everything that falls in their way, making foodstuffs "good to think with," as Lévi-Strauss would put it;[29] but it is also partly to be found in the nature of eating. "This way of eating on our feet, furiously, burning our mouths and throats, without time to breathe," Primo Levi writes, recalling his experience at Auschwitz, when food was only grudgingly and sporadically thrown in the way of laboring prisoners like himself, "that was *fressen,* the way of eating of animals, and certainly not *essen,* the human way of eating, seated in front of a table, religiously."[30] Animals feed; and except under dehumanized conditions, humans eat—"religiously," as Levi puts it, which is to say, with regularity, with respect for the occasion, with a semiotic as well as an ethical deference to the process. If there is something brutishly physical about the act of eating, a confrontation between a gastrological apparatus and the substance of the world, there is also in most cases of eating a symbolic dimension that determines the form, the duration, the location, the ceremonial significance, and even many of the sensual qualities of the physical confrontation. This symbolic dimension may be cooperative, coercive, or merely habitual and customary; but however it is conveyed and enforced, it is a nearly universal aspect of human behavior. To eat is not only to consume; it is also to communicate—with others, with oneself, with the nutritive substance of the world—and to communicate is to engage in a symbolic activity, determined by a symbolic structure of meaningful activity. "If there is no society without a language," Lévi-Strauss writes, "nor is there any which does not cook in some manner at least some of its food." Accordingly, food is related to culture in much the same way as language is related to culture. Indeed, food is itself a kind of language, a system of communication.[31]

Food is not a *closed* system of communication, however. Anthropological studies often have to struggle with this idea: for they are based on the very useful concept of the "foodway" of a culture: a relatively closed or finite system, comprised of the chains of events, messages, and material facts involved in provisioning a people.[32] The "foodway" model is especially helpful in that it ties the culinary life of a culture together as a whole; it highlights interrelatedness. It thereby explains the conservative function of food: social groups sustain traditional identity by availing themselves of a traditional system of food production, preparation, consumption, and symbolization. But the example of Sir Andrew's remark cautions us against adopting the idea too strictly. For if there is doubtless an element of English self-awareness in Sir Andrew's remarks and a humorous appeal to or parody of English national identity, there is also an element of self-assertion and even defiance in what he says. "*I* am a great eater of beef, and *I* believe that does great harm to *my* wit." But if "*I* thought that, *I'd* forswear it." Foodways are powerful determinants of behavior; but they operate in concert and sometimes in conflict with personal choice and the innovations of self-assertion, of personal identity.

Moreover, foodways operate in flux. A well-known article on food habits among Italian Americans in Philadelphia shows how, in order to accommodate cultural pressures felt from both their Italian heritage and their American experience, homemakers alternated the styles of their meals. On some days they served a "platter," an American-style meal with meat and potatoes and vegetables all on one plate; on other days they served a "gravy," an Italian-style meal, centered on tomato sauce ("gravy") and pasta and including several courses served in succession.[33] In cases like this, what food practices highlight is the commonly hybrid quality of cultural life. Food practices are formed by social groups who live not in absolute spatial and temporal isolation, but rather in contact with other social groups and other regional practices; historical developments frequently displace the ethno-ecological determinants of cultural conservatism and in all events supplement and qualify them, leading to conditions of hybridity or creolization. Italian Americans inhabit their Italian-ness in view of a history in which they have also acquired American-ness. Italians even in Italy might be said to inhabit their Italian-ness in the context of a history in which they have also inhabited the micro-regional domains of particular provinces (Tuscany, Sicily, the Mezzogiorno) and the macro-regional domains of zones like the Mediterranean world and the Atlantic world, not to mention other forms of cultural influence like class and religious affiliation, all of which, as it were, bring a flux of new culinary items and structures to the table. The results of contact, addition, subtraction, and segmentation often crystallize into distinctive grammars and lexicons of food. The Italian American "platter," as it were, makes a substantive out of meat, adjectives and adverbs out of its condiments and vegetables, a sentence out of the assembly of the individual platter, choosing its "words" from an Anglo-American lexicon. The Italian American "gravy," speaking a different sort of language, seems rather to make a substantive out of a sauce, a verb out of its pasta, and adjectives out of items like meatballs and grated cheese, choosing most of its vocabulary from a southern Italian or Sicilian lexicon. There are rules for each kind of meal, rules of selection, combination, and sequentialization; rules of exclusion, reference, and idiomatic exception; rules that operate not only syntactically and semantically but also psychologically, socially, epistemologically.[34] The Italian Americans in this study almost always served "gravy" on ceremonial occasions; they often served "platter" to non-Italian guests. "A menu" says the narrator of a novel, "can embody the anthropology of a culture or the psychology of an individual; it can be a biography, a cultural history, a lexicon; it speaks to the sociology, psychology, and biology of its creator and its audience, and of course to their geographical location; it can be a way of knowledge, a path, an inspiration, a Tao, an ordering, a shaping, a manifestation, a talisman, an injunction, a memory, a fantasy, a consolation, an allusion, an illusion. . . ."[35] Food practices are orderly activities, and both individual menus and whole cuisines generally follow according to orderly grammars, lexicons, and, in Primo Levi's terms, "religious" considerations. But these orderly formulations are momentary crystallizations in the flux of human history, temporary systems of rational physicality that get composed, decomposed, and recomposed in response to the shifting needs, desires, material circumstances, technologies, and values of the people who abide by them.

Early modern England, from the fifteenth to the eighteenth century, was another cultural hybrid, although assertions of national/ethnic purity become increasingly adamant and even shrill over the course of the centuries. "The English are great lovers of themselves, and of everything belonging to them," complained a Venetian visitor in about the year 1500; "they think that there are no other men than themselves, and no other world but England."[36] "God hath given us a world of our own, wherein there is nothing wanting to earthly contentment," wrote Joseph Hall in 1616. "Here grows that wealth. . . . Here is that sweet peace. . . . Here is that gracious and well tempered government. . . . Here all liberal arts, etc. . . ." And not to be forgotten: "for pleasure, either our earth or our sea yields us all those dainties which their native regions enjoy but single. . . ."[37] Like many another nation, early modern England was a hybrid (of Welsh, Danes, Saxons, Britons, Normans, Huguenots, Dutch) founded on notions of communitarian identity, which in turn made a set of resemblances, contiguities, and shared perceptions into a value. But ideas alone do not a culture make, and nations are not merely ideal or "imaginary" communities. They are also what I call "aesthetic communities," composed of networks of more or less voluntarily shared (and thereby symbolically asserted) sensations, feelings, and perceptions. In fact, a vast body of resources and skills are mustered by most any society simply to cater to the sensations, feelings, and perceptions of its members by way of providing for and organizing the experience of consumption. A great deal of symbolic capital was expended in early modern England no doubt to convince its subjects that they inhabited a "world of our own" worthy of admiration. But a great deal of capital, symbolic and material alike, was also expended in putting beef on the English table. To be a great eater of beef was at once to take one's pleasure and to assert one's membership in an aesthetic community — a prestigious community to which all well-to-do English subjects were induced to belong — even if this was a community that ancient authority would not have condoned, that contemporary educated Italians (among others) would have taken little pleasure in, and that even to assert, for all its commonplaceness, was to evoke such proto-Bergsonian and proto-Freudian undercurrents of feeling as exposed one to laughter. It was to act in concert with fellow English subjects over and above the hybridity out of which the English people had been made. For better or worse, food is a great homogenizer.[38]

The period (early modern, from, say, 1450 to 1740) whose chronological center Shakespeare's Sir Andrew occupies saw a great many changes in the European diet and in the symbolic uses to which food practices were put. Products from the New World like potatoes and maize and from the East like coffee and tea would eventually enter into the repertoire of consumption. A greater variety of vegetables and fruits, in greater quantities, would become a normal part of the diet of many. Manners would alter, not only (most famously) as people began to adopt the use of forks and to become more fastidious about sharing plates and spoons, but also as households reorganized, with common dining areas contracting and dining becoming more private, and as orders of service and the progressions of dishes underwent what people of later ages thought of as "refinement," the condition of "politesse" and "délicatesse." All this is part of "the civilizing process," as social historian Norbert Elias first called it — a long-term transformation in the practices of everyday life, to which we will turn on several occasions in what follows. Cookbooks began to appear in print in 1470. They became more and more elaborate, prestigious, and popular. In 1570 the first edition appeared of a cookbook by a man designated as the "Cuoco Secreto di Papa Pio Quinto," an elegant, arty production by Bartolomeo Scappi, whose publisher entitled it, simply, *Opera*. In 1652 a veritable explosion of cookbook publication was initiated in France and England with the appearance in print of *Le cuisinier françois* by Pierre de La Varenne. The center of gravity of professional European cookery shifted definitively to France. Even in England and Italy, fashions in food preparation shifted to French techniques and models (although this shift in taste should not be exaggerated — regional preferences and professional differ-

ences were also being emphasized at this time), and the heavily spiced and complicated cookery for which the Middle Ages are notorious gave way little by little
to an ethic of what a modern historian calls the quest for "la saveur propre des
aliments"[39]—"the proper, individual taste of foods." Meanwhile, what may be
thought of as a change in the relations between food and words took hold: increasingly, the food practices were submitted to the discipline of the word, especially the printed word, and the ramifications of what one ate and drank and
how one ate and drank multiplied exponentially. That scientific, agricultural,
and demographic revolutions were in the making only compounded the complexity of the intervention of the discourse on consumption, juxtaposing new
models and modes of physicality against the old. Not as only a subject of discipline but also as an object of wishes did food and food practices change. The medieval Land of Cockaigne and its impossible, laughable super-abundance gave
way to the Renaissance utopia and its rationalized, egalitarian sufficiency. The
fantasy of profusion underlying the Cockaigne myth gave way to a desire either
for cosmopolitan refinement or for rustic simplicity, and the medieval fear of the
sin of gluttony gave way both to food fads like vegetarianism and to the new ideal
of the gourmet, the man or woman of "taste."

In the face of these changes, Sir Andrew's preference for beef would seem to
be both unremarkable and conservative. The "quelque choses" he associates
with dance steps but not overtly with food would have been a more interesting
preference from a culinary point of view; but it is just such "somethings" that his
choice of beef would seem to eschew. "Oh, what nicety is this," wrote the killjoy
Puritan Phillip Stubbes two decades earlier about what he took to be the new extravagance of English food,

> what vanity, excess, riot, and superfluity is here. Oh farewell former
> world. For I have heard my father say, that in his days, one dish, or two
> of good wholesome meat was thought sufficient, for a man of great wor-
> ship to dine withal. . . . A good piece of beef was thought then good
> meat, and able for the best, but now it is thought too gross: for their ten-
> der stomachs are not able to digest such crude and harsh meats. . . .[40]

The would-be gallant Sir Andrew Aguecheek evidently fails in his gallantry not
only in misunderstanding what he is doing, but in choosing as a sign of his British
vigor a preference for beef, he has failed to keep up with what was already known
as the "à la mode"; he has failed to keep up with fashionable changes in the diet
and thus to demonstrate the quality of refinement or *délicatesse,* what the Puritan
Stubbes calls "nicety." Most likely, since even among fashionable people in En-

gland the custom of using forks had yet to take hold, he eats with his hands, off a trencher of bread, helping himself with hands, a knife, or a spoon from a common platter.[41] Along with Sir Toby, he drinks the imported wine of the aristocrat, it is true, and not the local beer of the masses. And if his beef makes his culinary repertoire unrefined, a throwback to that simplicity that Stubbes extols, it may also show him taking part in the movement toward "la saveur propre des aliments." Aguecheek's beef, like any important commodity, belongs to a complex world of signs and a history of continually transmuting material practices, determined by economic forces from below and by ideological impulses from above. It is to this world of signs, material practices, and discourses that a foodstuff like Aguecheek's beef really belongs. That one would actually also eat the stuff is not beside the point; it is in eating the stuff that one warrants one's membership in an aesthetic community. But one doesn't only eat the stuff. One eats one's *Dasein* too.

SIR TOBY: Does not our life consist of the four elements?
SIR ANDREW: Faith, so they say, but I think it rather consists of eating and drinking.
SIR TOBY: Thou'rt a scholar; let us therefore eat and drink.

III

Here is a recipe for "baked meats" from a cookbook published in London in 1587:

To make baked meats.

Take a leg of Lamb, and cut out all the flesh, and save the skin whole, then mince it fine and white with it, then put in grated bread, and some eggs white and all, and some Dates and Currants, then season it with some Pepper, Cinnamon, Ginger, and some Nutmegs and Caraways, and a little cream, and temper it all together, then put it into the leg of the lamb again, and let it bake a little before you put it into your pie, then put in a little of the Pudding about it, and when it is almost baked, then put in verjuice, sugar, and sweet butter, and so serve it.[42]

To "bake" a meat in Tudor England was to cook the meat in a covering pie shell, also known as a "coffin." In this somewhat typical recipe, a joint of meat is minced; mixed with bread, eggs, spices, and cream; and heated in an oven in the vessel of a "coffin." It resembles what today we would call a pasty, or a savory meat pie. But the lamb in this dish isn't simply minced and mixed with flavoring and binding agents; it is taken out of the leg, with the skin left whole, and then placed back into the skin of the leg. The whole reconstituted leg (minus the bone), pre-heated separately in the oven, is what is then placed into the coffin, surrounded and topped by a separately prepared pudding mixture, the making of which the recipe fails to specify or explain.

To restore a minced-meat mixture into a whole skin was a common practice in the aristocratic cookery of the Middle Ages. Plenty of examples of such pro-cedures are to be found in surviving medieval recipes from England and France as well as in the first printed cookbook in an early modern vernacular, *Le viandier* (1486), compiled after the example of other compilers by the Frenchman Taille-vent, aka Guillaume Tirel.[43] Also typical of late medieval practices are the flavor-ing agents mixed in with the minced lamb: currants, dates, pepper, cinnamon, ginger, nutmeg, and caraway seed, along with verjuice (a sour fruit juice, used like vinegar), sugar, and butter. Recipes a century later would usually eschew the mannerism of baking what is reconstituted to look like a natural whole lamb leg in the vessel of a pie; they would drop piquant or heavy spices like ginger and car-away, though they might still include pepper and add fresh fruits like grapes and apples and/or fresh vegetables like artichoke bottoms and asparagus. That would not, to this writer's taste, mean much of an improvement. But it would indicate a change in the repertoire of cookery. Even in England, though at a slower pace, a movement was afoot to emphasize the "saveur propre" of fresh ingredients, and local herbal aromatics like parsley were taking the place of eastern spices.[44] In continentally inspired recipes, like the baked beef described in the cookbook printed from the notebooks of the seventeenth-century virtuoso Sir Kenelm Digby, the "coffin" would be dropped, the baking would be done in a heavy pot, and seasoning would include parsley, "a few Sweet herbs (Penny-royal, Winter-savory, Sweet-marjoram, Limon Thyme, Red-sage)," and "an Onion if you will."[45] From the custard-smothered leg in 1587 to the mid-seventeenth-century potted beef of Digby's recipe, we may observe not only changes in taste, significant as those may be, but also changes in the lexicon of cookery, determined in part by changes in the cultivation and distribution of ingredients (fresh fruits, herbal aromatics), and in part by changes in the technology of cookery.[46] Digby's potted beef, left in the oven to slow-cook for eight hours, depends on a vessel, an oven-friendly metal pot, that is simply not mentioned in earlier English texts — sig-nifying recent improvements in the art of casting metals and fashioning metal vessels.

Plays like *Twelfth Night* and the very nearly contemporary *Hamlet* belong to an earlier period in the history of cookery, when dishes like the baked stuffed lamb were still common. The differences should not be exaggerated. Herbal aromatics were used in Tudor cookery too, and there was already a trend toward adopting the fashions of continental cookery. Many professional cooks in England were already receiving some of their training in France, and English cookbooks already record some recipes that were allegedly "à la mode." That is why Puritans like Stubbes can complain about the niceties and superfluities of fashionable tables and why Sir Andrew can refer to fancy "kickshawses." It is why William Harrison can write in the late 1580s that "in number of dishes and change of meat, the nobility of England (whose cooks are for the most part musical-headed Frenchmen and strangers) do most exceed."[47] But still, when one fashioned a "baked meat" in Tudor England, one prepared a savory, spicy meat pie, containing a whole joint of meat inside, cooked in what was known as a "coffin."

And that is what Hamlet is alluding to when he engages in the following exchange with Horatio:

> HAMLET: But what is your affair in Elsinore?
> We'll teach you to drink deep ere you depart.
> HORATIO: My lord, I came to see your father's funeral.
> HAMLET: I prithee do not mock me, fellow-student;
> I think it was to see my mother's wedding.
> HORATIO: Indeed, my lord, it followed hard upon.
> HAMLET: Thrift, thrift, Horatio. The funeral baked meats
> Did coldly furnish forth the marriage tables.[48]

Food may be funny. In this passage it is gruesomely, angrily funny. "In Hamlet's bitter jest," writes Stephen Greenblatt, "food prepared for his father's funeral has been used for his mother's marriage, a confounding of categories that has stained both social rituals in the service of thrift."[49] In point of fact, the serving of real "leftovers" at a wedding banquet (that is, the remainders of partly consumed portions of food) would have been unthinkable, and unless the wedding had been held within about a week after the funeral (a detail about which the text is suggestive but ultimately silent), it would have been technically impossible too. Although commentators including Greenblatt have seen a swipe at bourgeois values and what Greenblatt goes on to call more ingeniously "an economy of calculation and equivalence" in Hamlet's remark, the main point of the jest is that *only* by marrying within a few days of the funeral would it have been possible to serve pies originally prepared for the funeral. Such pies would not be already partly eaten. On the contrary, one of the virtues of savory pies before the invention of refrigeration was that the crusts served to seal the cooked ingredients in a relatively airtight container. Visitors to museums of early modern cookery like the kitchens of Henry VIII at Hampton Court will be familiar with the spectacle of wax puffed pies scattered about the facilities like so many packaged sausages, available to be opened and consumed at any time. Within a reasonable amount of time, a pie could be cooked, stored in an air-cooled buttery or pantry, and served on later occasions.[50] They may have been special treats when served fresh, but they were made to be served over several days or more, and even when fresh they must have been allowed to cool to lukewarm or even to room temperature first (and "coldly furnish forth") to make them easier to handle.

Looking at food practices in the early modern period, again we come in contact with some of the literal, material references underlying fictional texts: Aguecheek's beef, his kickshawses, his capers, Hamlet's funeral baked meats. And clearly, too, we come in contact with the symbolic milieu within which the items the texts refer to were encountered. Aguecheek eats his beef within a continuum of traditional practices and associations, on the one hand, and of "à la mode" pretensions, on the other. Hamlet, further research shows, observes the consumption of baked meats in a context where elaborate banquets were an essential custom, a quasi-religious ritual of liminality. Funerals and weddings alike were (and of course still are) ceremonial occasions marked by the formalities of food consumption. But it is also remarkable that as Aguecheek's beef represents both a customary observance and an act of self-assertion, so Hamlet's baked meat is both a common item and something specifically chosen by Hamlet for its rhetorical effect.

Yet there does not seem to be any particular food reserved for funerals in early modern England. Historian Christopher Daniell re-creates the surviving record of an early sixteenth-century funeral banquet, as follows:

> On the day of burial . . . bread and cheese were given to the poor men, and the priests and gentlemen were given lamb, veal, roasted mutton and two chickens in a dish. For the following morning's breakfast the priests and other honest men were given a calf's head and boiled beef. Dinner was a much more elaborate affair. . . . The poor . . . received "umbils" (that is, offal) of beef, roasted veal in a dish and roasted pork. The richer people and priests had two courses. The first course was a potage of capons, mutton, geese and "custard." The second course included a potage of broth, capons, lamb, pig, veal, roasted pigeons, baked rabbits, pheasants and *gelie* [either chicken or aspic]. A list of

necessary spices was also included, including saffron, pepper, cloves, mace, sugar, raisins, currants, dates, ginger and almonds.[51]

Again, we are in the midst of residual medievalism with much of this cookery. The later funeral banquets discussed in David Cressy's *Birth, Marriage, and Death* feature a different sort of fare, including the "barrel of oysters, cake, and cheese" that Samuel Pepys claims to have "fallen to" at a funeral in 1664.[52] In any case, though baked meats were an option at early modern funerals, they do not seem to have had a privileged status. One did not associate baked meats with funerals any more than chicken soup or custard.

So baked meats are chosen as Hamlet's example because they could in fact be served on a date after the occasion for which they were prepared (unlike, say, chicken soup, which spoils quickly once taken off the heat). The material fact of a specific food practice—the making of pies in preservative "coffins"—determines the choice of a telling joke. As in the case of Aguecheek's beef, the joke seems to work even for modern readers who miss the main point. But as is also the case with Aguecheek's beef, when we examine the joke in detail, with a view to the symbolic milieu surrounding the material fact, we find a deeper, more serious current of meaning at work. Only in this case the serious meaning is everything. A hint of it is to be found in the kind of dish Hamlet seems to have in mind. Our recipe for baked leg of lamb has an undertone or under-image, as it were, of interment, disinterment, and embalmment; it even evokes a sort of re-presentation of the dead. The meat is scooped out of the skin, mixed with enhancing preservative flavorings, put back together, placed in the pie shell, and covered with an earth of pudding. It is then, after baking and cooling, fit to be eaten either right away or after several days, its whole joint ready to be disinterred whole and presented to diners like a corpse in an open coffin. Nor was the recipe unusual for its day. Here is another, from a similar cookbook:

To Bake a Capon with yolks

When the Capon is made ready, truss him into the Coffin: then take eight yolks of Eggs sodden hard, and prick into every of them five cloves, and put the yolks into the Coffin with a Capon. Then take a quantity of ginger and salt, and cast it on the Capon, and let it bake three hours, then take two raw yolks of Eggs, beaten into a goblet of verjuice, with a good quantity of sugar sodden together, put it into the Coffin, and to serve it.[53]

Here salt and ginger, eventually bound with an egg-yolk-infused, sweetened fruit juice, serves to bury (as it were) a whole piece of meat—a whole capon. The custom must seem strange to us. The pies must have been very big, much bigger than the little pasties strewn about the Hampton Court kitchens, or else the animals being interred in them must have been rather small. Many of these "pies" were actually encrusted joints of meat, the pie crust—not made to be eaten, but to be cooked in—molded around the flesh like a second skin (see fig. 1.3). But whether or not there is any accounting for taste—a matter to which I will turn later in this volume—the fact of the suggestive imagery of the baked meat is before us. Clearly dishes like this were designed for their witty, celebratory potential; they marked the inventiveness specifically of culinary art and exulted more generally the ability of art itself not only to transform the raw into the cooked but to outdo nature by enchanting it. Yet, as Shakespeare for one was aware, the enchantment of the flesh in this case came at the cost of death and decay.

In a famous critical work that is very much of another era, when criticism and cheerleading often went hand in hand, Caroline Spurgeon insists that "Shakespeare has an unusually large number [of images] drawn from the daily work and occupations of women in the kitchen and living room" and that Shakespeare eventually developed an "extreme sensitiveness about the quality, cooking, freshness and cleanliness of food."[54] But whatever we might want to say about Shakespeare's interest in the woman's sphere, we obviously need to qualify Spurgeon's remarks about Shakespeare's sensitivity to food. For there is a mischievous, unsavory undercurrent of thought about food in Shakespeare's corpus as well. Consider how these baked meats must have been eaten. Not in slices, as we eat pies today, since a whole leg of lamb or a whole capon or some such item was inside. Indeed, even in Tudor times a dish prepared so that it could be eaten by the slice was usually called a "pie," not a "baked meat." The baked meat in a coffin had to be opened up, its crust either portioned out and served on the side or else discarded, while the main ingredient was brought forward for display and then carved and parceled out.[55] So again, an image of interment and disinterment and of revisiting the dead underlay the consumption of the dish. If the thrifty baked meats serve as a profane yet otherwise innocuous reminder of "an economy of calculation and equivalence," they also remind us of something still more unsettling, something more on the order of cannibalism than of the exquisite sensitivity to which Spurgeon alludes.

King Hamlet's death, at least as the ghost represents it, was itself a matter of confusing and violating the sacred categories of human existence, killing a king at rest and "full of bread," as Hamlet would later put it, by way of what some Elizabethans considered the most repugnant of means, poison,[56] in the process

seafon it with nutmeg and pepper, then lay it in your pye
or pafty with a few whole cloves, and flices of raw bacon
over it, and butter; clofe it up in pye or pafty of fhort
pafte, and bake it.

To bake wilde Bore.

Take the leg, feafon it, and lard it very well with good
big lard feafoned with nutmeg, pepper, and beaten ginger,

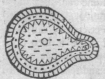

lay it in a pye of the form as you fee,
being feafoned all over with the fame
fpices and falt, then put a few whole
cloves on it, a few bay-leaves, large
flices of lard, and good ftore of butter, bake it in fine or courfe cruft, being baked, liquor it with good fweet
butter, and ftop up the vent.

If to keep long bake it in an earthen pan in the above-
faid feafoning, and being baked fill it up with butter, and
you may keep it a whole year.

To bake your wilde Bore that comes out of France.

Lay it in foak two dayes, then parboil it, and feafon it
with pepper, nutmeg, cloves, and ginger; and when it is
baked fill it up with butter.

To bake Red Deer.

Take a fide of red deer, bone it and feafon it, then take
out the back finnew and the skin, and lard the fillets or
back

Figure 1.3 Illustrations of baked meat, with recipes, from Robert May, *The Accomplisht Cook* (1660). Reproduced by permission of Special Collections, Leeds University Library.

violating the most intimately integrated of the king's natural functions. The poison caused the elder Hamlet's body almost literally — or perhaps even literally — to spoil and rot from within, to transform itself into a kind of putrefied food:

> Upon my secure hour thy uncle stole
> With juice of cursed hebonon in a vial,
> And in the porches of mine ears did pour
> The leprous distillment, whose effect
> Holds such an enmity with blood of man
> That swift as quicksilver it courses through
> The natural gates and alleys of the body,
> And with a sudden vigor it doth posset
> And curd, like eager droppings into milk,
> The thin and wholesome blood. So did it mine;
> And a most instant tetter barked about,
> Most lazar-like, with vile and loathsome crust,
> All my smooth body.[57]

The image of the "porches" and "gates and alleys of the body" derives from a standard medical metaphor of the period. The corrosion of the body from within that the ghost describes correlates with medical lore as well. So, indeed, is the ghost's representation of "thin and wholesome blood," blood being thought to be in the best condition when most "thin" and known to "curdle" when heated. But more originally, in a complex figure of speech that combines metaphor and simile with medical language that *we* read as metaphor but that early moderns read as literal description, the operations of the poison are compared to the making of a "posset," a thickened dairy product similar to today's eggnog, a favorite dessert of Samuel Pepys, made by adding an acidic (i.e., "eager") ingredient like wine into warm milk. As the blood thickens, first it "possets" and then it "curds," deteriorating from the tasteful smoothness of a good posset to a distasteful coagulation. The result is that the flow of blood is stopped, and the expiring body, "lazar-like," takes on the unsmooth symptoms of leprosy. This leprous body is then likened to spoiled cheese, its skin coated with a "loathsome crust"—though the "crust" may of course remind us of the skin of a cold moldy pie as well, or indeed of something like that "damned venison pasty that stunk like the devil" that Pepys was once offered as a gift.[58]

The concept of "putrefaction" or "corruption"—the words are usually interchangeable in Tudor and Stuart English, as they were in the Latin from which the English words derive — is of course much on Shakespeare's mind in the context of *Hamlet.* If the comedy of *Twelfth Night* dwells on the energetic consistency of life, the *Tragedy of Hamlet* dwells on the putrefying implications of mortality. If *Twelfth Night* frequently alludes to the "quick" and the "fresh" in the context of ruminations on love, life, and hunger,[59] *Hamlet* alludes to that which is "eager" and that which is a thing of "vigor" in the context of explaining how life turns into death and how the healthy body "full of bread" ends up rotting from the inside. Love, life, and hunger—that is, "appetite," a supremely significant word that will be discussed in the following chapters—are not unproblematic in *Twelfth Night;* but in *Hamlet* their correlates are disastrous. And they are disastrous because of their investiture in corruption, in things that are "rotten" or "rank and gross" and thereby "loathsome."

It is as if, in *Hamlet,* Shakespeare were determined to take the brilliant vitality foregrounded in *Twelfth Night* and transport it, naturally and sequentially, to its next dimension, loathsome death and decay. "Rank corruption, mining all within, / Infects unseen," Hamlet complains. In the world of *Hamlet,* corruption is always already present and eager, as it were, to gnaw at life from the inside. Yet the fact of mortality by way of the corruption of the flesh is not the whole of what vexes Hamlet. Hamlet is *offended* by the corruption of the flesh: in Hamlet's view, and in the governing view of the play as a whole, the very thing that eats at life from the inside is also a thing that affronts our senses and appalls our moral faculties. In language that both captures the inward bite of corruption and evokes the aesthetic and moral repugnancy of its effect, the world is thus "an unweeded garden" possessed entirely by things "rank and gross in nature." Sometimes the body of a man will "rot" even before he is dead, as "we have many pocky corpses nowadays," or a man, failing to rise to the occasion of his obligations, will impassively stay still like the "fat weed / That rots itself in ease of Lethe wharf."[60] The aesthetic and moral offensiveness implied by these words for the corruption of the flesh needs to be kept in mind—"rank," "gross," "pocky," "fat." A mother may be castigated for having left off "feeding" on a "fair mountain" in order to "batten"—glut herself—on the "rank grass" of a "moor," that is, the scummy moss of a swamp, and be abjured not "to live / In the rank sweat of an enseamèd bed, / Stewed in corruption. . . ." (The metonymy of sex and food in these last lines is significant: a "stew" is a whorehouse as well as a stew, and an "enseamèd" bed is one that has been greased up or larded).[61] The examples could be multiplied. Antithetical as such a sentiment may be to modern sensibilities (of which *Hamlet* also provides us with many a hint), or the stoic point of view that at several points Hamlet tries to sustain, the world Hamlet confronts is generally the contemptible world of Augustinians, so overcome by its corrosive condition of morbidity that neither worldly wonder ("What a piece of work is a man") nor moral conviction ("How all occasions do inform against me") can withstand it. To be "rotten" in the state of Denmark—a significantly chosen term, in this context— is thus to traffic, repugnantly, in triple corruption, at once physical, aesthetic, and moral: "O horrible, O horrible, most horrible!" the ghost exclaims. The repulsive figures of eating that permeate the play are signs of that triple corruption. The "funeral baked meats," material signs of the corrupt condition of the royal wedding feast, serve the guests with putrefied matter rigged up to celebrate, with unbeknownst irony, the triumph of culture over nature, the defeat of natural processes by way of the enchantments of art.[62] The fate of King Hamlet's body, rotted like a fungus-encrusted wheel of cheese, acts as if it were an outward expression of the murderous and incestuous corruption responsible for the king's death, demanding our indignation on any of several levels of response.

Strictly in a literal sense, in the Elizabethan context, though with a bit of a twist, what happens to King Hamlet's body even before it putrefies in the aftermath of death is already a function of "corruption." Corruption was a critical concept of premodern medical lore, particularly in conjunction with the all-important idea of digestion or "concoction." "Oppilations [obstructions] and putrefaction," writes Levinus Lemnius, are "the original cause of diseases."[63] Thomas Paynel tells his readers how luxury and overindulgence lead to a "corrupting" of the "digestion" and how drunkenness leads to "corruption of the liver's complexion."[64] Gilbertus Anglicus refers to how a loss of appetite might be caused by a "corruption of the stomach."[65] Grataroli cites Avicenna to the effect that eating fish after vehement exercise is dangerous because the fish "will soon be turned into corruption and so also corrupt the humors." Ficino notes approvingly the common doctrine that "the blood is corrupted when the digestion itself is corrupted." He also cautions his readers that "those foods which are rather moist or rich," unless they are seasoned with "sharp spices," will "produce a moisture which is very alien to the members and putrid; and if they supply any of the moisture which is necessary to nature, they present it in a condition subject to very quick corruption, just as watery wine is quickly disturbed and corrupted."[66] In a work that is more important to *Hamlet* than Grataroli's is to *Twelfth Night,* Timothy Bright makes a number of assertions like the one where he says that the very condition of "melancholy," with its "vain fear" and "plain desperation," is caused when the residue of a humor in the body, not being properly digested, "corrupt and degenerate farther from itself and the qualities of the body."[67] Corruption is the name for what happens when, as Othello once put it, "nature errs from itself." That is, it is a case where nature operates in such a way as to undermine its own integrity and so wastes rather than preserves its life: corruption is nature denaturing itself, what in English translations of Aristotle is sometimes called "degeneration" or "passing away." (The Latin verb *corrumpuo* has its etymological roots in the idea of something "breaking apart.") Today we associate the term only with what happens after death, but in the premodern body, corruption was a fact of life, constantly emerging from and adjoining itself to healthy natural functions. Nor was it, as we might assume today, only something that happens when the body goes cold. Premodern medicine recognized both "cold and wet" and "hot and dry" corruption.[68] What Avicenna and Ficino worry about in the examples cited was cold and wet corruption, caused by consuming "cold and wet" foods, like fish, under "intemperate" conditions; but what Bright worries about is a hot corruption, a degeneration (which could be triggered by eating "melancholy" foods like beef) that heats the body and overcooks the humors comprising it, a condition known as "adustion"—a word which in English also inevitably brings to mind "dust" and thus "ashes to ashes and dust to dust." To go corrupt by this latter hot process was to turn "adust," and thus abhorrent. "And yet to me," Hamlet consequently complains, thinking about the nature of a man, "what is this quintessence of dust?"

The body of King Hamlet, having been rendered corrupt from the inside by an "eager" poison, seems to have been even doubly damaged, subjected to both a hot and a cold corruption at once. This poison, sharply acidic—like the wine, vinegar, or beer that would cause milk to "posset and curd"—would seem to have cooked its poor victim from the inside, coagulating his blood like a cooked milk separated into curds and whey. But acids, including vinegar, were also often thought of as being cold, not hot (and the opposite therefore in this respect from wine). An "eager" wind, like the one that assailed Hamlet and Horatio on their first stalking of the ghost together ("The air bites shrewdly, it is very cold." "It is a nipping and an eager air") was a cold wind, bitingly cold. And so a coagulation of the blood, like a curdling of milk, could be thought of as a cold corruption, a "chilling" of the blood, like warm milk made cold by a cold acidic liquid, or like warm cheese made cold by aging, putrefying, and going deader and deader. So the poisoning is both at once—in another morbid "confusion of categories," where the confusion underscores the horror—hot and cold, a burning and a chilling, a cooking and a cooling, a turning adust and a putrefying. It is not only a feat of poetic ingenuity that thus likens King Hamlet's poisoning to the making of milk into cheese. By the terms of premodern science, the processes were akin. To be poisoned, to be corrupted from within, was like being transformed from a raw state (to put it in Levi-Straussian terms) to a rotten one: hot and cold at once, neither quite cooked nor quite raw, putrefied and adusting.

At issue here, in all of these allusions to repulsive yet natural processes, is a daunting magnification of the medical, moral, and aesthetic facts of life, as the common wisdom of the day understood them. The jest about funeral baked meats gruesomely inflates the preposterousness of the artifice and violence entailed in the practice of the human *essen:* a funeral baked meat—in effect a buried animal or animal part, allowed to be eaten cold and past its time—leads along a chain of signifiers to a poisoned corpse, corrupted from without and within, like a milk turning into cheese and cheese aging past its time and going rotten. The violence either way, when one thinks about it deeply, is alarming, especially when one thinks about it—as both Hamlet and the author of *Hamlet* inevitably do—in terms of how human life requires it, requires it in order to live. Shakespeare was a student of Montaigne, who openly complained (especially in "Of Cruelty") about the treatment of animals at the hands of carnivorous humans. Shakespeare was also an avid reader of Ovid and especially of the latter's *Metamorphoses,* which begins by idealizing the vegetarianism of the Golden Age and ends by recounting the mystical vegetarianism of the philosopher Pythagoras, who condemned eating flesh as cruelty. In *As You Like It,* Shakespeare himself put remarks in the mouth of an admirable character that object to the killing of innocent animals for food. The melancholy Jacques breaks out into tears at the sight of a hunted-down stag, a "wretched animal" that "heaved forth such groans / That their discharge did stretch his leathern coat / Almost to bursting."[69] So Shakespeare knew that if, when Elizabethans thought about food, they could be thinking about festive cakes and ales, they could also be thinking about slaughtered, skinned, and eviscerated animals, doomed to be buried in pots and pastry shells, as in so many coffins.[70] Hamlet's jest begins to touch on this—it places one anxiety, concerning his mother's hasty and incestuous marriage, under the sign of another anxiety, concerning the ontology of food and the brutality of eating meat. Similarly, the ghost's invocation of the "barked about" corpse magnifies the implicit horror of the identity of the body with natural processes generally, and hence with corruption and putrefaction. The ghost has perhaps found just the right sort of terms to provoke the tender-minded Hamlet into action; already aghast at the rankness of corporeality, Hamlet is especially vulnerable to evocations of the terrors of mortality. Where Aguecheek's beef evokes a comic Bergsonian objectification of cattle and eating, Hamlet's baked meat and his father's tettered body evoke a horrific objectification of killing and feeding. As Sir Toby and the audience have to laugh at Sir Andrew and his beef, so the audience has to shiver at Hamlet's funeral baked meat, and Hamlet and the audience alike have to recoil in revulsion at the image of the murdered, spoiled-food-like king.

But there is more: symbolic cannibalism, the third of the chief figures of repulsive eating in *Hamlet,* which apparently completes them. If "rank corruption infects unseen," in the view of Hamlet and *Hamlet,* that which is corrupted from within and rots becomes, not a waste material — to be discarded and forgotten, like the waste material of a healthy body — but a material incorporate with other bodies, a part of, not apart from, the lives of others. The waste of corruption is not wasted at all; rather, it itself is food, fodder to another creature, as the wasting and eating of bodies moves up and down along the great chain of being: "We fat all creatures else to fat us, and we fat ourselves for maggots." "A man may fish with the worm that hath eat of a king, and eat of the fish that hath fed of that worm."[71] One eats and thrives, by this point of view, and inevitably one dies and rots and one is eaten. The very process through which one thrives (since, after all, "life consists of eating and drinking") is also a process inevitably entailing the appalling, general corruption and cannibalism of the cosmos. That is why Polonius is to be found "not where he eats but where he is eaten"; and that is why the king's body, whose inward corruption stemmed in fact from poisonous intentions introduced "unnaturally" from without, ends up so rotten that one may wonder what worms would be able to stomach it, although Claudius and Gertrude are willing to make a symbolic feast of it. ("Discretion," as Claudius puts it, has in his and Gertrude's case "fought with nature.")[72] What may seem like Hamlet's personal pathology — whether his Elizabethan "melancholy" or his Freudian Oedipality — is thus really apiece with a view of the world that found its way from the high road of theological and medical treatises to the low, gruesome world of stuffed legs of lamb, temporarily (and only temporarily) preserved in a pie crust. Human bodies die corrupted by the same kind of process through which a cheese is fashioned. They end up as the dinners of worms. And within the multicourse feast of the great chain of being, what cheeses have done to them and what the worms do is not dissimilar from what humans suffer and do. There is more than one way to respond to the symbolic life of food, and there is more than one way to eat one's *Dasein* too.

IV

If food can make us laugh, it can also disgust us. The mutuality of preference and aversion in food practices is well known, if not yet entirely understood. Food taboos are commonly reinforced, phenomenologically, by aversion. Food aversions that lead to anorexia were already known to the ancients. (Contrary to popular opinion, anorexia is neither a recent phenomenon nor a recent diagnosis; it is only "anorexia nervosa," an explanation of the illness based on "nerves," that is new.) Food aversions of all types were well known to the early moderns, as in

Castelvetro's response to beef. But the reason food can disgust us is not merely a function of the natural and psychological phenomena of preference and aversion. Hamlet himself betrays no literal morbidity with respect to food and drink. But in his melancholy, he is contemptuous of natural processes in general.[73] And so, it would seem, is the play as a whole. The appetite that in *Twelfth Night* is a sign and function of vitality is in *Hamlet* a token of morbidity. In *Hamlet* what humanity hungers for is death, and what humanity and indeed the whole of creation feeds on is death. A universally corrupted appetite feeds on a universal condition of corruption. In the end, the melancholy of Hamlet and *Hamlet* suggest, it is the dead who coldly furnish us forth, and we are only too avid thus to be furnished.

Readers who know Shakespeare may well recall that the universal cannibalism that Hamlet complains about has even more odious applications in other plays, like *Titus Andronicus*. (*Timon of Athens, Coriolanus,* and *Troilus and Cressida* also contain cannibalistic imagery.) The vengeful Titus, in *Titus Andronicus,* literalizes the imagery of the baked meat when he threatens to execute his adversaries and profane their corpses by cooking them and serving them in a pie to their mother, a threat he will shortly make good upon:

> Hark, villains, I will grind your bones to dust
> And with your blood I'll make a paste
> And of the paste a coffin I will rear,
> And make two pasties of your shameful heads,
> And bid that strumpet, your unhallowed dam,
> Like to the earth swallow her own increase.[74]

The same unseemly vision of humanity and the cosmos that Hamlet's rhetoric may raise to the level of a universal truth can also in Shakespeare, in the rhetoric of a less admirable character, betray the psychopathy of evil. Only the pastry coffin — Shakespeare's innovation, apparently, as this is the only version of this ancient story I have come across that bakes the children this way (they are usually stewed and sometimes roasted) — only the pastry coffin really remains the same.

But where do such reflections lead? I started here with Aguecheek's silly yet serious choice of beef. I have concluded with Hamlet's dark contempt for a ceremonial pasty. Focusing on such things may run the risk of reducing matters of high sentence — the comedies and tragedies of Shakespeare — to the level of the trivial, the ridiculous, or the merely loathsome. Certainly it takes us away from the antiquarian curiosity that still motivates a good deal of research on early modern food today — examinations of what people supposedly cooked and ate in a remote era, whose dishes we may sample like time-traveling tourists. It may make us pause before adopting a purely sociological approach to the subject too — examinations of the social principles and statistically verifiable practices according to which people cooked what they cooked and ate what they ate. I have adduced a number of conventionally antiquarian facts in this chapter: recipes for baked leg of lamb, complaints about fancy dishes in the popular press. I have also underscored a number of sociological and sociohistorical principles. Food practices, I have suggested, are a form and medium of communication. They bind individuals together while providing outlets for individualistic self-assertion. They are a medium for what I have called "aesthetic community," the more or less voluntary sharing of sensations and feelings within the customary context of a society. They are historically and geographically specific. They entail a cultural appropriation of physicality. Coming to terms with them requires coming to terms with the moral, aesthetic, and intellectual life of a specific time and place, along with the economic practices that enable and constrain its morals, tastes, and ideas. But to point out these things — recipes for baked lamb, principles of sociological study — one is not in need of Shakespeare. Much less is one in need of a craven Aguecheek or a delirious Hamlet, however much "greatness" may be found in the former's appetite, or "method" in the latter's madness. But Shakespeare and his characters and their choices of images and ideas alert us to a wider, deeper, and more ambiguous dimension of the history of food practices. The joint of beef or the baked meat pie are parts of that dimension. Not just as examples of the everyday life of days of old or as indices of ethnographic trends are Aguecheek's beef and Hamlet's baked meat significant, but as complex signs of the indefinite ambivalence of culture.

All cultures may probably be seen to entertain some equivocalness with regard to food (as to so much else). Since there is no known society that "does not cook in some manner at least some of its food" and that does not organize food preparation and consumption as a symbolically significant, orderly activity, we may expect that in any case we turn to we shall find, if not both tragedy and comedy, at least some form of moral and perceptual ambivalence. The ambivalence means, among other things, that when we study the food of a culture, we have to study nuances of feeling and meaning, of connotation and denotation, of attitudes and assumptions, that may lead in many different directions. The virile roast beef of an Englishman is also a sign of an order of existence where the Englishman is food for worms. If music be the food of love, as *Twelfth Night*'s Orsino puts it, the funeral baked meat may coldly furnish forth a wedding table. When we examine documents about food, we have to be alert to context, to situational parameters, to rhetoric, to genre. The comedy of food, the tragedy of food — to

which list may also be added the romance of food, the burlesque of food, and so
forth, along with such discourses as are promoted by religion, science, aesthetics, and ethics — such things are not only conditions for representing practices
and values, they are also constitutive of the plurality of approaches, the multi-
valence of the *Dasein,* of the Heideggerian "being there," through which humans
in society go about accommodating their hunger.

Here in *Twelfth Night* we encounter a comedy informed by ancient and recent medical lore as well as recent social and technological developments, a comedy that clearly celebrates food and the material explanation of life — only we
know that we can only assent to this view so far; we know that there are problems
with it; it makes us laugh. Here in *Hamlet,* in turn, we encounter a tragedy similarly informed by medical lore and social and technological developments, yet
where medicine, social thought, and technological awareness have all been
inflected by pessimistic, otherworldly strain of Christianity, as well as a psychological disposition — Hamlet's — favoring not universal vitality but universal
morbidity. We can only assent to this view up to a point as well. If tragedy is
cathartic — a term referring by analogy to the same natural processes of digestion
as delight Sir Toby and appall Prince Hamlet — tragedy is not then a pronounce-
ment on the human condition; it is mimetic homeopathy. To surrender to the
same dismay at the universal cannibalism of nature as Hamlet would then be to
make the same mistake as Hamlet; failing the healing effects of cathartis, it
would be to subject oneself to the same madness. And so we accept Hamlet's
point of view just as we accept Sir Toby's — as part of a process, full of insight,
thought, Aristotle's *dianoia* . . . yet only so far.

Ambivalence is the continual result of such interjections as can be made in
the context of the culture of food: ambivalence, not indifference; undecidability,
not relativity or impassivity. To live in a world of food and drink and all the discourses that infuse them — genres like comedy and tragedy, discursive formations like classical medical lore and Christian *contemptus mundi* — is to live amidst
a cornucopia of irresistible and irreconcilable options. We shall have to live in a
world of cakes and ales, *Twelfth Night* implies; and we shall have to live in a world
where the cost of life is death, *Hamlet* responds, so that what is "eager" in our dispositions is also murderous. And we shall have to live in both worlds at once.

Or not "we," of course. For the parameters are specific. The aesthetic community of Shakespeare's world, like the larger framework of early modernity to
which it belongs, is historically and geographically specific, and the ambivalence
lived in conjunction with that community is specific too. Early modernity had its
own vocabularies of food and food practices: "beef" could mean "dim-witted."
Early modernity had its own science of food and food practices too: a "hot stom-

ach" was necessary to the consumption of "cold" commodity like beef, because of the inexorable laws of classical physics. Moreover, as we will see in more detail in what follows, early modernity had its own ways of transmitting the arts and science of food, by way of both technologies of literary output and transmission. There was the cookery book, the diet book, the conduct book, the travelogue, and for that matter the short story, the novel, and drama. And these vocabularies, sciences, and literatures were only the beginning. As the early modern mind confronted its own symbolizations, knowledge, and literatures of food, it also encountered its dreams of eating and drinking, its wishful images of consumption. What would it mean to eat exactly what wanted, to eat one's fill, to eat well, to eat wisely, or eat beyond the reaches of eating, to eat one's way to God? Such questions were not idle. They were the very stuff of what it meant to be alive and act as a rational being. Yet at the same time, the early modern mind encountered the idea of its limitations, its insufficiencies, its depravity. What did it mean to live in a world where one could not really eat one's fill, or well or wisely, or to live in a world where access by way of consumption to the divine had been cut off, barred, so that, by contrast, the very means by which one nourished oneself betrayed one's profanity, or sinfulness, or imperfection? These questions, too, were far from idle. The Italian humanist Marsilio Ficino wrote in the late fifteenth century about how one could ingest the "quintessence," the "power of the sun" and the "life of the world."[75] But at the same time, the anonymous author of the French *Le compost et kalendrier des bergiers,* or *Kalendar & Compost of Shepherds,* was warning, in words Hamlet echoes, that "they that nourisheth well the flesh prepareth meat for worms."[76] The whole business, in the *Kalendar'*s account, was shameful, and sinful to boot.

And what, then, for the early moderns, is our *nature?* Of what does life *consist?* What is our nature in view of the fact that though we always need to eat, our needs are symbolic as well as material, emotional and spiritual as well as physical? Or that our needs are personal as well as social? Or that we must find ourselves in an aesthetic community to which we are capable of not wanting to belong? Or that all of our natural needs—emotional, spiritual, physical—seem to come upon us, as it were, already written, already inscribed in the texts and disciplines of a culture of food that precedes us?

Both Sir Andrew Aguecheek and Hamlet in effect rebel: they each begin with this world, where beef is both proscribed and endlessly supplied, where baked meats are both ceremonial treats and morbid crystallizations of the murderousness of the sublunary cosmos; and they insist on attempting to go their own ways, on trying, impossibly, to stand apart from the system that determines them. Sir Andrew will do what he will. (*What You Will,* it will be recalled, is the subtitle of *Twelfth Night*.) Hamlet will exact his revenge. Or will he? "What is a man," Hamlet asks, "If his chief good and market of his time / Be but to sleep and feed?" Surely there must be more. Surely to stay within the system and to sleep and feed is not only to be only all too human, but even, as Hamlet complains, to be "a beast, no more."[77] Yet the system determines the form that the discontent of rebelliousness can take; "sleeping and feeding" and "eating and drinking" provide opportunities for resistance and transcendence. And so for the purposes of this study, it all comes down to moments like the one where Sir Andrew Aguecheek complains about beef and where Hamlet complains about pie — moments that point us toward the existential choices that early moderns faced, given the aesthetic communities to which they belonged. We are about to discover many more such moments. A seventeenth-century cookbook will be earnest about the healthfulness of eggs, in reaction against their potential "excrementitiousness"; a political satirist will maliciously recount the brutality involved in flaying a pig, while recommending a flayed pig for dinner; peasants, humanists, and Puritans will cry out at the excesses of the rich and the inequality of food distribution generally, often at the cost of appreciating the savor of food; Milton's Eve will pluck her first apple, and the earth will "feel the wound"; a colonialist will cry out against starvation and its gruesome corollary, the temptation to cannibalism, while himself appreciating the value of eating human flesh; a gourmet will rhapsodize over tasty flying fish landing on the deck of a transatlantic cargo ship, where a hold, deep in the bowels of the ship, will have been set aside for the transporting of slaves, for whom, he will claim, a diet of plantains is all but enough; a conduct-book writer will admonish her readers to keep quiet at the dinner table and observe their place in the hierarchy, in order to rise above it; and Robinson Crusoe's Friday, having already wordlessly tasted his first raisin, will garrulously dine on his first piece of animal flesh, a stewed joint of goat meat. He will instantly be converted from the single-minded cannibalism of the innocent savage to the copious, sacrificial carnivorousness of the Christian.

Chapter Two

THE SENSATIONAL SCIENCE

I

HERE IS AN ENTRY ON FOOD from a popular text. It is not a recipe but an item on eggs and their nutritional value, taken from what was commonly called a "regimen of health":

Eggs

Eggs and chiefly those of Hens, are a Food much used and esteemed amongst us; an Egg consists of two parts, the Yolk, and the White. The yolk is moderately hot and moist, and very corroborating; the White is cold and dry, and affords also much Nourishment, and lasting enough, but hard of Concoction.

The Newest Eggs are the best, and Nourish most and soonest, and yield good Aliment [i.e., nutrition], but the stalest are the worst, and the Corruption of Eggs is most dangerous, for we say . . . the best Food Corrupted, becomes the worst and most perilous. They do not well agree with those whose Liver and Stomach are filled with Vicious Humors, and in Choleric and hot Stomachs they are easily Corrupted, and turned into choler; as for the Cooking of them they are best when the Yolk is soft, and the Rest hardened to a White Color, and so supt up, being boiled in Water, they may easily be given to a weak Stomach; they are stronger in taste, boiled in the shell than poached, especially if Roasted, but the worst way of Dressing [i.e., cooking] them, is to fry them in a Pan.[1]

The language is riddled with terms of art: "corroborating," "hard of Concoction," "Vicious Humors." The terms are not difficult to translate one by one, however, if one has an *Oxford English Dictionary* close at hand: to "corroborate" was to strengthen or invigorate; to be "hard of Concoction" was to be difficult to digest. As for the viciousness of "Vicious Humors," though it may be hard to separate the term from the moral connotations we associate with other "vicious" things, and it may even have been hard for some early modern people to do so, the word could simply mean defective or harmful, so that a vicious humor was an elemental bodily substance (a "humor") that was in a noxious condition. The language is strange but not opaque, and the advice the entry gives is straightforward. Eggs are good for you, especially if fresh, and especially if soft-boiled or poached, and they make you feel good when you eat them. They do not agree with all stomachs and, like the beef that is dangerous for people inclined toward melancholy, they are counter-indicated for people inclined toward certain psycho-physiological ailments, especially "choler."

Entries like this were extremely important to the gustatory universe of premodern times; they were even more important to the culture of eating than the recipes in cookbooks. They circulated in printed texts both scholarly and popular, and spread through oral culture as well. Entries like this structured what Shakespeare's characters had to say about beef and baked meat. They structured what a lot of people did when they sat down to the table, and what a lot of cooks and servers had to do in order to cater to their needs. And they were systematic: not simply compilations of words and their meanings and their practical applications, based on a mixture of observation and tradition — though they were that too — they were the product of the vast scientific apparatus, a comprehensive system of discourse, knowledge, and practice.

We shall be doing this a lot over the course of this study, looking at snatches of language and literature that refer in some way to eating and drinking. We may note them first off as interjections, as eruptions of language that command attention: "I am a great eater of beef." "Eggs . . . are a Food much used and esteemed amongst us." (*Esteemed,* the directive puts it.) The eruptions of language call attention to the distance between our current way of thinking about these things and early modern habits. But these eruptions are not only quaint or colorful, they are also symptomatically significant, and our aim will be to look at them analytically, historically, and sociologically. Frequently, as in the case of both Aguecheek's beef and the medical writers' well-esteemed eggs, we will find that they call attention to a system. Not just a habit or an attitude, but a whole frame of understanding, of behavior, of life, is often revealed through expressions of these kind. And here then — though it is not alone in the world of discursive frameworks having an impact on eating and drinking in the early modern period, and it is not even entirely commensurate with the others — is the most pervasive, influential, and primary system of them all. "Eggs . . . are a Food much used and esteemed. . . ."

The language of early modern cookbooks, which we will turn to in the following chapter, also conveyed a system. "To make baked meats . . ." "To Bake a Capon with yolks . . ." The language of cookbooks operated in keeping with a systematic code of word use, and it disseminated a system of practice, from kitchen to kitchen, from household to household, from estate to estate, from town to town. So food preparation acquired a cultural form, based on shared conventions and habits and shared means — both linguistic and technological — for satisfying a conventional and habitual demand: the demand to eat well, in keeping with fashion.

But here is something else. Beef "maketh gross blood, and engendreth melancholy." "The yolk is moderately hot and moist, and very corroborating." And so forth. Reporting on the "powers" or "virtues" of foods, as ancient physicians had originally put it, statements like these conveyed a system for communicating with and by way of food, a system for establishing a chain of communication between the subject, the foodstuff, the subject's body, and the social world to which subject, food, and body alike belonged. The system had its origins in the Hippocratic writers of the fifth century B.C. and found its most influential codifications in second-century Rome and twelfth-century Persia. Generation after generation of classically trained physicians and medical writers — in ancient Greece and Rome and throughout the Roman Empire; in medieval Europe and the Middle East, including Christians, Muslims, and Jews, all the way through to the end of the seventeenth century — studied, absorbed, and applied it. When writers popularized the science, they produced examples of what was called the "regimen of health," the *regimen sanitatis,* which came to be known in one form or another to just about every cultivated corner of the early modern world.

Here is an egg, yes. But what shall we say about it? And what therefore should we do about it? Or, by the same token, what should we avoid doing about it? Anything at all? There was really only one kind of answer. The science of the diet in the premodern world was a system of saying and doing, of prescribing and adapting, of analyzing and inferring, which placed all known foodstuffs in a multiform but coherent, regimented framework. Everything was related to everything else: the material object to other material objects; the chemical or humoral composition to every other chemical or humoral composition; the "powers" or "virtues" of a foodstuff to every other power or virtue; the processes of ingestion, digestion, excretion, and assimilation to all other natural processes, up and down the scale of the great chain of being, leading in one direction toward well-being and health, leading in another direction toward corruption and death. The edible egg may appear to be an isolated phenomenon, a thing-in-itself. But the science of edible things took it up as the expression of a network of meanings. It made it not only into an object of systematic discourse, where all such items were subject to the same rules and principles of analysis and use, but a discursive object, the symbolic object of a symbolizing, synthetic science.

The science was not all-embracing, and it was subject to historical change as well as momentary disagreements. Ken Albala has demonstrated how it appeared in early modern letters in three consecutive stages: one in which early modern writers mainly cribbed their science from classical and Arabic authorities like Galen and Avicenna, a second in which they adopted their traditional science for contemporary readers and contemporary conditions, and a third in which original experiment, experience, and speculation greatly modified the science.[2] (He also discusses what he could have added as a fourth: the stage when, in the late seventeenth century, the science and its guidebooks went out of style, victims of the scientific revolution.)[3] The English rejection of Galenic authority in the late sixteenth century on the subject of beef would be a case not only of a specific disagreement about a specific phenomenon, but the expression of a stage in medical discourse when popular writers felt free to modify received opinion according to clinical experience. But the science — at once a specialty of learned doctors, the subject of popular but learned textbooks, and an oral tradition that pervaded all aspects and levels of daily life — was nevertheless comprehensive; it determined in advance the conditions under which food, health, and the body could be understood and healthy life ordered.

The reach of the science should not therefore be underestimated. When diners in the early modern period approached a cooked egg, they not only encountered an object capable of being consumed. They also encountered a discourse. And the discourse they encountered did not only describe or account for the object; it reached into the terms by which they experienced, internalized, and assimilated the object; it reached into the sensation of consumption and digestion, and indeed became a part of that sensation, a formative quality of sensation. That *sensational* aspect of the science is really what is crucial about it. For if, on the one hand, the science amounted to a "discursive formation" and indeed a "strategic formation" of discourse (as Foucault taught us to think about these things) whereby for nearly two thousand years academically trained physicians and eating subjects organized the concepts, grouped the objects, and articulated the symbolic dimensions of food,[4] on the other hand, what the discourse identified, formed, and expressed was a "little world," a microcosm of sensation. In spite of the rigorous imposition of what Galen called "first principles" to the science of diet, and indeed to the dismissal of what Galen thought of as the incoherence of the approach of mere "empirics," what the science really expressed was a symbolic relation of the subject to his or her sensations — sensations reaching from the palate and the gullet to the intestines, the rectum, and indeed to all the organs and extremities and functions of the body, all the little world to which that the body of the individual was thought to amount.

When an egg yolk is said to be "corroborating," a quality of the object that in the first instance belongs to it as an entity — as after all, with a little heat egg yolks harden and bind, like glue; their corroborative properties made them suitable as a base for paint — is ascribed, in the second instance, to a relation to the subject. The egg yolk "corroborates" the subject, the individual eating. The egg yolk feels good as well as tastes good; it refreshes; it slides down the gullet and fills the belly; it makes one feel as if a sort of glue, a medium of binding and strengthening, were being assimilated by the system. And the science of sensation that the premodern world called the regimen or dietary of health gave that effect of the egg yolk both a language and an explanation.

II

Our friend Gugliemo Grataroli, enemy of beef eating, can help orient us to the science. Better known as the author of a book on mnemonics, *The Castel of Memorie*, in his lesser-known work Grataroli addresses himself to devising a *Direction for the Health*, as the English translator puts it, *of Magistrates and Studentes* (in the original Latin title, the health of "*literatorum*" and "*eorum qui magistratibus*").[5] The reason we need a book just for us is that "the natures and complexions of men be divers," and therefore "require a diverse trade and order in diet and exercise." There is a diversity in "bodies" and in "trades of living," and "it cannot be that any one absolute way should be appointed to serve every nature in every faculty generally."[6] Moreover, different kinds of recommendations must be given to different individuals so far as they are *capable* of following different regimes. So in the same way a Hollywood actress might be advised to keep her youth by way of a regimen of vacations at exotic spas, mid-sixteenth-century physician Grataroli offers his nostrums to those who are able to eat what they want and exercise as they see fit, and have "convenient leisure to surcease from their charges and offices according as their calling and vocation is." An underling — and most people in early modern Europe were either peasants or underlings — may well have to eat what his master provides for him and live as his master gives him leave, but a man of letters or a magistrate will be able, when his public responsibilities aren't too pressing, to look after himself and "tender" his health.[7]

The freedom of the magistrate or student, however, takes what may seem to be a peculiar form as Grataroli and others like him articulate it, for the subject finds himself exercising this freedom from the predominantly passive position of a "patient." The physician is the active agent in matters of health; he is "the minister of Art and the deputy of Nature," and in that capacity something of a military man. "The Physician and the disease do mutually oppugn one another and strive for mastery," he writes, in a metaphor that originates in Hippocrates.[8] The patient, by contrast, plays a more passive role, even if he is also the site of the war between the doctor and illness. He is "the subject and party in whom this conflict and combat is arraigned." In fact, what happens in his body and his mind — mental health was also figured into the general category of "health" among the early moderns and was often emphasized — is much like the battle of the church and the devil for the soul of a man or (as in John Donne's sonnet about the battering on the heart of the "three-personed God") of two conflicting armies for the possession of a town. The patient, if he does "wisely and politically," will "resist the summons of his enemy Sickness"; he will direct "the order of his diet and daily visage by the Dial of the Physician's learned prescription and counsel"; he will thus "abstain from things hurtful and inconvenient by practicing that which is wholesome and expedient." Not quite the master of his fate, "he is joined in commission and made (as it were) fellow in office with the Physician against all raging assaults of Sickness." What is required is that the physician and patient both be "thus firmly confederate and linked together," so that "the disease and Sickness shall be easily driven to a narrow exigent and glad to disclaim his interest, and great hope is to be conceived of the victory and upper hand."[9]

Yet by the terms of this confederacy, the patient has to do what he can to take preventive measures. And so in his "directions," Grataroli focuses on five categories of health-related activities that the patient can take charge of on his own behalf, five "non-naturals" as they had been called since the Middle Ages: "Labor or exercise, Meat, Drink, Sleep, and the act of carnal copulation." If these things are "orderly, conveniently, and competently used," he adds, they have "great power and efficacy to keep a man in health, and in them chiefly . . . consisteth the whole poise and cause of healthiness."[10] Note, however, that our author says "great power," not "absolute power." For it was known that following the rigorous "regimen" could not prevent every kind of disease, and that the practice of medicine included invasive and restorative procedures: pharmaceuticals, surgery, and, by way of pharmaceuticals and surgery, the endless round of purgings and evacuations for which premodern medicine is so rightly notorious. But "regimen" or "diet"—the words are almost interchangeable—this was the main line of discipline through which the patient could manage his physical and mental condition, resisting the "summons" of disease while maximizing the wholesomeness of his condition. Regimen was a "technology of the self," to use another Foucauldian concept, a rational art of the self, a prosthetic craft of the self.[11] In keeping with principles that began with the Hippocratic writers, found systematic development under the Roman Empire with Galen, and worked its way into early modern medicine by way of the Semitic doctors of the Middles Ages, health was a matter of balance. Galen called this condition *eucrasia,* a good or happy "temperament" (*crasis*), "natural *eucrasia*" being "the cause of the function of every organ."[12] Sleeping well, getting enough exercise, copulating on occasion, drinking the right fluids, and above all eating well were the keys to maintaining a happy temperament. (Other writers following Hippocrates would also concern themselves with the air one breathed, the situation of one's residence, the quality of one's evacuations, and the state of one's emotional life, making for as many as eight non-naturals in all.) Since disease was understood to be not the result of an invasion of the body by noxious agents or "germs," but a condition of imbalance or *dyscrasia* (in early modern English, "distemper"), the key to health was keeping one's life in balance with the elements within and without oneself. If the body on its own tended toward a condition of "natural *eucrasia*," food, drink, sleep, air, exercise, habitation, evacuation, and sex were all factors over which one could exert some control and exercise an art of the self. "We study *Health*," Donne wearily observes, turning the idea toward the common metaphor of the well-tempered body as an edifice, "and we deliberate upon our *meats,* and *drink,* and *Air,* and *exercises,* and we hew and we polish every stone, that goes to that building; and so our health is a long and regular work. . . ."[13]

One of the most distinguishing features of the regimen was the relation it attempted to establish between the self—the "patient"—and medical authority.[14] On the one hand, most regimens spoke from that authority. The authors of regimens had studied medicine, which meant that they had absorbed the Greek and Latin classics on the subject, and many of them had practiced medicine as university-trained physicians.[15] But on the other hand, the regimens gave readers the tools to manage their health on their own. The rules about what to eat and drink and so forth were complex and nuanced; only an established authority could know how to devise them. And yet the emphasis of the regimens was almost always on the potential autonomy of the patient. Thus the title page of Thomas Elyot's *Castel of Helthe* (another work adopting an architectural metaphor to explain the little world of the subject and his discipline of health) claims that the text, gathered "out of the chief authors of physic," may be a tool "whereby every man may know the state of his own body, and preservation of health," and even "how to instruct well his physician."[16] Having learned the rules and the guidelines, the patient was enjoined to live by the lights of a craftiness of his own, to closely observe his physical and emotional sensations, and, in keeping with his observations, to govern his everyday life. It was important that the patient come to know himself as a physical being and, knowing himself, learn how to pursue at the very least what Epicurus called "the pleasure that consists in freedom from bodily pain and mental agitation."[17] Ultimately, the regimens tried both to submit their readers to a universal scientific discipline and to empower them to be their own caregivers. Writing in a spirit more liberal than Grataroli but not out of keeping with the rhetoric of regimens generally, Andrew Boorde asserts that "there is no man nor woman the which have any respect to them self that can be a better Physician for their own safeguard, than their own self can be."[18]

The regimens were popular. In England alone, some 153 medical titles were published by 1605, 33 percent of them regimens of health and related explanatory texts. The early vogue for regimens in English began in 1528 with the publication of Thomas Paynel's English commentary on the centuries-old *Regimen sanitatis Salerni,* along with three original texts, Thomas Moulton's *This Is the Myrour or Glasse of Helthe* (ca. 1531), Elyot's *Castel of Helthe* (1539), and Boorde's *Dyetary of Helth* (1640).[19] By the last years of Elizabeth's reign, Moulton's text had been printed in seventeen editions, Elyot's in sixteen editions, and Boorde's in six. These texts would be joined in print by a slew of new regimens written in England, Italy, and elsewhere. The Italian Platonist Marsilio Ficino, the Belgian Jesuit Leonardus Lessius, the French poet Du Four de la Crespelière, the Italian physician Castor Durante, and the English Puritan William Vaughan are only some of the kinds of names associated with regimens during the fifteenth, sixteenth, and seventeenth centuries. The most well-known dietary guide of all, the medieval *Regimen sanitatis Salerni,* is said to have been printed 240 times in a variety of vernaculars in Europe up to the year 1846.[20] If Grataroli's *Direction,* one of the more impressive texts of the genre, is relatively obscure (it was never printed in England but once), it is because it was swamped by the competition.

Certain qualifications may nevertheless be in order. There was not only the usual gap between theory and practice; increasingly, there was outright resistance to medical lore — perhaps in response to increased awareness of it, perhaps as an expression of a growing spirit of individualism and experimentalism, or of hedonism. Indeed a number of regimens were quite clearly on a preemptive offensive against this resistance. In the eyes of the authors of the regimens, too many people ate what they wanted however they wanted, and thereby ate too much or too greedily or just ate the wrong things, regardless of medical advice. In Italy a work like Bartolomeo Platina's *On Right Pleasure and Good Health* thus endeavors to distinguish between the "self-indulgence" expressed in the consumption of a "variety of foods" from "that pleasure which derives from continence in food and those things which human nature seeks." It wants to show its readers how a "right pleasure," an "honesta voluptate," can be pursued, which is also, contrary to the usual pursuits of pleasure common to the day, a pursuit of "honesta valetudine."[21] With less tactfulness, Luigi Cornaro—writing, as we will see (in chapter 5), a regimen that both precedes from classic principles and attempts to move beyond them—inveighs against his countrymen, those same Italians whom the English knew to be "famous for temperance." "O wretched and unhappy Italy," Cornaro writes, "canst thou not see that intemperance kills every year amongst thy people as great a number as would perish during the time of a most dreadful pestilence, or by the sword or fire of many bloody wars! And these truly immoral banquets of thine, now so commonly the custom,—feasts so great and intolerable that the tables are never found large enough to accommodate the innumerable dishes set upon them . . .—must we not brand them as so many destructive battles!"[22] In England we often find the same thing. "These things considered," Elyot writes about the doctrine he extols,

> it may seem to all men, that have reason, what abuse there is here in this realm in the continual gormandizing, and daily defying [dining] on sundry meats at one meal, the spirit of gluttony triumphing among us on his glorious chariot, called welfare, driving us afore him as his prisoners into his dungeon of surfeit, where we are tormented with catarrhs, fevers, gouts, pleurisies, fretting of the guts, and many other sicknesses, and finally cruelly put to death by them, oftentimes in youth, or in the most pleasant time of our life, when we would most gladly live.[23]

Thomas Paynel goes so far as to claim that he was motivated to provide a vernacular discussion of diets because "men in time past were of longer life, and of more prosperous health than they are nowadays." The reason is clear: "Surfeit and diversity of meats and drinks, letting and corrupting the digestion, enfeebleth man, and very oft causeth this shortness of life."[24] Such writers are responding to prosperity—gluttony's "glorious chariot, called welfare." They see the pleasure people take in "gormandizing." They see that local customs, particularly among the aristocracy, encourage a sort of dietary *copia:* the more dishes of different kinds served at a single meal the better. (We may recall the killjoy Phillip Stubbes inveighing against the "vanity, excess, riot, and superfluity" involved in serving a number of fancy dishes at a single dinner.)[25] They may be taking offense at the ceremonial punctuation of dining habits, where even among the poor all kinds of occasions called for ritualistic feasting and overindulgence, never mind that a number of occasions called for fasting or abstemiousness too. One thing more: the writers were also responding to the crushing fact that, for all the prosperity of the elite, for all the evident care and pleasure they take in ministering to their appetites, there was death everywhere. Adam lived 930 years, Galen 140, Paynel notes, "but nowadays alas, if a man may approach to 40 or 50 years, men repute him happy and fortunate."[26] The most popular regimen in English in the sixteenth century was preoccupied with preventing the plague and delivered its nostrums for the "learned and lewd, rich and poor" so that "every man woman and child [may] be their own physician in time of need against the vengeance and corruption of pestilence that now is reigning with other diseases many more."[27] Diet, of course, was one of the author's main bulwarks against an early death by the plague. One hundred fifty years later, John Archer can be found still complaining that people "live negligently, and do eat and drink they care not what, so it be good in itself, thinking it cannot be bad for them, so it please the Palate," the problem being (in words taken from a proverbial saying) that "thereby many dig their graves with their Teeth."[28]

In any case, clearly not everyone was practicing the rational art of eating that the regimens preached. The regimens promulgated a fixed and artificial discipline in opposition to traditions of behavior that operated more ceremonially, on the one hand, and more intuitively, on the other. In this respect, the regimens can be seen to be a piece with what a number of scholars have considered to be the repressive dimension of the "civilizing process" at work in the Renaissance.[29] The regimens encouraged their readers to be finicky eaters, fastidious in their conduct at the table and choice of food items, ever rational and restrained in the way they ministered to biological need; they thus encouraged them to adopt a system of self-monitoring through which they internalized the discipline of regimented, "civilized" behavior as a whole. Yet resistance to regimens and the medical profession authorizing them was not merely a matter of engaging in a revolt of the lower faculties. A highly educated and self-absorbed, even hypochondriacal aristocrat like Montaigne could show little evidence of familiarity with regimens of health, and much antipathy toward dietary medicine generally, while still paying tribute to the notions of healthy living and careful eating that animated official thinking on the subject:

Both in health and in sickness I have readily let myself follow my appetites and give great authority to my desires and inclinations. I do not like to cure trouble by trouble; I hate remedies that are more nuisance than the disease. To be subjected to the stone and subjected to abstaining from the pleasure of eating oysters, those are two troubles for one. The disease pinches us on one side, the rule on the other. Since there is a risk of making a mistake, let us risk it rather in pursuit of pleasure.[30]

One could say that Sir Andrew Aguecheek is a Montaignian in this respect: a man who follows his appetites, without regard to the science of authorities. But Montaigne believed that in following his appetite he could inductively discover the rational principles governing his own health. The promptings of his appetite were evidence of auto-regularity of the system; they were symptoms of the order of nature within. And making discoveries of this kind was not at all out of keeping with the spirit of the regimen of health. As Platina puts it:

Not all foods suit all people, but as there are various elements and various appetites of men according to their humors, as well as various tastes, so ought there to be various foods so that each may acquire what is agreeable, flavorful, and nutritious. To my mind, no one eats what fills him with distaste, or harms, or pains, or kills. Whoever thinks about what is suitable to his nature and eats that kind of food, or of the type which can nourish his body without harm, will remember that saying of Socrates, that we should eat to live and not live to eat.[31]

We have already encountered Thomas Elyot similarly emphasizing the importance of preference, saying that those things which one has habitually consumed, which have shown themselves to be agreeable to one's nature, and "which do much delight him that eateth" are to be preferred before things recommended on the basis of a priori medical doctrine.[32]

So Montaigne, like many others, was both inimical to professional medical lore and in agreement with much of the spirit by which it was tendered. If experience trumped science, as experience was more reliable and less "trouble," experience itself for subjects like Montaigne was already animated by a discourse of sensations and practices, of stimuli and responses, that was as common to skeptics as to true believers. Despite their evident impatience with what one writer, in a dedicatory verse, stigmatized as "our luxurious age," in expectation of "some new invention to devour / Estates at mouthfuls," the regimens by and large spoke for the common wisdom of the era.[33] Whatever people ate and drank, in whatever quantities and combinations, individuals needed to heed the summonses of their bodies and feed themselves in harmony, moderately, with their constituent, healthy needs. It was in subscribing to this regimen that individuals constructed their "castles of health," defending themselves against the great usurper Disease.

Yet it can come as a surprise, as our brief look at the discourse of the egg has perhaps already indicated, to find what — besides listening to one's own body and feeding it moderately — the dietary manuals recommended. To build one's castle of health or to govern one's commonwealth of health meant taking into account a vast range of foodstuffs and cooking techniques. It meant learning about the qualities of foodstuffs and how cookery affected them in keeping with a compendious system for classifying and assessing those qualities. Each and every edible was a complex substance capable of any number of behaviors — sending bile to the spleen, blood to the heart, heat to the liver, coldness to the head, elation to the spirits, desire to the genitals, blurriness to the eyes, or despair to the soul. An edible could loosen or obstruct, stimulate or deaden, nourish or corrupt, delight or annoy, gladden or depress. It could procure subtleties and spirits or putrefied matters and "evil" humors. Protecting one's health by regulating one's diet consequently meant understanding the sensational behavior of foodstuffs, the "power" of foodstuffs, as Galen had called it — from the moment they touched against the tongue and the palate to the time they percolated in the belly; liquefied into the blood; underwent refinement in the liver, the veins, the heart, and other organs and tissues; became assimilated into tissue or got excreted through sweat, phlegm, urine, or feces; and either entered into the healthy life of the body or else went awry, causing discomfort and disease. "Hot and cold," "moist and dry," as we have already seen eggs characterized, and in addition "corroborating" but also possibly "vicious"—the terms of art by which foodstuffs could be categorized and experienced identify not so much an apparatus of scientific error as a system of life, rooted in the vital little world of digestion and sensation.

III

The science was comprised of at least three related parts, and I am going to discuss them one by one in what follows: the *doctrine of the humors and temperaments,* the *doctrine of intake and discharge,* and the *doctrine of sensory affect.* All three bear further scrutiny. The first articulated the symbolic system that underlay the universe of things — elements, combinations, dispositions, spirits, and energies — comprising the digestive microcosm that was man. The second articulated the fundamental processes and functions of digestion, as well as how the individual bodies and minds could takes measures to regulate and control them. The third articulated the experience of the digesting subject, given the things and the processes the subject had to accommodate.

The *doctrine of the four humors* and the corresponding four elements, four seasons, and four temperaments is the most familiar of the three. If all the bodies in the world were compounded out of earth, water, air, and fire, and if these "elements" were understood not as atomic substances but as material allocations of fundamental "qualities" or "powers"—coldness, moistness, dryness, and heat—then all conditions of all the bodies in the world could be assessed according to their quadrilateral composition, their "temperament" (the Latin-derived word) or "crasis" (the Greek word) with respect to the four qualities. A historian of Galenism calls attention to the paradox embedded in this habit of thought by accounting it a "medical materialism" whose material processes are "animistically conceived."[34] First, we have the material element and the bodies compounded out of them: a hot and dry body, for example. But second, we also have the animistically conceived fact that this body has the power to act heatedly and drily. This animistic quality is the more important. What is crucial to know about this body isn't the air and fire that we might think is dominating its composition, as we think of hydrogen and oxygen dominating the composition of salt water or milk, but that the body behaves according to its two primary animistic tendencies, heat behavior and dry behavior. Of course, the hot and dry behavior of, say, a burning log is rather different from the hot and dry behavior commonly attributed to garlic or arugula (of which more below) or to an individual gripped by a frenzy, another "hot" condition. And the word "animistic" is in some respects unfortunate. Whatever its anthropological meanings, in premodern discourse the "anima" one attributed to things like food — that is, the "soul" or "spirit" or "life force" attributed to them — was a philosophic concept that was subject to dispute. But the general point is clear. Given the doctrine of the four elements and four qualities, bodies could be explained according to their physical composition, on the one hand, and the quality or power of their behavior, their animated tendency, on the other.

The doctrine thus provided the early modern subject with a heuristic, a system for discovering the nature of things encountered in everyday life. All the entities of the world could be located according to a set of four coordinates, four vectors of qualitative animality. To know a thing by this heuristic was to discover its distribution along the four trajectories, its particular quotient of elemental components and tendencies. Once one discovered that distribution, and once one could account for the relation of the components of the thing in keeping with its various qualitative inclinations, one could determine the temperament, the *crasis,* of the thing. This temperament in turn dictated both the general behavioral quality of the entity—whether hot, dry, moist, or cold, or some combination of them—as well as its health, its favorable or unfavorable disposition with regard to well-being and morbidity.

In human bodies all this was found to operate materially by way of the four humors—hot and wet blood, cold and wet phlegm, hot and dry yellow bile (choler), and cold and dry black bile (melancholy)—and the conditions of their "compounding" with one another. The classic statement of the doctrine is found in a Hippocratic writing:

> The body of man has in itself blood, phlegm, yellow bile and black bile; these make up the nature of his body, and through these he feels pain or enjoys health. Now he enjoys the most perfect health when these elements are duly proportioned to one another in respect of compounding, power, and bulk, and when they are perfectly mingled. Pain is felt when one of these elements is in defect or excess, or is isolated in the body without being compounded with all the others. For when an element is isolated and stands by itself, not only must the place which it left become diseased, but the place where it stands in a flood must, because of the excess, cause pain and distress.[35]

In fact, such a doctrine did not quite hold up to developments in anatomical science. Galen put himself forward as a champion of Hippocratic science and frequently reiterated the supremacy of the doctrine of the humors. But as an anatomist, Galen found all sorts of things that were not exactly humors — bone tissue, for example, or the "dark matter" that was excreted in the feces and other "superfluities" that coagulated in the gut. Yet the effect of Galenic medicine was to refer all the parts and substances of the body to the humors composing them (in the variety of "temperaments" possible given the rules of combination), and then to distinguish between defective, excessive, and corrupt humors, on the one hand, and sufficient and healthy and thereby balanced humors, on the other.[36]

Eventually, in the next few centuries after Galen, the doctrine of the humors came to account not only for the different substances of the body but for the temperaments of each of its parts and for the temperament, overall, of individuals. The heart, for example, might therefore be considered a warm and moist part of the body, made out of what balanced out as hot and moist humors, and a thigh bone a cold and dry part of the body. And an individual could be said to be constituted by any of four dominant temperaments or "complexions," the sanguine (hot and wet), the phlegmatic (cold and wet), the choleric (hot and dry), and the melancholic (cold and dry)—these temperaments determining character or personality as well as physical predispositions. Largely responsible for handing down this last development of the theory was the thirteenth-century didactic poem the *Regimen sanitatis Salerni,* where both parts of the body and individuals as whole beings were understood to be dominated by one of the four temperaments. If scholars would come to learn about the theory of the temperaments through the original writings of Galen and Avicenna and other medical authorities, the doctrine entered into the common wisdom of the time by way of the *Regimen sanitatis Salerni,* and this *Regimen* greatly simplified matters while adding the notion of the "temperaments" corresponding to the humors. "Four humors reign within our bodies wholly," the *Regimen* dogmatically informs us, in the 1609 translation by Sir John Harington, better known as the inventor of the water closet.[37] The compounding of the humors divides individuals into four different sorts of "complexions" (another word for temperaments) that align with mental and physical health, personality, habit, and even one's "inclination" toward virtue and vice. The *Regimen* redacts the notion of temperaments into a notion of character, in a Theophrastian sense. Each of the four main temperaments, the *Regimen* says, correspond to a particular complex of mental dispositions, habits, feelings, and body types, and all men (the text says nothing about women) are disposed toward one of the temperamental types. The *Regimen* thus describes a happy-go-lucky "sanguine" man, an aggressive and nervous "choleric" man, a dull and sluggish "phlegmatic" man, and an unhappy, gloomy "melancholic." Mood dominates the characterization—whether happiness, anger, dullness, or depression—but many other aspects of personality, behavior, and physical traits are incorporated besides. Here, for example, is the "sanguine" complexion:

> The *Sanguine* game-son is, and nothing nice,
> Loves Wine, and Women, and all recreation,
> Likes pleasant tales, and news, plays, cards & dice,
> Fit for all company, and every fashion:
> Though bold, not apt to take offence, not ireful
> But bountiful, and kind, and looking cheerful:
> Inclining to be fat, and prone to laughter,
> Loves mirth, & music, cares not what comes after.

In sharp contrast comes the choleric individual, dominated by the hot and dry humor.

Sharp *Choler* is an humor most pernicious,
All violent, and fierce, and full of fire,
Of quick conceit, and therewithal ambitious,
Their thoughts to greater fortunes still aspire,
Proud, bountiful enough, yet oft malicious
A right bold speaker, and as bold a liar,
Of little cause to anger great inclin'd,
Much eating still, yet ever looking pin'd:
In younger year they use to grow apace,
In Elder hairy on their breast and face.[38]

The *Regimen* cautions its readers that the doctrine may be more complex than it initially appears to be; but the overall effect is of a simple and even simplistic division of men into one of four dominant temperaments.

A regimen like this wants its readers to recognize some part of their characterizations in themselves and identify with one of the four complexions. "It behooveth . . . every man upon perfectly and thoroughly to know the habit and constitution of his own body, which consisteth in a temperament and mixture of four qualities," wrote Levinus Lemnius in the mid-sixteenth century.[39] The complexion or temperament of the individual as a whole was thought to have a predictive value. If you knew what your temperament was, you knew your physical and mental predisposition, and so you had a good idea about what was good or bad for you: you could predict which "non-naturals" were particularly suitable or harmful. "Meats must be used according to the diversity that is in bodies," writes Grataroli. And so, for example, "they that have very melancholic blood, must use moist and hot meats, they that be Choleric must use cold and moist, etc."[40] To give another example, from Andrew Boorde: "Melancholy is cold and dry, wherefore Melancholy men must refrain from fried meat [which gets dried out], and meat which is over salt [which is also dried out]." And by contrast, "Choler is hot and dry; wherefore Choleric men must abstain from eating hot spices, and to refrain from drinking of wine, and eating of choleric meat. . . ."[41] "Meat," in English, it may be recalled, was a word that denoted either the flesh of an animal or anything that was edible, from bread and salad to confections. A "choleric meat" is a food item that can for one reason or another be classified among the hot and dry. A strong, astringent wine might even be included among the "choleric meats": though liquid, its extra alcoholic "heat" and its chewy, tannic dryness both express hot and dry behavior in themselves and, in a man given to anger and boastfulness, promote the hot and dry behavior of a bellicose drunkard. It is because of such purported danger of hot and dry items for the choleric personality that Petruchio, in the often-cited dining-room scene in *The Taming of the Shrew*, justifies his refusal to allow Kate to eat dinner. The meat that Petruchio's servants set on the table and that Petruchio has dashed to the floor "was burnt and dried away," Petruchio tells Kate—whatever its "natural" qualities, it has been overheated and overdried and so become temperamentally "hot and dry":

> And I expressly am forbid to touch it;
> For it engenders choler, planteth anger,
> And better 'twere that both of us did fast,
> Since, of ourselves, ourselves are choleric,
> Than feed it with such overroasted flesh.[42]

IV

But there is more. So far as food and drink were the most important factors determining health, this doctrine of the humors and the temperaments was always coupled with what I call the *doctrine of intake and discharge*, the two poles of what in Hippocratic language were known as "the four natural functions" or "vegetable functions" of the body—attraction, retention, concoction (a general term for digestion), and expulsion.[43] The fundamental premise governing the Hippocratic and Galenic model was that, given first of all the nature of elements, humors, and temperaments, health and illness alike came into the body mainly through the non-naturals and primarily through what individuals ate and drank and thus "attracted" to themselves. "Digestion is the root of life," Avicenna is often quoted as saying.[44] The body was a consuming organism. What it attracted, consumed, and processed were the nutrients that made it grow and prosper, that gave it well-compounded tissues and energy, along with, inevitably, the feeble nutrients or non-nutritional matters that could undermine its health. The trick was to ingest what was good for it, to digest or "concoct" the things well, converting them into beneficial humors that could then be used by the various parts of the body for energy and growth; and then to expel those things that were either bad for it or of no use to it. Digestion was the root of life because digestion was the main point of contact between the body and the world, the place where products were assimilated and converted into human substances and "parts" or "members." The stomach, writes the anatomist Thomas Vicary, "is a necessary member to all the body; for if it fail in his working, all the members of the body

shall corrupt. Wherefore Galen sayeth, that the stomach was ordained principally for two causes: The first, that it should be to all the members of the body, as
the earth is to all that are engendered of the earth, that is, that it should desire
sufficient meat for all the whole body: The second is, that the stomach should be
a sack or chest to all the body for the meat, and as a Cook to all the members of
the body."[45] Not the brain, the "governor" of the body, and not the heart, "Lord
and King of all members," the stomach is the first container, conduit, and en-
genderer of life—as it were, "cooking" food for consumption by all the parts.
Digestion was not completed in the stomach, however; apart from the further
processes of elimination, salutary nutrients underwent further digestion in the
liver, the veins, and other parts. The whole of the body was in this sense a digestive organ. In the heart, for example, it was said that well-digested blood underwent a third digestion (after the operations of the liver) where the blood was refined into "a spirit that is clearer, brighter, and subtler than any corporal or bodily
thing that is engendered of the four Elements; for it is a thing that is a mean between the body and the soul."[46] But the stomach was generally understood to be
the last organ within the framework of the digestive body that was under some
sort of conscious sensory control. What the liver did with the chyle sent to it by
the stomach was largely an unconscious, automatic process; what the stomach did
before was directly, consciously sensible to the subject, and to that extent a part
of the subject's sensory awareness and cognitive processes.[47] Note that Vicary, by
ancient authority, claims that the stomach is required so that the body should
"desire" the food it needs. The thought is seconded with more technical reasoning by anatomist William Harvey, who notes that as "the orifice of the stomach
seems entirely made of nerve," so "there is great sympathy between the brain and
the stomach and vice versa." And most tellingly, therefore, the mouth of the
stomach "is the seat of the appetite" ("hic sedes appetitus").[48]

With the framework of this idea, Galen made a distinction that others reiterated but with less clarity. The humors, Galen argued, were everywhere in the
human body. The healthy body was dominated by the warm and moist humor
blood and inclined toward combinations of humors that maintained the moisture and heat of life. Thus "the cause of the natural functions"—that is, the ruling
principle of the healthy functioning of the body—"is eucrasia of the Warm."[49]
But though the humors were manufactured out of the concoction of foodstuffs
in the belly, the humors were not in the foodstuffs themselves. Rather, "the genesis of these humors is accomplished in the body." Food in, humors produced and
retained, and waste materials out. This principle accounts for the fact both that
the same foods had different effects on different people and that one could not
explain the temperamental effects of foodstuffs in the body simply by their ob-

vious sensory qualities. "For if all articles of food contained bile from the beginning and of themselves, and did not produce it by undergoing change in the animal body, then they would produce it similarly in all bodies; the food which was bitter to the taste would, I take it, be productive of bile, while that which tasted good and sweet would not generate even the smallest quantity of bile."[50] Yet it was "known" that honey caused biliousness in old men. So bitterness and biliousness were not the same thing, no more than sweetness and biliousness were the same thing: but the bile produced in a human body, whether out of something bitter like lettuce or something sweet like honey, was always bitter.

Good digestion and good health required both the proper functioning of the body as a digestive organ—which functioning can be attuned by such nonnaturals as getting enough sleep and exercising regularly—and the proper regulation of the intake of food. Individuals needed to make sure that they ate enough food, and enough of food that was good for them, and not too much. And they needed to make sure that they evacuated as much as possible of the things that were not needed or not good for them, the "dross" of foodstuffs, the inevitable "superfluities." Eating too little was obviously deleterious. "Abstinence," Hippocrates writes, "has upon the human constitution a most powerful effect, to enervate, to weaken, and to kill."[51] But more importantly, as this is the condition that physicians were generally called upon to treat and authors of regimens felt called upon to prevent, eating too much was dangerous. To eat too much, to "surfeit," was the chief cause of the production of excessive, imbalanced, or "corrupt" humors in the body and thus, generally speaking, the chief cause of illness among those who were lucky enough to overindulge. "For the wise man sayeth, that surfeits do kill many men, and temperance doth prolong the life."[52] So far as the human body was a digestive organ, anything that caused too many humors to be produced or that caused humors to sit in the body unused or out of balance with other humors had to be avoided. Too much of a given humor could lead directly to a temperamental imbalance or "distemper": too much yellow bile in the head, for example, would lead to too much anger in one's thoughts. Too many foodstuffs in the belly of whatever temperament, moreover, could lead not only to a dyspeptic condition, preventing further healthy digestion, and to an overall sluggishness of the body, but to the overlong remaining of food products in the belly, which might then "corrupt and putrefy" and transform into "evil humors." "For when there is abundance of humors in the body, it cannot be those but Agues must needs be engendered of that continual obstruction and putrefaction: and a store of diseases must needs spring out thereof, unless those excrements by continual labor and convenient exercise be purged, and the humors reduced into good blood."[53]

Moreover, mixing different foodstuffs in the belly inhibited—indeed, "corrupted"—digestion:

> To keep good diet, you should never feed
> Until you find your stomach clean and void
> Of former eaten meat, for they do breed
> *Repletion,* and will cause you soon be cloyed.[54]

Elyot similarly says "that sundry meats, being divers in substance and quality, eaten at one meal, is the greatest enemy to health that may be . . . for some meats being gross and hard to digest, some fine and easy to digest, do require divers operations of Nature, and divers temperatures of the Stomach."[55] When writers complain about the *copia* of banquets, they are applying a general principle of ancient and medieval medicine, for they are protesting not only against the provision of more food than is needed for good digestion and nutrition, but also against taking too many different kinds of foods at once. To eat right was to eat the right foods, in the right amount, in the right combination, in the right intervals, at the right time of day and the right time of year (cooling salads in the summer, hot pickled brawn in the winter), and generally speaking to eat simply, on the side of caution, not allowing the system to be overcome with too much of a thing or too many things. Moderation was always the rule to follow; the readers of regimens were cautioned always to leave off eating before feeling full and suffering "repletion." "Let the strength of thy concoction be always thy best guide," writes James Hart, "and keep rather within, than at any time exceed the strength of thy stomach."[56] They were to leave the table with still a little appetite left over.

V

Third and finally comes the *doctrine of sensory affect*—perhaps the most difficult part of the science to understand, since it requires us to imagine not only a theory but a regime of sensation that we no longer experience. It suggests to us that individuals could actually feel their bodies in the experience of eating differently from how we feel them now, and that they felt their bodily experience in this way because of an idea, a language, or a semiotic structure. The theory of the humors and the doctrine of intake and discharge were always correlated to corporal experience; indeed, they stemmed from corporal experience. And experience itself, by the same token — far from being (as the pure empiricist might suppose it to be) a bundle of sense perceptions given explanatory order after the fact by induction and reference to a theory — was already correlated with ideas and language and semiotic structures. The sensational science of nutrition, the common heritage from erudite Greeks and, in etiolated form, from popular folklore, intervened in the structure of sensory experience and both supplemented and determined it. It organized sensory response by way of its quadrilateral heuristic of things, qualities, and tendencies. It elicited certain kinds of sensory responses, discouraged others, and always framed them by way of a language that was at once in conversation with unmediated gustatory sensations and in conflict with the very idea of unmediated response. It imposed a formal order on matter, though the forms were held to be *in* the matter, governing the matter at all points too. If it was closely correlated with what one might feel in parts of the body, with what one *sensed* in them — sourness in the gullet, congestion in the lungs, heaviness in the legs, itchiness of the skin — it also imposed a hermeneutic structure of signatures, correspondences, and causalities upon them. A "dry" meat from the point of view of its supposed temperament (for example, salt fish) might also be dry in the mouth, dry in the stomach, dry in the blood, dry in the loins, dry in the eyes (causing myopia), and dry in the skin — all the dryness embedded in corresponding (but not mechanically equivalent) signatures, derived from the same purported cause. Or a "cold" food like lettuce might be cold in the mouth, cold in the stomach, cold in the blood, and so forth, which would explain both its sometimes noted effect on excretion — lettuce was an aperient, cooling the bowels — and its often noted effect on sleep: lettuce was a soporific too, as it cooled the brain, putting it to rest. But the lines of qualitative tendencies and causes and effects were not always so simple as these continua of dryness or coolness — a point that Galen and Hippocrates hastened to make, as when pointing out that sweet honey in old men produced the rather unsweet bitterness of a bilious affect. Lettuce itself, a coolant, could nonetheless be recommended for cool and wet melancholics, so far as it cooled and moistened and therefore helped purge hot and dry humors that were causing the melancholic to produce more cool and dry melancholia. But one way or another, the language of food took its vocabulary from sensation and imposed itself upon experience as a system for organizing sensation, even as it also claimed to be a science of what the Greeks called "hidden causes" and "rational principles." As Hippocrates writes, when trying to determine how much and of what quality a person ought to eat, "no measure, neither number nor weight, by reference to which knowledge can be made exact, can be found except bodily feeling [tou somatos ten aisthesin]."[57]

The sensational science that appeared in dietary manuals not only explained sensations and their causes, but also attempted to control how people experienced them; it placed their gustatory lives within a context regimenting aesthetic response. Sometimes the discourse was inflected toward what was called, as in Platina's work, "right pleasure," so that if it wasn't designed to maximize enjoyment, at least it was bent toward encouraging the individual to experience a condition of virtuous sensuality: not only Epicurus's "pleasure that consists in freedom from bodily pain and mental agitation," but also a positive and even lusty hygienic "delight" in the "dainties" of the table. This attitude became more popular in the seventeenth century. Sometimes, by contrast, and even also in the seventeenth century, the scientific language of food was inflected toward asceticism. Freedom from pain and care was enough in such cases, and the regimen of food was a regimen of self-denial for the sake of a more spiritual relation to the demands of the body. A number of writers of the early modern period maintained, not without some evidence to back them up, that a sparing and "sober" diet leading to greater spirituality also led to a healthier, happier, and longer life. And at times, most notably in the case of the learned Ficino in Italy in the fifteenth century and the self-taught laborer Thomas Tryon in England in the late seventeenth century, the sensational science of food took on mystical dimensions, whether in the direction of Ficino's Neoplatonic copiousness — a diet that added gold and silver to wine and mixed tempering spices and flavorings with everything else — or Tryon's meager Quaker-inspired vegetarianism, where "Parsnips boiled in good Water, seasoned with Salt, Vinegar, Butter, and Mustard," are said to make "a brave substantial hearty Dish of Food."[58] In both cases, diet becomes a way for a man to bring himself closer to divinity. Similar to this was the emphasis on a specific regimen for scholars, who needed to take especial care for the body — whether by way of lusty enjoyment, self-denial, or mystical combinations — in order to maximize the potential of the intellectual soul and compensate for the scholar's constitutive melancholy.

Derived from a theory of humors that was at once material and animistic, adapted to an intake-discharge model of the vital functions, and both correlated with and imposed upon sensory experience the science called upon doctors and patients alike to take account of, monitor, and endlessly interpret the sequence of ingesting, digesting, assimilating, and excreting that was the primary modality of everyday life. The healthy individual could learn to stay on the lookout for discomfort, a sensory sign indicating a fall off of health, a snare in the system — acid indigestion, for example — and attempt to rectify the situation with familiar dietary and purgatory measures. The unhealthy individual — suffering from a rash, a fever, a pain in the sides — consulting a doctor, could have his or her body and excretions subjected to a "diagnosis" (a "knowledge by way of") through which discomfort and even insensible processes and products could be turned into scientifically devised "symptoms," from which followed etiology, prognosis, and treatment. The system was enormously flexible, capacious, and elaborate, even if for nonprofessionals it might have seemed to provide, if not the same diagnosis, then the same therapeutic response to each and every illness. Most diagnoses were discoveries of an excess of something in the body (though there were diseases of deficiency too), an excessive humor or an excessively "corrupted" humor "clogging" the body and causing it harm. The effects that most often counted were thus only those that could be expressed — and felt — in terms of excess, clogging, thinning, and removal, and the treatments most often prescribed were methods of ridding the body of what was excessive and obstructive in it. "Clisterium donare, / Postea bleedare, / Afterwards purgare," the chorus in Molière repeats in pigeon Latin. Give a clyster (an enema), then bleed, then purge. And if it doesn't work? "Postea bleedare, / Afterwards purgare. / Rebleedare, repurgare, and reclysterisare."[59] Molière subjects the Galenic system to a violently reductive logical analysis — give an enema, then bleed, then purge — in a spirit whose rigor and clarity may be associated with the new philosophy.[60] In actual practice, the byways of diagnosis could be far more empirical and varied, yet almost all also followed the main paradigm to which Molière reduced it. An earlier comic writer depicts the practice of cleansing and purging of obstructions in view of a giant who lives on the high seas and regularly dines on sailing ships and villages, along with their inhabitants. When indisposed, the giant had for a doctor, the narrator says, "a chimneysweep who he had take a long ladder and climb it and get into his belly by way of his asshole with his chimney scraper. The chimneysweep scraped his bowels and his belly and removed the anchors, tops, and masts which were stuck in various parts of his belly: and after having removed and scraped and cleaned everything he climbed out of the bowels and mounted into the giant's body and went out by his mouth. For illness the giant never used any other medicine or any other doctor."[61]

But this is ridiculous. Consider the serious analysis and care tendered by a French physician for the "green-sickness." Technically, "green-sickness" is most commonly another word for "chlorosis," an anemia that sometimes afflicts young women at the age of puberty, giving their skin a pale green cast, and that frequently leads to amenorrhea and a morbid appetite. For early modern physicians, this condition encompassed several other ailments as well, including menstrual pains, abdominal bloating, migraines, hyperventilation, and anorexia. We might today begin an analysis of such a disorder by accounting for hormonal imbalances triggered by the onset of puberty or by looking at a nervous condition, a psychological stressor: in the language of twentieth-century depth psychology, we might attribute at least some of the symptoms to "hysteria." In the hands of Robert Burton, writing in the early seventeenth century, at least one version of the green-sickness, the "love-melancholy" of the young maiden thwarted in love, is associated with an overwrought and unsatisfied sexual impulse; the best cure for such a disease might then just be to let the virgin "have her way."[62] A form of green-sickness was thus correlated with erotic frustration and its cure with satisfying the hitherto frustrated desire. But that is not exactly how the trained medical practitioner would see things. Our physician Lazare Rivière begins his characterization of the ailment by saying that it is a disease of "obstruction"; that is, it is a product of a fault in the system of elimination. It comes, he says, from "an evil concoction of the bowels." A second- or third-order digestion of foodstuffs has in such cases gone awry. "And from thence their Body is full of Crudities, which, being carried forth, make an evil Habit."[63] "Crudities" were ill-digested matters, not feces necessarily but insufficiently processed items lingering in the system, like the solid matter that can sometimes be found in vomit, or the supposedly useless particles that can be found in dried blood, or the material of inflammations and tumors, or whatever it was in the fecal matter that prevented it from being eliminated.[64] Rivière imagines that "crudities," perhaps even of microscopic dimension, are being "carried forth" through the chyle and the blood, and remaining there, cause havoc. Not only are the lower bowels affected, although a lower bowel disorder is central to the analysis. The wandering crudities "produce diverse Symptoms in the Hypochondria [the upper bowels or belly, above the intestines], [including] a swelling of the bowels, by which the midriff is oppressed. . . ." It is this pressure against the diaphragm "which causeth shortness of breath." Ultimately, the swelling in the bodies produced arrhythmia and migraines: "And because gross blood and wind are carried by the Branches of the hollow Vein, and great Artery into the Heart, which contend against them for fear of suffocation, by often moving of its Arteries, there is a palpitation of the Heart, and often a beating of the Temples." Anorexia and other eating disorders may be consequents of this "obstruction" too. "Besides, they have in this Disease a loathing of meat, because the Stomach is filled with crude Excrements by reason of its evil Concoction and distribution: which excrements having gotten an evil quality by a peculiar kind of corruption, causes a desire of evil meats, and things not ordained for nourishment, as Salt, Spices, Chalk, Coals, Ashes, and the like, which disease is called *Pica Malacia,* or strange Longing. . . ."[65]

So a complex of well-identified and correlated symptoms, grouped together under the heading of the "green-sickness," like just about any other disease a Galenic physician might treat, ends up being a digestive disorder. Menstrual pains, headaches, arrhythmia, hyperventilation, eating disorders — all this, found with some frequency in this particular combination in pubescent girls and young maidens, turns out to be caused by an "obstruction" that begins in the bowels and travels through other parts of the body. The etiology of the disease is even rooted, however surprisingly to us, in poor eating habits. "The Causes of the Obstructions of the Veins, of the Womb, and the Hypochondria, are thick, slimy, and crude Humors, coming commonly from evil Diet: for these Virgins drink great droughts of Water at bed-time, or in the morning fasting; or early Vinegar, Herbs, unripe fruits, Snow, or Ice: hence it is they lose their Natural heat, and there is abundance of crude Excrements."[66]

The cure hence involves changes in the diet, the usual bleedings and purgings, warm baths, and, as in Burton, sex. "The Cure of the Disease is by opening Obstructions, by emptying the filthy Humours from the whole Body, and correcting the distemper of the Bowels, and strengthening them." But when the symptoms are mild and "the disease is less, and comes only from the Obstruction of the Veins of the Womb, in young women it is cured by Marriage." "Copulation, if it may be legally done, after the use of opening Medicines, is very good; and thereby the Natural heat is stirred up in parts Natural, by which the vessels of the Womb are much enlarged." As Rivière ultimately directs a good deal of his attention to therapies like warm baths and sex and to the symptomology of the womb, we may find that his main concern is with the uterus, as well it might be since this is exclusively a disease of women and includes menstrual pains. But the womb is only part of the picture for him. His therapeutic regimen treats the person instead of the disease — it is "holistic" — and includes a whole range of manipulations of the "non-naturals." And even so, the disease is conceptualized as a failure of the intake-discharge system, beginning with the ingestion of the wrong food and drink, or else with fasting, and ending with an "obstruction" of the system that needs to be eased by relaxing the system, by heating it up (whether through baths or sex), and still more importantly by purging the obstruction, breaking up and eliminating the "thick, slimy, and crude Humors" clogging the system. Sex, too, besides heating the body (though Rivière prudishly avoids going into this detail) was considered an eliminative or "excremental" process: at climax the woman expelled her seed along with phlegmatic fluids (perhaps the "slimy" humors Rivière refers to), and thus also eased the obstruction gripping her belly.[67]

There is nothing unusual about Rivière's analysis. An English physician of the seventeenth century, one John Symcotts, diagnoses a woman's repeated miscarriages, in a letter to her as follows:

Madam,

Upon inquiry of your present condition, I heard (to my grief) that your stock was lessened which you carried from Melchburn, still disposed to often miscarriages, and frequently troubled besides with a decumbency of humors causing much pain and lameness. For my part, I ascribe all this to the ill concoction of your stomach, perverting and depraving the good nourishment it receives and possessing it with intemperate qualities; the expulsive sends down a good proportion of it to the more remote and ignoble parts as not consistent with the temper of the more vital; and that which remains in the veins (upon the same grounds) power enough to irritate nature to expulsion, and with that, of the grateful fruit of conception.

For remedy hereof . . . I'll give you my opinion. 1. I think it very convenient that as soon as you find any symptoms or forerunners of the aforesaid recumbency of humors, that you please to take a vomit, and in less than a week, a second, in like manner (in case you vomit with as much facility as I have known you to do), the third also, especially if yellow or green humors were voided thereby. 2. After this it will be good to clear your blood of such degenerate humors as are mixed therewith, by effectual purgatives, for three or four days together as your strength will permit. 3. Then, omitting these for a time you may please to take ass's milk for twelve days or a fortnight. And all this while (which will be your worst task) to drink for your ordinary beer or barley-liquorice water. . . .[68]

"Clisterium donare, / Postea bleedare, / Afterwards purgare." And drink some milk. Whatever is wrong with you — and I have intentionally chosen far-fetched ailments, female disorders experienced in the uterus, the chest, and the head, in order to make the point clear — it ends up having its origin in the digestion system, and its cure in non-naturals that amend the intake-discharge apparatus: not because the stomach is king, but because the whole body is a digestive organ, with the stomach at its center, and because therefore the condition of the body is governed by what goes in it, what is assimilated by it, and what goes out.

The grand illusion of early modern medicine is that all of this cannot only be *explained,* but also *sensed.* Before the famous Cartesian split between body and mind, a split that the doubtful Molière would seem to be embracing, doctors and diners assume that the body-mind continuum can sense what happens to it in matters of health. It can feel the "corroboration" of eggs, the "coldness" of lettuce. The heart, center of the "spirit," can sense corroboration and so forth: when "feeling" enervated — that is, lacking in spirit — it can be lifted by a "cordial," a heart-stimulating beverage. The brain, center of reason and imagination, can sense a "cooling off" when it is headed toward shutting down and going to sleep;

it can similarly sense heat when it has had too much too drink or been aroused by too much choler. The relaxed individual is "cool." The angry individual is "hot." And so is the whole digesting mind-body apparatus, filling up and burning and depleting its store of goods, dissolving and moving things along, or failing to dissolve and move them along, generating obstructions, getting blocked up and too cold or too hot, suffering pain, bloating, constipation, failed pregnancies, failed appetite, headaches and nausea, fever and delirium, or even depression or frenzy, feelings of worthlessness, delusions of grandeur, lycanthropy (the illusion that one is a wolf, thought to be a common ailment), or the mad dancing illness of Saint Vitus' fire. What wonder that in this sensational world of feelings, emotions, and thoughts, a woman rendered desolate by a history of miscarriages would be advised to undergo catharsis, while soothing herself with milk and warm baths, or a giant would find it beneficial to swallow a chimney sweeper and have his ass and his belly regularly scraped clean.

VI

It is time now to look at how foods were actually categorized and analyzed, and how the system of interpretation operated both dogmatically, on the basis of an authoritative theory going back to the Greeks, and empirically, on the basis of the actual experience of bodily sensation. But where to begin? Not all regimens take an encyclopedic approach to the subject; some seem to assume familiarity with the encyclopedias of food available elsewhere and some, asserting that the encyclopedic regimens are too complicated, uninteresting, or irrelevant, go on ways of their own. Not all encyclopedic regimens begin the same or end the same. But those that go the whole route include dozens of entries on meat, fowl, fish, shellfish, breads, fruits, vegetables, dairy products, and beverages, and they universally impose some order or other on their materials. Frequently they categorize their items precisely according to their food groups: they discuss venison along with lamb, mutton, veal, beef, kid, and pork; lettuce along with spinach, parsley, borage, cucumbers, asparagus, and cress. But the system underlying their remarks is not always clear. A group of entries in one food group may be interrupted by a series of entries about foods in other groups. The text may digress and move on to medicines and tonics, or, as is the case with Platina's *De honesta voluptate*, talk about cookery at length, adding recipes to the dietary entries. Galen starts with grains, beginning with wheat flour and bread; Boorde starts with beverages; Platina begins with salt, bread, fruit, and oils. There is no dietary pyramid; indeed, the closest thing to our food pyramid is probably the system, adopted by some, of discussing foods according to how healthful or detrimental they are to individuals of each of the four complexions. Nor are there any criteria for analyzing the food groups except by the triple doctrines of the temperaments and humors, the intake-discharge system, and sensory affect. By the first doctrine, every food was compounded out of the qualities that would then yield humors in various concentrations (and hence be good or bad for people of different complexions). By the second, every food was provided a quantity of "nourishment," to provide more or less for the making of "good juice" ("good" chyle) and hence of "good blood," or, by contrast, to include superfluous or corrupted substances that provided no nourishment and needed to be excreted or purged. In a non-Galenic medical text of antiquity, which also had some influence in the early modern period and which jibed with Galenism in a number of ways, Celsus divides foods into categories both according to how "strong" a nourishment they provide and how much "good juice" they yield, the two not being the same at all: beef, for Celsus, is the strongest nourishment but provides a poor juice; pork, by contrast, is a weak nourishment but yields a good juice.[69] (One of the indicators of how "strong" a nourishment a food provides, according to Celsus, Galen, and others, is how little of it passes through the system as excrement: pork chops are better nourishment than apples because the former seem to get entirely assimilated by the body, whereas the latter mainly seem to get excreted.) Yet however tempered or "strong" a foodstuff may be, by the third doctrine, the rule of sensory affect, every food could be seen to be primarily important in terms of the impact it had on sensory qualities and virtues observable in the human body. One foodstuff, in addition to its temperamental quotient, may be thought to clog the stomach and restrain the flux. Another might stimulate the stomach, ease the kidneys, and soothe a sore throat. A third might clear the lungs, burn the intestines, and arouse a longing for love. Foods make themselves felt in the human system, and a large part of dietary science involves predetermining what the resulting feelings are.[70] Many of the determinations have to do with a food's density; texture and taste against the teeth, tongue, and palate; and its impact on the stimulus of gastric acids and systolic response, and hence of feelings that early moderns would describe as provoking, cloying, biting, embittering, heating, strengthening, mollifying, comforting, burdening, drying, obstructing, easing, cooling, or ventilating. Integrated into the descriptions and analyses of foodstuffs were the sensational aspects of food—how welcome an item tasted and felt in the mouth, how light or heavy and warm or cold it felt in the belly, how it aroused or arrested further appetitive longing, what eventual pains or comforts, obstructions or reliefs it caused in the bowels and the urinary tract, how light-hearted and clear-headed or depressed and lethargic one felt as it went through first, second, and third digestion. And sometimes these sensational aspects played an unspoken role in organizing the listings. Clearly Platina's order of foods reproduces a traditional Latinate sensibility about eating—at the beginning, salt, bread, fruits (including olives), and oils, Platina only gradually working up to heavier foods like red meat. We find in the Italian Castor Durante's more systematic, *Il tesoro della sanità* (1586) much the same thing. Yet in Platina's text, the listing of different kinds of foods by food groups also follows the order of service that the regimen recommends. Even in the fifteenth century, for example, there was some controversy over whether salad should be served as a first or last course; and it was not so clear as we assume it to be today that sweets ought always to be served as one of the last courses.

As for individual food items, one can begin anywhere. Pork, bread, apricots, milk, cheese, broad beans, and borage: all of the items are interlinked, and some of the items are more "nourishing" or otherwise more serviceable, but no item has *logical* priority. Yet all foodstuffs are subjected to more or less the same kind of analysis and the same kind of rhetorical treatment. Beef, we have seen, is universally accounted to be "cold and dry" as well as "gross" and "hard," and usually considered to be of "poor nourishment" and dangerous to melancholics, leading to dry skin diseases and depression among other noxious conditions. Pork is usually considered to be warm and moist as well as light and easy to digest, and, in the words of Castor Durante, most "copiously and praiseworthily nourishing" ("dà copiosissimo, & lodevol nutrimento").[71] "Of all foods," Galen observes, noting the great similarity between the flesh of swine and the flesh of humans, "pork is the most nutritious."[72] Usually pork is also said to "provoke urine," a good effect, but wild boar is preferred to domestic pigs because boar is less moist.[73] Most fish are usually considered "cold and moist," though some more than others; they are commonly held to be dangerous to phlegmatics and for all eaters prone to "corruption" in the stomach. (In Lent-observing societies, this traditional understanding of fish created not a few conceptual and practical problems, which were partly solved by the preponderance of salted fish.) Fruits are usually cold and moist and of poor to middling nourishment (a problem in regions rich with orchards), but most vegetables are warmer and drier and of greater nutrition than fruit. Because of their fleshiness, asparagus and artichokes are frequently admired for their nutritional value. Bread, especially white bread, is usually recommended as a warm and dry and quintessentially nourishing food when taken with a liquid like wine, particularly by Mediterranean writers. Rice, by contrast, is held to be cooler and wetter and not as sound a source of nutrition. Spices are usually "hot," and so, though they add little nutritional value otherwise, are good with foods that are constitutively "cold," "tempering" them and thus rendering them more suitable to eat. Spices are also good for melancholics, with their "cold" temperament, as they heat up the blood and dissolve the heavy "crudities" that might otherwise clog it: "Twice a day," Ficino recommends to the melancholic scholar, "eat food that is both moderate and light, and that is seasoned with cinnamon, mace, and nutmeg."[74] "Cinnamon," writes Grataroli, "over and beside the heat which it hath (for it is said to be hot toward the third degree) is also very good for the stomach and Liver. It openeth obstructions and comforteth them both, and also it dryeth up the humidity and moisture of the stomach and keepeth it from corruption and putrefaction."[75] Garlic, a more controversial item over the ages, is also a substance that "warms," according to Hippocrates. In addition, it "passes well by the stool and by urine, and is good for the body though bad for the eyes."[76] Grataroli recognizes the heat in garlic and related items like onions but thinks them "better to be forborne, as not fit for a Student or magistrate: unless peradventure in winter they that are phlegmatic may use them being boiled or in Sauces to purge phlegm withal."[77] Durante, more dispassionately, notes that garlic is "hot and dry in the fourth degree, and sharp, and has the power of biting, digesting, stimulating the appetite, and cutting."[78] William Vaughan says that if roasted or boiled or eaten after beets, garlic "may be taken to expel venomous humors out of the body, to clarify the voice, to encourage a faint-hearted man, and to dissolve wind."[79]

But let us return to our "Eggs," which I cite once more.

Eggs

Eggs and chiefly those of Hens, are a Food much used and esteemed amongst us; an Egg consists of two parts, the Yolk, and the White. The yolk is moderately hot and moist, and very corroborating; the White is cold and dry, and affords also much Nourishment, and lasting enough, but hard of Concoction.

The Newest Eggs are the best, and Nourish most and soonest, and yield good Aliment [i.e., nutrition], but the stalest are the worst, and the Corruption of Eggs is most dangerous, for we say . . . the best Food Corrupted, becomes the worst and most perilous. They do not well agree with those whose Liver and Stomach are filled with Vicious Humors, and in Choleric and hot Stomachs they are easily Corrupted, and turned into choler; as for the Cooking of them they are best when the Yolk is soft, and the Rest hardened to a White Color, and so supt up, being boiled in Water, they may easily be given to a weak Stomach; they are stronger in taste, boiled in the shell than poached, especially if Roasted, but the worst way of Dressing them, is to fry them in a Pan.

What we have here is one entry among many others, covering most of the common foodstuffs. Like all of the entries in this and many other texts, this entry on eggs is thoroughly typical and mostly derivative. It follows a generic pattern, which follows from the mode of analysis and presentation that Galenic medicine encouraged. The item, the egg, is broken down into its parts; its temperament and nutritional value is explained. The reader is then told how to choose among examples of the item. Drawbacks of the item, according to the temperament of those who would eat them, are listed. Medicinal uses are then mentioned. Finally, directions for cooking the food, in keeping with principles at once having to do with science and gastronomy, are mentioned. Whatever the typical reader probably already knows about the subject, by generic convention the complete entry accomplishes at least five things: (1) it explains what the item is and analyzes it according to its temperamental qualities; (2) it specifies how "nourishing" the item is; (3) it specifies how readily the item is digested; (4) it explains to which people and with which complexions the item is most agreeable, to whom it is least agreeable, and under what conditions it may also have additional powers or virtues in the body; and (5) it prescribes how and when they are best chosen and prepared.

By now it should be clear under what conditions, by way of what "strategic form" such an entry can be included in a dietary manual. The heat and moisture of the yolk, the coldness and dryness of the white, the "corroborating" powers of the yolk, the less palliative but still strongly nourishing white—all such characteristics follow from applications of a general quadrilateral heuristic to perceived sensory qualities. "There is a great difference in the parts of an egg," wrote Thomas Cogan a century earlier, "for the yolk is temperately hot, the white is cold and clammy, and hardly digesteth, and the blood thereof engendered is not good."[80] The distinction between those for whom eggs may be especially beneficial or harmful, depending on their complexions, the explanation of the distinction by reference to "Vicious Humors," specific body parts, and "corruption"—all this follows from the "grouping of objects" that Galenic science institutionalized, a grouping according to the categories of the salutary and the noxious, the vital and the corrupt, and so forth, and that found confirmation both in the observations of things and the correspondences and signatures that may be discovered by way of observation. Thus, Ficino at one point also compares the egg yolk to an overheated, corrupted "yellow, fiery, and thick form" of bile—not that egg yolks are bilious, but that bile, in its noxious form, can be like an egg yolk, which reveals a potentially noxious character in the egg.[81] And finally, the recommendation to choose fresh eggs over old ones, poached eggs over roasted ones, soft-cooked eggs over hard-cooked eggs, and to avoid eating fried eggs if one can, all for the sake of ease of digestion in the all-inclusive sense of "digestion"—all this follows from a type of enunciation, which connects medical advice with cookery and includes culinary recommendations along with medical analysis, in keeping with the practical experience of a trained, food-recommending physician. "Eggs cooked in a frying pan," the great Galen had written, "have the worst nourishment in every way, because as they are cooked they become greasy, and besides producing a thick juice they also contain something bad and excrementitious."[82] The advice here need not at all correlate with culinary practices and common attitudes. "There is so much known about fried, roasted, and scrambled eggs that it is not necessary to speak about them," said one fourteenth-century cookbook.[83] The sensational science made pronouncements of its own, according to its own impulses and logic. But its complexity as a language at once of authority and experience should not be underestimated. The sensational science followed byways that combined reliance on authority with personal observation, a priori categories with experience, an abstract model of nutritional strength and the "warm" soundness of the blood with a "grouping of objects" in terms of sensory affect, a textual strategy or "type of enunciation" with a sociopsychological habit of dietary choice. But the effect was felt throughout the ages. In 1615 Gervase Markham advised the housewife to make collops and eggs (i.e., bacon and eggs), cooking the eggs separately: Once the bacon is done, "take your eggs, break them into a dish, and put a spoonful of vinegar unto them, then set on a clean skillet with fair water on the fire, and as soon as the water boileth put in the eggs, and let them take a boil or two." When they are cooked through, she adds, "dishing up the collops, lay the eggs upon them, and so serve them up: and in this sort you may poach eggs when you please, for it is the best way and most wholesome."[84]

Following the lead of the Hippocratic writers, the great Galen provided a precedent according to which for fifteen hundred years educated cooks and diners often studiously avoided fried eggs, apparently because in the frying some of the oil or butter burns and darkens and turns a little bitter and solid particles derived from the egg, the pan, or the oil itself are suspended in the precipitate, and because therefore, given the sensational material obviously at hand, notable to the senses of taste, sight, smell, and even touch, something "bad and excrementitious" hovered over the *language* of eggs.

This was not, as we will see in the next few chapters, the only language that hovered over products like eggs. Food was also the subject of an art—cookery—

along with the language that developed to disseminate it. It was furthermore the object of dreams and the language of dreams. It even became a tool and symbol of "civilization." But first of all it was always, like the egg, a combination of the hot and dry and the cold and wet, a substance either invigorating or dulling, or somewhere in between, a substance spurring or obstructing, good or evil, filling or excrementitious — out there, in the object, objectively conceived, and also in here, in the body, the subject of sensation.

Chapter Three

THE COOKBOOK AS LITERATURE

I

"INCIPIT LIBELLUS DE ARTE COQUINARIA," the manuscript starts off: "Here begins the little book on the art of cookery." Its first entry, with a heading in Latin and a recipe in Old Danish, reads as follows:

Quomodo fiet oleum de nucibus.

Man skal takae en dysk mæthe nutæ kyænæ, oc en æggy skalæ full mæth salt, oc latæ them samæn i en heet mortel oc stampæ thæt wæl, oc writhæ gømæn et klæthæ; tha warthær thæt oly.

The modern editor renders it in English thus:

How to make walnut oil.

One should take a dish of walnut kernels and an eggshell full of salt, and place them together in a heated mortar; pound them well and wring through a cloth. Then it becomes oil.[1]

The "little book" may be the oldest surviving manuscript of its kind written in a modern European language, though similar manuscripts show up from about the same time, perhaps only a few years later, in Italy, France, and England. Dating from about 1300, the book is a carefully produced, decorated manuscript bound in codex along with a text on plants (that is, an "herbal") and a text on the art of stonecutting. Its headings are all in Latin: "De salso ad carnes recentas apto" (About a sauce for fresh meat); "Quomodo conficatur pastellum de medullis cervorum" (How to prepare a pasty of deer marrow); "Item aliud temperatum pullorum" (Another way of preparing chicken). The rest is in idiomatic Danish, though with some borrowings from other European languages. Editors have long suspected that the collection is a translation of an earlier work written in Middle Low German, which itself may have been based on a text of Mediterranean origin; and slightly later versions of the text appear in Icelandic and Low German as well as a second Danish manuscript. It is not a lengthy or elaborate book. In its first extant version, it contains only twenty-five recipes and speaks to only a small repertory of ingredients and procedures. But the text is not unsystematic or lacking in thoroughness. After it explains how to make walnut oil, it goes on to specify the making of almond oil, almond butter, and almond milk. Then it discusses sauces of various kinds, made of basic vehicles like almond milk, vinegar, broth, and honey, to which seasonings like mustard, cinnamon, cloves, nutmeg, garlic, and ginger are added. Next it gives directions for serving fish with sauces, preparing a pair of custards and a pair of gruels (including a "hwit moos," which the translator renders as "white mush"), deer marrow pasty, and a number of chicken dishes, where the chicken is either stewed, roasted, or baked. The food is typical of what we know of thirteenth- and fourteenth-century cookery in western Europe, although the dishes are not as complex or heavily spiced and sweet as in other texts of the same kind. An especially interesting dish that appears toward the end is "Chickens Hunter Style" (in Old Danish, *honær* [chickens] *inder iæghæt*), perhaps the earliest recorded recipe for a preparation that is still common today in the form of *pollo alla cacciatore* and *poulet au chasseur*:

About a dish called Chickens Hunter Style

One should roast a hen and cut it apart; and grind garlic, and add hot broth and lard, and wine and salt and well beaten egg yolks, and livers and gizzards. And the hen should be well boiled in this. It is called "Chickens Hunter Style."

Though most of us are most familiar with a cacciatore where sautéed chicken parts are finished in a sauce of fresh tomatoes and mushrooms, one also finds southern Italian versions *in bianco*, made as in the Danish recipe with stock and egg yolks. A quick search of the Internet even shows recipes where the chicken, as here, is roasted rather than sautéed before it is steeped in a liquid.[2]

Recipes were nothing new even in the Middle Ages. But it was one thing to pass recipes along by oral demonstration, as most had been passed on from cook to cook since the beginning of cooking, and another thing to do so by written communication. The written recipe contains an added element of what historians of the book call "fixity."[3] Reducing an abundance of practical operations and sensory experiences to a minimally adequate set of instructions, it precipitates the culinary experience into linguistic form, codifying its operations and materials and fixing the experience once and for all. It thus forestalls variation, while at the same time allowing for greater precision and complexity. Hot broth *and* lard *and* wine *and* salt *and* egg yolks, the latter *well beaten,* all belong to this signature "Hunter Style" preparation, which will thus always be pretty much the same. It is because all of these operations and ingredients are included that this precise dish, named and categorized and in this way enshrined, can be duplicated in a kitchen — can be duplicated, in fact, in a kitchen far away in time and place from the kitchen where the recipe originated. In view of such a process, the contributor to the eighteenth-century *Encyclopédie* entry on "Cuisine" cites a passage from the comedy *Adelphi,* by Terence, where a household steward tells one of the kitchen servants, after complaining about dishes that he considered ill-prepared, "Illud recte; iterum fic memento."[4] (This is done right; remember how to make it again.) So one of the chief impulses behind the recording of recipes is memory. Because in the flow of production and consumption when something is "done right," one needs to remember how to do it again. And many of the recipes that have survived in manuscript would seem to have originated in just this way. We find them not only in the context of formal cookbooks but also in household accounts and commonplace books, where housewives and household workers both male and female sporadically recorded the how-tos and what-abouts of daily experience. We find them mixed in with instructions for preparing a salve for wounds or hand soap or eye shadow, juxtaposed with lyrics from a song and notations about animals bought and sold. Something in the kitchen was not only done but "done right"; it therefore needed to be remembered because it needed to be done again. Only, the aide-mémoire of a recorded recipe can be directed not only to oneself but to others. "Remember how to make it again" easily becomes an interpellation, "You there [take my advice], this is how to make it." The "it," the dish now memorialized, becomes the object of a code that "you" may indefinitely reiterate, from kitchen to kitchen, a code to which you the cook, and cook after cook indeed, are summoned to deploy. *Quomodo fiet*... How to make ... *This* is how to make ... *This* is how to make *it*... *You there*... For this reason, much is often made of the probable etymology of the "recipe," until recently more commonly known as a "receipt"—in French "recette," in Italian "ricetta," in German "Rezept"—the recipe or receipt being an order received.[5]

Somehow, then, in the midst of a tradition of cookery that was mainly handed down by oral tradition and demonstration, the first extant copy of the *Libellus de arte coquinaria* was recorded. It was mildly thorough and systematic, supplementing tradition with the fixity of the written word. But it was heterogeneous in character too, and its origins are hard to pin down. The book mixed two languages and included borrowings from still other languages.[6] It also mixed different kinds of ingredients, procedures, tastes, and styles. It has no identifiable author. We cannot even be sure who the scribe was, although he was evidently associated with a monastery.

Culinary philologists producing modern texts of early cookbooks in manuscript are often on the lookout for an original text, in a single language, with a single style of cookery, by the pen of a single author, from which other, compromised, copies derive. This Danish-Latin book would seem to be a case of this: a mixed-up and "corrupted" text that would seem to derive from a more singular-minded source, with a more singular vision of cookery, which is unfortunately lost to the predation of time. But philologists may perhaps do well to consult Foucault's famous challenge to the idea of absolute textual "origins." Apart from the empirical pursuit, which sometimes finds an earliest text from which other texts may be conjectured to stem and more often does not, a theoretical premise underlies the hunt for textual origins that culinary philologists may do well to jettison. It is assumed that a fully self-present moment of origination, a pure expression of unmixed and unprecedented intentions, usually lost to time, lies at the core of most any early modern cookery book. Yet such an origin may well be not only difficult to find — given the difficulty of recovering manuscript material from six, seven, or eight centuries ago — but inherently mythic, a researcher's fantasy. Even the individual recipe may lack an "original." What masterly *incipit* can be found for chickens hunter style, say? When did the "livers and gizzards" get added to the pot? What about the egg yolks? When precisely did a roasted chicken steeped in liquid of a certain kind, with certain additives like livers and egg yolks but not certain other available additives (like onions or saffron), become "hunter style"? One will never find out in many cases, not only because the traces of origin have been lost to legend, but because the recipes themselves often function less as inventions sprung from the mind of a creator than as momentary codifications of sensual experience that afterward *take on* the appearance of original inventions. Although individual writers and compilers certainly play a role in recording recipe collections, what is first of all in question is less an invention newly strung from the pen of a master cook than an impersonal engagement in the process of a writing of a certain kind — something Jacques Derrida calls the function of the "scriptor" — though which a variety of codes referring to the production of individual dishes are assembled.[7] To this assemblage and the engagement in writing it involves, a Foucauldian author *function* is often added, either after the fact or as part of the scribal enterprise. The most famous of these named functions is one Taillevent or Guillaume Tirel, assigned "author" of *Le viandier,* a manuscript (or series of manuscripts; there is no original) of the Middle Ages, that when printed went on to become the most prominent and best-selling cookbook of the Renaissance in France. Taillevent became the legendary "Name of the Text," although "he" was certainly not its creator, since some manuscripts predate the birth of the famous chef; if he was involved in the manuscript, it was only as its most prominent compiler.

Thus, again: though we may find an author function in some of the early collections and individuals at work in compiling them, we seldom find an actual author. The collection is a site where diverse impulses from diverse sources have been assembled; it does not spring full-blown from the mind of a single-minded author, to whom a name and a biography may be assigned. The multilingual, multifarious nature of a text like the *Libellus de arte coquinaria* is a sign of that. Latin vies with Danish. Terms adopted from French, Italian, and German vie with the Danish. A dish of meat baked in dough — not unlike our Hamlet's "funeral baked meat" — is in one case a Romance-language *pastel* shaped like a cake and in another case a Scando-Germanic *koken* formed like a pie. Soon the whole guide gets absorbed into an Icelandic variant, where a *pastel,* a *pastil,* and a *koken* sit side by side. By the same token, ingredient vies with ingredient in such a text. After the walnut oil come the products made from almonds, which are then incorporated into several composed dishes. But almonds do not naturally grow in Denmark. Walnuts do.

Recipes migrate; collections migrate. An account book from fourteenth-century Florence includes the names of dishes served whose first known recorded recipes stem from contemporary Venice and the Mezzogiorno.[8] A dish of mixed meats made in a single pot, given by the Burgundian "Taillevent" in 1300 as a "hutpot" and by an Anglo-Norman writer as an "hochepot" (in both cases, meaning "stir pot," from the verb *hocher*), appears in Netherlandish villages as a "hutspot." Eventually it becomes known in the Low Countries as a national dish, even while in fashionable London households it is promoted as an exotic, complex preparation, giving rise to the word "hodgepodge," for a mixed stew of things. At some point it emerges as a humble Lancastrian casserole with potatoes known as a "hotpot" — which often goes unstirred.[9] So recipes are always on the move. And as recipes migrate, so do texts like the *Libellus.* They move from writer to reader, from study to study, from kitchen to kitchen, and on to new writers and new readers (and cooks and kitchens), changing with every known copying or reinscribing, crossing national and linguistic boundaries, and eventually, despite the conservative effect of "fixity," varying and evolving.

None of this is to say that the medieval cookbook is without intentionality. According to Bruno Laurioux, to whom almost everything I have to say here is greatly indebted, the sudden appearance of a number of cookbooks like the *Libellus* in the late thirteenth and early fourteenth century (nothing in Europe appears before then in a vernacular, going back to the fall of the Roman Empire) bespeaks a change in the relation of cooks to both their craft and their patrons.[10] Clearly, professional cooks were mainly responsible for the inception of the manuscripts, cooks who were now, after centuries of oblivion, accorded a more prestigious role in princely households, and who accordingly imagined their craft in more exalted terms. Recruited from the ranks of learned men, raised in social status, and charged with overseeing larger and larger staffs, whose members need to be directed by more and more precise instructions, the cooks were readers and writers. They wrote things down; they read what others had written down. They copied some things; they invented or improvised some others. And on occasion by their labors a document in the form of a coherent, comprehensive text took shape. Although it is not always the case in medieval manuscripts, the various editions of the *Libellus, Le viandier,* and some others of the period articulated an orderly and general view of the culture of the kitchen, from rudimentary preparations (oils, condiments, and sauces) to complex variations of major dishes.

By the end of the earliest extant version of the *Libellus,* the reader has participated more or less systematically in a repertoire of tastes and textures and the means for producing and combining them. The available ingredients and protocols are of course finite. No iguana or jellyfish appears; nor does galingale, pimento, or soya, nor even, in this Danish text, rice. (Hence, unexpectedly, it contains no recipe for the famous "blancmanger," the blend of rice and minced chicken so prominent in other medieval cookbooks.) If roasting, stewing, and baking are the usual operations, there is no frying, sautéing, fricasseeing, or smoking. But the ingredients and protocols included, which of course have their source in traditional practices — in the foodstuffs and technologies that had been adopted by this time in the northern European kitchen — are not only finite: they are made, in the context of the cookery reproduced, to work together, for the sake of producing a coherent set of varieties and variations. This coherence is what the attentive reader is meant to walk away with.

The recipes for chickens hunter style and related dishes provide an example of how the system works. The collection includes eight chicken dishes in all. There are three boiled chicken dishes: one very simply boiled with bacon; another boiled with spices — pepper, cinnamon, and saffron, to which are added bread for thickening, livers for a garnish, lard, vinegar, and salt; and a third also boiled with bacon, as well as sage, vinegar, and salt. There is a dish of boiled dumplings made with diced chicken meat, binders, and seasonings including cumin and wine. There is the chickens hunter style, another boiled dish, later thickened and garnished with innards, where the chicken is first roasted and then cooked in broth as well as other liquids, and garlic is added. There is a dish somewhat related to this in which chicken pieces are served heated in a sauce made of chopped hard-boiled eggs and vinegar, thickened with egg yolks, and seasoned with pepper, cinnamon, cardamom, saffron, and salt. Then there are the two baked meats, the *pastel* or pasty, and the *koken* or pie, neither of which uses minced chicken but rather chicken parts. The *pastel* is made of a hen cut in two, covered with sage leaves, and seasoned with bacon and salt. The *koken* is made of "pieces" mixed with bacon, pepper, cumin, saffron, and egg yolks.

From all this, one can not only compile an inventory of goods, but also distinguish a common pattern of selection, combination, and variation. The chickens hunter style, it is apparent, is not only something unique, of mysterious origin, and of a winning quality that would make for its centuries-long popularity; it is also a variation culled from a standard repertoire of ingredients and techniques. A seething liquid of broth, wine, lard, and salt — this is little different from any of the other boiled dishes, except for the use of broth rather than water, the absence of vinegar (though a vinegar-like role is played by the wine), and the addition of garlic (which appears elsewhere in the text, in a fish sauce). A garnish of livers is also standard. Egg yolks used as thickening agents are ubiquitous. So this unique signature dish is really in the first place an expression of a grammar and lexicon of cookery that animates the whole; and what is really remarkable, if one admires the dish, is how out of such common materials and procedures so distinct a variation of it could be created.[11]

The *Libellus* is not only brief but rudimentary. For all the attention paid to almonds, for example, it says little about what to do with almond products. For all the attention paid to chicken, it says little about other forms of flesh, although it mentions venison, pork, and several kinds of fish along the way. By contrast, the *Le viandier* has close to two hundred recipes, including thirty recipes for roasted meats alone, from wild boar to stork, and some of them are far more complicated than anything imagined in the *Libellus*. The *Le viandier* will add more spices, like grain of paradise and long pepper, and add touches like gilding roasted meats with egg yolks before serving, fixing their crusts and causing them to glow attractively as they come to the table (modern uses of this are said to be *doré*). The contemporary Middle English *Forme of Curye* likewise includes about two hundred dishes, many with complex instructions and more exotic spices.[12] But the *Libellus* provides us with a glimpse of the literary dimension of late medieval cookery, and it bears witness to something even more important for our purposes: it goes to show how remarkable an achievement the cookbook is.

As early as 1300, without any extant precedent, a text appears in multiple editions in several different nations, attesting to a form of cookery that is at once local and international. It is neither a guide for novices nor a book for the masses. Like most early books of cookery, it usually omits to specify exact quantities of ingredients and cooking times, or to explain cooking techniques. The book assumes a certain level of experience and competence on the part of its cooks, as well as the availability of a certain repertoire of supplies and cooking apparatuses. But the book is in the main concrete and specific in its suggestions: there is little doubt, even to a reader of some seven hundred years later, as to how these dishes were made and what they tasted like. Yet again, the book could have been of little direct use for the great majority of kitchen workers, who in 1300 would certainly have been illiterate. Nor, given the rarity and expense of books before printing, would the book have been available to many households. However rudimentary it may often be, a book like the *Libellus* is a work bespeaking privileges: the privileges of power, of master chefs and stewards over apprentices and laborers, of cosmopolitan patrons (who seek literate and cosmopolitan chefs) over locally minded, parochial ones, and of men over women. (It would be another two centuries before we find recipe collections that take the traditional control of the kitchen by women into account, and a third century before a cookbook written by a woman would be published.) Yet this advanced, elitist, and masculinist oeuvre is all the same a sweet science. It opens a window onto a system for adding taste, texture, and variety to the diet. It appeals to the appetite, to the pleasures of the table and of the community of the shared dish. It adds value to the meal and the necessities, biological and social, that the meal is designed to serve. Indeed, it adds meaning to the meal. The dishes have names. They have provenance. They have status. They come to the table not only as an item for consumption, catering to hunger, but as a distinctive product of craftsmanship or art. They may serve not only to gratify the appetite but to instill a sense of pride in what is being served, whether in the kitchen workers who produced them, the diners invited to the table, or the head of household presiding over the meal, all of whom may well invest a good deal of ego in the food they are involved with. The dishes, to put it another way, are tokens of a civility that has been encoded and encouraged by labors of learning. Situated in the midst of a practical culture where a certain range of products are available for use, where cooks will be brought up in the kitchen and understand basic operations, but where a certain presumably sophisticated form of cookery, with a certain range of dishes, textures, and tastes, needs to be transmitted and repeated, the early cookbook succeeds in providing the text, at once cogent, useful, and orderly, of a portable culinary ethic appealing to pride and disseminating civility.

Other texts would follow. The explosion of cookery manuscript circulation in the fourteenth century in Italy, France, Germany, and England is such that in 1997 Laurioux was able to identify 139 extant texts before the advent of print, many of them duplicates or fragments, to be sure, but all the same an impressive total. And toward the end of the century, printed recipe collections begin to appear: in Italy the already discussed *De honesta voluptate et valetudine* of Bartolomeo Platina (ca. 1470), *De re coquinaria* of "Apicius" (1498), and Giovanni de Rosselli's *Epulario* (1516); in Germany *Küchenmeisterei* (1485), a frequently reprinted book adopted from a manuscript; in France Taillevent's *Le viandier* (1486), based on one of the manuscripts, an edition that would be "reprinted twenty-three times between 1486 and 1615 by thirteen different publishers";[13] and in England *This Is the Boke of Cokery* (1500) and the *Boke of Kervynge* (1508), both of them also transcribed from manuscript material. Later in the sixteenth and early seventeenth century, Italy and England would see the publication of the first books of cookery designed originally for print—including in Italy the courtly *Banchetti* of Cristoforo di Messisbugo (1549) and the landmark *Opera* of Bartolomeo Scappi (1570), and in England a number of more modest efforts specifically addressed to housewives, including the three books consulted in chapter 1, *The Treasurie of Commodious Conceits, and Hidden Secrets; or, The Good Huswives Closet of Healthful Provision* (1573), *The Good Huswifes Jewell* (1587), and *The Good Huswifes Handmaide for the Kitchin* (1594). Then, in the middle of the seventeenth century, the huge third wave of cookbooks would appear in England, France, and elsewhere, Pierre de La Varenne's *Le cuisinier françois* (1651) leading the way on to works as diverse as Robert May's magisterial *The Accomplisht Cook* (1660), the anonymous *L'escole parfaite des officiers de bouche* (1662), Hannah Woolley's *The Cook's Guide* (1664), the posthumous *The Closet of Sir Kenelm Digby Opened* (1669), and the notorious (because of its preface) *L'art de bien traiter* by an otherwise unidentified L.S.R. (1674).

Obviously, early modern recipe collections are akin to the writings on the diet discussed in the previous chapter. They represent another intervention in eating and drinking at the hands of the written word. Here, too, writers and compilers are concerned with encouraging a system of practices, over which the prestigious prescriptions of the book will preside. But if the regimens of health proceeded from authority and for many centuries formed a single, if supple and variable discourse, writings on cookery followed a more uneven course of development, evolving in fits and starts, by way of a mix of experiences, traditions, and innovations, and being transmitted across uneven lines of dissemination. For its own period, the *Libellus* was something of a rarity: a text found whole (though each version varies from the other) in three different manuscripts. In other books, recipes are often interpolated with other textual material — the most famous case of this in the Middle Ages being the so-called *Menagier de Paris* (ca. 1394), an inclusive guide to practical life presumably written by an aging burgher to his fifteen-year-old wife, which, side by side with advice on the care of stables and admonitions to be gentle in all things, includes a long section of cookery, with dishes mainly culled from a version of the *Le viandier*.[14] In some instances the most significant and influential visions of cookery are seen to come from texts that do not quite fit with the "book of cookery" tradition, but belong to a mixed form of discourse: general guides to practical life, directions for household management and regimens of health. The conquest of the "book of cookery" as a literary form (the word "cookbook" is a recent American neologism) may be said at least in England and France to find definitive form only in the late seventeenth and eighteenth century. Yet meanwhile, as recipe collections multiply from 1470 on, mixed forms continue to play a major role in the discourse of cookery, and something else begins to happen as well. The book of the art of cookery enters into the general literary life of European culture; it enters into European consciousness, or to put it another way, into the European life of the mind.[15]

II

The results can be surprising, as when a book in the very form of a recipe collection, mostly expressed with a straight face, reciting real and worthy recipes, appears in 1664 as an anti-Cromwellian satire, or when Thomas Tryon provides his recipes for such "noble" dishes as boiled turnips by way of directing people into a life of ethical vegetarianism. Even when not particularly surprising, as it enters into print and comes to cater more and more self-consciously to the needs of a reading public, the recipe collection becomes the vehicle, as I have elsewhere discussed it, of a highly literate rhetoric and even a systematic epistemology.[16] That is, it adopts, in the first place, a language of persuasion and, in the second place, a language for organizing knowledge. It sways readers both to act in a certain way and to value the act in a certain way. It informs the reader about a variety of substances and methods, and it organizes the system by which the reader may come to recognize, categorize, and comprehend substance and methods.

The grammar and the lexicon of the cookbook, the system through which the cookbook communicates an art that is at once exactly reproducible and subject to innovation, is based on a systematic methodology for identifying, classifying, and generating meaning out of the items and procedures of a foodway.[17] So there is much going on in the recipe collection in view of its literary functions. In the seventeenth century, recipe collections were so common that still another aspect of literary life became an important part of the recipe collections: authors (often insisting on their rights as authors and not just as what we call author functions, and rooting their works in autobiography) were aware that they were competing with one another for prestige and sales. They therefore redoubled their efforts to appeal to the reader, finding more elaborate bases for establishing authorial distinction, for targeting and shaping potential readerships, and for justifying the place that their books assume in the conduct of culture as a whole.

In Italy, because of conditions of literacy and publishing, the process of entering the cookbook into the life of the mind began immediately. The first printed book of recipe collections is in fact the hybrid *De honesta voluptate et valetudine* by Bartolomeo Platina, a text that has previously been touched on in view of its medical implications. At once a regimen of health and a recipe collection, *De honesta* is based in part on a compendium of classical learning relating to the diet and in part on a modern cookery manuscript: the mid-fifteenth-century *Libro de arte coquinaria* of Maestro Martino, also known as Martino of Rossi and Martino of Como. Platina claims Martino as a friend and inspiration, and Platina may have had a hand in transcribing parts of one of the Martino manuscripts we have.[18] The second half of *De honesta* is basically a compilation of recipes from Martino with added editorial comment. Since the first half of the book, the regimen of health, is far more original, and because the Martino recipes are now available in several modern editions, critics have been inclined to emphasize the regimen material. But what is really intriguing about *De honesta* is its yoking of the two things together.[19]

Martino's *Libro* is important in its own right. Though it adopts a number of its recipes from earlier texts and editions, it is a work of great authority, originality, and thoroughness. In the longest extant copy, not quite identical with the copy Platina must have used but similar enough, it is divided into six chapters and contains over 260 recipes, some simple, some complex, marking a transitional stage between medieval and Renaissance cookery. The text in every version caters to a recognizably Italian palate, although many touches common to all elite food on the Continent—like seasonings of sugar and saffron—are found as well. One can turn to this text to learn how to make local versions of *blancmanger,* a large variety of relatively light soups, sauces, *torte* (pies, pasties, and the like), fried dishes (*frittelle*), fish, and meats, and a good variety of pasta dishes: a *macharoni romaneschi* and a *macharoni siciliani,* to give two examples. But for our purposes, what may be most significant about Martino's *Libro* is its systematic organization of the art of cookery. It is not only encyclopedic, dividing its material by foodstuffs, the first chapter being devoted to meats, the second to soups and pastas, the third to sauces and condiments, the fourth to *torte,* the fifth to the *frittelle,* the sixth to fish; it is also magisterial. The variety of dishes is stunning. The text bespeaks a command over the world of foodstuffs and cookery that rhetorically approximates to a command over the world itself. The text begins, as if in imitation of Genesis, with a separation of kinds and a set of commandments that control the conditions for cooking meat depending on their kinds: "Beef and cow's meat ought to be boiled, and breast of veal also, but the back . . . requires roasting. You will reduce their hams to small pieces. You will boil a whole sheep with no harm, and good roasting can be done with legs and hams. . . ."— and so on, on to pork, kid, goat, deer, and eventually birds, who are divided between water- and land-based fowl.[20] (A similar separation of the kinds opens the English *Boke of Cokery.*) Such virtuosity pervades the whole of the text. The recipes are individually masterly. Though the dishes are often elaborate (for example, a gourd pie [*torta di zuche*] made with pastry shell and pastry leaves, gourds, milk, cheese, sowbelly, butter, sugar, ginger, cinnamon, eggs, and rosewater), the instructions are precise and easy to follow. They take the unusual step for the time of including precise quantities. These recipes would be repeated in other texts. Most notably, they form the basis of Giovanni de Rosselli's *Epulario,* or to give one of its long titles, *Opera noua chiamata Epulario: La quale tracta il modo de cucinare ogni carne, ucelli, pesci, de ognisorte, et fare sapori, torte, pastelli, al modo de tutte le prouincie, et molte altre gentilezze,* a text that would be the most popular cookbook in Italy for a hundred years and that would find some success in French and English translations as well.[21]

For Platina to take such a text and combine it with a regimen of health may in retrospect look like a muddling of categories, which the passing of time would eventually straighten out. But Platina himself is aware of combining two forms of discourse, and indeed of needing to do so. In part that is because he is concerned with the dietary care of the self, and in quattrocento intellectual circles a preoccupation with such mundane matters as fixing dinner was not therefore out of the question. "As much care as runners habitually take of their legs, athletes of their arms, musicians of their voice, even so it behooves literary scholars to have at least as much concern for their brain and heart, their liver and stomach," writes the contemporary Marsilio Ficino.[22] Such a care of the self, as we have seen, is meant not only to keep the mind and body well, by chasing away melancholy and other "obstructions" to health, but to exalt them to a higher plane of existence. The gold-colored condiments Ficino wants the scholar to have added to his dishes are meant to bring the scholar to a goldlike, sunlike, and therefore godlike state of the self.[23] But in combining the discourse of diet with the discourse of cookery, Platina does a couple of other things as well. He endeavors to open up a space where the pleasures of the table can be conjoined with the pleasure of health, to the end that both can be accepted by the culture of the church, which for all the splendor of the papacy was still the living heir to the doctrines of contempt for the flesh and the practices of asceticism that codified it. In addition, and perhaps even more importantly, Platina tries to bring the value of a healthy pleasure into the management of everyday life, even among, or especially among, the cultural elite of fifteenth-century Italy. To take pleasure seriously is not, for Platina, merely to articulate the principles of making health and pleasure into a material practice — it is wisely to plunge into the material practice itself.

The space of "right pleasure" is articulated cautiously, and not without inconsistency. "Far be it from Platina to write to the holiest of men," Platina writes in the dedication to his patron, Cardinal Baptista Roverella, "about the pleasure which the intemperate and libidinous derive from self-indulgence and a variety of foods and from the titillations of sexual interests. I speak about that pleasure which derives from continence in food and those things which human nature seeks." The idea is far from original to Platina; it is classical, directly related to the classical regimens of health as well as to the classical discourses of morality. Self-indulgence is bad; temperance is good. Self-indulgence entails a pursuit of "variety" for the sake of piling on the pleasures; and such indulgence in food is tied, by way of a persistent metonymy, to indulgence in sex (see chapter 6). But if there is a wrong pleasure, there is also an "honest" one, a "right pleasure" as the early modern English would put it. Platina lists a number of authorities on right pleasure, among whom Cicero takes pride of place. He defends his enterprise by appealing again and again to health and even favorably compares the enterprise he is engaged in with traditional enterprises of military valor: "just as in the past he who saved a citizen in battle seemed to deserve civic honors, he seems to deserve more [than a soldier] who would save many citizens by asserting a rational plan for food." It is as if Platina was arguing for a healthy way of living that would both pay respect to such needs of the body as a wrong-headed asceticism would neglect and forestall such dangerous excesses as a less rational plan for food could license. In language that seems to stem more from Roman satirists than from direct observation, although it is presented as if from the latter, Platina goes on to say that if people were to follow his example, "we would not see today so many so-called cooks in the city, so many gluttons, so many dandies, so many parasites, so many most diligent cultivators of hidden lusts and recruiting officers for gluttony and greed."[24]

"Right pleasure"—a term of art that would be important in debates about food up to the nineteenth century—would seem then, no less than the *eucrasia* sought after by classical medicine, to entail a militant defense against extremes. But that is not quite how the rest of *De honesta* actually reads. The regimen half of the book expresses a copious, gratifying system of consumption. The cookery section, based on Martino, is given an erudite gloss, which sometimes seems to try to rein in the pleasure of cookery; but what the text mainly expresses is a love of fine food and the systematic cuisine, Martino's, that epitomizes it: a cuisine that strives after splendor. "One should have a trained cook with skill and long experience," Platina writes in an early part of the regimen, a cook "patient with his work and wanting especially to be praised for it." Discernment, cleanliness, and understanding are all desirable qualities. If possible, "he should be completely like the man from New Como [Martino], the prince of cooks of our age, from whom I have learned the art of cooking food."[25] As for including the section on cookery that begins with book 6, Platina asserts, "Although the nature and force of those foods which humans customarily eat has been explained, I would seem really to have done nothing thus far if I were not to offer a plan, in order, which cooks and chefs use for preparing foods, for the cooking of all dishes is not the same, nor is their seasoning the same nor their cooking in the same time."[26] No: the cook whom Platina takes as his model aims not only for complexity, variety (in spite of Platina's protestations against "variety"), inventiveness and depth, but for what in painting is known as "finish." Here is a recipe for a porridge made with hemp seeds, as transcribed in a slightly abridged form by Platina:

> Make a hemp dish for twelve guests this way: cook a pound of well-washed hemp until it splits open. When it is cooked, add a pound of almonds. When it has been pounded with bread crumbs in a mortar, moisten it with lean stock, and stir it into a pot through a sieve. Then, when it has been placed on the hearth, stir frequently with a spoon. When it is almost cooked, put in a half pound of sugar, a half ounce of ginger, and a little saffron with rose water. When it is cooked and apportioned on serving dishes, sprinkle with rather sweet spices.[27]

A humble porridge from a lowly grain—derived from what Alberto Capatti and Massimo Montanari call the "food of the poor"[28]—is here elevated to a complex concoction with the addition of luxury items like almonds and "lean stock" (the

Martino manuscript specifies that this can be either of lean meat or lean chicken), along with specifications about cooking times and such refinements as stirring the whole of the pounded cooked porridge meal through a sieve, in preparation for a second round of cooking, and such lordly spices as sugar (used in large quantity), ginger, and saffron. And then it is "finished": placed on serving dishes and sprinkled with "sweet spices." In the same spirit, Martino cooks his fresh-made "macharoni romaneschi" in a "rich broth"—a *brodo grasso*—and finishes it "in a pan with cheese, butter, sugar, and spices."

It was a hallmark of all late medieval and Renaissance cookery that, aside from rarities like venison and game birds, common ingredients and combinations from the "food of the poor" like hemp seed were elevated into striking culinary artifacts. The impulse is the same as we saw in the case of baked meats— chickens or lamb joints baked whole in a pie. The triumph of culture over nature, the defeat of natural processes by way of the enchantments of art, as I called it in chapter 1—this deep meaning, which gets attached in the civilized and luxurious world of western Europe to its chicken and veal no less than to its grand palaces and cities—finds expression both in the foundations of cookery, hemp seed mixed with almonds, wheat dough rolled into macaroni, and in its finishing touches: "cheese, butter, sugar, and spices." No question, as many writers have emphasized, the appearance of food was important to the great households of early modernity: devices such as gilding roasts and baked goods with egg yolks just before serving, or of adding saffron and its rich goldlike color to almost any dish that will take it, devices that Martino is every bit of fond of as the cooks of *Le viandier*—these are methods for making food impressively glow as it comes into the dining hall and onto the table.[29] But adding "sweet spices" or "cheese, butter, sugar, and spice" at the very end—this is at once to layer flavors, in the interest of complexity, and to take care for the savor of ingredients as they are brought to the table. Sprinkled atop an already complete dish, the cheese, the butter, or the spices burst with fresh odors that ascend immediately to the nose, inviting the diner to enter into a deeper polyvalent relation with the food.

This kind of cookery has two lives. In one, partly by way of *Epulario,* which plagiarizes Martino's work, it becomes a part of Italian culinary tradition, the dominant text of cookery in Italy until the second half of the sixteenth century. In the other, it becomes a part of learned culture. Platina's book would have many readers. And even the recipe section of the text keeps bringing the reader back to conventions of learning. At the end of the recipe for gourd pie, Platina adds: "Let Cassius [apparently, the code name of one of Platina's humanist friends] not eat this because he suffers from colic and the stone. It is likewise difficult to digest and nourishes badly." At the end of the recipe for a hemp dish, he adds, "I think this is very similar to *baricicoli* of the people of Siena, for an extraordinary dish has been made from many ordinary things, but it is also difficult to digest and creates squeamishness and pain."[30] It is as if, having enticed his readers into gourmandism, Platina wants to end by playing the spoilsport. Indeed, the book concludes with a section "On settling troubles," drawn chiefly from Cicero, admonishing his reader to practice moderation in all things.

But Platina's most interesting editorial content comes at the end of his recipe for *blancmanger,* the rice and chicken dish, to which Platina has added decorative refinements, such as serving half of it white and half of it colored with egg yolk and saffron. Platina then explains:

> I have always preferred this to the Apician condiments, nor is there any reason why the tastes of our ancestors should be preferred to our own, for even if we are surpassed by them in nearly all arts, nevertheless in taste alone we are not vanquished, for in the whole world there is no incentive to taste which has not been brought down, as it were, to the modern cooking school, where there is the keenest of discussion about the cooking of all foods. What a cook, oh immortal gods, you bestowed in my friend Martino of Como, from whom I have received, in great part, the things of which I am writing. You would say he is another Carneades if you were to hear him eloquently speaking ex tempore about the matters described above.[31]

The "Apician condiments" to which Platina refers would be the concoctions of Apicius, presumed author of the Latin *De re coquinaria.* Manuscripts of *De re coquinaria,* based on either of two ninth-century manuscripts based on fourth-century material and lately brought to Italy, were circulating in Platina's Rome in the mid-sixteenth century. It is not clear that Platina actually saw or read a copy. His allusions to it are vague. One recipe that seems directly to stem from Apicius, "Lucanian Sausage," has nothing to do with the *Lucanicae* featured in the Roman text, except for the fact that it, too, is a sausage. Martino, for his part, says nothing about the Roman "Lucania" in the Italian text; he simply calls the dish *salsicce,* sausages. Platina possibly only knew of Apicius and the prestige attached to his name by hearsay; at best, if he saw the manuscript, he did not take the time to study it carefully. But perhaps Martino was familiar with the Roman cookbook: his impulse to devise a systematic guide to cookery may have been inspired by the model of *De re coquinaria,* for that text is systematic and magisterial too, divided into ten chapters, each devoted to a different group of foodstuffs, from wines and sauces to fish, and conveying a mastery of a great number of ingredients and forms of preparation.

In any case, manuscripts of *De re coquinaria* certainly circulated in quattrocento Italy and were discussed in humanist circles, and in 1498, in two separate editions — one from Venice, one from Milan — the ancient cookbook was reproduced in print, making it only the second book of cookery published in Italy, after Platina's hybrid text. But the effect was literary rather than culinary. Although a historical interest in antiquity, including its mundane customs, only grew with the centuries, there is no record of anyone in Renaissance Italy actually trying to serve an ancient Roman dinner.[32] In all likelihood, some tried. But as Platina indicates, whatever poets or painters did in their relation to antiquity and the *rinascimento* of learning, cooks had little use for Roman precedents.[33]

In some respects, that may have been a shame. The Lucanian sausage that Platina alludes to is rendered by Apicius as follows:

> Pound pepper, cumin, savory, rue, parsley, mixed herbs, laurel-berries, and *liquamen,* and mix with this well-beaten meat, pounding it again with the ground spice mixture. Work in *liquamen,* peppercorns, plenty of fat and pine-kernels, insert into a sausage-skin, drawn out very thin, and hang in the smoke.[34]

This is far more interesting than Martino/Platina's *salsicce.* Martino doesn't know how to add texture and brightly contrasting tastes to a sausage as Apicius does with his laurel berries and pine nuts; nor does he avail himself of fresh herbs. The cuisine that unfolds in *De re coquinaria* speaks for a cuisine that is perhaps more copious in the range of ingredients and combinations of tastes it procures than anything the medieval kitchen could produce. Apician cookery is the product of an empire with vast material resources and far-flown commodity exchanges — oil from Greece, wine from Crete, spices from Egypt, seafood from the Iberian Atlantic as well from the whole of the Mediterranean, livestock from Gaul, fruits and nuts from northern Africa, grains from everywhere, not to mention good supplies of fresh produce from local providers — and it provisions an elite with as complex and varied and wide a palate as it can contrive for it, without exceeding the limits beyond which lie incoherence. The results — fermented fish sauces and currylike stocks for braising, stewing, and seasoning (*garum* and *liquamen*), helpings of olives, figs, ground herbs, spices, honey, oils, and breads, served up with main dishes like stuffed, steamed mullet, stewed peas "Vitellius," and oven-roasted dormice, served with honey and poppy seeds — were capable of being corrupted into the coarse luxury that Petronius's *Satyricon* satirizes in its chapter "Dinner with Trimalchio." And even the modern reader may on occasion feel that the recipes go too far, that they challenge the palate rather than pleasing it. But no less than the rudimentary *Libellus* or Martino's masterly *Libro de arte coquinaria, De re coquinaria* of Apicius re-creates a culinary world that, however far-flung, expresses a unified vocabulary and syntax. Apicius has a way of making things.

Consider as a last example the dish in Apicius that comes closest to chickens hunter style. Apicus calls his dish "chicken à la Varius"—"pullus Varianus"— possibly referring to the emperor Varius Heliogabalus.

Chicken à la Varius

Cook the chicken in the following liquor: *Liquamen,* oil, wine, to which you add a bouquet of leek, coriander, savory. When it is done pound pepper, pine-kernels, pour on two cyathi [1/6 pint] of *liquamen* and some of the cooking-liquor from which you have removed the bouquet. Blend with milk and pour the contents of the mortar over the chicken. Bring to the boil. Pour in beaten egg-white to bind. Put the chicken on a serving-dish and pour the sauce over. This is known as white sauce.[35]

Not quite a double-cooked chicken, and far more richly seasoned than any familiar chickens hunter style, the dish nevertheless follows the same principles. A chicken will be steeped in a seasoned liquid, and this liquid, to which binding and flavorings are added toward the end, will then serve as a thickened sauce to be poured over the chicken upon serving. The chief differences are three: (1) the liquid is a combination of oil and wine—Apician cuisine features a heavy hand with both ingredients, possibly as a sign of luxury; (2) the seasonings feature a number of herbal aromatics as well as members of the onion family, combined with texture-adding ingredients (pine nuts, here, although the use of almonds in late medieval food is not entirely different); (3) one of the flavor bases is a *liquamen,* a salty fermented fish sauce condiment similar to the fish sauces of contemporary southeast Asia, which is all but ubiquitous in Apician cookery.

Challenging or not, what is most striking about *De re coquinaria* in the current context is that it existed and persisted primarily as a literary phenomenon.[36] If it was seldom if ever used for cooking, fine Latin editions were nonetheless published over the next few centuries in places as far off as Antwerp, Basel, Lyon, Leipzig, Zurich, and London. The *idea* of Apician cookery became a part of erudite society. And this idea included several notions that would be important both for the history of cookery and for the history of literature. First of all and above all, though the word itself would not appear in this sense for quite some time (early moderns rather doing with such words as "manners" and "habits"), the text of Apician cookery presents Roman food as a vehicle of culture.[37] We will see other examples of this later, as when English colonists in Virginia would confront the food habits of the Powhatan Indians. But here, already, an erudite class is alert to the idea that a people remote in either time or place would have its own culinary culture, and that this culture amounts to a kind of edifice of production and consumption. The kitchen and the dining room were known to be structures, in other words, of aesthetic community. But secondly, Apician texts celebrate the notion that cookery itself is an art form of some distinction, and that to master this art would require a high level of expertise and learning, a mastery akin as much to the fine arts as the handicrafts of artisans. And as such, civilized cookery is a *literate* discipline.

III

In some respects, the literary effects of the cookbook are impossible to assess. References to cookbooks are relatively rare: if we can suspect that Shakespeare understood how a baked leg of lamb was prepared, we cannot be sure that he ever actually read a cookbook. The reference is to the baked meat, which our familiarity after the fact with an actual recipe helps us understand; the reference is not to *The Good Huswifes Jewell*. Every now and then, it is true, we encounter a stunning example of the literary life of cookbooks, like the Cromwellian cookbook previously alluded to. In the midst of the early Restoration, some ten years after the explosion of cookbook publication in England and France heralded by La Varenne's *Le cuisinier françois*, we find printed *The Court and Kitchen of Elizabeth Commonly Called Joan Cromwell, the Wife of the Late Usurper*. Most of the book is a straightforward compilation of recipes, much the same as other recipes being circulated at the time. But sometimes one comes across a recipe like the following:

To bake a pig

This is an experiment practiced by [Elizabeth Cromwell] at Huntingdon brewhouse, and is a singular and the only way of dressing a pig. Take a good quantity of clay, such as they stop barrels' bungs with, and having molded it, stick your pig and blood him well; and when he is warm, arm him like a cuirassier or one of Cromwell's Ironsides, hair, skin, and all (his entrails drawn and belly sewed up again) with this prepared clay, thick everywhere, then throw him below the stoak-hole under the furnace and there let him *soak*. . . .[38]

What are we to make of it? If one looks closely at the language of this recipe, one will find not only a satiric reference to Cromwell's wartime machine, but a rhetorically powerful manipulation of language, including internal rhymes and near-rhymes, alliteration, surprising rhythms, and an intentionally violent diction that makes what is in fact a common, homely way of "dressing a pig" into a caustic evocation of the wartime cruelty. The anonymously authored book deliberately sets up a contrast between the plain home economics of a housewife whose modest origins are constantly and inaccurately mocked (he accuses her for example of "sordid frugality and thrifty baseness" and of being "fitter for a barn than a palace") with the aggressive, unscrupulous ambitions of "the late usurper"— sometimes by making a homely recipe resemble a Cromwellian act of aggression. Much else can be said about this curious text.[39] First of all, however, it needs to be noted that as this text takes the literature of cookery as a vehicle of satire, it both attests to the growing literary presence of cookbooks in the public life of England and to the ability of mainstream literature to appropriate and hence contribute to its literary value.

But the literary life of cookbooks is more evident internally, in how the books come to communicate with their readers. As they moved from manuscript culture to print culture, cookbooks become more and more self-consciously constructed as verbal performances, designed for public release and prepared as acts of communication, an "author" to a "reader." They would increasingly come to incorporate tables of contents and indices and groupings based on classes of ingredients and preparations as well as explanatory material, indicating how not only the lessons of Apicius, Martino, and Taillevent had been generally absorbed but how writers and compilers became aware that their books were *addressed* to a readership, a readership that needed to be *oriented* or even *trained*. More specific quantities, cooking times, and technical details would be increasingly annexed to the bare instructions of the traditional recipe. The books themselves would come from the press as finished artifacts, often with glorious title pages, frontispieces featuring fine portraits of their proudly self-identified authors, and a variety of illustrations. However books were actually prepared, celebrity chefs, known to be embraced by a prestigious patron, often served as a drawing card to readers. One popular book of the seventeenth century, *The Queen's Closet Opened* (1655), made the exiled Stuart queen into a kind of authority on the basis of which the contents of the book was to be commended. She was not the author—one W.M. takes credit for most of that, including a section entitled *The Compleat Cook*—but the queen was nevertheless a kind of authorial receptacle or object, like a queen bee: once recipes were "presented" to her and, presumably accepted, they acquired an aura of majestic originality. Attempting to appeal to readers, cookbooks adopted the editorial apparatuses of other kinds of books, the prestigious author, the prestigious patron, the frontispiece, the catchy title — they took their place in the general literacy of the period, subscribing to the same conventions of production, packaging, marketing, and sales.

The history of these books, as I have suggested, is uneven. The glory of Renaissance Italian cookery reached its highest literary achievement in the mid-sixteenth century. The French press, meanwhile, was relatively silent. England, for its part, unproductive for most of the Renaissance, was the most active site of cookbook publication at the end of sixteenth and in the early seventeenth century. At mid-seventeenth century there was the explosion of cookbook publication in France and England; while after 1667 the press in Italy was relatively silent. So there is no one line of development from country to country or even within a single country. Yet we should not confuse these waves of publication and silence with waves of vigor or senescence in cookery itself. If the Italian press released few original books in the seventeenth century, for example, it was nevertheless reprinting familiar books from the sixteenth century and eventually translating material from the new cookery in France. If the English press produced a dozen or so books from 1573 to 1642, reprinting some of them as many as twenty times, many of the books were unoriginal, if not downright plagiaristic, and cookery (apart from confectionary) wasn't going anywhere by them. Cookery is one thing; the book of cookery is another. The relationship between them is complicated — especially given the fact that even in the late seventeenth century most kitchen workers probably could not read.

It is true that the cookbooks of the late seventeenth century articulate new styles of cooking both in England and in France, and that these new styles were increasingly adopted by fashionable households in both countries. There is no doubt that a heightened interest in the literature of cookery that begins with *Le cuisinier françois* signaled a heightened interest in cookery both for its own sake and as an expression of other social trends. The cookbooks themselves attest to this. Popular cookbook writer "E. Smith," possibly one "Eliza Smith," prefaced her text *The Compleat Housewife* (1723) with what amounts to the Enlightenment's anthem to cookery, approximating cookery to the discourse of progress generally. "Cookery, Confectionary, &c. like all other Arts," she writes, "had their Infancy, and did not arrive at a State of Maturity but by slow Degrees, various Experiments, and a long track of Time." After a period when "the Art of Cookery was unknown" and humankind subsisted on a natural vegetarian diet, cookery came into "use" as a household necessity to cater to the tender appetites of people inhabiting a more complex, meat-eating world. Yet "Cookery did not long remain a bare Piece of Housewifery, or Family Economy; but in Process of Time, when Luxury entered the World, it grew to an Art." She means "art" in the sense of a fine art, like architecture or poetry, and she speaks of it with the same pride and resignation as other artists spoke of the state of their own arts at the time. "This Art being of universal Use, and in constant Practice," she says, "has been ever since upon the Improvement; and we may, I think, with good Reason believe it is arrived at its greatest Height and Perfection, if it is not got beyond it, even to its Declension. . . ."[40] As food became an art in this sense, it could be assimilated to the latest notions of civility, of politeness and wit, of refinement and excellence. The cookbook is understood by writers like Smith to be an agent and record of progress, and even a bulwark against decline. Yet the heightened interest in cookbooks and cookery could become the object of satire too. In 1712 the Scribleran William King responded to the publication of a new edition by physician and traveler Richard Lister of Apicius's *De re coquinaria* with a parody, *The Art of Cookery*.[41] "Let me tell you," he writes in a preface; "I hope in the first place, it [Lister's edition of Apicius] will, in some measure remove the Barbarity of our present Education: For what Hopes can there be of any Progress in Learning, whilst our Gentlemen suffer their Sons at *Westminster, Eaton,* and *Winchester,* to eat nothing but *Salt* with their *Mutton,* and *Vinegar* with their *Roast Beef* upon Holidays? What extensiveness can there be in their Souls?"[42] Skeptical of the whole business, yet a sharp observer of the contemporary dining scene as well, King presents an edition of Horace's *Ars poetica,* in Latin, against which, on opposite pages, he includes an original poem modeled on *Ars poetica,* which he calls *The Art of Cookery.* A preface from the publisher to the reader claims that King is showing his esteem for Horace and the values Horace espoused, above all Horace's contempt for luxury. He adds that the author "desires little farther than that the Reader would for the future give all such Booksellers [who print cookbooks] no manner of Encouragement."[43] The poem compiles not recipes but rather a poetics of food, often to comic effect, but with a serious aim in mind as well: King was trying to do for cookery what his friend Alexander Pope was doing for poetry. He was skeptical about the reliance of cooks on cookbooks just as Pope was skeptical about the reliance on imitation at the expense of "nature." " 'Tis a sage Question," he therefore remarks in the course of the poem,

> if the Art of Cooks
> Is lodg'd by Nature, or attain'd by Books:
> That Man will never frame a noble Treat
> Whose whole Dependance lies on some Receipt.
> Then by pure Nature ev'ry thing is spoil'd,
> She knows no more than stew'd, bak'd, roast and boil'd.
> When Art and nature join the Effect will be
> Some nice Ragout, or charming Fricassee.[44]

If the relation of cookbooks to cookery is complex, as cookbooks become a part of the general literacy of Europe, even that complexity becomes subject to literary treatment.

But let us return to the *internal* literariness of the cookbook, a view of which will also provide a glimpse into actual practices of cooking and dining. I want to call attention to two features of early modern cookbooks in general, the menu and the preface.

IV

Historians have paid remarkably little attention to the first of these, the menu.[45] That may stem in part from the fact that unlike individual recipes, early modern menus do not *read* well. Apart from propounding a redundant profusion of dishes brought to the table in "courses," they often don't seem to make much sense; they show "no obvious organizing principles," as one historian says about medieval menus.[46] But the agglomeration, the redundant profusion that is characteristic of the bills of fare featured in sixteenth- and seventeenth-century cookbooks, is in fact the main point: the profusion and the redundancy alike — which together made for a culinary version of what literary artists admiringly called copiousness — were what the public was intended to appreciate.

Here, for example, is a relatively brief English bill of fare that originates in 1500, in *This Is the Boke of Cokery,* and then gets repeated in both *A Proper New Booke of Cokereye* (1575) and later in the same cookbook, published in England in 1587, Thomas Dawson's *The Good Huswifes Jewell,* that gave us one of Hamlet's dishes of baked meat.

> Here followeth the order of meats, how they must be served at the table, with their sauces for flesh days at dinner.
>
> The first course.
>
> Pottage or stewed Broth. Boiled meat or stewed meat. Chickens and Bacon. Powdered [i.e., salted] Beefe. Pies. Goose. Pig. Roasted Beef. Roasted Veal. Custard.
>
> The second course.
>
> Roasted Lamb. Roasted Capons. Roasted Conies [rabbits]. Chickens. Peahen [female peacock]. Baked Venison. Tart.[47]

The first thing that may strike and puzzle the reader today is the quantity of meat and lack of anything else except for a "pottage" and a "custard" in the first course and a "tart" in the second. The next thing is the lack of variety in the meal. The heading promises to inform the reader about the sauces that should be served with each dish, presumably varied in the medieval fashion—brown sauces, green sauces, mustard, and so forth—but the text omits to mention them. All the menu leaves us with is a gathering of meats, poultry, and pies. Moreover, the dishes are not only uniform, but, except for the opening pottage and the concluding custard and tart, presented in no readily discernible order of service. Either all the dishes were to be brought out at once and displayed simultaneously, or they were brought out in succession; but in either case, the "order" according to which these particular items in these arrangements was served is difficult to decode. The sequence of service would seem to demand a good deal more than a list of meats, poultry, and pies that can be consumed in any order; nor, it would seem, were early moderns unaware of such demands. We have already seen that the order in which foodstuffs were consumed was of some concern to medical writers—particularly with regard to the hotly debated point whether salads and fruits should be eaten first or last. There is the often-cited case of Montaigne's conversation with an Italian steward, who discoursed at length and vainly, according to Montaigne, on "the difference of appetites: the one we have before eating, the one we have after the second and third course, the means, now of simply gratifying it, now of arousing it and stimulating it"—after which the steward "entered upon the order of serving, full of beautiful and important considerations."[48] In fact, when we consider the extravagant banquets in Italy whose bills of fare have been recorded, we begin to see something like the steward's concern about the progress of the appetite. But in the main, at least until the late seventeenth century, meals in Italy, France, and England alike, though varying in their choices of items, seem to have followed the same bulky style as this menu from Dawson's *Good Huswifes Jewell;* and what seems to be valued above all by way of this style is the mere redundancy that it communicates: this menu features not an orderly progression of items, from one appetite to another, but a profusion whose parts either duplicate one another or can be substituted one for the other.

Along with certain gestures toward preference, availabilities, and the technical range of the early modern kitchen, this redundant profusion, again, is the menu's governing principle. "The order of meats, how they *must* be served at the table," the cookbook tells us (emphasis added)—this *imperative* takes into account the kinds of items that can be cooked together in a kitchen: in the first course, for example, two heavy roasts, a probably roasted fowl and a possibly roasted pig (though "sousing" pigs in a briny broth was also popular) that could

Figure 3.1. A line of serving men bring finished dishes to the table at a palatial feast, from Bartolomeo Scappi, *Opera* (1570). Reproduced by permission of Special Collections, Leeds University Library.

be turned on their spits simultaneously at different heights above the fire; a long cooked pottage and a probably more shortly simmered stew, prepared in separate pots placed at different positions over the fire; a couple of baked dishes that go into the oven; a separately prepared custard, probably made in advance. Every menu, from the humblest to the most extravagant, will necessarily attempt to accommodate the limited range of early modern kitchens. In addition, they will attempt to accommodate the theoretical diversity of appetites that diners brought to the table. The imperative—"how they *must* be served at the table"—also addresses itself to what particular diners at a particular place may be anticipated to expect and prefer, bringing desires to the table that are products not only of individual experience but of that vast apparatus of the culture for provisioning itself, from property relations to agronomics, from trade patterns to household management, that was required to make common and not-so-common items available. Lamb, capons, rabbits, chickens, peahen, venison, and tarts — these are all items of consumption that are both objects of preferences and commodities

that the economics of the country estate had been configured to produce. But redundant profusion — over and above the limits imposed and the variety enabled
by habit, economics, and technology — serves at least three more purposes: it
contributes to the ceremonial value and the prestige of the meal; it provides certain aesthetic and dietary advantages; and it helps ratify social distinctions.

We hear all three purposes appealed to in William Harrison's *Description of
England,* published as part of the second edition of the famous *Holinshed's Chron-
icles* (famous, that is, because of Shakespeare's use of it) in the same year as Dawson's cookbook: attestations of jingoistic pride in profusion for its own sake; ap-
proval of the aesthetic and dietary considerations that profusion additionally
serves; and appreciation of the deference to rank and wealth that it can be used
to promote. "In number of dishes and change of meat," he thus notes, "the nobility of England . . . do most exceed. . . ." He may have been right, although
records show that ceremonial Italian banquets of the period were far more extravagant, as were some French banquets too. In any case, the reason for this
claim to superiority is that "there is no day in manner that passeth over their
heads wherein they have not only beef, mutton, veal, lamb, kid, pork, cony, capon,
pig, or so many of these as the season yieldeth, but also some portion of the red
or fallow deer, beside great quantity of fish and wild fowl, and thereunto sundry
other delicates wherein the sweet hand of the seafaring Portingale is not wanting."[49] They have all these things, Harrison wants to emphasize, and they have
all of them *daily:* not only beef, but veal, not only mutton but lamb, not only pork
but pig (the latter designating a young hog), and not only the flesh of domestic
livestock but wild deer, fish, and fowl, not to mention sweetmeats, made available by virtue of the sugar imported from Portuguese merchants, plying the
trade between Mediterranean and eastern Atlantic sugar plantations. It seems
that part of the order of service at households of this kind, and even the not necessarily "noble" household to which Dawson directs his cookbook, is variety, or
at least a variety of flesh, for its own sake, which is to say for the sake of maximizing the exploitation of resources at the wealthy household's command — exploitation for the sake of exploitation, one might call it, a strategy that has the
advantage both of putting power on display and of generating increased production: to challenge the limits of a household's culinary economics was to encourage the production of wealth for the sake of wealth.

But two other elements of order also enter into the picture: on the one hand,
aesthetic and dietary benefits; on the other, social deference and stratification.
As for the first, as Harrison attests, with all the profusion on display, no one either would or could eat all the dishes available: "each one feedeth upon that meat
him best liketh for the time." The mass profusion of the dinner gave individual

diners leeway to make individual choices: guests were not obliged all to eat the same thing, and they could make choices, as the ambiguity wrapped up in the expression "him best liketh for the time" suggests, both for hedonistic and for health-related purposes. A diner might simply have a taste for a certain dish at that moment. Or again, a diner might have a taste for being tempted by a multitude of choices and wish to make as many picks from the multitude of items as good manners allowed. Indeed, we can see in that sort of temptation and moment of decision a sensual experience that was unique to premodern ceremonial dining: the profusion of meats passing before one's eye and under one's nose — lamb, rabbits, chicken, peacock, and venison — among which one had to make a choice or two or three. That was a pleasure, a hedonistic teasing of the senses. As for health, the diner may also be thinking of what "him best liketh" in the medical sense — though as we have seen, in the pre-Cartesian world of the sixteenth-century diner, medical choice was neither detached nor abstracted from gustatory sensation. One person may have decided on veal as a medically preferable dish, because it went down better; another may have decided on beef for the same reason; a third on neither, but rather on a fowl like goose or "chickens and bacon." Similarly, for more analytically predetermined medical reasons, one person, like our self-identified choleric friend Petruchio, may be inclined to take a liquefying stew, another, feeling a bit wet inside with a cold, inclined to indulge in a dry roast or, maybe better, the pottage or broth offered at the start of the meal: "wet" dishes that were nevertheless known to dissipate congestion.[50] However, for all the care for the individuality of the diners that this redundant profusion caters to, as Harrison also attests, the profusion also enabled diners to observe rank. "The beginning of every dish," Harrison writes, is "reserved unto the greatest personage that sitteth at the table, to whom it is drawn up still by the waiters, as order requireth, and from whom it descendeth again even to the lower end, whereby each one may taste thereof."[51] There is little inherent precedence of one dish over another on Thomas Dawson's hypothetical table, but the highest-ranking diner is thereby given leeway, according to his own particular tastes, to determine which among the dishes is to be accorded priority. In this respect, the bulky order of service that Dawson's menu prescribes serves to provide high-ranking individuals with occasions for asserting their degree. And not only asserting it. Once the breast of the goose or the shoulder of the suckling pig has been carved for the presiding lord's plate, the breast and the leg have not only been accorded a high status; they have been removed from circulation. To the privileged official, the breast and the leg signify the priority of rank; to the rest of the diners, they signify, for lack of the proper rank, what can no longer be acquired and consumed.

In *Simplicissimus,* a comic novel published in Germany in 1669, the narrator thus tells the story of what happened when, as a newly established court page, he was given a job on the occasion of a "princely entertainment" to "help bring up dishes, pour out wine, and wait at table with a plate in my hand." The first day on the job, he goes on, "there was big fat calf's head (of which folk are wont to say no poor man may eat) handed to me to carry up." Never mind that today we recoil from the idea of such a dish, not to mention the part of it (as we will see) that strikes the page's fancy: in the mid-seventeenth century, on the Continent, the dish and the part in question were delicacies. Having grown up as a poor rustic, never having been exposed to such things close up before, Simplicissimus could not resist the dish, with its "whole eye with the appurtenance thereof hanging out; which was to me a charming and a tempting sight, and the fresh perfume of the bacon-broth and ginger sprinkled thereon alluring me." While still carrying the dish into the hall, knowing better but following his "desires," he stealthily scooped out the eye with a spoon, and gulped it down; then he brought the dish to the head table, minus an eye. The lord of the manor is scandalized when he sees the calf's head served without one of its eyes, and, in front of his guests, sets about interrogating the staff to see who is responsible. When he discovers that Simplicissimus is the one, the boy defends himself by demonstrating how he did it. He takes out his spoon, scoops out the second eye, and gulps that down too. The company laughs at this comic bit of impertinency, and the boy is forgiven. "Yet my lord warned me," Simplicissimus adds at the end, "to play him no more such tricks."[52]

Giovanni Francesco Straparola, a century earlier in *The Facetious Nights,* tells a less happy story:

It happened one day that a German and a Spaniard, having arrived at the same hostelry, took their meat together, being served many delicate viands of all sorts and in great abundance. As they were thus dining the Spaniard handed to his servant now a morsel of meat and now a morsel of fowl, giving him to eat now this thing now that. The German, on the other had, went on eating silently, swallowing one thing after another without thinking in any way of his servant. On this account there arose between the servants a feeling of great jealousy, the servant of the German declaring that the Spaniards were the most liberal and regardful of men, and the servant of the Spaniard confirming what he said. But after the German had finished his, he took the dish with all the meat therein, and, handing it to his servant, he bade him take his supper thereof. Whereupon the servant of the Spaniard, being filled with envy

RECIPE FOR *A POTAGE OF A CALVES HEAD*

Take a good fat Calves Head that is very fresh, and scald it, raise the Skin a
little, and put it a-boyling; and when it is boyl'd take out the Bones, the
Brains, and the Eyes, which you must afterwrd put into their places again;
then take the Flesh and hash it with Beef-Suet, or rather Marrow, and the
Yolks of Egs, raw, to bind your Farcing and season it well, and farce your
Calves Head; and when you have so done, put the Brains and the Eyes into
their places again, and sew up the head, and put it into cold Water to wash
it, then put it into the Pot with some good Broth, and make it boyl very
well; and to make Garnish for it, take Calves Feet and half boyl them in
Water, then cleave them in the middle and toss them up in a Ragoue with
Butter and Bacon, and put them into your Pot with a few Capers and so
let them boyl, then steep Bread in slices, and put your Calves Head upon
it, and garnish your Head with the Feet that were boyl'd with it, but forget
not the Capers; but you must take notice that there is other Garniture, for
they say a Dish is well garnished when it is full, or the Meat in it.

From *A Perfect School of Instructions for Officers of the Mouth,* trans. Giles Rose (London: 1682), 301.
The original text is *L'escole parfaite des officiers de bouche* (Paris, 1662).

at the good luck of his companion, recalled the opinion he had just
given, and murmuring to himself spake these words: "Now I know well
that the Germans are liberal beyond other men."[53]

But we digress. The menu clearly articulates a context in which a formal
meal may be served—a context bespeaking early modern notions of affluence,
deference, and exclusivity, as well as pleasure. It clearly provides a key as to how,
given the apparatus of the early modern kitchen, a meal bespeaking these values
was to be physically orchestrated, from the fire and the stir pot to the serving
dish. But it also plays a documentary role and helps structure the text of the
cookbook as a whole. The menu is a primary *register* for the early modern cookbook in print.

In fact, though by itself it is has much to tell us about preparation and consumption, the flesh day dinner discussed above only hints at the range of experiences registered by early modern menus. The flesh dinner is only the first of several: there follows a service for supper, another much larger and more elaborate

THE COOKBOOK AS LITERATURE : 95

service for dinner, and then a large and elaborate service for fish days. Fish day services are especially grand in the sixteenth and seventeenth centuries — obviously registering, though without a hint of irreverence, the idea that in certain households, the self-denial dictated by religion for such a day can be overcome by bounty and ingenuity. If the profusion of meats on flesh days is impressive, on fish days the variety of seafood, prepared in as many ways as possible and adorned with as many additional "Lenten" ingredients as may be available, is in many of the menus magnificent:

Service for Fish days

Butter. A sallet [salad] with hard Eggs. Pottage of sand Eels and Lampreys. Red Herring, green broiled, strewn upon [with spices or sauce]. White herring. Ling. Harbourdine. Sauce, Mustard. Salt. Salmon minced. Sauce, mustard and verjuice, and a little Sugar. Powdered Conger. Shad. Mackerel. Sauce vinegar. Whiting: Sauce, with the Liver & Mustard. Plaice: Sauce, Sorrel, or wine, and Salt, or Mustard, or Verjuice Thornback: sauce, Liver and mustard, Pepper and salt strewn upon, after it is bruised. Fresh Cod: Sauce, green sauce. Dace. Mullet. Eels upon Sops. Roach upon Sops. Perch. Pike in Pike sauce. Trout upon sops. Lench in jelly or Greslle [?]. Custard.

The second course.

Flounders or flukes. Pike sauce. Fresh Salmon. Fresh Conger, Bette, Turbot, Halibut. Sauce Vinegar. Bream upon sops. Carp upon sops. Soles or other fishes fried. Roasted Eel: Sauce the dripping. Roasted Lampreys. Roasted Porpoise. Fresh Sturgeon. Sauce Galantine. Crayfish, Crab, Shrimps. Sauce Vinegar. Baked Lamprey, Tart, Figs, Apples, Almonds blanched, Cheese, Raisins, Pears.[54]

And this is only Tudor magnificence. Italian magnificence was of a higher order. Compared to what is registered in the two most important Italian cookbooks of the sixteenth century, the Tudor's bountiful service of forty-six items, including almost forty different kinds of seafood and freshwater fish, was merely a quantitative achievement. In Italy the elaborate courtly cuisine of Cristoforo di Messisbugo and Bartolomeo Scappi, as featured in their books of 1549 and 1570, respectively, record meals on the occasion of princely banquets whose ingenious complexities, contrasts, and harmonies go far beyond mere profusion. The Italian meals were designed to re-create the effect of magnificence, featuring many more dishes and more elaborate inventions, and even to approximate the condition of works of art. They were made to be continuous in spirit with the courtly music, architecture, poetry, and painting that their masters patronized, and even to be coordinated with them. Messisbugo's *Banchetti composizioni di vivande e apparecchio generale*, along with providing instructions for composing dishes (*vivande*) and organizing the kitchen and dining room (the *apparecchio generale*), includes accounts of fourteen ceremonial banquets the author had presided over, complete with descriptions of the entertainments provided along with the actual menus. The first and most elaborate is a banquet given in honor of several members of the Este family, the rulers of Ferrara, by the Estes themselves. (This detail, which commentators usually overlook, is itself important: when the Estes gave great dinners, they did not need the excuse of weddings, funerals, religious festivals, or diplomatic ceremonies; all they needed was themselves and the will to give great dinners.) At the banquet, Messisbugo informs us, fifty-four diners in all were in attendance. They were regaled for about seven hours, not only with food but with musical performances designed to complement the food, and were given eighteen different courses to eat, each including eight separate dishes. A first course included marzipan biscuits, a field greens salad, asparagus salad, anchovy salad, dumplings filled with sturgeon meat, and cold sliced mullet; a second course included hard-boiled eggs in "French sauce," more sturgeon, fried sea bream, a "white soup," "Catalan pizza," and fried "small fish" from the Po. As the dinner proceeded, there appeared lamprey, tench, pike, sturgeon with a garlic sauce, sturgeon fried in butter along with "English sauce," sardines, trout, turbot, crayfish, shrimp, oysters, eel, and caviar among the seafood items, more salads, pastas, cheese dumplings, savory tarts, salads, hot vegetable dishes like "fried greens with pine nuts and eggs," spinach several ways, "Sicilian rice," olives, artichokes, mushrooms, fava beans and "honey milk." The meal ended with a course of sweetmeats including citrus fruits, sugared nuts, nougat, and ices, consumed like all the courses to the sound of music, in this case to a concerto played under the direction of one M. Alphonso, featuring voice, viola, lute, guitar, trombone, flute, recorder, and piccolo.[55]

No doubt one of the animating principles of Messisbugo's menu is the same redundant profusion characteristic of the English menus. But in Messisbugo the profusion is more a product of the ingenuity of the cooks than the resourcefulness of their purveyors, and redundancy seems less designed to cater to individual tastes than to punctuate the meal with repeated yet varied themes. Although it is inconceivable that any single diner could have partaken of each and every dish — and, given the ample quantities that Messisbugo also records, there must have been a good deal of waste (no doubt passed down to the servants and the hordes of non-invitees who attended such banquets as spectators) — the idea of the menu is to tease and coax along the appetite of the guests, "now gratifying it, now arousing it and stimulating it," so that the whole of it may be consumed the way an operagoer consumes an opera.

Not to be outdone, in his own *Opera* (meaning "Works"), Bartolomeo Scappi records still more elaborate feasts. This "private cook of Pope Pius V," as he is identified on the title page, devotes thirty pages of material simply to illustrating how to equip a kitchen, not to mention how to provision it. Scappi intends to write the definitive book on princely cookery; and in fact when historians talk about the "classic" food of the Italian Renaissance, it is to the recipes and meals of Scappi that they refer. A feast he recounts on one October 28 includes a total of 159 dishes, from "marzipan biscuits" accompanying dishes like pasta and roast turkey to dried fruits and candies. Extending over six pages of small type, it reads like a Hollywood production, with the proverbial cast of thousands.[56]

The first purpose the menu seems to serve is commemoration. The menu immortalizes notable achievements in the history of cookery. But the menu also plays a normative role. Whether intended as an exact imperative applicable to future meals, as the English cookbook implies, or as a suggestion about how things can be done, if they are to be done splendidly and well, the menu provides a model for other cooks and hosts to emulate. Yet in the context of the cookbook as a written document, intended to be studied, the menu plays still another role. If the cookbook is at bottom a guide to a style of food preparation, the menu provides a synthetic view of the whole. The style of food preparation a cookbook features may not be immediately clear; it may take a good deal of study and practice to come to terms with it, let alone to master it. And not all of it may quite fit together, at least in any obvious way. There may be inconsistencies. But the menu is a helpful key; it brings a number of diverse preparations into the focus of a single table, the script of a single comprehensive performance. To the reader coming to an early modern cookbook and wondering, "What is this thing called cookery?" or "What is the art of cookery as this particular text envisages it?" the best answer will often be: Look at the menu. It is in the menu that the impulses of a cuisine come together and articulate a concrete structure. To borrow a term from Immanuel Kant, the menu is the *architectonic* of early modern cuisine.

V

Prefaces tell another story. By prefaces I mean many different sorts of prefatory matter: dedications, commendatory verses, notes from the printer, and notes to the reader, along with formal introductions explaining the subject, scope, or rationale of the text. Given their prolixity, the extended titles of cookbooks may also be considered as examples of prefatory matter. It goes without saying that if the menu structures the reading of the cookbook, prefatory material is meant to induce that reading, to lead it along. But there is more to the art of induction than that.[57] Why buy this book, or why, if one is a dedicatee, consent to patronize its publication? Why *use* this book? How should one use it or at least peruse it and keep it on one's shelf? At once seducing and impressing the reader, advertising itself and supplying information, prefatory material provides provisional answers to questions like these. And in doing so it inevitably reveals a good deal not only about the text to follow but also about the society in which readers encounter recipes and the books that contain them. As cookbooks become increasingly commonplace — so that, on the one hand, the competition for readers becomes more fierce and, on the other hand, the literature of cookery becomes a more familiar feature in the intellectual landscape of the time — the prefatory material of cookbooks comes to focus on the larger question of what values the reader will assent to in purchasing, reading, or using this book. These are values referring not only to types of cookery, but to ways of life and the arts of living. Turning one's serious attention to the refinements of cookery being promoted in a given book — this is a practice of everyday life that prefatory matter must not only render attractive and engaging in advance, but also justify. Prefatory material assimilates a style of cookery into the realm both of things that may be done and of things that ought to be done.

In that masterwork of sixteenth-century Italy, Scappi's *Opera,* the cookbook is presented as a fait accompli, and unlike its predecessor, the work of Platina-cum-Martino, it expresses no anxieties about what it represents. The author has devised a princely and authoritative system of cookery; the reader — though this primary reader must also be the major domo at a princely household, since none other would be equipped to follow Scappi's instructions — has only to follow the system to reproduce equally authoritative cookery. Certain of the canonical status of the cookery he reproduces for the reader and certain, too, both of his own social status as a chef as well as the status of the employer who authorizes his labors — none other than the pope himself in this era when the pope is the most powerful prince in all of Italy — Scappi needn't make any excuses for his text or any allowances to the readers his book is intended for. Yet his preface is fulsomely apologetic, attributing all kinds of excellencies not to himself but to the masters of the households he has worked in as well as the nobles who have patronized his labors, and making half a dozen apologies for his chutzpah in attempting to provide a guide for the cooks of the future and for "the benefit of mankind." The cookbook was destined to lead a complicated life, it would appear, both as a prescriptive record of meals to be prepared and as a textual object, an intervention in the discourse of food. If that was clear even in the case of the magisterial *Opera* of the lordly Scappi, it would be even more evident in the next waves of cookbook publication. One of these waves, beginning in the late sixteenth century, was unique to England: the issuing of texts specifically addressed to "housewives," usually spelled "huswives"—a term whose connotations may be unexpected, since it could refer at once to a wife, a female head of household (married or not), and an impudent woman (i.e., a "hussy").[58] Until Hannah Woolley's work in the Restoration, all of the published works addressed to housewives were written by men, and when the authors wrote their prefaces, they put their own masculinity as well as the femininity of their readers into play. So, too, did they put into play the value of cookery in and of itself, as well as the purposes it served in household management as a whole. At the same time, they raised the issue of the role of household management in the conduct of society, the kinds of households in which advanced arts of cookery were to be practiced, and the kinds of cooks (or housewives) who would supervise such cookery. Looking at these books published between 1574 and 1642—about a dozen in all, many in multiple editions with revision and additions—we are far removed from the professional and princely cookery represented by Scappi, and far from the self-confident authority of a "Cuoco Secreto di Papa Pio Quinto." And in this one, the world of Tudor England, the role of culinary pleasure in life and the practice of catering to it cannot be taken for granted. The "housewives" to whom these books were addressed were not expected to work alone: they had servants, some of whom may have been recruited from the ranks of professional cooks in places like London or trained in distinguished households in England or abroad. The housewives might not even be expected to get their hands dirty in the kitchen. But they were in charge, however hands-on their role in the kitchen may have been. And what they were in charge of was an institution, the formal meal, which was a site of supreme symbolic significance and, therefore, potentially of conflict and controversy. As we saw earlier in the case of Phillip Stubbes complaining about the "vanity, excess, riot, and superfluity" of diners not content with a "good piece of beef," the English had to struggle with the idea of fine cookery pursued for its own sake. That "housewives" were being asked to be the standard-bearers of fine cookery. That this cookery not only featured a few complicated foreign dishes, like the "boiled meat after the French ways" (which browns the meat first before stewing it) prescribed in Dawson's *Good Huswifes Jewell,* but also a good many confections — marzipans, comfits, candies — made it only more challenging for writers to carve out a social and moral space for their readers. Luckily, the

Ætatis Suæ 71
1660

What: wouldst thou view but in one face
all hospitalitie, the race
of those that for the Gusto stand,
whose tables a whole Ark comand
of Natures plentie, wouldst thou see
this sight, peruse Mays booke, 'tis hee

For Nathaniell Brooke, att the Angell in Cornehill; La: Parry.

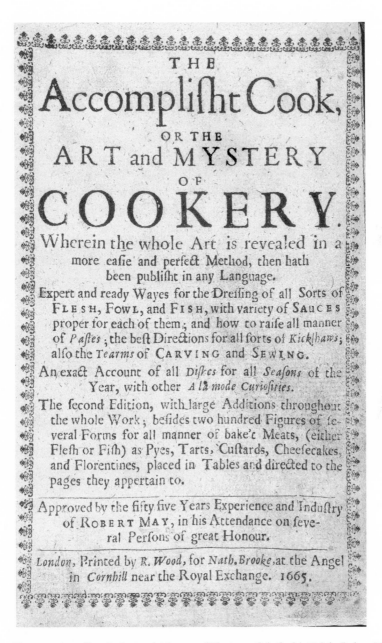

THE
Accomplisht Cook,
OR THE
ART and MYSTERY
OF
COOKERY.

Wherein the whole Art is revealed in a
more easie and perfect Method, then hath
been publisht in any Language.

Expert and ready Wayes for the Dressing of all Sorts of
FLESH, FOWL, and FISH, with variety of SAUCES
proper for each of them; and how to raise all manner
of *Pastes*; the best Directions for all forts of *Kickshaws*;
also the *Tearms* of CARVING and SEWING.

An exact Account of all *Dishes* for all *Seasons* of the
Year, with other *A la mode Curiosities*.

The second Edition, with large Additions throughout
the whole Work; besides two hundred Figures of several Forms for all manner of bake't Meats, (either
Flesh or Fish) as Pyes, Tarts, Custards, Cheesecakes,
and Florentines, placed in Tables and directed to the
pages they appertain to.

Approved by the fifty five Years Experience and Industry
of ROBERT MAY, in his Attendance on seve-
ral Persons of great Honour.

London, Printed by R. *Wood*, for *Nath. Brooke*, at the Angel
in *Cornhill* near the Royal Exchange. 1665.

Figures 3.2 & 3.3. Frontispiece and title page of *The Accomplisht Cook* (1660), by Robert May.
The dedicatory poem beneath the portrait of May, like other dedicatory material that follows,
joins May's work to the tradition of poetic hospitality with origins in Ben Jonson and such
poems as "To Penshurst" (see chapter 4). Reproduced by permission of Special Collections,
Leeds University Library.

practice of housewifery was also understood to include hygiene and medical matters, and books promoted to housewives per se usually included plenty of recipes for soaps, "waters," and medicines like a "powder peerless for wounds" that Dawson recommends. So long as it was tied to the general care of the household, fine cookery had its uses, its defensible uses. Still, the appeal to practicality was seldom sufficient by itself; other kinds of claims — to pleasure, to exoticism, or, by contrast, to profit, propriety, and the conservation of resources — would often make themselves felt, and producing a book of recipes for this new class of readers thus required some fancy rhetorical footwork.

The most well-known example of this rhetorical footwork is Hugh Plat's *Delightes for Ladies* (1602) — which would go into twenty-two editions through the middle of the seventeenth century — where Plat dedicates his text to "all true Lovers of Art, and Knowledge," and then, having reminded them of his earlier work in popular science, alerts his readers that "now my pen and paper are perfum'd"; for, as he goes on to say,

> Rosewater is the ink I write withal
> Of sweets the sweetest I will now commend
> To sweetest creatures that the earth doth bear
>
> According to each Lady, her delight,
> I teach both fruits and flowers to preserve,
> And candy them . . .[59]

Whether on the part of the author or the reader, according to Plat, the moral foundation for a serious preoccupation with food preparation with a focus on sweetmeats is, in a word, gender. Sweets for the sweetest, by the hand of someone whose own instruments — pen, paper, and ink — have become sweets. The recipe book is a fashioned for women's work, and the code for this work is the woman's "delight." The economic functions of housewifery are elided in favor of a notion of feminine superfluity, to which this masculine author is pleased to bend his efforts and make an appeal, even if Plat's recipes include directions for such mundane things as making candles, rendering salad oil, and preparing ointments for acne, as well as more delightful products like puff pastes, jellies, marmalade, pickled cucumber, clouted cream, Polish sausage ("Polonian sawsedge"), foundation powder, rouge, and hair coloring effective enough to turn dark hair chestnut or even "faire yellow."

But a still more interesting case of prefatory rhetoric may be the first of these cookbooks for women, John Partridge's *Treasurie of Commodious Conceits,*

Figure 3.4. From Bartolomeo Scappi, *Opera* (1570). One of a number of fine engravings accompanying Scappi's recipes, here a contented cook waves to his spectators from his roost at the spit. The illustration serves mainly to identify the proper equipment and organization of a professional, palatial kitchen. Reproduced by permission of Special Collections, Leeds University Library.

which set the fashion for all the other texts to follow. Consider the title itself, in the first editions rendered as

> The treasurie of commodious conceits, & hidden secrets. and may be called, the huswiues closet, of healthfull prouision. Mete and neces-sarie for the profitable vse of all estates both men and women: and also pleasaunt for recreation, with a necessary table of all things herein con-tayned. Gathered out of sundrye experiments lately practised by men of great knowledge.

Out of the "experiments" of men — presumably male chefs and apothecaries — comes a "treasury" of conceits and secrets, which shall serve as a "closet" for the use of the housewife, in her capacity as a guardian of the household's "healthful provision." The terms, which are used together in this way (in print) for the first time, would remain popular through the end of the seventeenth century.[60] "Con-ceits" are at once ingenious ideas and inventive recipes or dishes. "Hidden se-crets," an expression that would become a commonplace for describing the release of recipes to the public, originally refers to the trade secrets of arts and crafts: the "secrets" of shoemaking would be the expertise acquired when learn-ing the gentle craft as an apprentice, expertise that was supposed to stay within the guild. The closet — literally either a private chamber, a cupboard, or a cabinet for private effects, including correspondence — is metaphorically a repository for commodious conceits and secrets, which is to say recipes. The closet, in other words, is a commonplace book or bundle of documents in manuscript where in-structions about foodstuffs have been collected, only now transformed into a public document, a book. (It may be worth noting that many English cookbooks, like Partridge's *Treasurie*, were published in octavo; that is, in very small books, easily "secreted" in one's pockets or elsewhere among one's private effects.) All this is for the "huswives." Typically for English texts, the language is also com-posed to specify, in not-so-mock Horatian fashion, that the recipes are at once "meet" and "necessary," at once "profitable" and "pleasant." Somewhat typical, too, is the notion that the book will be of value to "all estates": the text admits no distinction between great and lesser households, which says something both about the book and about the households the book imagines: in point of fact, the recipes here, though indeed useful and pleasurable, are, on the one hand, some-what homely yet, on the other hand, out of the reach of most actual households in England at this time. The baked capon that we looked at in terms of the fu-neral baked meats in Hamlet's household required not only a capon and pie crust, but also sugar, ginger, cloves, eggs, lemons, and verjuice — except for the eggs all precious commodities, affordable to either a master shoemaker or a peer of the realm, but not likely to be found in a peasant's hut. Yet most peculiar is the addition of the expression "both men and women," that is "meet and necessary for the profitable use of all estates both men and women." The expression is ambiguous. Is the "huswives' closet" useful to both men and women in the sense that both men and women can use the closet, which is to say prepare food and medicines from it, or in the sense that the food and medicines are good for both men and women? There are no references in the culinary literature of early modern England to differences in food preferences between men and women, except in the case of pregnant women or of women suffering from female diseases, like the "green-sickness." Even the sweetmeats that books like Partridge's promote, and that critics have associated with the woman's sphere, can in the hands of male dramatists serve as tokens of masculine revelry and aggression.[61] At the end of a play contemporary with *Hamlet, Antonio's Revenge,* the enemy of the protagonist gathers his men together and calls for "banqueting stuff" to be brought in. "Bring hither suckets, candied delicates, / We'll taste some sweetmeats, gallants, ere we sleep," he says. To this the revenger Antonio, hidden from the others, replies in an aside: "We'll cook your sweetmeats, gallants, with a tart sour sauce!"[62]

The reference to "men and women" would in any case be dropped in later editions. So the ambiguity would disappear. But either way, neither the first edition nor those that follow would let the matter rest with the long discursive title and its pretensions to Horatian balance. First comes a note from the printer, which makes still another adjustment in the readership for which the book is hopefully intended:

> The Printer to all that covet the practice of good Huswiverie, as well wives as maides.
>
> Good Huswives here you have a Jewel for your Joy,
> A Closet meet your Huswivery to practice and employ,
> As well the gentles of degree, as eke the meaner sort,
> May practice here to purchase health, their household to comfort,
> And as the proverb proveth true, to remedy each grief,
> Amongst the rest of Physics' helps, the huswives' help is chief.
> Therefore good huswives once again, I say to you: repair
> Unto this Closet when you need, and mark what you find there.

Another figure of speech, which would also be popular for the next one hundred years, is added to the repertoire: the cookbook is a "jewel." It goes without saying that only books intended for women are ever "jewels." But the printer never-theless makes this "jewel" an object of profitable use only: whether for the "gentles of degree" or for "the meaner sort"—the book consistently trying to appeal to broad classes of housewives—the book is meant "to purchase health," "to comfort" the household, to "remedy" ills. Even, as the note goes on to say, "conserves and syrups sweet" are depicted as profitable rather than pleasurable commodities; for the book is said to provide recipes for them "to comfort heart and brain."[63]

The author himself is not so prudish. In a Chaucerian note of the author to his book, Partridge allows that his reader should "use thy commodities as well she may / To profit her friends for health's preservation, / And also to pleasure them for recreation."[64] In an epistolary dedication, he broadens the context. Not only does he embrace pleasure as well as profit; he puts pleasure in the context of Renaissance magic, proposing that what it offers are "fine conceits, as well of meats as of Conserve and Marmalades, as also of sweet and pleasant waters, of wonderful odors, operations, and virtues." In making that move, from health to pleasure and from pleasure to magical virtues, his appeal is not to a feminine readership, although he claims that "a certain gentlewoman" initially encouraged him to publish, but to "the public benefit of all men" and to the instruction of "all manner of person and degrees." Of course, the dedication is written to a man, one "Richard Wistow, Gentleman and Assistant to the Company of Barbers and Surgeons." Perhaps there is some confusion or uncertainty on Partridge's part as to who his public really is, a confusion that would be cleared up after the book was first published and Partridge benefited from feedback from booksellers and customers. But like Hugh Plat after him, Partridge was an author of popular science and history books, well versed in humanist concepts of publication. And in publishing this newfangled thing, a woman's recipe book, he was aware of releasing previously secreted material, which various purveyors would prefer be kept in the closet. This notion would also be repeated by authors of recipe books over the next one hundred years and more; however female-oriented and housewifery-oriented a book of this kind may be, what was at stake in its publication was the release of the material that is conventionally understood to be unfit for print because it belongs (as some writers would put it) to a "mystery," a private fellowship of craftsmen. Partridge's language is almost identical with the language poets would use when publishing poems, where the act of printing is held to be or at least pretended to be somewhat indecent, and therefore requiring defense. "After that I had . . . taken some pain in collecting certain hidden secrets together, and reduced them into one *Libello,* or pamphlet, for my own behoove and my familiar friends," he writes, "yet at the instance of a certain gentlewoman, being my dear and especial friend, I was constrained to publish the same, and considered with my self the saying of the wise: which is, That good is best, which to all indifferently is of like goodness, or effect: or which without respect of person is good to all indifferently." He has thus decided to "communicate unto the view and public benefit of all men, this little book, the contents whereof do instruct and teach all manner of person and degrees to know perfectly the manner to make divers and sundry sorts, that have not hitherto been publicly known: which fact of mine I know will be not only dislike of some, but altogether condemned: Not for that it is evil, but that their fine heads cannot digest, that any other beside themselves should enjoy the benefit thereof, having for their Maxim, that such things are of small price as are common to all men. . . ."[65]

The success of this book would in any case be the inspiration for the release of many more. Partridge himself would go on to publish *The widowes treasure, plentifully furnished with sundry precious and approoued secretes in phisicke and chirurgery for the health and pleasure of mankinde: hereunto are adioyned, sundry pretie practices and conclusions of cookerie* — another text that would go into many editions and where the readership and use of the text is a complex issue, the idea of addressing the book to widows being an especially interesting innovation. Perhaps the best known of these books today is one that came out fairly late, Gervase Markham's *The English Hus-wife* (1615), which we have encountered before in the case of collops and eggs. His inspiration being a French husbandry manual and conduct book, and his instincts being conservative, Markham prefaces his recipes with admonitions: "A housewife must be religious": "She must be temperate." As for her diet:

> Let her diet be wholesome and cleanly, prepared at due hours, and cooked with care and diligence; let it be rather to satisfy nature than our affections, and apter to kill hunger than revive new appetites; let it proceed more from the provision of her own yard, than the furniture of the markets, and let it be rather esteemed for the familiar acquaintance she hath with it, than for the strangeness and rarity it bringeth from other countries.[66]

Markham could not be clearer about the binary terms in keeping with which housewifery and cookery was to be practiced: nature vs. affection, hunger vs. appetite, satisfaction vs. revival — what Partridge was among the first to call "recreation"—home provision vs. the "furniture of the markets," familiarity vs. strangeness, commonness vs. rarity, national tradition vs. foreign imports.

But in spite of all the attention Markham has attracted among literary critics, his book was by no means the most popular of its type, and Markham did not, in any case, have the last word in cookery literature. By 1615 a new mood was becoming prominent, signaled by the publication of John Murrell's *A New Booke of Cookerie*. What is new is the spirit of cookery as "fashion," and fashion as a characteristic of the cosmopolitan lifestyle:

> A New Booke of Cookerie [the title page asserts]. Wherein is set forth the newest and most commendable Fashion for Dressing, or Sowcing, eyther Flesh, Fish, or Fowle. Together with making all sorts of Jelleyes, and other made-Dishes for service; both to beautifie and adorne eyther Nobleman or Gentlemans Table. Hereunto also is added the most exquisite London Cookerie. All set forth according to the now, new English and French fashion. Set forth by the observation of a Traveler.

Murrell makes no bones about this. Although he is aware of the female public of the cookbooks of the last forty years in England and addresses himself to a female patron, he is the messenger of what would soon be called *le monde,* "the world" of high fashion. "Of this *Name* and *Nature,*" he writes in his dedication to "the virtuous, and well-accomplished Gentlewoman, Mrs. Francis Herbert,"

> . . . many small *Books* and *Pamphlets* have heretofore been published; the most of which nevertheless have instructed rather how to mar then make good Meat: but this (in credit of my knowledge, and strict observation in Travel) is experimentally such as it pretends to be in the Title-Page thereof. Whereof I can say but this, and this it will perform for the sayer, That it gives each Meat his right for the manner of dressing; each Dish his due, for the order of serving. . . .[67]

Openly appealing to fashion and cosmopolitanism—"London Cookery" itself being a sign of fashion and cosmopolitanism in Murrell's text, since it is quietly promoted in opposition to non-London, which is to say provincial cookery— Murrell mocks official ideas that have been circulating at least since William Harrison's account of English food, and that at the time Murrell was writing was finding its way on the English stage, as in Philip Massinger's comedy *The City-Madam* (1632). Hostile to tradition and provincialism, disdainful of the mere housewifery promoted by earlier texts and especially by the contemporary *English Housewife,* the "Traveler" promotes not pleasure, but newfangled, far-fetched propriety. His language on this head coincides exactly with the language that would soon be promoted in France, when after a long period of dormancy, French cookery literature would suddenly flourish: the idea that good cooking gives "each Meat his right" and "each Dish his due." In other words, good cookery pursues the "saveur propre des aliments"—the own taste, the individual taste, the proper taste, of its main ingredients.

When a few years later Murrell published what he called *The Second Booke of Cookerie* — appending it to a new edition of a more conventional text he called *A Delightful Daily Exercise for Ladies and Gentlewomen* (first edition, 1614; second edition, 1621)—he kept up the pressure. The second book was said to contain *"many of the best and choicest works, that are used at this day, both of the French and Dutch fashions."*[68] It was said to *"set forth the newest and most commendable Fashion of Dressing, Boyling, Sowcing, or Roasting, all manner either Flesh, Fish, or any kind of Fowle. Together with an exact order of making Kickshawes, or made-dishes of any fashion, fit to beautifie either Noblemans or Gentlemans table. All set forth according to the now new English and French fashion."* It featured such "Novelties as *Time, Art,* and *Diligence* (the Perfecters of each *Faculty*) doe daily devise" and was therefore fit "to give all contentment to the curioust palate." Nor, according to Murrell, was there anything at all suspicious about the new emphasis on catering to "curious" taste: "I take [it] to be no sinful curiosity," he says; it "is rather a sin to mar a good meat with ill handling."[69]

VI

A systematic handling of a coherent style of cookery, brought forth with persuasive and scientific language out of a network of texts and practices; an engagement with artfulness that had a cachet of antiquity and an intricate involvement with the performance of princely grandeur (or, more humbly, with household welfare); a textual practice that increasingly became a part of the intellectual life of the era and as a sign of that increasingly engaged with the architectonics of the menu and the rhetorical negotiations of prefatory matter—that is what the cookbook looks like when it is viewed as literature. Also, of course, the cookbook was a vehicle of gustatory pleasure — but the pleasure of the gustatory was never an unmediated sense perception, a "taste" that one book after another attempted to delight, albeit with different means. When, beginning in 1651 in France and a couple years later in England, cookbook writing would, as it were, explode into print and a new age of cookery be professed, no formal literary innovations would be introduced. But the content of cookery literature would undergo a revision, aiming toward new experiences of pleasure and taste, and indeed toward new definitions of pleasure and taste. The French cookbooks would be far more inventive than the English in this period, whose own tastes seem to have remained fairly steady. English books were self-consciously consolidating, refining, and codifying earlier traditions, taking a cautious approach to innovation and to English culinary identity.[70] French books were self-consciously refashioning the world of cookery, creating a "nouvelle cuisine" that would eventually be called an "haute cuisine," and that in any case signaled a major change in how the pleasures of the table were to be managed.[71]

Pierre de La Varenne initiated the cookbook explosion with *Le cuisinier françois,* soon translated as *The French Cook.* The text, as its most perceptive student demonstrates, would stand out from everything that had gone before, at least in France, in at least seven ways: (1) It would abandon the heavy spices of medieval and early Renaissance cuisine. (2) It would introduce instead an emphasis on indigenous aromatic seasonings, including the bouquet of bay, parsley, and thyme. (3) It would introduce new criteria of culinary prestige: delicacy (*délicatesse*) and rigor, exhibited through the newly systematized structure of the meal and designed to demonstrate not so much the bounty as the good taste of the master of the household and his chef. (4) It would emphasize the use of butter as a cooking element, liaison, and finish—a practice already under way in the sixteenth century in France but now a dominant element in it. (5) For the largely acidic sauces and condiments of medieval and Renaissance cookery, it would substitute fat- and *fond*-based sauces and would in general favor round, fatty flavors over sharp, acidic ones. (6) It would replace sugar as a main flavoring ingredient with salt: fewer salted meats being used in favor of fresh ones, salt would be added to dishes as their distinguishing resonance, and sweet flavors would be exiled to dessert courses. (7) On the whole, it would emphasize the *saveur propre* of foods: chicken dishes would taste predominantly of chicken, with seasonings, sauces, and garnishes being used to intensify the taste of the chicken, rather than to transform it into something else. The "defeat of natural processes by way of the enchantments of art," a conceit so important to medieval cuisine, would finally become passé, in favor of a protocol that was no less artificial, not to mention time-consuming and fussy, but that was supposed to accentuate rather than transform the nature of foods.[72] Taken together—although some of these qualities can be found in English and Italian cookbooks well before 1651, and although the change in approach that La Varenne signals must surely have developed in France over a long period of time in the absence of a cookbook codifying it—these changes represent an impressive shift in the style of fine cookery. One expert makes the further claim that in the hands of La Varenne and his successors cookery itself, as the new cookbooks taught it, became a different sort of practice. La Varenne is the first, Barbara Ketchum Wheaton observes, to organize cookery according to modules of ingredients and modes of preparation, so that a variety of dishes with varied flavors and textures could be put together out of an orderly repertoire.[73] In that claim, I think, she points to something new about the nouvelle cuisine of seventeenth-century France, but she also exaggerates, since a modular approach of some sort can be found as early as the Danish-Latin *Libello*, not to mention the architectural guidelines of Scappi. What La Varenne initiates is a new fashion of modular organization that would remain constant through the twentieth century, where cookery begins with the preparation of stocks and *fonds*, and where dishes would be assembled according to the similitudes and contrasts that could be added to the *saveur propre* of a main item with the assistance of various modes of preparation, which follow according to basic rules of preparation. That in itself is revolutionary. In fact, it would herald the characteristically French approach to food — still dominant in such post-French innovations as "California cuisine"—where, although sensitivity to fresh and subtle tastes would seem to be everything, cookery in fact elevates principles over experience, methods over substances, and style over things: taste itself, in fact, becoming elevated from a quality of sense perception into a principle of cookery.

La Varenne doesn't quite explain it that way, it is interesting to note. In his own prefatory remarks, he would frame his accomplishment in terms of his relation to his patron and make a more cautious appeal to the tastes of his readers. This changer of culinary fashions throughout Europe would lay claim to many things: to propriety and pleasure in the name of "délicatesse"; to the possession of a secret now finally worth bringing to the attention of the public; to the authority of a patron and a treasure of a unique taste; and even to the achievement of a "masterpiece." But he would hesitate to make any claims to originality and would avoid appealing to fashion altogether. I quote La Varenne here from the English translation of *Le cuisinier françois* published in 1653, which I have glossed with some of the original French:

> *My Lord,*
> *Although my condition doth not afford me a Heroic heart, it gives me nevertheless such a one as not to be forgetful of my duty. During a whole ten years employment in your house, I have found the secret how to make meats ready neatly and daintily [le secret d'apprester delicatement les Viandes]. I dare say that I have exercised this profession with a great approbation of the Princes, the Marshals of France, and of an infinite number of persons of quality, who did cherish your Table in Paris, and in the Armies, where you have forced Fortune to grant*

Figure 3.5. Title page and frontispiece of *The French Cook* (1653), by Pierre de La Varenne. Reproduced by permission of the British Library (E.1541.(1.)).

your Virtue some Offices worthy of your courage. I think, that the public ought to receive the profit of this experience of mine, to the end that it may owe unto you all the utility, which it will receive thereby. I have therefore set down in writing what I have so long practiced in the honor of your service, and have made a small Book of it, bearing the title of the Clerk of your Kitchen. But, as all what it doth contain, is but a lesson, which the desire of pleasing you hath cause me to learn, I have thought that it ought to be honored with our name, and that without sinning against my duty, I could not seek for it a mightier prop than yours: It is a token of the passion which I have always had, and which I shall have all my life time for your service. Therefore, my Lord, use your accustomed generosity, do not despise it, though it be unworthy of you. Consider that it is a treasure of the Sauces, the taste whereof did once please you [dont le gout vous a contenté quelque fois]; and to conclude, that it is the Masterpiece of the

*coming from the hands [c'est un chef d'oeuvre qui part de la main] of one who
will ever, etc. . . .*[74]

However one assesses the changes in French cuisine brought about by La Varenne,
the rhetoric of this cuisine looks backward as well as forward and recalls no
precedent more than Scappi's *Opera* of eighty years earlier.

For a complete embrace of the new on the part of the master chef, one would
have to wait not just for new approaches and new things, but for a cook and author who fully embraces the rhetoric of the new. Such is the notorious case of the
man known only by his initials, L.S.R. A fine cookbook writer in his own right,
L.S.R. in many recipes is not all that different from La Varenne, though his cookery is more elaborate and detailed, his general presentation better organized,
and his instructions more exacting. Getting things right for L.S.R. means mastering time and space as well as the material at hand — knowing precisely when
to take a sauce off the fire, or when a chicken has been sufficiently *mortifié,* or
when to add garnishes and liaisons to a potage, where to place a roast on the
table, how to arrange side dishes, and how to add flavors with ingredients the
sight of which may be unpleasant to the eye. It means knowing what is most "polite" and the "most approved" as well as to good sense. Where La Varenne is still
revealing a "secret," in *L'art de bien traiter* L.S.R. claims to demonstrate "the veritable science of properly preparing, arranging, and serving" food. This positive
science aims at "the exquisite choice of meats, the finesse in seasoning them, the
civility [politesse] and the propriety of serving them, the quantities proportion-
ate to the number of guests, and finally the general ordering of things which
make an essential contribution to the quality and the embellishment of a meal
where the mouth and the eyes are equally charmed by ingenious diversity. . . ." As
for earlier cuisine — including La Varenne's, which he characterizes as a "prodigious overflow" and "confused heap" of different things — L.S.R. wants to reject
it entirely:

> I know well that in the matter of novelties it is not easy to please every-
> one, and tastes are as different as humors; but if one wants to take the
> trouble of reflecting on the subject that I am addressing today, in ways
> altogether opposed to those by which several old authors have spoken
> after their fashion, one can discover and even avow that I am right to
> reform that antique and disgusting manner of preparing and serving
> things, whose disharmony and rusticity produce nothing but useless
> expense without direction, excessive profusion without order, and
> finally inconvenient superfluity, without profit and without honor.[75]

VII

As literary artifacts, cookbooks insert themselves into the world of practical life, both as advocates of things to be done and as expressions of ideas to be read and thought. As we can see, the pleasure that particular recipes can afford the diner are only a small part of what the cookbooks themselves are aiming to provide. Indeed, the idea of pleasure for its own sake remains somewhat problematic for most early modern cookbooks. Or, to put it another way, if pleasure of some sort is indeed the final goal to which early cookbooks address themselves, looking at cookbooks as literature goes to show that the pleasure entailed is mediated by a variety of other considerations that bear less on the taste of food than on the rules of preparation, presentation, and appreciation, along with the social values such rules are intended to serve. Profusion and splendor, refinement and subtlety, propriety and hierarchy, or for that matter wholesomeness and frugality — these are all values according to which early modern cookbooks could chose to define and realize the pleasures of the table, given certain rules for culinary self-expression. When John Murrell begins writing about the "latest fashions" of foreign countries or when L.S.R. condemns the disharmony, rusticity, superfluity, and unprofitable dishonor of his predecessors, the pleasure of the table is being redefined, mediated by new formalities, and expressed by way of new discursive conventions, in keeping with new values: whether or to what extent food actually *tastes* different, or yields more pleasure, is almost secondary to the drive to express culinary value.

A food writer who does not quite get this point once complained in print about what is still among the best editions of Apicius, Barbara Flower and Elizabeth Rosenbaum's *The Roman Cookery Book* (1958). The recipes in the edition, she writes, "have not been adapted for the modern cook, excepting the occasional comment in the notes, and the book is mainly of scholarly, rather than practical, interest."[76] Poor impractical scholarly interest! It would seem that scholars have missed the point. But if the focus is on the historical and cultural contexts of food practices and the texts that guide them, the distinction between the scholarly and the practical doesn't hold, for it is precisely the nature of the practical that scholarly examinations of cookbooks as literature must endeavor to explain.

The pleasure of the practical, and the practicality of pleasure, can only in the barest sense answer to the universals of antiquarians or, more seriously, of experimental psychologists, who after many years, in my opinion, have not been able to go beyond the observation that some people like some things and other people like others (but all children like milk).[77] It would be fun to try a roasted Roman dormouse served with poppy seeds with honey, or to know why exactly I have become so fond of the unlikely product radicchio, a bitter herb. But we can never taste what the Romans tasted because we can never dine in an authentic Roman context, with genuine Roman ingredients, within the flow of time and the structures of space and sociality that ingredients and dinners were served and consumed in Rome. Nor, at least given our current understanding of the psychology of taste, will we be able to devise a rule that would predict my keenness for radicchio and your indifference or aversion to it. Taste doesn't work that way. The history of cookbooks explains the problem in part because what it attests to is this aspect of taste; it attests to the history—and historicity—of pleasure, the way pleasure answers to the continually evolving foodway of a culture and the erratically shifting nuances and fashions of culinary language. "There is nothing more insupportable or disgusting," writes L.S.R., "than seeing oil float as it were on the surface of soups and other preparations, which is capable of taking our appetite away and even provoking nausea. . . ."[78] Therefore he always skims his soups. But he also always serves soup over a sop of bread (a *mitonnade*) and he always adds cullis, or *coulis* (a reduced and strained stock) to the broth. You can serve a soup without any garnishes and the soup will lose nothing by it, he says, but "you will not be able to forgo two principal things, namely the sop and the cullis: one is the foundation of the building, the other is the covering and the crowning."[79] The argument makes sense, but only if one also understands the rest of the world of culinary sensations over which L.S.R. intends to stand guard—a world where taste is always for the delicate (though delicacy does not militate against an intensity of flavors, which is rather one of the goals of *la nouvelle cuisine*), and disgust to the point of nausea (L.S.R. actually refers to a *vomissement*) is an ever-present danger.

Chickens hunter style, a serviceable dish in 1300 that would continue to be popular in our own time the way an old fairy tale is continually retold and admired, is a concrete example of the issues under discussion. With a name, a provenance, a recognizable "style," and a familiar taste, it is still being reiterated on tables around the world, especially given the recent spread of Italian food (and hence *polla alla cacciatore*) as a world cuisine. Sometimes this tale is told with a white sauce, as it was told in medieval Denmark; more often it is told with a red sauce, using an ingredient, the tomato, that wouldn't become acceptable, outside of Spain, until the eighteenth century.[80] But it is noteworthy that in the seventeenth century, during the revolution of cookery and the outpouring of books that defined it, the dish falls from view. John Murrell could not include it in his *New Book of Cookerie* under any name; though a self-professed connoisseur, Murrell doesn't know how to do anything with chickens but stew them. His cookery does not have a way of double-cooking anything, and it does not use fry pans for constructing or finishing sauces. No chickens hunter style is possible in it. Similarly, French cooks would also be incapable of including chickens hunter style (by any name) in their repertoire. Yet their inability to do so was not due to the fact that they weren't familiar with the procedures involved. Rather, the "style" of the dish as the Danish recipe presents it failed to fit into their modules of preparation or to follow their criteria of delicacy and propriety. Though mushrooms continued to be an important addition to a simmered dish, the French cook did not throw gizzards or livers into them; they reserved the gizzards and livers for other things and preferred items like sweetbreads and artichoke bottoms. And more important, though the basic idea of the dish as it appeared in the Danish text was still present in their cookery, the idea was subsumed perforce under new categories of preparation and identification. La Varenne makes a *poulardes en ragoût, ragoût* being the key term. Small larded force-fed chickens (*poulardes*) are cut in half, quickly browned in a frying pan, put in a pot with broth and a bouquet *garni,* and cooked with truffles and mushrooms, or otherwise with small slices of roasted mutton or pork, and then garnished with pistachios or lemon.[81] The ragout being a kind of unthickened stew, the final element, the egg yolk liaison, is not considered. But the liaison gets supplied in one of the next important cookbooks of the period, *Le cuisinier* by Pierre de Lune (1662):

Fricassée de poulets à la sauce blanche.

Cut the chickens, brown them in a frying pan with lard, put them in a terrine with stock or water or a glass of white wine, a bouquet, salt, pepper, three or four mushrooms, nutmeg; when you are ready to serve it, mix in three or four egg yolks with verjuice or lemon.[82]

As for L.S.R., that chef would feature the fricassee of chicken as one of the signature dishes of a well-set table. His recipe is over two pages long and comes in two variations. The second one begins with cut-up chicken browned in butter and lard; seasoned with salt, pepper, cloves, parsley, and thyme; and accompanied with *ciboulettes hachés,* chopped mushrooms, and either artichoke bottoms or asparagus tips. To this either boiling water or bouillon is added, as well as, "according to the season," sweetbreads, more mushrooms, and morels or *mousserons* (another kind of mushroom). Finally, "when your fricassee is reduced by boiling to four or five ladles of sauce, take it off the fire, add a half-dozen egg yolks mixed with verjuice, and as much flour as it will take. Pour the mixture into a small cauldron or casserole dish, and stir five or six times in the warmth, and serve as is without again putting it on the fire, lest the eggs curdle."[83] We need to be careful here of falling for the saying, *plus ça change,* and leaving it at that. The continuity of European cookery from 1300 to 1700 is one thing; the continuity of cookbooks is another. As a dish, the chickens hunter style undergoes a series of alterations and complications, in keeping with a steady attitude toward the substance of right eating and a continuous ecology of husbandry. As a recipe, it moves from being something obscurely and loosely recorded for reasons that are not entirely clear to the expression of a "veritable science" that openly defies tradition and purports to change the way the world of the privileged sits down to a meal.

Chapter Four

✳ ✳ ✳ ✳ ✳ ✳ ✳ ✳ ✳ ✳ ✳ ✳ ✳

THE FOOD OF WISHES,
FROM COCKAIGNE TO UTOPIA

✳ ✳ ✳ ✳ ✳ ✳ ✳ ✳ ✳ ✳ ✳ ✳ ✳

We found there a large and beautiful plain where the people of the
country planted eggs with hoes, just as people in France plant beans
with hart's horns.

These eggs sprouted in the earth and threw up shoots higher than
a lance, which produced pods a fathom long, and each pod contained
at least thirty or forty eggs.

On such things the people of the country subsist, for they do not
have any other sort of fruit but these eggs, which are considerably
larger than a goose egg, and they are very good and of good digestion,
and they engender good blood, as I know from experience. And the
country is named by its inhabitants the Island of the Coquards.[1]

I

THE DREAMS CAME IN MANY FORMS, as well they should have
done. "The appetite is a creature of dreams," writes Roland Barthes; "it is at once
a memory and a hallucination," ever allied with "the fantastic." Food, already fantastic, must then become the subject of fantasy, the fantasy of a fantasy, and ultimately transcend itself. "Two apples in my hand and the third in my mouth," says
an old English proverb.[2] We can have all we want, just as we want, whenever we
want, however we want, and even more; we can have it and eat it too, although
the fantasy of doing so — regressive, childlike, yet also mature and providential
since it refers to the future as well the past — involves an impossibility: eating the
third apple without one's hands, which are busy holding on to the first and second apple. On the other side of the equation from the realm of cookery dealt
with in the previous chapter lies the realm of dining, and with that the fantasia,

the fantasy of the fantasy of feeding and being fed. The redoubled fantasy may revert to childhood: every apple we eat is the first apple we tasted, spooned into our expectant mouths mashed and sweetened with maybe a little milk or cheese added in, and we can never get enough of it. Food is a primal joy and feeding is a riot. But the fantasies may also look forward, expressing our civility, our good manners, our understanding of nutrition and fashion, our rational response to the need to eat and preserve ourselves for another day — "two apples in my hand" — as well as our desire for higher orders of pleasure: for food as spiritual matter and feeding as sublimation. We will have more than one occasion to observe this phenomenon. To the early modern imagination, the merest apple could be the vehicle of magical transformation, translating innocence into knowledge and matter into spirit. While Rabelais himself was still a child, still perhaps calling for "Some drink, some drink, some drink" from his nurse, a courtly Florentine could thus spin out an erotic fable where a sorb apple — served at a glorious, elegant, allegorical banquet — betrayed such an "unspeakable sweetness of taste" that one felt "as though the ideal form had been dissociated from the gracious material."[3]

Yet in the early modern period, the food of wishes could also be a food of regret: not only abundance and joy, but temperance, frugality, and methodical self-denial could be objects of desire. The simple abstemious meal, penitential abstinence, vegetarianism, and even weight watching could all be projected onto the screen of culinary desiderata. Apicius aside, the heritage of late antiquity, both Roman and Christian, encouraged diminished and grudging wishes of this kind. So did newer strands of thought, including both humanism and the new science of the scientific revolution. We will dine on a green salad, says the host of Erasmus's dialogue *The Godly Feast.* And then the host says, "Perhaps we can have a hen from the coop." What more could one wish for? Or, more to the point, what else but this should be the substance of our wishes? "Food not bought," as he says, prepared with homely integrity, is what we desire.[4] We fantasize over something that is actually available to us, feeding and being fed in a homely setting with sparing simplicity, lubricating the occasion with a moderate amount of estate-made wine and a goodly amount of learned, godly conversation. To desire more is to desire the wrong thing. A salad, a chicken, a loaf of homemade bread, a glass of homemade wine, conversation. Or even, as in the case of vegetarian Roger Crab, a diet of "corn, bread, and bran, herbs, roots, dock-leaves, mallows, and grass," washed down with nothing but water from the well down the road.[5]

We will get back to this food of regret in the next chapter, however. For now the subject is the food of wishes in a positive sense. "Room, room! Make room for the bouncing belly," as Ben Jonson has it said in the opening of his masque

Pleasure Reconciled to Virtue. "First Father of sauce, and deviser of jelly: / Prime master of arts, and giver of wit . . ." The belly, along with the gullet, the tongue, the palate, the nose, and the eyes — the organs of appetite, as the early modern period conceived them, which leveled their demands not only on the world but also on the mind. The menu itself, as we have seen, could be a field of dreams — collocations of twenty-dish courses, featuring half a dozen different cooking techniques and dozens of different kinds of ingredients, wild game and livestock, puddings and polentas, spices and herbs, roasts and fricassees, potages and stews. The feasts and banquets the menus recorded were themselves sites of desire. Thought to embody the values of good government, hospitality, and "freedom," serving important ceremonial as well as practical purposes, they raised the need to eat to the level of a political daydream. They were perhaps the single most important, since the most frequent, venue for putting "power on display" or for disseminating a palatial "illusion of power," although the best scholars of Renaissance power have seldom paid much attention to them as such.[6] One attended a banquet not only in the hopes of a good meal and a generous helping of liquor, but in the spirit of yearning observance, situated as one was within a belly-pleasing idealization of the court, the presiding family, the great manor, the civic association, or the body politic as a whole.

Increasingly, first in Italy and then in France and the other parts of the north, one also encounters appreciations of food for its own sake, that is to say for its sheer aesthetic qualities. "Everybody writes in praise of drinking," says the comic writer Paul Scarron, at about the same time as *Le cuisinier françois* was put it into print. "And me . . . / All I want to do is eat." "If our body is charmed" by good food, he goes on to say, "Even more charmed is our soul." "O my dear friend," he concludes, ". . . I'm all for eating: / There's nothing like being a glutton [glouton]." The merest slice of melon, insists Scarron's contemporary Antoine Gérard de Saint-Amant, with such an odor, such a heft, and such sweet flavor, will "tickle the soul . . . strengthen the heart . . . satisfy the appetite . . . ," and overwhelm the senses, reducing them all to the sense of taste.[7] In their painting *The Feast of Archeloüs* (ca. 1615; Metropolitan Museum of Art), Peter Paul Rubens and Jan Brueghel the Elder turn a somewhat lugubrious moment in Ovid's *Metamorphoses,* when the river god Archeloüs tells the story of his despair and isolation, into the occasion of a great seafood dinner, where spirits of the sea bring forth lobsters and bream, oysters and cockles, out of their own wild domain to deck an elegant table, where one also finds such delicacies as a herring pie, fixed in a grotto at the edge of the sea, set with a fine white tablecloth and silver platters, hard by an even more elegant sideboard from which wine is served. What Ovid wrote contrasts the progress of Roman society with the pathos of

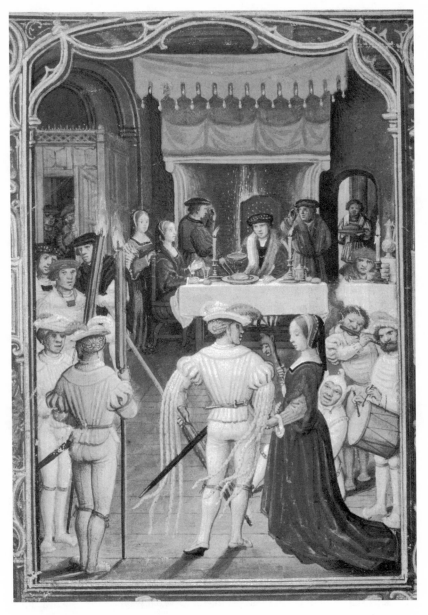

Figure 4.1. Feasting. South Netherlands (Bruges), late fifteenth century. Reproduced by permission of the British Library (Add. 24098).

natural life. What Rubens and Brueghel represent is a banquet of overwhelming pleasure: nature and culture united to stimulate desire and provide for a surplus of satisfaction, even as Archeloüs tries to point to the world of suffering from which he has come. This kind of insistence on the sheer aesthetics of the feast, over and against the cares of the world, is an especially prominent feature of the baroque. The still life of food for which Dutch painting is rightly famous — the glimmering breakfast of fruit and bread, of seafood and wine — is a case in point. There are always reminders in these paintings of something else, rejoinders about the hard labor that goes into the provisioning of every good meal, or the vanity of human wishes. Meals are interrupted; glasses are overturned; mischievous cats reach out for human consumables; reflections in the silver of the platters and flatware tease the mind. Still, the exuberant physicality of the food and drink on display all but overpowers any morality the paintings may be trying to inculcate. Food and drink are good for their own sake; and good food and drink, the artists of the baroque imply, are more than good. They become a standard against which even the most spiritual of goods may be measured, or a medium through which other sorts of values may begin to communicate themselves.

Before the baroque era, nevertheless, the discourse of the food of wishes often moved in a different direction. If the double fantasy of food could incline toward the idealization of the household or the state or the noble labor of the bourgeois household and its moralized hedonism, it could also transcend the limits of the everyday world. It could become what Ernst Bloch calls the "wishful image": an escape from the everyday that is also possibly an inspiration — a consolation, a spur to labor, a "liberating laugh" alleviating fears, and perhaps even an impetus toward agitating for social change.[8] The conditions of producing and consuming food in premodern Europe — conditions where surpluses could not be taken for granted, where the distribution of goods was obscenely unequal, where the rhythm of life was also a rhythm of uneven consumption, and where the hopes of whole classes could thus be fixed upon the foodways of the world — meant that utopia itself, in almost any of its forms, was necessarily and first of all a utopia of food. Two apples in my hand and a third in my mouth: regressive and progressive at once, the wishful image of the utopian food of wishes expressed the aspirations of whole classes of people in the premodern world. They also, however, expressed the limits of such aspirations. What was it that one could wish for in the realm of food? What was the purpose in wishing for it? What was possible, beneficial, or stimulating to desire — to desire to imagine, to desire to experience, to desire to put in one's mouth? The demand for primal delight and de-repressing riot contended against the aspirations for civility, security, and transcendence. The bouncing belly was a voracious organ, but it was also a master of arts, a giver of wit.

II

Let us begin with the Middle Ages and with a special kind of dream of transcendent abundance, the Land of Cockaigne, which will eventually be adopted, modified, and then rejected. We will then go on to some of those adaptations, modifications, and rejections, including some that are already noteworthy in the Middle Ages and others that we will look at some detail, the products of humanists like Rabelais and Sir Thomas More. In the post-medieval period, the Land of Cockaigne is no longer so persuasive a daydream; it is often irrelevant. But let us begin with the medieval Cockaigne, and let us begin with a high-culture Italian version.

In Boccaccio's *Decameron,* then, a fourteenth-century collection of short stories, a simple-minded painter is regaled by his mischievous friends about "'a Basque province, in a district called Bengodi, where vines are fastened to the stakes with sausages, and a goose can be had for a penny, with a duckling thrown in for good measure.' A wonderful mountain was also to be found in that country," the narrator adds, ". . . all made of grated Parmesan cheese, and inhabited by folk who spent all their time making macaroni and ravioli, which they boiled in capon broth and then spilled out pell-mell, so that whoever was the nimblest obtained the biggest share. And last but not least, a stream of the most delicious wine you'd ever hope to taste, with not the tiniest drop of water in it, flowed close by."[9] So there we have it. Boccaccio's version is one of the earlier recorded instances, and the first in Italian, of that comic, mythic land of satisfied desires. As Herman Pleij emphasizes in *Dreaming of Cockaigne,* the Land of Cockaigne — also known as Luilekkerland in Dutch, Schlaraffenland in German, and in Boccaccio's tale as Bengodi — was more than just a place where one could eat one's fill; it amounted to a full-fledged medieval utopia, a fabulous far-off place where all sorts of needs were permanently accommodated and many perceived injustices in real society were restituted.[10] As elements of the Cockaigne myth were told and retold, an impossible abundance of food — mountains of cheese, fence posts of sausage — became the chief projection of a utopian longing that also reached into political arrangements and the social order, not to mention classical learning and religious teaching. Yet food was nevertheless the main preoccupation of most Cockaigne fantasies, which form a crucial backdrop to the moral life of food in the early modern era. And what we find in them is a remaking of the objective reality of food into something strange, wonderful, and renegade.

The details of the fantasies are always significant. Macaroni, ravioli, and grated cheese are the stuff of Italian Cockaignes. North of the Alps, the foods desired are sausages, cakes, meats, poultry, fish, bread, and spices, to which are

added wine or beer, milk, and honey. A version from Lyon, not surprisingly, includes a lot of melted cheese. Context is crucial in these myths, and the selected
foods in fact present themselves in any of four contexts: the architectural, the
natural, the animalistic, or the social. In the architectural context, buildings are
made out of food: pillars and fence posts of sausage; shingles of cake; rooftops of
pies; windows and doors of salmon, sturgeon, and cod; streets paved with ginger
and nutmeg. In the naturalist context, rivers run with wine and the other desirable beverages (as in the Boccaccio account, water is banished from the Land of
Cockaigne); when it rains, custards, pancakes, figs, or eels descend from heaven.
The animals are not only plentiful and tame, including otherwise wild animals
like deer and boar; they may also offer themselves for consumption: geese fly
about at mouth level already roasted and ready to swallow; pigs wander about
with knives stuck in their sides, asking to be sliced into bite-sized portions. As
for the social contexts, it is often mentioned that one never has to pay for one's
food, or otherwise labor, or compete with other people for resources. In Cockaigne consumption itself is rewarded with honorifics and money, so that the
more one consumes, the greater the reward.[11] Indolence is rewarded as well: one
should eat without expending effort. Along with all this, it almost goes without
saying, everything is usually held in common.

Current scholarship encourages us to read the varieties of the legend as
specific articulations in specific historical situations, and not simply as an ur-myth
with unchanging features. Boccaccio's version, placed in the context of a comic
story about tricksters playing a joke on a simpleton, expresses the dream of Cockaigne to far different effect than the Middle English version, recorded by a monk,
who seems to be somewhat serious about the Cockaigne fantasy, finding in it a
genuine if impossible satisfaction of instinctual desires, though his main impetus
is to satirize life in the monastery. Boccaccio is already jaded, though in a high
fashion. The monk is longing for the world, objecting to the vow of poverty and
the hypocritical authority keeping the world outside the gate. And both of these
versions contrast with the two contemporary rhyming texts in Dutch, which are
told straight, without any framing devices or other contextual apparatus.[12] So the
Cockaigne story does not from case to case really mean the same thing. Nevertheless, some consideration of the structural elements of the legend still seems
called for. The myth almost always includes these four basic motifs:

1. Food becomes architecture (or, perhaps better, architecture becomes
   food).
2. Nature flows, sprouts, and pours, providing an excess of nourishment, of
   its own accord, without labor.

3. Animals are at once alive and cooked, and they freely offer themselves for consumption.

4. Society rewards indolence and consumption.

These, it bears repeating, are only the culinary elements of the myth. Other elements that show up in many versions—a reward for sleep, free love, communism, a fountain of youth, a donkey that defecates eggs or gold, and the subversion of the liturgical calendar (so that fast days are all but abolished, and holidays are multiplied)—are no doubt important too. So is the geography of Cockaigne: this haven of culinary wishes is usually imagined as a faraway land, which requires some effort to reach, although the effort may be, in principle, the opposite of effort: for example, in some versions one has to eat through a three-mile-wide wall of polenta to get there. Added up, such features may well amount to a potentially revolutionary image, as Mikhail Bakhtin, Piero Camporesi, and Herman Pleij suggest: a horizon of hope, where the injustices and deprivations of life as most people know it are overcome.[13] There is something of the idea of Cockaigne present in the Peasants' Rebellion in England of 1381, the Peasants' War in Germany during the early sixteenth century, and the Digger movement in revolutionary England in the middle of the seventeenth century. "*Worke together, Eate Bread together, Declare this all abroad,*" the leader of the Digger movement learned to propound, he said, in a mystical trance.[14] We like to think of peasant revolution in Europe as being political and religious in nature, but the dream of a common abundance commonly consumed and an end to unsatisfied appetites is certainly part of it as well. And as with peasant rebellion and revolution, so with the Cockaigne myth, which addresses itself first of all neither to politics, communism, the fountain of youth, nor sexuality, but to the relation of the individual and society to food.

All four imaginary elements in the relation of individuals and society to food as the myth imagines it involve inversions of the psychological, social, and natural orders. The Land of Cockaigne is a world turned upside down. The inversions express both conscious grievances and infantile wishes—grievances aimed against society in the world that is right side up, infantile wishes that have no use for society of any kind except so far as it is gratuitously and indiscriminately accommodating. If architecture becomes food, the real use of architecture is spurned. It is turned on its head and used for purposes for which it is not intended, and it is shown to be hollow; for whatever it is (and in premodern society's palaces and cathedrals, architecture could be glorious), it does not help to satisfy first needs first. Meanwhile, the childlike inhabitants eat. Similarly, if nature supplies "of its own kind, all foison, all abundance," as a character in Shakespeare puts it, in a context related to the myth of Cockaigne,[15] the basic relation of humanity to the natural world is rejected, in favor of something more primal: instead of providing a supply of food that human effort is required to husband, nature is food ready-made, and almost nothing but food, giving itself to humanity. Private property and the inequality that follows from it may thus become unnecessary. And the childlike inhabitant eats. Again, if animals can fly or crawl about ready-roasted and offer themselves up for consumption, then even death and slaughter have been rejected — but not meat eating itself or the desire for living off the death of others that meat eating demands. Desire is left intact, even as it is also endlessly accommodated. The childlike inhabitant need only open his mouth, and the food flies in. As for the rewards for laziness and consumption, in premodern society these rewards most clearly invert things for which the individual is more likely to be punished. Unpunished, in the fantasy, the poor man is unsuppressed. He can do whatever he wants; he can do nothing. The unpunished child, meanwhile, is unrepressed too: the child is a good girl or boy just for eating and sleeping.

We need to take seriously the experience of hunger that would motivate a daydream world like the Land of Cockaigne. The hard life of the peasant, subject to cycles of dearth and plenty, of plentiful seasons and meager ones, of existence only occasionally above the level of bare subsistence, vulnerable to famine, and educated in ideologies — Christian asceticism, on the one hand; deference to the privileges of the wellborn, on the other—which demanded self-sacrifice for the benefit of higher causes, was the empty cart of bricks out of which the impossible abundance of Cockaigne was constructed.[16] The architectural, the flowing, the flying, and the ready-sliced food all together form an image that acts not only as a projection of primal demands but as a response to lived experience, both of the hunger that threatened and the luxurious abundance of things from which one was debarred. Indeed, taking hunger seriously also means taking seriously the complicating circumstances of the discourse of Cockaigne. The "excessive profusion without order" that L.S.R. saw in the banquets that preceded those of his own more refined age finds a mirror in the profusion of foods without order—sausages, codfish, and cakes, joined by roasted flying geese — that tantalize the appetite in Cockaigne. Only now the profusion is available to all, without respect of persons or occasion or other formalities. The two visions of plenty, Cockaigne's excess and the aristocratic banquet's luxurious profusion, are two versions of the same thing. Nor was this banquet logic and the hungers underlying it the only determining contexts for the discourse of Cockaigne. The myth was articulated in dialogue with still other myths and other realities. As a "lying tale" and a "laughing tale," the *conte à rire* or fabliau that the French versions advertises itself to be puts it alongside other tall tales and other forays into the realm of what Bahktin called the "grotesque body."[17] Whatever the legend may have meant in the age before the written records of the late Middle Ages and early Renaissance, by the time it was written down it was clearly a tale without a plot that no one was expected to take seriously. The myth was a floating island. It was a comedy, absurd and delightful, that drifted along among a variety of social and discursive contexts to which it was related or against which it abutted.

Among those contexts, beside the harsh realities and fears that living at a subsistence level brought about, is the holiday feast and the well-known "battle of Carnival and Lent" that formed a part of the festivities at the most raucous and substantial of the feasts. "You have no right here," Lent tells Carnival, in a French fabliau on the subject, as they argue in the halls of a palace. "You lie!" says Carnival. Lent leads an army of fish against Carnival and an army of roast meats, poultry, and legumes seasoned with lard, along with cheese and milk. The battle finally turns in Carnival's favor when his army is reinforced by Father Christmas, leading a troop of hams.[18] In Rabelais's retelling of the story (in *Book Four* of *Gargantua and Pantagruel*), Lent is defeated when, in the midst of battle, a giant pig rushes onto the scene of battle.[19] This is "Mardi Gras," symbol of the celebration that bears his name and at the same time a token, a visitor from the otherworld of Cockaigne, where no conflict between fish and meat, or between the observance of Lent and the observance of the feast, is conceivable. Many versions in fact openly advertise the simultaneous availability of fish and flesh, and ban Lent for periods of twenty years or more.

Still another context was the folktale in general. Cockaigne was one tale among many. And in fact, the legacy of the European folktale tells a somewhat different story about peasants, wishes, and food. If Cockaigne elements appeared in many folktales, they were placed in complicating contexts. The Grimm Brothers' "Hansel and Gretel" is the best known version, where starving children encounter a house built of "bread and covered with cakes."[20] But like "Hansel and Gretel" and its analogues and precedents, the many tales about hungry children and impoverished peasants and the magical means by which their problems are solved embraced an ethic where the easy plenitude of Cockaigne was eschewed for more realistic, not to mention unpleasant, assessments of the nature of food and feeding. Inside the house in the woods — in many versions at first a welcoming home, presided over by a kindly housewife, but not a house made of food — there dwells a cannibalistic ogre who has to be outwitted and killed. In a fabliau recounted by Giovanni Francesco Straparola in his *Facetious Nights* (1556), a monk is reviled in this monastery because of his gluttony. The monk "had a platter he jestingly termed his oratory of devotion, and this platter was big enough in size to hold seven ladlesful of soup." He not only empties his platter at every meal, but "all the leavings which remained as overplus on the plates of the other monks, whether they were many or few, were gathered up as gifts to the oratory and put to the uses of devotion." He greedily devours the leftovers "however foul and dirty they might be."[21] Chastised by his abbot, the monk replies, "If I had the chance of filling my belly with rich and delicate food after the fashion of those who sit in high places, [I] would assuredly eat vastly less of the stuff which I now swallow; but, seeing that I eat rough simple food which is not very easily digested, it seems to me in no wise a shameful thing to eat a good quantity of it."[22] A similar idea is recorded in Hans Sachs's *The Grand Inquisitor in the Soup* (ca. 1560). "What's left over," from his own rich meal, one monk says to another, "we'll give to the poor at noontime when they line up outside the cloister. Make a kettle for them and mix in some herbs, peas, and radishes. That's enough for them. Like the proverb says, 'If the poor have a lot—then they eat a lot.'"[23] All told, apart from the obvious anti-clerical satire, a more general complaint is being leveled: the powerful eat meat and live well and behave well; the poor eat meager soup and live poorly and behave poorly. The greedy belly is a product of deprivation and the dependence of the poor on the meatless leftovers of others.

To give one more example: In "Vardiello," a modernized folktale recounted by Giambattista Basile in *The Pentamerone* (1634–36), a simpleton, charged with keeping house while his mother goes out to the market, inadvertently kills the chicken whose eggs he was supposed to see hatched, then spoils the eggs, spills all the wine in the house, and when sent on a consolation mission to sell a bolt of cloth, gives the cloth away to a statue, thinking that he was doing a good deed. The cloth soon disappears, as a passerby filches it. Later, returning to the statue, the simpleton inadvertently but illegally comes across a cache of gold coins, which he brings home to his mother. At home, while he is resting outside with his back to a wall beneath a window, the money safe inside, his mother showers down a rain of figs and raisins upon him, which he gladly stuffs himself with, thinking it a reward from heaven. The mother uses the story the simpleton then tells about raining figs and raisins to have him locked up as a madman, forestalling any rumors that her son actually acquired a treasure of gold coins and making sure she can keep the money for herself. So the rain of food, a frequent element of Cockaigne fantasies, is shown to be a device to gull simpletons withal.[24]

In these and similar cases, elements of the myth of Cockaigne are used to deconstruct the myth. The house of plenty houses a cannibal. The delight in the "oratory" of endless quantities of food is an outcome of social inequality. The rain of food is a delusion: what really counts is money. The childlike response to the need to eat that the myth encourages—let the world turn into food for you, and devour everything you can — is not the lesson that even the simplest of those to whom the story was told would be expected to infer. The primal demand is not rejected, exactly — rather, appropriations of the myth of Cockaigne continue to register the demand: they acknowledge the demand and look kindly upon it. But they urge the need to move beyond it in favor of pragmatism. Raining figs, banquets of meat for which one does not have to labor, houses made of cake, rivers flowing with wine — these wishful images of peasant culture are in their own way normative, inspirational, and consolatory, but they are understood to be wishful only: they are not imperatives; they are not even to be desired. If the wishful images of food that crystallize in Cockaigne motifs are at bottom utopian, they are also — as is the fate of many utopian speculations — of no account, derisory, and hopeless.

III

Whatever the case may have been among the folk of the Middle Ages, by the sixteenth and seventeenth centuries the myth of Cockaigne was no longer innocent. It had a past. It had its limitations. It was known to have a source not only in the fables of the peasants but in classical learning — for example, Lucian's *A True Story,* to which Erasmus referred, filled with such elements of the lying tale as rivers of wine and a fountain of youth. It continued to have its uses — most spectacularly in food-lusty writers like Rabelais and Jonson. However, in the hands of humanist writers — most of whom derived not from the peasantry but from the bourgeoisie and the gentry, and many of whom had experience in the households of the great — other fantasies about food would be more vital. It was not that people were less hungry in the sixteenth and seventeenth centuries. Probably the opposite was the case, on the whole. But the discourse of the food of wishes was being used in new and different ways, and was responding to new experiences.

In cases where the myth of Cockaigne persisted, it was in modified retellings of the myth and in appropriations of its motifs and symbolism for other purposes. Fairy tales like "Vardiello" (first recorded in the early seventeenth century, although the motifs are much older) are examples of the latter. So are episodes in Rabelais and in Rabelais-inspired works like *Le disciple de Pantagruel,* also known as *Les navigations de Panurge* (1538), and the "Familière description du très vinoporratimalvoise et très envitaillegoulmente royaume Panigonnois" (1600). In the former a voyage on the high seas takes the narrator to the region of a sailing giant who eats whole ships and towns along with their inhabitants for dinner.

We have already seen, in chapter 2, how the giant avails himself of medicine when he suffers from indisposition. After coming upon an island of bloodthirsty wild men (*les Farouches*), an island inhabited by sausages (*les Andouilles*), and a Lantern-land (the lantern being a common symbol of carnival celebrations), the narrator goes on to visit Cockaigne-like regions: an island with a mountain made of butter, a river flowing with milk and running with fish, and trees bearing hot sausages; a flatland where hot pasties and fresh eggs grow out of the ground, larks fall from the clouds already roasted, and the rooftops are shingled with pies. There are lands with giant vegetables as well: immense gourds, cucumbers, lettuce, cabbage. But when he finally returns home, the narrator sets up house for himself and his men and establishes "a manner of living for the whole week for these people, and according to the food of the day." The food has little to do with Cockaigne:

> Au Lundi poix au lart.
> Au Mardi canes & canartz.
> Au merquedi pastés de loches.
> Au jeudi chapon en broches
> Au vendredi poissons de mer.
> Au Samedi tard à diner.
> Et au Dimanche, boyrons tous ensemble.[25]

Peas in lard, ducks, loach in pastry, brochettes of capon, on Friday seafood, on Saturday "late to dine," on Sunday drinking together—the point of *Le disciple de Pantagruel* is unclear. The work is an amateurish pastiche of folkloric motifs, though expressed with a tone of smug superiority, since the narrator constantly jokes about whether he is lying or not and claims affiliation with Pliny, Solon, Strabo, and Lucian, as well as Jean de Mandeville, author of the infamously exorbitant fourteenth-century *Travels*. But one thing is unmistakable: after the adventure, the narrator leaves the gastronomy of Cockaigne behind and lives with his fellows like a moderately prosperous abbot.

As for the "Familière description," this later work is written in accomplished ten-syllable verse, and although it contains vivid evocations of life in a Cockaigne-like kingdom, employing the usual motifs, it is framed as a challenge to the readers who would find such a place wholly attractive. "Come forth you lazy ones," it begins. And later: "Do you not want to undertake the quest / For this place, which without labor brings / Everything that suits people of your sort?" In spite of the moralized context, the description is effusive. It not only reiterates in fine form familiar elements of Cockaigne, beginning with a mountain of porridge and trees of butter, houses built of meat and streams running with wine; it also introduces certain Renaissance refinements. The wines themselves are lovingly named: white hypocras and "exquisite Malvoisie" (a white wine), "much better than the wines of Arbois and Beaune, or anywhere else." In this Kingdom of Panigon, named after a minor character in Rabelais, moreover, there are policies to help "move the appetite" of the citizens:

> By the streams running with such excellent wine,
> Little by little one sees
> Corned beef, *boutargue* [salted mullet roe], and hams.

What is new is not the meat; what is new is the way it is presented as a stimulus to the appetite, although, it is true, the appetite in question seems to be the thirst for more wine from the wine-flowing streams. The inventory of foods and food practices, in any case, eclipses earlier expressions of the genre. Here there are not only sausages; there are at least four different kinds. Here the fish aren't only numerous: they are served "stewed, roasted, and cooked in a hundred fashions." The anonymous author of this text is familiar with what, in the homes of the wealthy, passed as fine dining, and his fantasy reflects the new refinements and developments of taste. And yet again, in the end, the moralizing returns. If the happiness of man consists in virtue joined with honor, the speaker says, this is not really the best of places. "To me it seems a brutal life." "Work then," he concludes, "and do your duty. / Try to do good and you can have the good. / Follow virtue, and above all love honor."[26]

The author of the "Familière description" was probably influenced by Hans Sachs, whose *Das Schlauraffenland* (i.e., "Sluggard's Land," ca. 1530) had been circulating for some time. A contemporary of Rabelais, a shoemaker turned prolific author, scholar, and defender of both popular traditions and the Reformation, Sachs also includes a few ample catalogs. His Schlauraffenland has fish swimming either "boiled, roasted, salted, stuffed, or fried," and it has trees dropping with "fine figs, or cherries, / Plums, peaches, apples, or blackberries." Toward the end his tale turns nasty, however: "He who with his hand / Would work, is banished from Sluggard's Land / With all who honor modesty, / Morality, or industry." It concludes with an unconvincingly harsh moral lesson:

MORAL

> This fable is a tale of old,
> To careless children often told,

To show how bad the world would be
Were honor lost, and modesty;
Were people greedy, indolent,
Or only on low pleasures bent.
Here is set forth an allegory
Showing, in its quaint marvel-story,
How love of ease and sweets may lead
To utter worthlessness and greed;
How the indulgences of sense,
Or idle dreams of indolence
Can only end in foul offence;
That happiness can never be
Without a life of industry:
So let the olden fable stand,
This picture of the Sluggard's Land.[27]

This moralism was a common feature of the "Meistersinger" versions of Cockaigne in Germany of the sixteenth century, of which Sachs's version is the most prominent example.[28] And it would seem in these Renaissance renditions, as in the "Familière description," that readers and writers wanted it both ways: both to take delight in an amusing fantasy, speaking to needs, and to imagine themselves better than the fiction, seeing it placed in the context of good bourgeois, post-Reformation values, which of necessity reject the relevance of the Cockaigne myth. A similar situation obtains with the Dutch text of 1546 transcribed by Herman Pleij. The details proliferate in this longish work in prose. But from the beginning, the reader is cautioned that "until now this land was unknown to all except those rogues and rascals who first discovered it." The reader is alerted as well to the shabby behavior of its inhabitants. Where earlier versions took a silly pleasure in the idea that one might be paid in Cockaigne for sleeping, drinking, or doing nothing at all, here the description shades off into brutishness. "Bullies who tease and torment honest folk earn two shillings a day. Liars also earn good money. . . ." "Anyone leading . . . a virtuous and upright life is hated by everyone and eventually banished from the country. Likewise anyone who is wise and sensible is scorned and despised and treated badly by everyone." The text ends with cautionary advice in verse, whose tone is unmistakable:

From the pen of old folk this tale has sprung,
To serve now as a lesson to the young,
Accustomed to a nice and easy life,

Where intemperance and laxity are rife.
To Cockaigne these youths must now be sent,
Till their excessive energies are spent,
And they acquire a taste for honest work,
For in their sloth a host of vices lurk.[29]

We are on our way to the absolutely sour view of gluttony taken in the Cock-aigne-utopian fantasy of the English clergyman Joseph Hall in *Mundus alter et idem* (1605), later translated and adopted by John Healy in *The Discovery of a New World* (1608), which represents a Land of Plenty that is absolutely appalling. The great gluttons in Hall's antipodes are senators, whose chins reach to their paunches and whose paunches reach to the ground, elected in recognition of the greed with which they feed themselves.

Camporesi writes about what he calls the "twilight of the myth of Cock-aigne" that begins in this period and that eventually smothers both the joy of Cockaigne and its "call to liberation." No longer an expression of peasant culture or of peasant longings for a more just and substantial way of life, it becomes re-placed by visions of aristocratic hedonism, on the one hand, and by sour moral-istic complaints, on the other. An Italian text from 1588 that he records, *Il piace-vole viaggio di Cuccagna,* recounts a journey to Cockaigne that takes the would-be visitor on a month-long meander in lands increasingly decadent, where one feasts and dallies with the ladies, takes in the scenery, grows indolent, and gives up one's sense of obligation. Finally one arrives at the River of Forgetting, and once you cross it, "you pass safe to the Land of Cockaigne, and here ends my tale. There you may enjoy yourself in merriment, for ever more. And anyone who mentions this world is to be beaten about the head and arms and driven out forthwith."[30] The rejection of innocent childlike demands is complete. Here it is only adult needs that the story imagines satisfied—whoring and gaming among them, and a taste not for wonderful adventure but hedonistic tourism. The story ends at the objectionable forgetfulness at which an adult's true, contemptible, childlike indulgence would begin.

This is not to say that the myth didn't have its sunny uses in the sixteenth and seventeenth centuries. The celebration of the artisanal class in Thomas Dekker's comedy *The Shoemaker's Holiday* (1599) concludes with a Lord Mayor's Feast where Cockaigne imagery invades the pleasure of the moment. "There's cheer for the heavens," reports one of the participants: "venison-pasties walk up and down piping hot, like sergeants: beef and brewis comes marching in dry-fats, fritters and pancakes come trowling in wheelbarrows; hens and oranges hopping in porters' baskets, collops and eggs in scuttles, and tarts and custards come quavering in malt-shovels."[31] In the classic manor-house poem "To Penshurst," Ben Jonson adapts Cockaigne motifs to convey a form of civility. Addressing himself to the lord of the manor, he praises the Penshurst estate for its self-supplied bounty:

> The painted partridge lies in every field
>   And, for thy mess, is willing to be killed.
> And if the swoll'n Medway fail thy dish,
>   Thou hast thy ponds, that pay thee tribute fish,
> Fat, aged carps, that run into thy net.
>   And pikes, now weary their own kind to eat,
> As loath, the second draught, or cast to stay,
>   Officiously, at first, themselves betray.
> Bright eels, that emulate them, and leap on land,
>   Before the fisher, or into his hand.[32]

It may seem at such moments that Jonson is indulging in a *conte à rire* or even a lying tale, but Cockaigne motifs in this poem hover over realistic details, which signify a community of man and nature for the benefit of man that is both ecologically sound and technologically masterful. The partridge is "willing" because it keeps coming back and doesn't fly away at the approach of hunters. Carp and pike do in fact "betray" themselves, swimming close to the surface and, in season, running right into the fishermen's nets. When baited, eels may in fact squirm out of the water in pursuit of nourishment, as if to make themselves more readily available. So both Dekker and Jonson avail themselves of Cockaigne motifs, adjusted to approximate realistic details, in order to depict the triumph of civil society, the one from the point of view of the working bourgeois and the other from the point of view of the landed aristocracy. The original Cockaigne myth is in "twilight," indeed. And one might be tempted to leave it at that, except that we find in another later manor-house poem that the realism is dropped. Writing during the darker days of the reign of Charles I, imitating Jonson but describing a different kind of place, Thomas Carew writes to the lord of the manor at Saxham how when he visited

> The pheasant, partridge, and the lark
> Flew to thy house, as to the Ark.
> The willing ox of himself came
> Home to the slaughter, with the lamb,
> And every beast did thither bring

Figure 4.2. An open-air banquet. Cologne, Germany, 1605–15. The golden liquid (*upper left*) seems to be flowing from a spigot in a tree, as if honey from a bough. Reproduced by permission of the British Library (Add. 18991).

> Himself, to be an offering.
> The scaly herd more pleasure took,
> Bathed in thy dish, than in the brook;
> Water, earth, air did all conspire
> To pay their tributes to thy fire . . .[33]

The Cockaigne myth returns in full, not to celebrate the ideal of public civility, but rather the more private values attached to domesticity and hospitality.[34] Naturalism abounds in this description: the birds indeed fly into the woods and fields of the estate and the birdhouses and traps set to lure them; the ox and the lamb indeed return to the barns without protest. The characterization of the intentions of the animals, however, is deliberately absurd. These motifs from Cockaigne idealize the manor, making the creatures and even the elements — or at least water, earth, and air — sacrifice themselves to the altar of domesticity: the animals *come home* to the home of the lord of the manor; the elements pay tribute, not unlike the tribute, the taxes and rents, that the peasants really had to pay to their lords: goods, services, and cash payments that arrive at the hearth of the manor. The transformative fire of the hearth, where all things are received and altered for redistribution, is the symbolic center of the manorial home, which here takes the place of the peasant's Cockaigne and altogether annihilates its populist message.

IV

Rabelais, writing in the early sixteenth century under the spell of northern humanism, would seem to be the great poet of Cockaigne, but his Cockaigne, too, is significantly modified, even nullified in many ways. Apart from stray references here and there, mainly in a few brief episodes in *Books Four* and *Five,* there is no actual Cockaigne in the work of Rabelais. The myth might have resonance for the laughing monk—motifs in *Books Four* and *Five,* including Cockaigne material, may have been borrowed from *Le disciple de Pantagruel,* which appeared after *Gargantua* and *Pantagruel* were published but before *Book Four* and *Book Five,* and there are echoes of the myth throughout. But the myth of Cockaigne is never foregrounded in the novel. Rabelais wants to put certain impulses into action—impulses that lay behind the Cockaigne imaginary but that could be experienced and represented in other ways. He tries to make those impulses a part of a reformed (but not quite Protestant) contemporary civil society, where both the impulses and civil society are as a result redefined. That means, obviously, that civil society has to come to terms with the body and its digestive and sexual systems, that it has to make room for hunger and desire, for satiation and pleasure. But it means, too, that hunger and desire and satiation and pleasure need to be nurtured. They need to be kept alive and at once celebrated and civilized. The result is a twofold vision. On the one hand, Rabelais's novel embraces cyclical rhythms that provide for an energetic and varied existence: hunger and satiation, recreation and labor, war and peace, austerity and indulgence. These rhythms bespeak the energy and work of life, and allow for hunger to be at once cultivated, invigorated, and happy. On the other hand, though, the novel provides glimpses of an escape from cyclical rhythms that leads toward the civility of humanist self-fashioning and even toward an aristocratic, humanist utopia. For the logic of cultivation all but inevitably moves from encouraging hunger to eradicating it.

The complex semiology of the opening passages of *Gargantua* (i.e., *Book One*)—the second book Rabelais composed but the first in chronological sequence — provides a classic articulation of the issues. We meet Grandgousier, Gargantua's father, at a feast, in the following terms, which I cite from Thomas Urquhart and Peter Le Motteux's seventeenth-century translation:

> Grandgousier was a good fellow in his time, and notable jester; he loved to drink neat, as much as any man that then was in the world, and would willingly eat salt meat: to this intent he was ordinarily well furnished with gammons of Bacon, both of Westphalia, Mayence and Bayonne; with store of dried Neat's tongues, plenty of Links, Chitterlings and Puddings in their season; together with salt Beef and mustard, a good deal of hard rows of powdered [i.e., salted] mullet called Botargos, great provision of Sausages, not of Bologna (for he feared the Lombard bacon) but of Bigorre, of Longaulnay, Brenne, and Rouergue.[35]

Drink and food first, duly cataloged. Thirst and appetite first. And an appetite for salty products, as in the "Familière description," that encourage a thirst. All again, amply, even over-amply cataloged. Then the wife Gargamelle and sex and procreation are introduced. (Rabelais's misogyny is there for all to see.) And on to the first of the novel's feasts, held in early February, in advance of Mardi Gras: 367,014 "fat tripes," served up while the rest of the beef was to be salted and preserved, to which people from all the surrounding towns are invited. "They were so delicious," the narrator reports, "that every one licked his fingers." However, "the mischief was this, that for all men could do, there was no possibility to keep them long in relish; for in a very short while they would have stunk."[36] Here is one sort of viands that cannot be salted away for the future, and that therefore needs to be consumed on the spot, en masse, even though "these tripe were no very commendable meat"; eating them was like "the chewing of ordure," a "fair fecality," "such shitten stuff!" Told to be cautious, on account of her eleven-month-old pregnancy, Gargamelle downs "sixteen quarters, two bushels, three pecks, and a pipkin full." Her satiety stimulates both evacuation and childbirth, but because of medicine applied to stop the evacuation, the child is forced up from the mother's womb and out through her ear, at which the newborn infant cries aloud, "Some drink, some drink, some drink, as inviting all the world to drink with him."[37]

The choice of foods in the opening of the novel reminds us of the catalogs of food in the Land of Cockaigne, but there is a significant difference. Apart from the tripe, they all put one in mind not only of hard drinking (which is described in an intervening chapter) but of civil arrangements: all is preserved food, laid up for the future and prepared to suit the tastes of consumers, including the taste for having food that goes good with wine. The preserved meats even have provenance, another sign of culture: Westphalia, Mayence, Bayonne, Bigorre, Longaulnay, Brenne, and Rouergue. As for the tripe, it is significant for two reasons. It is in the first place a food that cannot be preserved, that must be eaten immediately upon the slaughter of beef. That places it not outside civil arrangements but securely within them, for the tripe is appropriated for a ritual of collective dining — a ritual of disorderly indulgence, to be sure, but a ritual all the same, placed in the context of the liturgical calendar and the rhythm of life it marks. As it is a food that cannot be preserved, so it is also, in the second place, a food that brings us symbolically and materially into the inside of the bodies of cows and humans involved, deep into the digestive tract of both those that are eaten and those that eat, but even this descent into the depth of the body has a cultural value. The first sign of this depth is fecal matter, found at once in the intestines that are being eaten and in the intestines of those who eat — Rabelais insists upon it, shoves it in our faces, as it were. But there is another sign of this depth too. In what seems to be a burlesque comment on the Augustinian notion of birth, where humans are born between "urine and feces," Gargantua is forced upward from the womb. Delivered far from the excrement and fluids of the lower extremities, he comes out the ear, not far from where the brainy Athena was born, an organ signifying language and orality. He comes out of the organ for receiving speech, that is, and immediately speaks. What he says is at once the cry of the infant, demanding liquid nourishment, and the call of conviviality: "Some drink, some drink, some drink. . . ." ("À boire, à boire, à boire!") From the oversated, overburdened lower extremities of the mother comes a creature who experiences and announces a renewal of desire, at once affirming primal need and articulating a civil ritual of sociality.[38]

Satiation is never for Rabelais the only satisfaction. Unlike the sluggards' meals in Cockaigne, the happy feasts in *Gargantua* and *Pantagruel* come as rewards for effort and as a signs of a cooperative and generous spirit. In this respect, the happy feasts (there are some unhappy feasts too) are differentiated from the banquets of the merely privileged and the merely gluttonous. Bakhtin thus calls attention to Rabelais's delight in the "merry triumphant encounter with the world in the act of eating and drinking, in which man partakes of the world instead of being devoured by it," and even to the "victory over the world in the act of eating" that Rabelais celebrates in the communal, carnivalesque feast. This is different from merely "private gluttony," which "expresses the contentment and satiety of the selfish individual, his personal enjoyment, and not the triumph of the people as a whole. Such imagery is torn away from the process of labor and struggle; it is removed from the marketplace and is confined to the house and the private chamber (abundance in the home); it is no longer the 'banquet for all the world,' in which all take part, but an intimate feast with hungry beggars at the door."[39] Bakhtin exaggerates, I think it is fair to say, the democratic impulses in Rabelais.[40] He does not perhaps exaggerate the distinctiveness of public dining in Rabelais or its symbolic and metaphysical implications. Nevertheless, the grotesque, communal, triumphant "banquet for all the world" is not the only wishful image that Rabelais attaches to eating. There are other triumphant forms of dining, and even some forms that Rabelais wishes to censure, as well as forms in which internal, personalized practices of restraint, for the sake of self-fashioning, are imposed.

On his sea travels in *Book Four,* Pantagruel encounters the Gastrolaters — worshipers of the belly. One would think Rabelais approves. But no, these Gastrolaters, by whom Rabelais allegorically means cloistered monks, are greatly "detested." "They stuck close to one another in knots and gangs. Some of them merry, wanton, and soft as so many Milksops; others lowering, grim, dogged, demure and crabbed, all idle, mortal foes to Business, spending half their time in sleeping, and the rest in doing nothing, a Rent-charge and dead unnecessary Weight on the Earth."[41] As far as Pantagruel is concerned, they are no better than "the Cyclops Polyphemus," saying, "I only sacrifice to myself (not to the Gods) and to this belly of mine, the greatest of all the Gods." Their feasts are cataloged; meat days feature over one hundred dishes, from wine and bread and "Fricasees nine sorts" and eleven sorts of pasties and pies, to over twenty-four different kinds of birds; fish days include about ninety different sorts of seafood, from salmon-trout to frogs. Along with Pantagruel, the narrator of Pantagruel's travels is nevertheless contemptuous. "'Twas none of their fault, I'll assure you," he says ironically, "if this same God of theirs was not publicly, preciously, served in his Sacrifices."[42] Though a great appetite seems to be one of the chief virtues Rabelais wishes to extol, these Gastrolaters are idolaters. The "God" they celebrate is personified in this episode by one Master Gaster, the principle of the belly, but Master Gaster is not what they think he is. Gaster "had the Manners to own that he was no God, but a poor, vile, wretched Creature." He is only the belly. Yet he stands for something too, something that the Gastrolaters don't appreciate, but the humanist Pantagruel is pleased to learn about it. What he stands for is ingenuity, humanity's inventive arts of living. He is said to have invented husbandry, industry, and cookery, as well military science, the better to defend the culinary resources of a people. The principle of the belly is the principle of civilization.

Other occasions also arise where the primal demands of the grotesque body are eschewed in favor of civil arrangements. Most telling is the story of the education of Gargantua, who as a child begins by leading a lazy and gluttonous life, but who then, under the tutelage of a new master, learns the art of temperance. This is Rabelais's version of Erasmus's *Education of a Christian Prince*. The young prince Gargantua learns to regulate his life according to a set schedule, rising early, fasting in the morning, getting plenty of healthy exercise, and devoting himself as much as possible to study. He learns to eat only as appetite requires. His daily fare, to be sure, is voluminous and lustily consumed and drowned in unlimited quantities of wine, but it is a reward for labor, a product of a rational rule of living, and an expression of a hearty love for life. It also shows him to be his father's son. "Because he was naturally phlegmatic," even the giant Gargantua being subject to the terms of the regimen for health, as well as heredity,

> he began his meal with some dozens of gammons, dried neat's tongues, hard rows of mullet called Botargos, Andouilles or sausages, and such other forerunners of wine; in the meanwhile, four of his forks did cast into his mouth one after another continually mustard by whole shovels full. Immediately after that, he drank a horrible draught of white wine for the ease of his kidneys. When that was done, he ate according to the season meat agreeable to his appetite, and then left off eating when his belly began to sprout, and was like to crack for fullness; as for his drinking, he had in that neither end nor rule; for he was wont to say, that the limits and bounds of drinking were, when the cork of the shoes of him that drinketh swelleth up half a foot high.[43]

Food and drink, again, are gigantically consumed, without inhibitions. But for eating and drinking alike (the "horrible draught of white wine") a system of self-control, a technology of the self, is at work as well. *Pace* Bakhtin, this is a triumphant form of dining that is individually experienced, egoistically regulated, and scientifically organized. It obeys both certain gastronomic inclinations and the general guidelines of a regimen of health (which, again, included a principle of following personal inclination). Gargantua's personal cheating use of the guidelines permits him to exceed the usual limits, to be sure, to eat to a late stage of satiety and drink with "neither end nor rule" ("poinct fin, ny canon"). But the prince's joyous routine of consumption is nevertheless practiced within the context of what Rabelais calls "la discipline de ses precepteurs Sophistes" (the discipline of Gargantua's wise tutors), and the convivial drinking with which it concludes is part of rhythm where that "without end" will actually conclude in early bedtime, from which Gargantua will rise early, to renew his fasting, his exercising, his studying, and his prayers.

One more form of triumphant dining in Rabelais needs to be highlighted, one that leads to an exit from Cockaigne altogether. In the Abbey of Thélème, described at the end of *Book One* and the crowning achievement of the story of Gargantua, Rabelais constructs his own rational utopia. On the surface, the abbey would seem to involve a return to the same primal pleasures of feeding that one encounters in Cockaigne. There is only one law in the abbey, we are told, "Do What You Will." Nothing could be more Cockaigne-like. But that is not how the law of freedom actually operates in the abbey. In this monastery without walls or rules, where men and women freely cohabited and all life was spent according to one's own "free will and pleasure," the Thelemites "rose out of their beds, when they thought good: they did eat, drink, labor, sleep, when they had a mind for it." But once freed from all constraints, they therefore acted according to a natural instinct toward "virtuous actions," an instinct called "honor." "By this liberty they entered into a very laudable emulation, to do all of them what they saw please one; if any of the gallants or the Ladies should say, Let us drink, they would all drink: if any one of them said, Let us play, they all played. . . ."[44]

In fact, there is no description of food in Thélème, neither of what the inhabitants ate nor of how and when they ate it. The narrative is much more interested in architecture and clothes, and the "grotesque body" so prominent in other parts of *Book One* is overlooked or banished entirely. For this reason, Bakhtin goes so far as to say that "Thélème is characteristic neither of Rabelais's philosophy nor of his system of images."[45] Expressive more of aristocratic and humanist values than the popular movements with which Bakhtin wants to associate Rabelais, the utopian abbey describes an ideal version of courtly life suffused with humanist values, where natural nobility is encouraged to flourish. Still, the absence of concern for eating and drinking in the description of the abbey is striking. Overlooking them, Rabelais perhaps inserts by their absence an ironic judgment of the aspirations of courtly life and the humanist utopia. But he calls attention as well to a fundamental principle of utopian fiction in the early modern period: though it will respond to the problem of inequality and hunger, depicting societies where both have been expelled and rules of egalitarian abundance have been planted in their stead, the utopia will subordinate eating and drinking to higher laws of community, justice, and worship. Instead of adventures in dining, the early modern utopia will feature dining as a sacrament. Solving the problem of how to live and how to organize society systematically, by way of a rational rule — even if that rule is a natural instinct toward virtue — the Renaissance utopia eradicates the emptiness of need, the clamoring of infantile demands, and the palliation of infantile satisfactions, however civilized the needs, the demands, or the palliation are supposed to be.

V

Dining in utopia in the early modern period means rejecting earlier plebeian food fantasies and adopting a more austere but also more communal and sacramental regimen. If Rabelais and the tellers of Cockaigne myths revel in catalogs of plenty, utopian fictions eschew the catalog; they don't dwell on eating, and they are diffident both about the items being consumed and the pleasures experienced when people are consuming them. The solutions to the problem of material life they propose do not include a preoccupation with food and shun the idea of culinary adventure. Utopia is sober.[46] But utopia is also a land without hunger and provides an answer to plebeian doubts and fears.

Let us look at some examples, beginning with the *Utopia* of Thomas More (1516), which invents the modern genre of utopian fiction and remains the most influential. In More's *Utopia,* as in many fictions to follow, we are told that "there is plenty of everything"; in Utopia "there will never be any shortage." Devised in part as a response to objections that can be raised against European society, that by its very design it causes misery and hence unnecessary suffering, crime, and cruelty, the nation of Utopia is a meat- and vegetable-eating garden republic, where food is produced collectively and distributed for free. Meals are usually taken in communal dining halls. "For while it is not forbidden to eat at home, no one does it willingly, because it is not thought proper; and besides, it would be stupid to work at preparing a worse meal at home when there is an elegant and sumptuous one near at hand in the hall."[47] The emphasis in the description of Utopia is less on consumption, though, then on work, distribution, and the minimal exigencies of ceremony. We know that "fish, meat, and poultry" are common. We are also told that at the great dining halls an elected official, the "syphogrant," presides at a dais, and the rest of the tables are arranged along the sides of the room. Women sit on the inside, for a strange reason, with no precedent so far as I have been able to determine: sitting on the outside makes it easier for them to get up from the table if they have labor pains. The men sit at the outside of the tables. Otherwise, seating is arranged by age, with elderly persons deliberately mixed in with the young. "The best food" is offered first to the infirm of either gender, and then to the rest of the diners, regardless of status.

Some contradictions arise here, to be sure. Though the women sit on the inside rows of the tables, the text later remarks that officials preside at the main table seated with their wives. The strict separation of the sexes, for dubious but rationalized ends, gives way to the importance of the integration of the sexes, to the end of marking prestige (what the French call *distinction*) in a society of equals.

Similarly, and more important, while there is supposed to be plenty of everything, certain delicacies are nevertheless in short supply. All food is not equal.
Nor does it seem desirable that all food should be equal. Yet in any case, "lunches
are light" and "suppers more generous" and "the dessert course is never scanted."
Pleasure is prized by the people of Utopia, we are told: Utopians are "inclined to
think that no kind of pleasure is forbidden, provided harm does not come of it."
The content of the pleasures of the table, however, is never discussed.

In Tommaso Campanella's *City of the Sun* (first written in Italian in 1602) a
similar picture emerges; in Campanella's city, food is likewise served communally
in great dining halls, though perhaps less ceremoniously. The men and women
again sit at separate sides of the table, and the people eat in silence. A little more
about consumption is expressed, but many of the details are otherwise familiar:

> Each [person] is served according to his needs with a main dish, some
> soup, fruit, and cheese. The physicians have the duty of informing the
> cooks every day as to what kind of food is the most suitable to prepare
> respectively for the old, the young, and the ill. The officials receive the
> most choice portions, and they often order that a part of the food from
> their table be served to some one or other who distinguished himself
> that morning in a lesson or discussion or military exercise. The recipi-
> ent regards this as a singular honor and mark of favor. On feast days
> there is singing at table. Because everyone takes a hand in providing,
> nothing is ever lacking.[48]

The brief mention of foodstuffs — with the inclusion of soup, fruit, and cheese —
takes us into the world of Italian cuisine. Note the sparing emphasis, in fact the
omission of the mention of meat, although the main dish, what Campanella calls
the "piatto di pitanza," might well have included animal flesh, particularly on the
"feast days" to which he refers. Note, too, that the tables in the City of the Sun
are less democratic than those in Utopia, precedence being given by rank rather
than age. Rank serves, however, as a spur to merit, and the general attitude toward dining is similar to that in Utopia, as is the structure of the arrangements
eating requires the Utopian polity to make.

In *Christianopolis* (1619), written by the Lutheran minister Johann Valentin
Andreä, we encounter something a little different. The general idea of communist distribution is still observed, and the items of consumption are much the
same as in *Utopia,* but the focus of the meal shifts from the great dining hall to the
private home:

Their meals are private to all, but the food is obtained from the public storehouse. And because it is almost impossible to avoid unpleasantness and confusion when the number of those partaking of a meal is so great, they prefer that individuals shall eat together privately in their own homes. Even as the food is distributed according to the nature of the year, so also it is apportioned weekly according to the number of families. But provision of wine is made for a half year. . . . They get their fresh meat from the meat shop, and they take away as much as is assigned to them. Fish, as also game, and all sorts of birds are distributed to them according to each one's proportion, the time and age being taken into consideration. There are ordinarily four dishes. . . . Serving men and serving women are a rare thing. . . . The husband and wife perform together the ordinary duties of the home. . . .[49]

Communism on a grand scale encourages communism on a small scale. Back in the north of Europe, the emphasis is on animal flesh. But again, there is little said about the contents or pleasure of dining.

All three utopias have important features in common. In each case, eating in utopia marks a rejection of the Cockaigne fantasy. Eating in these utopias is always moderate, disciplined, aimed at what are taken to be basic needs and indispensable pleasures rather than toward the unleashing of unregulated desire and hedonistic delight. Although many utopias including More's begin with the problem of scarcity and indeed seem to be devised precisely as an answer to the problem of scarcity, designing societies where "there is plenty of everything," abundance in itself is not what the utopias imagine or desire. Moreover, if the utopias reject the impossible abundance of the Land of Cockaigne, they also reject the mixed vision that emerges in Rabelais, apart from the tale of Thélème, where adventures in eating, ceremonial feasts, and hedonistic self-fashioning are embraced.

The utopia, solving the problem of social life systematically, for all time and all at once, puts an end to the unequal and unjust rules of consumption against which the Cockaigne tradition registered a futile protest. In the utopia, eating is a ceremony of community; it is a performance of community perfected. *"Worke together, Eate Bread together, Declare this all abroad"*—this clarion call to utopian community, as expressed by a landless and hungry visionary during the crises of the English Revolution, articulates a vision of the utopian ideal common to More, Campanella, Andreä, and a number of others. One never simply eats in utopia. One eats as an expression of utopian principles and in observance of utopian ends. Unlike other visions of the food of wishes, whether the Land of

Cockaigne or the aristocratic domains of "To Penshurst" and "To Saxham," this utopian eating is therefore in harmony with the conditions and dignity of labor. One indulges to one's contentment neither as a "sluggard" nor as a parasite; one feeds neither off the preternatural plenty of self-sacrificing nature nor off the self-sacrificing labors of others. "Because everyone takes a hand in providing, nothing is ever lacking," as Campanella puts it—that is, nothing is ever lacking because collective labor rationally undertaken will assure ample supplies; and everyone dines together, from the common store and by way of common social principles, precisely because "everyone takes a hand in providing." Moreover, if eating in utopia satisfies material need, it does so as a *symbolization* of the need and its satisfaction. Dining, again, is sacramental in utopia. It communicates, ceremonially, the value of general welfare that utopia has been designed to satisfy. It "declares" itself. It makes communitarianism speak. Gerrard Winstanley, again, puts the idea most compellingly. *"That the earth shall be made a common Treasury of livelihood to whole mankind, without respect of persons,"* as he puts it, to which purpose "I took my spade and went and broke the ground upon *George-hill* in Surrey, thereby declaring freedom to the Creation, and that the earth must be set free from entanglements of Lords and Landlords, and that it shall become a common Treasury to all, as it was first made and given to the sons of men."[50] From breaking ground in the name of freedom and the "common treasury" of the earth, the utopian idealist, whether in fact or in speculation, declares the principle that all alike shall work, and all alike shall eat (Winstanley's vision of this eating is nearly identical with Andreä's, by the way), and in working and eating together, the people will declare a new order of human existence: an age, as Winstanley often puts it, of the "Second Adam."[51]

Yet neither utopia nor its dining customs are born merely from the minds of their creators. Thinking about collective dining, as would seem to be appropriate in societies where private property has been abolished, More and Campanella, for their part, think in terms of both the great hall of aristocratic households and the refectory of the monastery. In these terms they consider the problem of delicacies and the best cuts and the order of seating, even if they also fashion paradoxes out of them. The collective banquet of the great household or monastery determines the architecture of dining and brings along with it the idea that dining, even in the face of abundance, involves gradations of quality and hence gradations of rank among the diners. Similarly Andreä, writing in seventeenth-century Germany, thinks in terms of contemporary social developments. When Andreä has his people of Christianopolis eat in private, he is registering a general trend in attitudes toward dining; meals in all social classes in the seventeenth century were beginning to be taken on a smaller scale, in more intimate conditions.[52] The narrator tells us that the people of Christianopolis dine in private for practical reasons: "to avoid," as he puts it, "unpleasantness and confusion when the number of those partaking of a meal is so great." But at the time Andreä is writing, the preference for smaller parties of diners is becoming commonplace. The great community of Christianopolis is wholly rationalized and wholly uniform from top to bottom, with priests and philosophers presiding over the city-state from the precincts of a tall central and centralizing tower. Nevertheless, Christianopolis is also a worker's paradise, populated in the main by urban artisans, and on the level of individuals and individual families, life is experienced on a small scale, in the privacy of small and independent households. Andreä's utopia is a model, pious, north German town. Winstanley's imaginary utopia — expressed in his last work, *The Law of Freedom in a Platform* (1652), where life is similarly both centralized and individualized — is little different, an urban community of tradesmen, joined with farmers in the countryside.

One is tempted to say that the chief difference between eating in utopia and eating in the real world in the early modern period was that in the former eating has been depoliticized. The prevailing dining customs ratified inequality; they made a political statement about who was in charge and who was not. Utopian schemes observed different priorities. The meal in utopia does not serve the interests of power the way the meal in life was supposed to do: power resides in the utopian meal and inequities reside in the meal, but the meal does not serve to ratify power by way of ceremonies of privilege and exclusion. Part of this stems from an age-old fight by philosophers against luxury. "Fear of want," as More puts it, ". . . makes every living creature greedy and rapacious, and man, besides, develops these qualities out of sheer pride, which glories in getting ahead of other by a superfluous display of possession. But this sort of vice has no place whatsoever in the Utopian scheme of things."[53] But "depoliticization" is not quite right. If political gamesmanship is bred out of dining in utopia, politics is nevertheless central to the utopian concept of eating: because writers like More and Campanella take care to depoliticize it in the interest of egalitarian and communitarian notions of sociality, and of making the communal meal a sacramental testimony to utopian values, they re-politicize it. They make dining both a central purpose and a symbolic focal point of the politics of communism.

In symbolizing the politics of communism, dining in utopia serves a higher purpose too. The speaker in More's *Utopia* calls it "voluptas"; but he means by that pleasure of a certain kind. The Utopians believe, we are told, that most human happiness "consists of pleasure . . . ," though only "good and honest pleasure" —*honesta voluptas,* again. "By pleasure they understand every state of movement of the body or mind in which we find delight [suava] according to the behests of nature." In this scheme, pleasures of the mind are to be found in activities like contemplation. As for pleasures of the body, these "they divide into two classes. The first is that which fills the senses with immediate delight. Sometimes this happens when bodily organs that have been weakened by natural heat are restored with food and drink; sometimes this happens when we eliminate some excess in the body, as when we move our bowels, generate children, or relieve an itch. . . ." "The second kind of bodily pleasure they describe as nothing but the calm and harmonious state of the body, its state of health when undisturbed by any disorder." "When we eat, they say, what happens is that health, which was starting to fade, takes food as its ally in the fight against hunger. While our health gains strength, the simple process of returning vigor gives us pleasure and refreshment." While the Utopians therefore recognize the value of eating for "immediate delight," they subordinate it to health. "As for eating and drinking and other delights of the same sort, they consider these bodily pleasures desirable but only for the sake of health. They are not pleasant in themselves but only for the sake of health."[54]

Behind the argument put into the belief system of the Utopians lies not only what is acknowledged to be a version of classical Epicureanism, close to what Epicurus himself wrote down, but the positive model of health handed down from the ancients through medical writings. The phrase gets repeated several times: "honest pleasure," *volupta honesta*. Books like *Utopia* can thus be seen as playing a role in the reintroduction of classical medicine to the peoples of Europe, the same reintroduction that led to the publication of books like *The Castel of Helthe* and, for that matter, *De honesta voluptate et valetudine*. And more generally, they can be seen as playing a role in the secularization, along classical lines, of the rules of material life. If one looks for the highest value that eating in utopia is designed to serve, the value to which even the sacrament of communitarianism may be said to be subordinated, this is it: health. One eats in utopia for the sake of health. And health is what the classical philosophers and medical writers said it was: a *eucrasia* of the warm.

Odd motifs and paradoxes nevertheless recur. If in Christianopolis "husband and wife perform together the ordinary duties of the home" and servants are unusual, collective dining in More's Utopia requires the labor of slaves. Not only do slaves play a part in preparing and serving the food, but they are given the most unwholesome work to do. Slaves alone are put to work in the slaughterhouses, which are located outside the cities, "where running water can carry away all the blood and refuse." "The Utopians feel that slaughtering our fellow creatures gradually destroys the sense of compassion, the finest sentiment of which our human nature is capable. Besides, they don't allow anything dirty [sordidum] or filthy [immundum] to be brought into the city, lest the air become tainted by putrefaction and thus infectious."[55] Among the devout, there is even a class of hardworking "celibates who abstain not only from sex but from eating meat, and some from any sort of animal food whatever." There is also, however, a class of the devout who "are just as fond of hard work, but prefer to marry." "Unless it interferes with their labor," these people "avoid no pleasure. They eat meat [carnes quadupedum], precisely because they think it makes them stronger for any sort of heavy work."[56] Freshly slaughtered meat, the staple of Utopia's urban citizens, is actually a problem, both in terms of processing it and in terms of consuming it. The requirements of hygiene and nutrition contend with democracy and piety. The open society must be sealed off against the pollution and cruelty upon which its sustenance depends. The pious life — depicted as a life of hard physical labor, voluntarily undertaken, in More's own satiric swipe at the proverbial laziness and greediness of monks — may entail a negation of one of the highest values of life in Utopia, the value of health (and hence of the honest pleasure that health requires); or else it entails a negation of the highest values of piety: pleasure-loving monks who marry and eat well, thriving on the flesh of quadrupeds.

Such contradictory quirks — where impulses toward vegetarianism, piety, and private asceticism come into conflict with impulses toward pleasure-loving, meat-eating, public dining and the classical concept of health — find their strangest expression in a late utopian fiction that is also something of a dystopian fiction, Gabriel de Foigny's *La Terre Australe connue* (1676). In the Terre Australe — a fictional Australia — not only human customs but human nature is found to have been altered, by comparison with which Europeans are at best what the Australians call "half-men." As a sign of that change in human nature, the environment seems to have changed as well. It is more benign. The climate is of an endless summer, and trees bear fruit — all kinds of luscious, healthy, psychotropic fruits — the year-round. Australians as a result are vegetarians, fruitarians in fact, and their attitudes and practices are in other ways different too, even to their habits of defecation. "We Europeans," the traveler Jack Sadeur reports,

> although often harmed by the defective foods we eat, take two or three times as much as we need for our nourishment, from which follow our fevers, colds, and upset stomachs, and many conditions unknown to the Australians. The latter are preserved from such ills by the great richness of their fruits and their admirable habit of eating only as much as they need. Far from reveling in eating and in sumptuous banquets, they steal away and eat in private, considering this a shameful animal func-

tion from which man should abstain as much as he is able. This means, too, that they experience so seldom the "call of nature" that they scarcely produce any excrement.[57]

Finally we arrive at a vision that challenges European notions not only of how food is distributed but of what people eat and what they do with what they eat. Taking its cue from travelers' reports on customs in places like Bali, where such practices and values were in fact known, *La Terre Australe* goes a step further than Christianopolis and wholly demolishes the public nature of eating that the early moderns took for granted. Eating in *La Terre Australe* is entirely asocial. The great political aspect of dining in the early modern period—which begins with the assumption that dining is a social activity to be governed by rules of sociality and thus the laws of status, distinction, honor and shame, and the etiquette that goes along with them—has been turned into an activity where politics is impossible because sociality is shunned; there are no rules of sociality to appeal to, and indeed eating itself has become something shameful, something that must be done in private, like defecating. It is a sacrament in reverse: penitence through self-revulsion. Eschewing all foods but fruit, the Australian diet would seem to demolish early modern notions of nutrition too. Doing so is not entirely unappealing—the fruits are all described as astonishingly delicious, better than the best pineapple. Nor in the atmosphere of the late seventeenth century—where fruits and vegetables were playing a bigger role in the European diet, and social and medical attitudes toward them had as a result undergone a revision—does the fruitarian diet seem altogether absurd. But de Foigny, a worldly monk who got himself into considerable trouble by his love of carnal pleasures, explodes the fruitarian vision for satirical ends. The reader eventually finds out that the health-obsessed and sexually diffident Australians (they are in fact hermaphrodites whose arts of procreation remain a shameful secret) practice euthanasia. An unhealthy life for them is not worth living. And when one's health begins to falter due to old age, individuals commit suicide by eating: the very fruits that give them their vigor and high spirits, their magical fruits, when eaten in a certain progression of excess end up killing them as if by poison.

VI

Not all utopian food fantasies after Rabelais are perplexed by the idea of hedonistic delight. Nor should it be assumed that the ambivalences and moralisms of humanists are wholly characteristic of the era. Feasting was feasting, whether at a royal banquet or a country holiday; it is to be assumed that few people willingly eschewed occasions to eat well. But the literature of the period seems more inclined to police the meal than to celebrate its pleasures.

In one utopia, described in a pair of little known texts published in London in 1580 and 1581, communitarianism triumphs at the expense of the merest hint of excess pleasure. In the first, *Siuqila: Too Good to Be True,* Thomas Lupton includes a condemnation of inequality and the suffering it causes in modern England, painting a picture much like what we have observed in the case of folktales:

> The poor with us, would think themselves happy, if they might have a mess of pottage, or the scraps that come from the Rich mens tables, two or three hours after they begin their dinner or supper, and to have the same given them at their door. But many of the said rich greedy guts, caring for nothing but for the hilling and filling of their own back and belly, cannot be content to go by their poor pitiful brethren and give them nothing, but they will most uncharitably and unchristianly rebuke them, chide them, rattle them, yea, and threaten them. . . .[58]

What Lupton prefers is a society governed by the rule of charity, where the rich ask the poor to dine with them, and where they even put the poor "at their own table: yea above themselves."[59] The poor, in fact, are so frequently patronized in Lupton's fictional land Mauqsun (that is, the Latin *Nusquam* ["nowhere"] spelled backward) that they only exist as a social category: economically, they aren't poor at all. Lupton distinguishes between those enjoying landed wealth and the rest of the nation's inhabitants, and between those who have the resources to bestow charity on others and those who have the need to accept charity. But those who have this need never go needy in Lupton's utopia.

As for what is eaten, or how, Lupton says little. But Lupton comes down on the side of austerity. Since hunger "is the most pleasant sauce of all other," an interlocutor puts it in the sequel, *The Second Part and Knitting Up of the Boke Entitled "Too Good to Be True,"* and hunger then "is the most delicate sauce for meat, and easiest to get, and of most virtue, and of least cost, none in our Country of Mauqsun on pain of death may use any other kind of sauce but that." That was not a misprint: the people in Mauqsun exact very strict and even harrowing laws against both sin and crime, and so to serve a sauce at a table may well be reckoned a crime deserving of capital punishment. To be sure, the speaker insists that one should eschew sauces for positive reasons. "If they in your Country"—that is, England—"would give over all sauces," he says, "and use that sauce [i.e., hunger] only, their bodies would not be so full of diseases, nor their purses so empty of money. . . ."⁶⁰ But as it operates by negatives, like other utopias *Too Good to Be True* counters a society felt to be too tolerant of excess, licentiousness, and the pursuit of pleasure for its own sake with a society absolutely intolerant of such things. The voice of *ressentiment* mixes with a proto-Puritan inclination toward the policing of everyday life to create a society where no one goes hungry, no one suffers humiliation at the hands of one's superiors, and no one is allowed to eat sauce, on pain of death. Given the customs of the English diet, which Lupton no doubt assumes, it is likely that Lupton nevertheless imagines allowing a little mustard with one's roast beef and a little extra broth with one's potted mutton.

But by contrast, on the subject of utopian dining, one should consider the case of the banquet described in Francesco Colonna's *Hypnerotomachia Poliphili,* first published in Italy in 1499. Colonna's erotic romance — one of the great achievements of the Aldine press in Venice and a well-known text throughout Europe in the early modern period — provides an example of what it could be like if feasting, at least Italian-style, were allowed the positive image of an erotic fantasia. In the endless dream he recounts, the narrator-protagonist finds himself a guest at the banquet of a queen, seated amid beautiful women, in a palace of costly and exquisite design. Every guest was tended by three servants — themselves beautiful women. One of the servants fed the guest, a second "interposed a plate beneath the food so that nothing should fall, and the third, on the left, elegantly wiped the guest's lips with a white napkin, soft and perfectly clean." This table service "was observed diligently for each of the guests, so that no one touched any of the food, but was fed willingly by the servant, except for the cup."⁶¹ Here in one of the swankest banquets described in the whole early modern period, the guests are fed, tended, wiped: they have made a perfect return to infancy.

As for the food, it comes in seven courses, not unlike the banqueting order that would be recounted in Cristoforo di Messisbugo's *Banchetti* of 1549. It includes at the outset a "cordial confection . . . a healthy compound made mostly of powdered unicorn's horn, the two kinds of sandalwood, ground pearls in brandy set alight so as to dissolve them completely, manna, pine nuts, rosewater, musk, and powdered gold: a very precious mixture, weighed and pressed out in morsels with fine sugar and starch." Indigestible as such a ground-up compound of bone, pearls, nuts, gold, and sugar may seem to be, the narrator assures us that "it is a food preventing every harmful fever, and for dispelling all sorrowful fatigue." In other words, it is both a prophylactic medicine and a euphoria-inducing stimulant. Later courses include the following numerically ascending dishes: "five cakes or fritters made from saffron-colored dough with hot rosewater and sugar, cooled and finely sprinkled with the same musk-flavored water and with powdered sugar," and served in five different ways, with fragrant oils. "Six cuts of fattened, blinded capon, moistened with its own fat, sprinkled with yellow rosewater mixed with orange juice, roasted to perfection and then gilded over. With this came six slices of snow-white bridal bread, and beside it a sauce of lemon juice modified with fine sugar mashed with pine nuts and the capon's liver, to which were added rosewater, musk, saffron and choice cinnamon." "Seven pieces of partridge meat, roasted diligently at the fire, and as many mouthfuls of yeasty milk bread. The sauce was sharp, with crushed almonds, thrice cooked sugar, starch, yellow sandalwood, musk and rosewater." "Eight morsels of choicest, succulent roast pheasant meat, and as many pieces of a light white bread. The sauce was thus: fresh egg yolks with pine nuts, orange water, pomegranate juice, Colossine sugar and cinnamon." "Nine mouthfuls of long-lasting peacock's breast, roasted in its juices, fat and well grilled. There was a sour green sauce with ground pistachio nuts, Cyrian sugar, starch, musk, wild thyme, white oregano and pepper." Next came a dessert course, including hot plums and a molded subtlety, an "excellent confection . . . made from date-pulp, pistachios ground with rosewater, sugar of the Isles and musk, mixed with precious pow-dered gold so that the entire thing seemed to be made of gold." Even with all its defiantly precious sauces, the narrator calls the meal a "frugal" feast at one point: and surely it was not the kind of meal of which Rabelais was likely to approve, not to mention L.S.R. (For Rabelais the meal would be too dainty, dandified, and sober; for L.S.R. it would be overly artificial and, in its preciosity, ultimately dis-gusting.) The narrator himself professes more pleasure at the spectacle of the meal than at the food itself, the food being served off elaborate serving carts with fantastic sculptures and trophies, and dished onto plates of precious stones and metals, set upon elaborately set tables, and each course being presented with a rare new tablecloth and setting: "The more I thought over all these excellent spectacles, the more ignorant and stupefied I was; but the intense admiration of everything certainly gave me extreme pleasure, as I beheld so many great and tri-umphant things. There was such lavish luxury, such incredible expense and extravagance, that I think it better to hold my peace rather than speak in-adequately of it."[62]

Nevertheless, another dessert course, featuring the sorb apple, comes in. A bush of "cinnabar-colored coral," standing upon "a hillock made all of emeralds," is carted into the dining room. Gemstone flowers seem to grow out of the coral bush, and inside five of the flowers are "five little apples — or rather sorbs." While a pair of "damsels" presents the coral bush, another offers a cup of "precious liquor, such as even Cleopatra never offered to the Roman captain." The serving

Figure 4.3. Banqueting scene, from Cristoforo di Messisbugo, *Banchetti composizioni di vivande e apparecchio generale* (1549). Not quite featuring the elegant erotica of Colonna, this feast humorously descends into hedonistic dissipation. A young couple embraces, while the lady of the house chides the master for an unspecified offense. The household pets, meanwhile (an encoded image of the poor or of non-invitees generally?), have to fend for themselves. Hardly a bone seems to have been thrown their way. Reproduced by permission of Special Collections, Leeds University Library.

maids, three to a guest, pluck the fruits from the bush with golden tongs. Then "they offered them for us to relish the taste. The unspeakable sweetness of taste that I felt was as though the ideal form had been dissociated from the gracious material."[63] In the drama of the dream, representing the sensualist ideals of the Italian Renaissance in the age of Botticelli, what is new is not the apple, however "unspeakable" its sweetness: the dream of such an apple was known to the Middle Ages, where such things were imagined to rain down from the heavens, or to be eaten, as here, without one's hands. What is new is that in the face of the policing of eating and drinking that would be so prominent in humanist discourse, and in advance of the return to the body that writers like Rabelais would propound, one early Renaissance writer could imagine a perfectly infantile scenario whose very pleasure expressed Neoplatonist ideals of art and the ascendance of the spirit: a sorb apple whose taste transcends materiality and rises to the level of an ideal form.

Chapter Five

FOOD OF REGRET

All that I eat or drink, or shall beget,
Is propagated curse.

Paradise Lost

I

YET THERE WAS ALSO, as I have said, a food of regret. The indefinite ambivalence of culture to which this study began by appealing would suggest the existence of such a different trajectory in the realm of dietary wishes. And, again, the nature of eating should suggest that too. For the rational biped, delight, abundance, and transcendence also entail their opposites. Countless flowing spigots of beer, tables where "nothing is wanting," sorb apples that exalt the spirit as well as the senses have their counterparts in polluted streams, scanty gruel, and the rotted "Sodom's apple," whose insides had the taste and consistency of ashes.[1] They have their counterparts, too, in clear running water and a handful of berries, nuts, or olives: the stuff not of delightful, abundant transcendence or of disgusting, miserable, mundaneness, but of still another set of values and still another set of wishes, which came with its own stories, its own mythic fantasies — narratives, in fact, of the beginnings and ends of time. The food of wishes had its stories too; but the stories of the food of regrets were more serious than playful, and more a matter of establishing the fundamentals of the historical world than of entertaining daydreams.

At first, according to classical legend — and it always came "at first" — there was a Golden Age, when

The fertile earth as yet was free, untouched of spade or plough,
And yet it yielded of itself of every thing enough.
And men themselves contented well with plain and simple food,
That on the earth of nature's gift without their travail stood,
Did live by Raspis, heppes and hawes, by cornels, plums and cherries,
By sloes and apples, nuts and pears, and loathsome bramble berries,
And by the acorns dropped on ground, from Jove's broad tree in field.
The Springtime lasted all the year, and Zephyr with his mild
And gentle blast did cherish things that grew of own accord,
The ground untilled, all kind of fruits did plenteously afford.
No muck nor tillage was bestowed on lean and barren land,
To make the corn of better head, and ranker for to stand.
The streams ran milk, the streams ran wine, and yellow honey flowed
From each green tree whereon the rays of fiery Phoebus glowed.

I cite this from Ovid's *Metamorphoses* in Arthur Golding's Elizabethan translation (1567).[2] The "loathsomeness" of the bramble berry is the translator's own addition and is not quite in tune with what Ovid was trying to say. (So is the "wine": except for the requirements of meter, Golding should have written "nectar.") Originating, at least for the written record, in Hesiod's *Theogony,* to whom Ovid was much beholden, the Golden Age was a time of innocence, a prelude to the consecutive descent of humanity into the guilty ages of silver, bronze, and iron. Free of technology as of law, neither being needed in order to sustain what Ovid/Golding calls "the truth and right of every thing," for readers of the Renaissance it represented a suggestive, classical parallel to the Garden of Eden; their readings of the Golden Age were impacted by the biblical story, and their readings of the biblical story were impacted by the Greco-Roman Golden Age.[3] The myth includes motifs that would recur in the tale of Cockaigne and other folk legends — for example, the river of honey — though not always to the same effect, since honey among the Golden Age classicists is more of a condiment than a beverage. The myth of the Golden Age provided a respectful, wistful image of pre-civil life, where men subsisted on a sparse, natural, vegetarian diet and had no need or desire for any other. Golding deliberately deemphasized the wistfulness of Ovid's verse, not desiring perhaps to give into a non-biblical nostalgia. He was one of Ovid's "moralizers." Another early English translator, George Sandys, writing in the seventeenth century, was more enthusiastic, in his own version sonorously emphasizing such words as "content," "happy," and "harmless" (that is, "free from harm"). Where Golding reminds the reader of the lean and barren land that in modern times muck and tillage would improve, George Sandys, more

faithful to the original and more mellifluously, writes that "Forth-with the Earth
corn, unmanured bears; / And every year renews her golden ears."[4]

Even if the Golden Age diet was rudimentary, it was not unappealing. The
catalog of foodstuffs — raspberries and cherries, nuts and pears, acorns, milk,
nectar, and honey — was deliberately variegated and attractive. However plain
the fare might be, the rhetoric emphasized a satisfied sensuality. "What the sun
and the showers had given," as Lucretius puts it in his own, more critical version
of the story, which predates Ovid's by a century,

> All that the earth produced of her own accord had bestowed without
> labor,
> Sated their hearts. Among acorn-charged oaks they secured, for the most
> part,
> Food for the body; and also the earth at that time used to gender
> Plenty of arbute-berries of much greater size than at present,
> Such as in winter you see becoming bright red as they ripen.
> Various other coarse kinds of food did the callow earth's freshness
> Bear; these were more than enough to provide for the needs of poor
> mortals.[5]

But it is important that the image of golden simplicity was a prelude to images of decline. One of the main uses of the myth of the Golden Age in both the
classical and early modern periods was the contrast it afforded between the
dietary depravities of contemporary life and an earlier, happier simplicity. To
extol a Golden Age of ancient ease was to express weariness with modern deca-
dence. Surely Ovid, Lucretius, and other ancient writers imagined it in this way,
and there are plenty of examples of the same thing from writers in the sixteenth
and seventeenth centuries. Having finished a simple meal with a group of goatherds straight from a pastoral romance, Don Quixote takes up a handful of
acorns and wistfully recites a paean: "Happy the age and happy the times on
which the ancients bestowed the name of golden. . . ." The law of mine and thine
was unknown, and "no man, to gain his common sustenance, needed to make
any greater effort than to reach up his hand and pluck it from the strong oaks,
which literally invited him to taste their sweet and savory fruit. Clear springs and
running rivers offered him their sweet and limpid water in glorious abundance."[6]
Quixote limits his imagination to acorns and water, not even bothering with
fruits and berries or milk and honey, while the goatherds are still eating roasted
goat meat and getting drunk on the liquor in their wineskins. Nor is Quixote's
modern age quite what an entirely sane individual of Cervantes's era would think

it is. Yet the contrast is clear, if also, in the hands of Cervantes, ironic. We now eat a complicated, omnivorous diet, in a spirit of selfishness; we require a good deal of labor to get our food and still more labor to make it palatable. In the early days we ate simply, limiting ourselves to fruits and nuts; we ate unselfishly and without labor. We have already seen this idea developed un-ironically in the cookbook of Eliza Smith:

> In the Infant Age of the World, when the new Inhabitants contented themselves with the simple Provision of Nature, viz. the Vegetable Diet, the Fruits and Productions of the Earth, as succeeded one another in their several peculiar Seasons, the Art of Cookery was unknown: Apples, Nuts, and Herbs, were both Meat and Sauce, and Mankind stood in no need of additional Sauces, Ragouts, &c. to procure a good Appetite. . . .[7]

Similar remarks are made in the French *Encyclopédie* in its entry on cuisine: "Milk, honey, the fruits of the earth, legumes seasoned with salt, and bread cooked under the ashes were the food of the first peoples of the world. They survived without any other refinements besides the gifts of nature, which only made them stronger, more robust, and less vulnerable to illness."[8]

The myth of the Golden Age had other uses for the early moderns besides culinary nostalgia. In the many allusions to the myth gathered by Harry Levin in *The Myth of the Golden Age in the Renaissance,* diet figures only sporadically. Innocence, virtue, communism, and euphoria are more important features for the early modern imagination. George Sandys, an accomplished world traveler who would pen much of his translation while working as a treasurer for the Virginia Company in Jamestown (ca. 1622–26), appended a long and original critical commentary, where his remarks on the Golden Age accentuated the social protest implicit in the myth:

> Then was there neither Master nor Servant: names merely brought in by ambition and injury. Unforced Nature gave sufficient to all; who securely possess her undivided bounty. A rich condition wherein no man was poor: Avarice after introducing indigency: who by coveting a propriety [property], alienated all; and lost what it had, by seeking to enlarge. But this happy estate abounding with all felicities, assuredly represented that which man enjoyed in his innocency.[9]

So Sandys, experienced with the real challenges of survival in so-called primitive lands, was less impressed with the culinary than the moral and economic meanings of the First Age. Torquato Tasso develops another popular motif. In *Aminta,* he has the chorus state specifically that the Golden Age was interesting "not just because streams ran / with milk, and trees the honeyed dew distilled," and so forth, but "because that vain / abstraction, empty word, / that erring idol of propriety"—honor—". . . mixed not anxiety / within the happy joy / of loving's faithful band."[10] In other words, the age was golden because people didn't scruple to have sex when they wanted to. Similarly, John Donne comically bemoans the fact that "The golden laws of nature are repealed, / Which our first Fathers in such reverence held," according to which "this title honor" inhibits free love. "How happy were our sires in ancient time, / Who held plurality of loves no crime!"[11] In one of Shakespeare's allusions to the myth, the Golden Age stands for little more than sylvan fellowship among men, who have given up their professions in favor of hunting and gathering. The wrestler Charles, in *As You Like It,* reports that Duke Senior "is already in the forest of Arden, and a many merry men with him; and there they live like old Robin Hood of England. They say many young gentlemen flock to him every day, and fleet the time carelessly, as they did in the golden world."[12] Economic egalitarianism, free love, promiscuity, the woodsmen's fellowship — in fact, Hesiod and Ovid mention only the first of these. There are no women in Hesiod's and Ovid's versions of the Golden Age, and no sex, and of course no hunting.

The legend of the Golden Age became a portmanteau of primitivist ideas that Renaissance writers could use for purposes that neither Hesiod nor Ovid had intended, and certainly in which "plain and simple food" had limited importance. In Shakespeare's *The Tempest,* where the counselor Gonzalo mixes up his ambitions of sovereignty with visions of a golden world without sovereignty, the treatment seems to be classical, but the pleasures of classicism are omitted. In this land,

> Letters should not be known; riches, poverty,
> And use of service, none; contract, succession,
> Bourn, bound of land, tilth, vineyard, none;
> No use of metal, corn, or wine, or oil;
> No occupation; all men idle, all;
> And women too, but innocent and pure . . .

And there too,

> All things in common nature should produce
> Without sweat or endeavor: treason, felony,
> Sword, pike, knife, gun, or need of any engine,

Would I not have; but Nature should bring forth,
Of its own kind, all foison, all abundance,
To feed my innocent people.

This world would indeed "excel the Golden Age," as the character next says.[13]
But Gonzalo omits dietary details, except by way of negatives, and thus says
nothing about consumption. He is more interested in his imaginary commonwealth as a site free of technology and competition. It may be the case that eating berries and nuts held no attraction for Gonzalo's creator. The only positive allusion to a fruitarian diet in Shakespeare appears in *A Midsummer Night's
Dream,* where Titania wants to feed Bottom "with apricots and dewberries, /
With purple grapes, green figs, and mulberries." But Titania is a fairy, Bottom
would prefer "sweet hay" or "a handful or two of dried peas," and in the universe
of the play it is possible to insult a person by calling her an "acorn."[14] As for the
negatively defined food of Gonzalo's utopian fantasy, it is probably crucial that
the main influence behind his speech is Montaigne's essay "Of Cannibals," where
Montaigne's people, excelling the Golden Age, eat meat, drink a sort of wine,
and, of course, are "cannibals."

The New World and its Golden Age "cannibals" are worth turning to later
(see chapter 7). When explorers and armchair ethnographers saw the New World
as a mixture of golden primitivism and ferocious cannibalism, they confronted a
new geography of eating, finding in it new opportunities, displacements, natural
laws, and economic principles, as well as reasons for both guilt and disgust. The
New World transformed the idea of the Age of Gold from a speculative myth to
a concrete reality. But the New World did not by and large inspire people to lead
plain and simple lives, without technology, and to do without "corn, or wine, or
oil," or for that matter meat or fish.

The rhetoric of a "plain and simple food" located in prehistoric times, regardless of whether such prehistoric realties found a remnant in the apparently
primitive cultures of the New World, worked somewhat differently. The rhetoric identified not a geography of eating but an alternative mode of being in the
realm of dietary morals. Even if the true story of human origins was to be found
in Genesis, the myth of the Golden Age provided interesting elaborations that
had the ring of truth. It helped explain historical processes that the Bible failed
fully to account for, and it identified an ideal way of life, primitive though it may
have been, to which moderns still needed to pay attention. If the Garden of Eden
could not be returned to, no more than a Golden Age in which "the streams ran
milk, the streams ran wine," the Golden Age at least cataloged something that
one could yearn for. One did not have to eat like one's contemporaries. Over and

against the satisfactions of the *homme moyen sensuel,* or of the fantasies of abundance that were the subject of the previous chapter, there was this countervailing fantasy, whose genealogy is the subject of this chapter. One could eat more
simply and honorably, less hungrily and brutally, more in keeping with the laws of
God and nature. That was what was done in the Golden Age. And that could be
done again. Or could it?

II

"Nor think that Moses paints fantastic-wise," the influential Huguenot poet
Guillaume de Salluste Du Bartas writes of the presumed author of Genesis, "A
mystic tale of feigned Paradise: / 'Twas a true Garden, happy plenty's horn."[15] The
Garden of Eden, for Renaissance humanists and reformers, had been a real place.
It was not just a metaphor. Contrary to an earlier branch of exegetical tradition,
according to which the legend was to be interpreted only as an allegory revealing
abstract truths and ahistorical moral imperatives, progressive intellectuals of the
early modern period (following the example of Saint Augustine) insisted on the
reality of Eden. Humanity, to the Renaissance mind, existed in a history in which
it had once actually inhabited Paradise and now inhabited it no more. And so the
story of the Garden and Eden and the Fall of man was the history, among other
things, of humanity's relation to food.

A characteristic model is found in Tasso's *Creation of the World,* written toward the end of the poet's life, when (in contrast to his Protestant contemporary
Du Bartas) he was under pressure to conform to Catholic orthodoxy:

> But when God fashioned this our world at first,
> he made all forests perfect with green leaves,
> where ripe, sweet fruits were visible through boughs
> instead of still unripe, commencing ones:
> already full and luscious, there they were
> waiting for every unborn animal,
> ready to rouse its hunger and its taste
> with the allurement of unknown delight.
> The pregnant earth at the divine command
> gave birth to roots and herbs and relished fruits
> wherein the native power lay concealed
> of an immortal, fertile seed

that was for almost all eternity
to renovate all perished things below.[16]

The similarity of Tasso's account with the classical Golden Age is patent — and,
sticking to orthodoxy, Tasso did not have to draw directly upon classical poetry
itself to fashion the resemblance. A long tradition of rabbinic, patristic, and post-
patristic commentary fashioned an image of Paradise in terms like these, as did
many Protestant writers. But Tasso also follows a main branch of biblical exe-
gesis in making a key distinction between prehistoric and historic needs. In the
state of innocence, as Tasso puts it, an "innocent food, unsoiled by blood or
death" was "granted both to man and animal." But the situation soon changed,

> when, rebelling 'gainst the holy word,
> [man] scorned his own Creator's high decree,
> all the wild beasts rebelled, in turn, against him,
> waging full war. Man's frail and helpless limbs,
> now doomed to be destroyed by fearful death,
> began to find their daily sustenance
> in blood-infected food — a mortal food
> given to wretched mortals in their new,
> less happy state . . .

After the deluge, humanity descends from a lush vegetarian diet, which it shares
in camaraderie with all the animals, to a meat-eating regimen. It survives on
"blood-infected" and "mortal" food. Interestingly, but again following tradition,
Tasso assigns the descent from vegetarianism to carnivorousness not to the Fall
but to the time when "after the waters swelled / in one great deluge that with
waving death / covered all mountains and annulled all shores." And he goes on
following tradition, of which Saint Thomas Aquinas was the prominent spokesman, when he nevertheless condones meat eating:

> Yet, because man, God's holy semblance, still
> keeps in himself his primal origin,
> he has not lost his natural and rightful
> lordship on every beast, and justly, then,
> in the fierce war that justly he declares,
> he still can seize and capture all of them
> for food or just to clothe his bare, weak limbs.
> This law, which is not wicked or unjust,

comes not from nature but from God himself,
who made all beasts obedient to man.[17]

In a doubly fallen state, first after the Fall, and second after the deluge, humanity is obliged by necessity and right—a right compared by Tasso to the right to wage a just war—to "seize and capture," not to mention slaughter and consume, the beasts.

The same model of historical descent was followed a few decades earlier by the anti-Catholic Luther, in his *Lectures on Genesis,* though with a different conclusion. Commenting on Genesis 1:11, Luther says:

> You see what sort of food [God] provides for us, namely herbs and fruits of all kinds. Hence I believe that our bodies would have been far more durable if the practice of eating all sorts of food—particularly, however, the consumption of meat—had not been introduced after the Deluge. Even though the earth was cursed after Adam's sin and later on, at the time of the Deluge, had also become very corrupt, nevertheless a diet of herbs rather than of meat would be far finer today. Indeed, it is clear that at the beginning of the world herbs served as food and were created for this use, that they might be food for man.[18]

Luther thus again makes a clear distinction between ante- and postdiluvian conditions and emphasizes bloodless culinary simplicity. There is only a slight rhetorical or modal difference between the two accounts. Tasso's poem acknowledges that we were better off before the Fall or the Flood. Luther's commentary emphasizes that we *would have been* better off had we kept, or been able to keep, to our antediluvian regimen. Still, in each case, rather than recommending a vegetarian diet for the present day, the author registers regret. The paradise of food is a paradise lost.

Inevitably, one comes to Milton when considering these matters. *Paradise Lost* has permanently altered our response to the story of the Garden of Eden, indeed our very idea of it. Hardly alone in dramatizing the myth—over a hundred narratives and dramas on the subject survive in print from the early modern period, not to mention an uncounted number of paintings, drawings, and sculptures—Milton nevertheless single-handedly altered its psychological, philosophical, and theological makeup. In terms of food, he both followed mainstream Protestant tradition, coming close to Luther among others in his attitude toward it, and included many ideas and motifs that stand far outside of tradition. We need not go too deeply into why at this point. There are many reasons, beginning with Milton's radical politics and his often heretical religious ideas.[19] But Milton raised the stakes of the story, for food as for everything else. If his epic poem is designed as a theodicy, intended to "justify the ways of God to man," along the way it constructs what amounts to a theodicy of food. Yet if Milton represents a "fortunate fall," on the whole, where, having been exiled from Paradise, his Adam and Eve may nevertheless think themselves "happier far" by cherishing a "Paradise within," the story of food in the epic may not yield so gratifying a result. The final attitude toward food in the epic may rather be mixed. Milton has many surprises up his sleeve and, perhaps appropriately, some of what he says about food before and after the Fall may be an elaborate joke. The tragedy of the Fall includes a comedy of food. It also includes some standard advice, enhanced by faith: "If thou well observe / The rule of 'not too much' . . . / So may'st thou live, till, like ripe fruit, thou drop / Into thy mother's lap." But the fundamental idea about food, which is also its fundamental problem, is perhaps best expressed by Adam, during his initial despondency at finding himself fallen from innocence. These were the words cited in the epigraph to this chapter: "All that I eat or drink, or shall beget, / Is propagated curse."[20]

III

The food of regret, in any case, had both a recriminatory and a utopian dimension. The recriminations were obvious. The reason the Golden Age or the age of Paradise was only a thing of the past lay in men, and it continued to lie in men. That was patent in the case of Christian thought and even classical thought too, which had never developed an idea of original sin. In Ovid, for example, though nature becomes more challenging to man in the Silver and later ages, and for no particular reason — the world simply changes from one condition to another — the depredations of life are wholly human.

> For when that of this wicked Age once opened was the vein
> Therein all mischief rushed forth: then Faith and Truth were fain
> And honest shame to hide their heads: for whom crept stoutly in,
> Craft, Treason, Violence, Envy, Pride and wicked Lust to win.[21]

To tell the story of the food of regret was thus to remind the public of the depravity of human nature. The situation was of course much more pronounced in the case of retellings of the story of the Garden of Eden, where one of the chief motives was to render in sorrowful detail the consequences of human sinfulness — and thereby to make sure it was understood that humanity, not God, was creepily responsible for this sorrowfully consequent sin. The homily of Eden was cruelly pointed. *This* is what you have lost. This is what *you* have lost. This is what you have *lost.*

The utopian dimension of either the Christian Paradise and the Golden Age, by contrast, was more equivocal. The Christian Paradise, according to orthodox tradition, was not to be *hoped* for, exactly. However one felt about it, one had to admit that whatever humanity lost by its sins, what it gained by salvation through Christ was by far the greater thing.[22] And so if Paradise represented the blissful condition that God originally intended for humanity out of his unqualified goodness, and if that blissful condition represented what humans would want to enjoy if they could enjoy anything in this world, it was still not the best condition that God has in mind for humanity, and it was not to be desired — anymore. This was the logic that informed Milton's "fortunate fall" — that is, the idea that humanity was ultimately better off by having been exiled from Paradise, "happier far" by the "Paradise within" — as it did for many post-Augustinian writers. Our utopia could not be in the past; it could only be in the future.[23] And our future could not be the Garden of Eden. God had better plans. Similarly, the classical Golden Age, subject though it was of intense backward-looking longing, could not, for classical and classically minded authors, be a practical objective. Though it begins with a story of creation that includes the legend of the Golden Age, Ovid's *Metamorphoses* thus concludes rather differently. At the very end, it celebrates — though not perhaps without some irony — the destiny of the Roman Empire and the deification of Caesar. Just before that, on the other hand, the poem includes an account of the anti-militarist, vegetarian mysticism of Pythagoras, who puts before the public less an object of a desire — the peaceful life, the nuts and berries of the fruitarian diet — than a prohibition against aggression. "Oh what a wickedness / It is to cram the maw with maw, and frank flesh with flesh, / And for one living thing to live by killing of another."[24] Ovid's Pythagoras cannot explain the fall from the Golden to the Iron Age and the present-day economics of food; he can only prove that it was and continues to be wrong, and suggest that it be rectified by way of a prohibition.

Exceptions abound, but they are exceptions that prove the rule. Millenarian belief sometimes put faith in a "Third Age" or a "Second Adam," where life for the godly would resemble the paradisial condition. This was "heresy." And yet a good number of advanced thinkers of the early modern period — though neither Luther nor Milton were among them—went even further and believed not only that Paradise had been a real place, but that it could be discovered again. Christopher Columbus, most notoriously, believed that he had sighted it from afar while sailing in the Gulf of Mexico.[25] What it would be like to live in Paradise once one found it, however, was unclear, since after all it wasn't just Eden that was lost, but humanity's Edenic disposition. One tradition had it that Paradise was now to be found on the moon. In a comic utopian fantasy, *The Man in the Moone* (1638), Francis Godwin does not hesitate to have his narrator tell us that as soon as he arrived on the moon he found a shrub whose leaves were so good that "I cannot express the pleasure I found in the taste thereof." Nor does he hesitate to have him remark that on the moon "food groweth every where without labor, and that of all sorts to be desired."[26] Authors in the classical tradition mark similar exceptions to the rule. In his Fourth Eclogue, Virgil includes the fantasy that with the birth of the child of one of his patrons, "shall the earth, untilled, pour freely forth / her childish gifts," while

> the plain by slow degrees
> with waving corn-crops shall to golden grow,
> from the wild briar shall hang the blushing grape,
> and stubborn oaks sweat honey-dew.

In his poem about making a salad (1569)—a serious work, in spite of what may seem to be its ludicrous subject matter—the French poet Pierre de Ronsard, leader of the Pléiade, enjoins his companion to

> Wash your white hand. Let it be clean and supple.
> Follow my heels, and bring a napkin with you,
> And we will gather greens, go out to take
> Our years' share of the season's fruitfulness.

And if this seems to be less than paradisial or golden, Ronsard adds that he is going on his salad-picking venture "In fields left fallow by the plowman, / That, left untilled, bear on their own all sorts."[27]

The exceptions skirt common sense. And however seriously or wistfully intended, what they reveal above all is how the paradisial and Golden Age fantasies included normative material. The utopian function of the fantasies, so far as their food of regrets was concerned, hinged not so much on aspiration as on ethical injunction. In practical terms, this meant that the Golden Age and the Gar-

den of Eden provided models for ascetic practice. Indeed, they provided models
for what it meant to "follow nature" in one's habits. "Nature" in this sense referred both to something immanent—already there, embedded within us and
without us—and something from which either civilization or original sin or
some combination of the two has caused us to be alienated. If nature is corrupt,
or if man is corrupt, either is "corrupted"—originally, etymologically (from *cor-
rumpo*) "break to pieces"[28]—from a condition of which the Golden Age or the
Garden of Eden stands as the model. If one wishes to challenge corruption, to
follow nature in its positive, regenerative sense more closely, one may therefore
adopt a practice either against civilization or against sin in keeping with which
one's life would be simpler or more innocent. And the early modern period had
both inherited a number of ways of doing this and come up with unique practices
of its own. By the seventeenth century, the practices included a scientific diet
based on a measured, reduced quantity of foodstuffs—the qualities of humoral
theory be damned—and vegetarian programs motivated at once by considerations of health, scruples against killing, and mystical desire.

Thus we find the great prophet of the scientific revolution making the following observation in his *History of Life and Death:*

> It seems to be approved by experience, that a slender Diet, and well
> nigh Pythagorean, or such as is answerable to the severest Rules of
> Monastical Life, or to the institutions of Hermits, who had Necessity
> and Scarceness for Rule, doth produce long life. And to this course ap-
> pertains drinking of water, cold air, slender food (to wit, of roots and
> fruits, and powdered and pickled flesh and fish, rather than that which
> is fresh and hot) the wearing of hair cloth, often fastings, frequent
> watchings, and seldom enjoyment of sensual pleasures, and the like.[29]

The forward-looking, militantly Protestant, and worldly Sir Francis Bacon is
obliged to note that the regular diet of his class, the "fresh and hot" meat-centered
cuisine of prosperous Englishmen, was inferior to a "slender" fare featuring
much-despised commodities that pagan Pythagoreans and Christian monks and
hermits of old confined themselves to. Yet he approves of the slender fare because
it has been "approved by experience." The science is what counts. Still, it is not
the life of the hermit or Pythagoreanism that he ultimately recommends, but
rather a diet "somewhat more choice then these rigors and mortifications allow,"
following the systematic example of the sixteenth-century Venetian Luigi
Cornaro, who, as we will see, came up with a more modern, secular scheme.

IV

Science and method, obedience to a higher ideal and vigilant self-discipline — these were the common supplements to dietary behavior for anyone responding to the food of regrets. So were the two parallel sources of mythological and historical understanding upon which the food of regrets was to be regretted: the two communicating, but separate models of classical and Christian tradition, each of which promoted contrasting models of asceticism and nostalgia. Classical tradition gave the early modern period the "simple life," the "frugal" life, *vita parva*, which we see Ronsard emulating in his poem about a salad. The *vita parva* took several different forms, to be sure. Epicureanism, Cynicism, Stoicism, Pythagoreanism, and Neoplatonism all found ways to promote a simple life and a sparing diet. A militarist primitivism, where dietary simplicity was associated with military valor, found expression too. Horace, Seneca, Caesar, Tacitus — all such major Latin writers, who formed a major part of the education and culture of Renaissance humanists — in one way or another subscribed to a food of regret, influencing early modern attitudes. Meanwhile, Christian tradition gave ascetic practice yet another pair of models: on the one hand, the Eucharistic experience and its analogues, where the ritualistic consumption of wine and bread signified the assumption of the body of Christ and through it individual redemption; and, on the other hand, the renunciation of "the flesh" for spiritual ends by way of abstinence and continence, so that the paradigmatic relation to food for all Christians came to entail eschewing it. If the myths of origins of the two cultures jibed with one another, the dietary asceticisms that followed from the myths found rather different developments.

Horace (65–8 B.C.) was not the only exponent of an Epicurean simple life among classical writers, but for the early modern period, he was the most influential. On at least one occasion, he fantasized about leaving the troubles of Rome, plagued as it was with civil war, for the Fortunate Isles of Greco-Roman legend, which were "set up by Jupiter for righteous men / when he debased the Golden Age." There "the land unploughed gives grain," "vines unpruned are never out of flower," and "honey flows from hollow ilex [a kind of oak tree]."[30] But the dominant strain in Horace's relation to food plays in a different key. What Horace mainly imagines is the simplicity not of living primitively according to nature in its original state but of living with simple needs, in keeping with the conditions of subsistence farming. "Fortunate the man who, free from cares, / like men of old," he writes in the opening of his Second Epode . . . but the "men of old" are farmers. The fortunate man, free of debt and isolated from the calls of warfare and political struggle, keeps herds of cattle; grows pears, grapes, olives, and salad herbs; hunts wild birds, boar, and hare; makes wine and cheese; and serves up lamb or kid on special occasions.[31] (This vision is adopted whole in Erasmus's colloquy *The Godly Feast,* cited in the previous chapter, as it also is in a dialogue by another author whose works have concerned us, Tasso's *Father of the Family.*) Trouble free, Horace's fortunate man does without products acquired from distant seas and lands: Lucrine oysters, turbot, parrot-wrasse, African guinea fowl, Ionian heathcock. What is needed, but also problematic, according to the irony of the poem, which is in fact spoken by a greedy merchant, is to learn how to give up one's urbane habits. "A man is doing well," Horace argues in another poem, "if God, with a thrifty hand, gives him enough." Self-sufficiency is its own reward: "A stream of pure water, a few acres of woodland, / and a sure harvest, make me more blest by fortune / than the governor of grain-bearing Africa in all his glory."[32] Haute cuisine Roman-style, which Horace knew well, is the target of two whole satires.[33] Roman luxury, to be sure, required an artfulness that had less to do with the showy bulkiness common in Renaissance feasting than a science of the palate and the ingredients and methods that served it best: "Give good heed to serve eggs of an oblong shape," Horace's gourmet advises, "for they have better flavor and are whiter than the round. . . . Cabbage grown on dry lands is sweeter than from the farms near the city." "It is not everyone that may lightly claim skill in the dining art, without first mastering the subtle theory of flavors."[34] The gastronomic advice actually follows the course of complex meal, from appetizers to main courses to digestives. But Horace's response to the gourmet's science is at best bemusement. In his satire extolling the benefits of frugal living (*vivere parvo*), he has his spokesman, an unlearned peasant, remark that the "chiefest pleasure lies, not in the costly savor, but in yourself." He cautions against being taken in by the costly splendor of things — "a big fish on a big dish," for example — as opposed to their real taste; but he also notes the difference between simple, delicious fare and the "mean style of living" (*sordidus victu*), which contents itself with the worst and cheapest of things merely out of avarice. As for the benefits of the simple life, they include the usual contributions to mental and physical health: less illness, more energy and acuity. They also make it possible really to appreciate feasts on special occasions.[35]

The simple life, according to Horace, is genuinely Epicurean. It is conducted as a true pursuit of pleasure, and though it means living temperately, it does not entail self-denial. This is an important point: the construction of the simple life in a Horatian mode means situating the self within the currents of society and nature for essentially egoistic ends, in obedience to the pleasure principle. Epicurus himself had expressed similar ideas:

We are firmly convinced that those who need expensive fare least are the ones who relish it most keenly and that a natural way of life is easily procured, while trivialities are hard to come by. Plain foods afford pleasure equivalent to that of a sumptuous diet, provided that the pains of penury are wholly eliminated. Barley bread and water yield the peak of pleasure whenever a person who needs them sets them in front of himself. Hence becoming habituated to a simple rather than a lavish way of life provides us with the full complement of health; it makes a person ready for the necessary business of life; it puts us in a position of advantage when we happen upon sumptuous fare at intervals and prepares us to be fearless in facing fortune.[36]

Seneca (4 B.C.?–A.D. 65) provides a different picture. A Stoic rather than an Epicurean, though not entirely out of sympathy with the Epicurean position, Seneca imagines a pursuit of simplicity that is less a matter of adjusting the goods one consumes and the way of life one follows than of overhauling the consuming body and the ego presiding over it. Seneca is even more contemptuous of Roman haute cuisine than Horace, but not, he claims, because it is unpleasurable. Pleasure itself is not to be valued — "For we stoics hold that pleasure is a vice" — although the use of the word pleasure (*voluptas*) to indicate the appropriate satisfaction of a need or a mental want is sometimes inevitable.[37] Seneca recommends occasional fasting, by which he means feeding oneself by an act of free will the way the poor feed themselves by necessity. Fasting prepares one against the vicissitudes of fortune and yields an honorable sort of pleasure: "For though water, barley meal, and crusts of barley-bread are not a cheerful diet, yet it is the highest kind of pleasure to be able to derive pleasure from this sort of food, and to have reduced one's needs to that modicum which no unfairness of Fortune can snatch away."[38] Even living on water and barley is not enough, however:

You are doing no great thing if you can live without royal pomp, if you feel no craving for boars which weigh a thousand pounds, or for flamingo tongues, or for the other absurdities of a luxury that already wearies of game cooked whole, and chooses different bits from separate animals; I shall admire you only when you have learned to scorn even the common sort of bread, when you have made yourself believe that grass grows for the needs of men as well as of cattle, when you have found out that food from the treetop [i.e., acorns] can fill the belly.

Seneca argues that it makes no difference what the food we eat tastes like, since all food goes to the same place and is subject to the same "corruption" as the modern translator puts it—or, to give a more literal rendering, "seized by the same fetidness" ("eadem foeditas occupabit"). But even learning to live on the most meager of foods is not enough for someone who would live like a philosopher. "For it is base to make the happy life depend upon silver and gold, and it is just as base to make it depend upon water and porridge." For "freedom comes not to him over whom Fortune has slight power, but to him over whom she has no power at all. This is what I mean: you must crave nothing."[39]

Thus Horace and Seneca, and two classical models of the simple life, one in pursuit of simple pleasures, the other in pursuit of indifference to pleasure. Both of them, for all their differences, were equally wistful about the Golden Age. Seneca quotes Virgil on the subject:

No ploughman tilled the ground,
No fence dividing field from field was found;
When to the common store all gains were brought,
And earth gave freely goods which none had sought.

He then exclaims, "What race of men was ever happier than these? They enjoyed all Nature in common. She sufficed for them as mother and defender of them all. Their defense was the secure possession of the common resources. Why indeed, should I not call them the richest race of mortals, since no poor man could be found among them?"[40]

But there was also the example of contemporary peoples who, if they did not exemplify the innocence (and vegetarianism) of the men of the Golden Age, at least exemplified a savage nobility. Caesar tells of the Nervii, who "did not admit traders into their country and would not allow the importation of wine and other luxuries, because they thought such things made men soft and took the edge off their courage."[41] He describes the strange, primitive inland Britons dispassionately and without comment: "Most of the tribes of the interior do not grow corn but live on milk and meat, and wear skins. All the Britons dye their bodies with woad, which produces a blue color, and shave the whole of their bodies except the head and the upper lip. Wives are shared between groups of ten or twelve men. . . ." Similarly, the Germans, as a whole, "are not agriculturalists, and live principally on milk, cheese, and curds." Writing over a century later, Tacitus concurs. The food of the Germans, he says, "is plain—wild fruit, fresh game, and curdled milk. They satisfy their hunger without any elaborate cuisine or appetizers." However, Tacitus's Germans drink beer, and "they do not show the same self-control in slaking their thirst. If you indulge their intemperance by plying them with as much drink as they desire, they will be as easily conquered by this weakness as by this force of arms."[42] The idea is never emphasized, but it persists. The barbarians are often very primitive; their primitivism is expressed in their simple diets, which do not depend on agriculture or at least on the bread-wine-oil triumvirate of Roman culture; and if there is something strange about them, there is perhaps something admirable as well. According to Arthur O. Lovejoy and George Boas, the Scythians, drinkers of mare's milk, attracted the most attention among Roman writers.[43] But Lovejoy and Boas fail to mention one of the more influential accounts, Dio Cassius's description of the ancient northern Britons, the Caledonians and the Maetae (i.e., the Scots and the Picts):

> Both tribes inhabit wild and waterless mountains and desolate and swampy plains, and possess neither walls, cities, nor tilled fields, but live on their flocks, wild game, and certain fruits; for they do not touch the fish which are there found in immense and inexhaustible quantities. They dwell in tents, naked and unshod, possess their women in common, and in common rear all the offspring. Their form of rule is democratic for the most part, and they are very fond of plundering; consequently they choose their boldest men as rulers. . . . They can endure hunger and cold and any kind of hardship; for they plunge into the swamps and exist there for many days with only their heads above water, and in the forest they support themselves upon bark and roots, and for all emergencies they prepare a certain kind of food, the eating of a small portion of which, the size of a bean, prevents them from feeling either hunger or thirst.[44]

Along with such accounts circulate stories of Roman warriors who learned to live in conditions of necessity no less stalwartly than the barbarians did. The best known is Plutarch's remark about Mark Antony during a difficult military campaign at Modena. "It was a wonderful example to the soldiers, to see Antonius that was brought up in all fineness and superfluity, so easily to drink puddle water, and to eat wild fruits and roots: and moreover it is reported, that even as they passed the Alps, they did eat the barks of trees, and such beasts, as never man tasted before."[45] Shakespeare transforms this passage, in *Antony and Cleopatra,* into a rebuke by Octavius to Antony for the life of luxury and licentiousness he thinks him to be leading while living in Egypt with Cleopatra:

> Antony,
> Leave thy lascivious wassails! When thou once
> Was beaten from Modena, where thou slew'st
> Hirtius and Panda, consuls, at they heel

Did Famine follow, who thou fought'st against,
Though daintily brought up, with patience more
Than savages could suffer. Thou didst drink
The stale of horses and the giddled puddle
Which beasts would cough at. Thy palate then did deign
The roughest berry on the rudest hedge.
Yea, like the stag, when snow the pasture sheets,
The barks of trees thou browsèd. On the Alps
It is reported thou didst eat strange flesh,
Which some did die to look on. And all this —
It wounds thine honor that I speak it now—
Was borne so like a soldier that thy cheek
So much as lanked not.[46]

Throughout most of such discourses, as indeed through most of the countervailing discourses of abundance featured in the previous chapter, the emphasis is
on men and masculinity. Again, there are no women in the Hesiodic and Ovidian
golden ages, and in other accounts, even in cases where free love between men
and women is admired, little thought is given to the homestead, the hearth, or
the role of women in providing for themselves and others. If the Golden Age
does without cookery, the meal, or the home, it does so by turning a blind eye to
women and femininity. When nature provides and no family life seems needed,
the home is superfluous, the meal has no fixed locality or customs, and women —
for those writers whose accounts of these things survive — are out of the picture.
And when the aim is not to return to the Golden Age but to replicate its features
by way of a valorous life of simplicity, as in Horace or Seneca, women are still out
of the picture. Nor do Roman ethnographers have much interest in women —
partly because it was not against women that Roman adventurers needed to
wage war, but partly because they were outside the equation of virtue to which
Roman men were taught to aspire. In both Plutarch's *Life of Antony* and Shakespeare's *Antony and Cleopatra*, Antony's brave and masculine mastery over hunger
is openly contrasted with the feminized self-indulgence he surrenders to while
living in peaceful, carnal Egypt.

Women would not be invisible in Judeo-Christian accounts of such matters.[47] Eve's role in both the happiness of Eden and humanity's fall from innocence made woman central to paradisial memory. The state of innocence was the
state of a couple, and the fall from innocence entailed an episode where one
member of the couple fed the other. Yet Christianized accounts of the simple life
also often marginalized conventional family life and hence overlooked the typi-

cal *habitus* of women. If the Genesis tradition provided grounds for a long tradition of misogyny, blaming Eve for the Fall — Eve having allowed herself to be seduced by the serpent and then having fed the forbidden fruit to Adam — it did
not, with regard to women and food, provide many grounds for a countervailing
tradition of gustatory feminism. The gustatory wishes of the simple life encouraged by Christianity, with or without women — though it might have reference
to the Garden of Eden so far as it included a vegetarian-inclined diet — moved in
other directions.

The two competing motifs of gustatory simplicity in traditional Christianity, again, were the Communion and the fast. On the one side, the simple pair
of the wine and bread of the Eucharist made eating and drinking, in a Mediterranean mode, central to religious experience. One partook of Christ by eating
his body, by drinking his blood. (Or did one? The controversy over this and its
cannibalistic overtones will be discussed in chapter 7: the Protestant Milton
from early in his career would refer to the host, in the plural, as "gods made of
bread.")[48] Wholly separate from Greco-Roman traditions in this respect, Christianity encouraged the idea of spiritual nourishment by way of matter. The motif
is frequently featured in Renaissance painting, where the Last Supper and less
exalted biblical events such as the Wedding at Cana reiterate the typology of
Communion while embracing the material specifics of food and drink and conviviality. Conviviality, it should be added, was central to the model too. Communion was taken socially, in a public ritual; one's personal nourishment in the
presence of the Host required a social setting whose nearest analogy was the
feast. And vice versa. "For truly," as Erasmus's host states in *The Godly Feast,* as
the guests sit down to dinner, "if a meal was something holy to pagans, much
more should it be so to Christians, for whom it's an allegory of that sacred last
supper which the Lord Jesus took with his disciples."[49] On the other side, however, the renunciation of the flesh through fasting made *not* eating, and even not
experiencing hunger in spite of one's fasting, central to religious experience. The
classic doctrine was expressed by the church father Saint Basil: Christian "conti-
nency," he wrote, was the "abstinence from pleasures which aims at the thwarting of the will of the flesh for the purpose of attaining to the goal of piety." Con-
tinency "destroys sin, quells the passions, and mortifies the body even as to its
natural affections and desires. It marks the beginnings of the spiritual life, leads
us to eternal blessings, and extinguishes within itself the desire for pleasure."[50]
The aim, as Basil and many others would express it, was at once to chastise and
liberate. One exacted punishment against the defective and culpable nature one
had inherited from Adam as a result of the Fall, but at the same time one freed
the soul from the defect; one removed an impediment to spirituality.

Figure 5.1. The Last Supper, from the *Sforza Hours* (ca. 1490). A Renaissance feast, served by comely servants, dished out on expensive plates and glass goblets, in a sumptuous setting. But the only food we see is bread and wine. Reproduced by permission of the British Library (Add. 34294).

Christian dietary asceticism had a long and sometimes surprising history. It reached one of its literary climaxes in the early medieval *Voyage of Saint Brendan,* where the dream of doing without labor, food, or hunger turns out to be not only a sign of spiritual purity but an open expression of the death wish. Brendan voyages in fact to a paradise, at the entry of which is a land of exceptional foods — fruits and nuts, of course. But the goal of the voyage is actually a paradise of the afterlife, where a desire expressed throughout the text, experienced by Brendan and his party again and again, the desire *not to have to eat,* would finally be satisfied.[51] Dietary asceticism reached another sort of climax in the late Middle Ages when the great hunger artists were predominantly young women who, either within the confines of a religious order or without it, placed themselves apart from the general run of society by athletic food refusal. Saint Catherine of Siena — who labored to feed the poor and tend to the sick, not stooping to feed on their filth or else on nothing at all, and who died, emaciated, probably from malnutrition — is one of the great icons of feminist asceticism.[52]

The early modern period, however, saw a dramatic decline in dietary asceticism. Food and hunger came increasingly under the wing of secular, scientific thought. The cult of suffering little by little became replaced with the cult of health. The Reformation, again, discouraged prolonged abstinence, whether in matters of marriage and sex or in matters of eating and drinking. Though it cannot be said that the early modern period gave women more opportunities for autonomy, the way to autonomy by monastic life being closed to many, even for those for whom monasticism remained open the inopportune secular world still seemed to offer more. Starving saints became "miraculous maidens," who were more an object of curiosity than models of living life according to God's commands.[53] Yet elements of Christian dietary asceticism continued to exert an influence on early modern attitudes, even merging with Galenic-inspired self-medication of purgings and cleansings.

Saint Teresa of Ávila, whose example looms large in the Counter-Reformation, was herself a troubled hunger artist, a fairly strict ascetic who was also a purger.[54] "For the last twenty years," she writes in her spiritual autobiography, "I have suffered from morning sickness, and cannot take any food until past midday — sometimes not until much later." The translator in fact engages in circumlocution; in the original Spanish, Teresa says she is subject not to "sickness" but to "vomits," *vomitos.* And Teresa's "vomits" are not entirely unintentional. "Now that I take Communion more frequently," she adds, somewhat mysteriously, since it is hard to see why taking Communion should have this effect, "I have to bring it on at night before I go to bed, with feathers or in some other way." She makes herself vomit by sticking feathers down her throat. She takes no pleasure in purging herself in this way, "but if I do not, I feel much worse."[55] What

Teresa recounts is a struggle with her own body, where she fights what is often a losing battle to gain a spiritual control over her flesh. "One night I was at prayer when the time came for me to go to bed. I was in considerable pain, and my usual sickness was coming on. When I saw how bound I was to my body and how my spirit, on the other hand, demanded time for itself, I became so depressed that I burst into floods of tears and was thoroughly upset. This was not the only time that I felt exasperated with myself. It happens frequently. . . ." Her pain in fact indicates over-attachment to the flesh, even as it also indicates the desire of her soul for freedom. Purging is thus both an evil and a good, a hindrance and a help, a sign of illness and a pathway to health. She claims she is not self-destructive. "I never fail to do what I see to be necessary for my life." Yet the wish behind her pattern of accommodating her needs and purging herself of what she has swallowed — "Pray God I not often do more than is essential" — seems to have much in common with the death wish behind the voyage of Saint Brendan: the craving for a transcendence of materiality and instrumentality that is impossible in this life, and yet has to be satisfied at any cost.[56] Among her models is a famous monk who nevertheless all but succeeded, Peter of Alcántara, one of her spiritual advisers, who was later to be canonized and celebrated as the patron saint of Brazil. "For forty years he had never slept more than an hour and a half between nightfall and morning," she reports approvingly. To achieve this "penance," as she calls it, "he always remained standing or on his knees. Such sleep as he had, he took sitting down, with his head propped against a piece of wood, which he had fixed to the wall. He could not lie down to sleep even if he wanted to, for his cell, as is well known, was only four and a half feet long." As for food, he was an ascetic athlete: "He usually ate only once in three days, and he wondered why this surprised me. He said that it was perfectly possible once one got used to it, and a companion of his told me that sometimes he would go eight days without food. This must have been when he was at prayer, for he used to have great raptures and transports of love for God, of which I was once a witness."[57] Peter, evidently, was not a purger. He didn't need to purge. His "lanking not," his pain-free, disturbance-free hunger artistry, was a sign of superior, Antony-like spirituality. (The "Catholic" Shakespeare was perhaps thinking of such saints when he added the detail of "lanking not" to the list of Antony's virtues.)

V

But eaters in the early modern period found many more clinical and unorthodox reasons to pursue a spare diet. Most famous and influential was the case of the minor nobleman from Venice, Luigi (aka Alvise) Cornaro, whose story was so important to Sir Francis Bacon. Born in 1464, he was famous for having lived well beyond the usual limits of life expectancy in the period, and then having written a book about how he did it. His *Trattato de la vita sobria* — which he wrote at the age of eighty-three and then supplemented with additional material over the next twelve years, so that his career as an author reached to the age of ninety-five — was translated from the original Italian into eleven different languages and released in over three hundred separate editions. In English, in which it was first translated by the poet George Herbert,[58] it appeared in no less than 169 editions, and its editors were still taking it seriously as a guide to good health and longevity as late as 1903. The appeal of Cornaro's treatise was twofold, its simplicity and its modernity. Cornaro held on to what I have called the intake-discharge doctrine of Galenic theory, and in principle held on to other Galenic doctrines as well; but his advice was such that no sophisticated knowledge of humors, temperaments, and animistic qualities was necessary. Cornaro's advice was to follow one's sensory awareness, and then to apply a method to it. Again, it was both simple and modern.

He explains the method by first of all telling his own story. Between the ages of thirty-five and forty, he writes, having lived in debauchery, he was often in poor health:

> The excesses of my past life, together with my bad constitution, — my stomach being very cold and moist, — had caused me to fall a prey to various ailments, such as frequent pains in the stomach, frequent pains in the side, symptoms of gout, and, still worse, a low fever that was almost continuous; but I suffered especially from the disorder of the stomach, and from an unquenchable thirst. This evil — nay, worse than evil — condition left me nothing to hope for myself, except that death should terminate my troubles and the weariness of my life. . . .[59]

Finally, however, he decided to take his physicians' advice and follow a strict invalid's regimen: "Having been instructed by my physicians as to the method I was to adopt, I understood that I was not to partake of any foods, either solid or liquid, save such as are prescribed for invalids; and, of these, in small quantities only."[60] What he has in mind are the many thin soups and gruels that doctors had been prescribing to people with fevers and other ailments since the time of Hippocrates — foods that genuinely soothe and that, once prescribed and consumed, in successful cases genuinely precede recovery. Many cookbooks — even La Varenne's *Cuisinier françois* — include recipes for such food for the sick. Here is one for capon broth, included in a book Cornaro probably knew, Platina's *De honesta volupta:*

> . . . take a pot which contains about five quarts of water. Put the capon in it, with the bones broken up finely and with an ounce of lean pork, thirty grams of pepper, a little cinnamon, not ground too much, three or four cloves, five leaves of sage, torn into three pieces, and two leaves of bay. Let this boil seven hours, or until it is reduced to two cups or less. Beware of putting in salt, for if it is salted, it becomes a cause of illness. . . .[61]

Concentrated and mercifully unsalted chicken soup, in other words, is what Platina here recommends for the infirm. As for Cornaro, having resolved to follow doctor's orders without cheating, he writes, "Within a few days I began to realize that this new life suited my health excellently; and persevering in it, in less than a year— though the fact may seem incredible to some — I found myself entirely cured of all my complaints."[62]

But Cornaro did not spend the whole year, or the rest of his life, subsisting on chicken soup. What made Cornaro's story paradigmatic for an era was, in the spirit of the medical advice he had been tendered but also in the spirit of self-directed experiment, his persistence in following a method, a method at once personal and scientific.

> Now that I was in perfect health, I began to consider seriously the power and virtue of order; and I said to myself that, as [diet] had been able to overcome such great ills as mine, it would surely be even more efficacious to preserve me in health, to assist my unfortunate constitution, and to strengthen my extremely weak stomach.
>
> Accordingly, I began to observe very diligently what kinds of food agreed with me. I determined, in the first place, to experiment with those which were most agreeable to my palate, in order that I might learn if they were suited to my stomach and constitution. The proverb, "whatever tastes good will nourish and strengthen," is generally regarded as embodying a truth, and is invoked, as a first principle, by those who are sensually inclined. In it I had hitherto firmly believed; but now I was resolved to test the matter, and to find to what extent, if any, it was true.
>
> My experience, however, proved this saying to be false. For instance, dry and very cold wine was agreeable to my taste; as were also melons; and among other garden produce, raw salads; also fish, pork, tarts,

vegetable soups, pastries, and other similar articles. All of these, I say, suited my taste exactly, and yet I found they were hurtful to me. Thus having, by my own experience, proved the proverb in question to be erroneous, I ever after looked upon it as such, and gave up the use of that kind of food and that kind of wine, as well as cold drinking. Instead, I chose only such wines as agreed with my stomach, taking of them only such a quantity as I knew it could easily digest; and I observed the same rule with regard to my food, exercising care both as to the quantity and quality. In this manner, I accustomed myself to the habit of never fully satisfying my appetite, either with eating or drinking — always leaving the table well able to take more. In this I acted according to the proverb: "*Not to satiate one's self with food is the science of health.*"

Being thus rid, for the reasons and in the manner I have given, of intemperance and disorder, I devoted myself entirely to the sober and regular life.[63]

Hillel Schwartz characterizes Cornaro's story as an early example of the "romance" of dieting. In this romance, "the dieter's battle against gluttony is a magical battle; every step taken against the glutton doubles the hero's strength, gives him at once more youth and power. Lighter, he is more agile and more alert. The longer the battle lasts, the more vigor he has."[64] This characterization is helpful. But in Cornaro the "battle" is really more of a divine comedy. There are no dragons to slay, no struggles against cravings, no purgings, no clysters up the behind or feathers down the throat in the Venetian's progress toward health and long life. Cornaro's experience is rather like those of the patients Peter Kramer describes in *Listening to Prozac,* who find their lives indefinitely transformed for the better without any side effects or costs.[65] There is no downside to the regimen:

> In a word, I grew most healthy; and I have remained so from that time to this day, and for no other reason than that of my constant fidelity to the orderly life. The unbounded virtue of this is, that that which I eat and drink, — always being such as agrees with my constitution and, in quantity, such as it should, — after it has imparted its invigorating elements to my body, leaves it without any difficulty and without ever generating within it any bad humors.[66]

How Cornaro was able to determine exactly what "agreed" with his constitution, or in exactly what quantity he should take his food he never quite says. But in that, too, his experience in controlling alimentary intake is rather like modern SSRI therapy. For Cornaro, food is dosage. One experiments with the compo-

nents and the quantity with which they should be consumed, and once one finds
the right dose, one sticks with it, religiously. And though Cornaro will not say
how he arrived at the proper dose, he is clear about the consequences of straying
from it, once it has been discovered. Thus he writes about what happened once,
when his relatives and friends

> observed how very little I ate, and, in unison with my physicians, told
> me that the food I took could not possibly be sufficient to sustain a man
> of an age so advanced as mine. They argued that I should not only pre-
> serve, but rather aim to increase, my strength and vigor. And as this
> could only be done by means of nourishment, it was absolutely neces-
> sary, they said, that I should eat rather more abundantly.

Arguing strenuously against them, Cornaro finally nevertheless relented.

> Now I did not like to appear obstinate or as though I considered myself
> more of a doctor than the very doctors themselves; moreover, I espe-
> cially wished to please my family, who desired it very earnestly, believ-
> ing, as they did, that such an increase in my ordinary allowance would
> be beneficial to my strength. So I at last yielded, and consented to add
> to the quantity of food. This increase, however, was by only two ounces
> in weight; so that, while, with bread, the yolk of an egg, a little meat, and
> some soup, I had formerly eaten as much as would weigh in all exactly
> twelve ounces, I now went so far as to raise the amount to fourteen
> ounces; and, while I had formerly drunk but fourteen ounces of wine, I
> now began to take sixteen ounces.

An interesting set of numbers: if we assume a rough equivalence between
Cornaro's measures and our own, calculate that liquid soup and bread constitute
75 percent of the total weight, and take account of the three glasses of wine he
consumed, Cornaro is consuming no more than about fourteen hundred calories
a day—a spare diet, indeed. Raising his intake by two ounces of food and two
ounces of wine, he consumes about sixteen hundred calories a day. But even this
small addition of food and drink had dire consequences, according to Cornaro,
so that he was forced as a remedy to return, joyfully, to his "sober" or "orderly"
life, on fourteen hundred calories a day:

> The disorder of this increase had, at the end of ten days, begun to affect
> me so much, that, instead of being cheerful, as I have ever been, I be-
> came melancholy and choleric; everything annoyed me and my mood

was so wayward that I neither knew what to say to others nor what to do with myself. At the end of twelve days I was seized with a most violent pain in the side, which continued twenty-two hours. This was followed by a terrible fever, which lasted thirty-five days and as many nights without a moment's interruption; although, to tell the truth, it kept constantly diminishing after the fifteenth day. Notwithstanding such abatement, however, during all that period I was never able to sleep for even half of a quarter of an hour; hence everybody believed that I would surely die. However, I recovered— God be praised!— solely by returning to my former rule of life; although I was then seventy-eight years of age, and it was just in the heart of the coldest season of a very cold year, and I as frail in body as could be.[67]

Cornaro's most important acolyte was Leonardus Lessius, the Flemish Jesuit, who translated *Trattato de la vita sobria* into Latin, publishing it in 1613 as an appendix to his own *Hygiasticon; seu, Vera ratio valetudinis bonae et vitae una cum sensuum, judicii, et memoriae integritate ad extremam senectutem conservandae*. It was the English translation of this text, *Hygiasticon; or, The Right Course of Preserving Life and Health unto Extream Old Age* (1634), that introduced the wider reading public of seventeenth-century England to Cornaro's ideas. Lessius in fact adds little of his own, except that he places the ideas in a high rhetorical context. Much more the scholar than Cornaro and better familiar with humoral theory, he nevertheless underscores from the start the chief difference between Cornaro's kind of diet and that of classical medicine, its methodical modernity. His language in this regard is reminiscent of Montaigne and anticipatory of Descartes, although it is also presumptuously moralistic:

> Many authors have written largely and very learnedly touching the preservation of Health: but they charge men with so many rules, and exact so much observation and cautions about the quality and quantity of meats and drinks; about air, sleep, exercise, seasons of the year, purgations, bloodletting, and the like; and over and above prescribe such a number of Compound, Opiate, and other kinds of exquisite remedies, as they bring men into a labyrinth of care in the observation, and unto perfect slavery in endeavoring to perform what they do in this matter enjoin.
>
> And when all is done, the issue proves commonly much short, ofttimes clean contrary to that which was expected. . . . For men forsooth will have their own minds, eat every thing that likes them, and to their fill: they will shape their diet according to the ordinary usage of the

world, and give in everything satisfaction to their sensuality and appetite.[68]

Lessius recommends a simpler resolution, in the fashion of Cornaro, to live the
sober life. And in place of the complexities of humoral complexions, the "non-
naturals," and medicinal remedies, he extols Cornaro's reliance on quantitative
measure: "a constant measure is to be kept."[69]

Such, too, was the main recommendation of Sir Francis Bacon, writing at
about the same time, who also provides a post-Galenic theoretical justification
for the method. Beginning with many of the assumptions of Galenic medicine,
Bacon attempts to move beyond them. "The continual course of nature, like a
running river, requires a continual sailing against the stream," he writes. Life, in
other words, is not only a *eucrasia* of the warm, but also a vital struggle, a contention between life and death, where the exertion itself is the substance of life.
It is the conduct of the contention, therefore, that requires regulation, for both
too much struggle and too little are enervating, and interruptions of the steady
state of contention can be fatal. "We see it in flames," Bacon writes about the
problem of too much consumption and thus too much digestive exertion, "that
a flame somewhat bigger — so it be always alike and quiet — consumeth less of the
fuel, than a lesser flame blown with bellows, and by gusts stronger or weaker."[70]
For Bacon the body has to be steadily but parsimoniously fueled.

> The spirits, to keep the body fresh and green, are so to be wrought and
> tempered that they may be in substance dense, not rare; in heat strong,
> not eager; in quantity sufficient for the offices of life, not redundant or
> turgid; in motion appeased, not dancing or unequal. It is to be seen in
> flames, that the bigger they are, the stronger they break forth, and the
> more speedily they consume. And, therefore, over great plenty, or exu-
> berance of spirit, is altogether hurtful to long life; neither need one
> wish a greater store of spirits, than what is sufficient for the functions
> of life and the office of a good reparation.[71]

In other words, the body is to be kept a little hungry, in order to keep it on edge,
its "spirits"—which the body itself concocts out of food — neither excessive nor
heavy. But it is not to be starved either, for its "spirits" need to be substantial. The
body has to be steadily fueled.

> The stomach — which, as they say, is the master of the house, and whose
> strength and goodness is fundamental to the other concoctions —
> ought so to be guarded and confirmed that it may be without intem-

perateness hot; it is to be kept ever in appetite, because appetite sharpens digestion. This also is most certain, that the brain is in some sort in the custody of the stomach; and therefore, those things which comfort and strengthen the stomach, do help the brain by consent.[72]

And so, again, Bacon admires the "pythagorical or monastical diet, according to strict rules, and always exactly equal." And "if the diet shall not be altogether so rigorous and mortifying" as among monks, it should at least "be always equal and constant to itself." "If one is not to be a monk or a vegetarian, then, there is no better model than the regimen and diet of Cornaro, the Venetian . . . who did eat and drink so many years together by a just weight, whereby he exceeded a hundred years of age, strong in limbs, and entire in his senses."[73]

VI

The "pythagorical" diet as such did not, so far as we know, have many enthusiasts during the early modern period.[74] Non-methodical vegetarianism — a diet based on grains and vegetables and possibly dairy products, with meat products or fish only occasionally added for flavoring and nutrition — was a custom imposed upon the peasantry for much of the time in many places. One did not choose this custom of non-methodical vegetarianism; one simply did not have any other choice. Meanwhile for those who could choose what they ate, the orthodox, liturgical rhythm of eating imposed a rule of fast and feast that made ritualistic vegetarianism mandatory. Lenten regulation only gradually came to allow fish and dairy products in the fast day diet; and although, from the evidence of menus, fast days could be occasions for great piscatory feasts, for the majority of early modern eaters the fast day was in fact a day of abstinence, whose chief requirement was the avoidance of meat, and whose usual observance meant a vegetarian diet with perhaps a small piece of fish or an egg thrown in.[75]

In some cases, to be sure, vegetarianism could be a deliberate choice. Monastic orders continued in many instances to practice vegetarianism — the eschewal of meat having traditionally been regarded as an effective mortification and sign of penitence — and in prosperous Italy, as we have seen, though meat eating was prestigious, vegetables, grains, oil, wine, and fruits dominated the diet of the majority of people as a matter of preference. Leonardo da Vinci, it is said, practiced a Pythagorean diet, being repelled by the cruelty of meat eating.[76] Leonardo and such isolated figures apart, there was a general trend in all Euro-

pean countries, stemming from Italy in the sixteenth century and moving north-
ward during the seventeenth century, toward the increased cultivation and consumption of vegetables.[77] An especially winsome expression of the spirit of such
vegetarian preference is to be found in Giacomo Castelvetro's scribal publication dedicated to the powerful Lady Bedford (the same woman to whom it is
sometimes thought that Donne wrote his "To His Mistress Going to Bed"), *A
Brief Account of all the Roots, Greens and Fruits that are Eaten in Italy either Raw or
Cooked* (1614).[78] "It is almost impossible to describe our delight in the delicious
green salads of [summer]," he says of Italians, in a characteristic remark.[79] Delight and health together meet in Castelvetro's praise of vegetables. Likewise, at
the end of the century appeared what would become the often reprinted *Acetaria: A Discourse of Sallets,* by John Evelyn (1699), where, alluding either to the
Golden Age or to the Garden of Eden, Evelyn asserts that "were it in my Power,
I would recall the World, if not altogether to their Pristine *Diet,* yet to a much
more *wholesome* and *temperate* than is now in Fashion."[80]

"Ethical" vegetarianism, vegetarianism chosen primarily out of scruples
about killing, nevertheless, was not often publicly advocated in early modern Europe, even if, as we have seen, ideas about the cruelty of slaughtering animals for
food were expressed in such prominent authors as Sir Thomas More, Michel de
Montaigne, and William Shakespeare. But ethical vegetarianism emerges as an
openly discussed alternative in the second half of the seventeenth century in England, partly as an expression of radical, sectarian Behmenism — a popular form
of Christian mysticism, based on the writings of Jacob Böhme — and partly as an
amateurish outgrowth of Galenic conventions.[81] Best known are the cases of
Roger Crab and Thomas Tryon, who were both hatmakers.[82] In the 1655 publication *The English Hermit,* Crab tells how he came to live the life of a recluse, dining
on nothing but "corn, bread, and bran, herbs, roots, dock-leaves, mallows, and
grass," and drinking nothing but water.[83] Crab gives reasons for his decision out
of Scripture, out of "experience," and out of "reason." None of these reasons by
themselves, as the publisher of the volume notes, is terribly convincing; but they
add up to an ethical vision of living according to God's commands, innocent of
the death of other creatures, and in better health to boot. Tryon, a better and
more prolific author, provides a systematic view of vegetarianism on similar lines.
As far as Tryon is concerned, it is God's command that we follow a vegetarian
diet, avoiding bloodiness alike in what we eat and what we are. But Tryon's rhetoric accentuates the positive. Indeed, Tryon claims to find inspiration in such authors as Leonardus Lessius.[84] And instead of harping upon the ethical imperative
of vegetarianism, he joins vegetarianism with the values of vigor, long life, and
gustatory pleasure, as well as spiritual redemption. The title to one of his major

works provides a synopsis of how he joins these things together: *Wisdom's Dictates; or, Aphorisms and Rules, Physical, Moral, and Divine; for Preserving the Health of the Body and the Peace of the Mind, fit to be regarded and practised by all that would enjoy the Blessings of the present and future World.* The ethical choice is also a prudent choice. The prudent choice brings one closer to the "blessings of the present" but it also brings one closer to the blessings of heaven. Here is a small sampling from Tryon's 290 aphorisms:

> 22. Whenever you Eat or Drink, Do it . . . *in Remembrance of me,* that is, fear my Name, and submit to the guidance of my Spirit, who will teach the Sons of Wisdom all things necessary.
> 23. Desire not variety of Meats nor Drink, for fear the Soul be overwhelmed in the dark Clouds of Wrath and Sorrow.
> 24. Eat not to dullness, for that is a token of Gluttony, and a forerunner of Diseases.
> 25. Delight not in Meats and Drinks that are too strong for Nature, but always let Nature be stronger then your Food.
> 26. Prolong not the Pleasures of the Palate, by improper mixtures of wanton sauces beyond the necessities of the Stomach, for whatsoever is superfluously received is a burden to Nature, and the Seed-Plot of Diseases.
> . . .
> 29. Do not Eat or Drink any thing that is hotter than your Blood, except in a Physical way, for fear lest you infect the Fountain of Life with a Scorbutic Humor.
> . . .
> 289. As it was Intemperance that shut the Gates of Paradise against Man, so Temperance and Order are the only Keys that opens them, and establisheth him again in Innocence and well-Doing.
> 290. For Temperance brings Man again near unto his first Innocent Estate, and fits him to live again in the Garden of Pleasure, amongst the innocent Herbs and Fruits, and prepares him for the Consummation of Happiness in the Celestial Paradise.[85]

This brings us back, of course, to the Garden of Eden and *Paradise Lost.* That "temperance," meaning methodical vegetarianism, could lead man "near" to his lost innocence — that is always the dream tied to the food of regret. Tryon struggles mightily to place this attempt at a return to innocence in the context of the latest developments in humoral physiology and longevity theory. It is not, of course, without significance that he comes upon vegetarianism as a solution to the pain of life when living in a society where meat eating was the rule rather than the exception, where penitential fasting was relatively rare, and where dissenting opinion over God, worship, and the conduct of life had by then become a decades-long tradition. In Western society, vegetarianism can be a solution only where vegetarianism is not already a problem, and the enthusiastic reinvention of the rules of eating such as Tryon articulated can only come, perhaps, where a spirit of innovation is encouraged. For Tryon, the spirit of innovation came on two fronts: the sectarian religion that burst onto the scene during the 1640s — a sectarianism that had even by 1648 found expression in such "heresies" as the avoidance of blood — and the scientific revolution of which people like Cornaro and Bacon were harbingers, which by Tryon's time was in full swing. But like Tryon's nostalgia for the age of innocence before the Fall, most of what could be said of Tryon in relation to recent trends in religious, scientific, and social thought could also be said of many other writers. Yet Milton provides us with a rather different picture.

VII

It is a picture placed in a mythopoeic context, a rewriting of the story of the Creation, and a picture that is more apt to leave us with questions than to provide us with answers. *Paradise Lost* is not a how-to book. We do get apparently straightforward advice from an angel, to be sure, when, after the Fall, Michael explains to Adam what human life will henceforth be like. Adam wants to know if there is no way to experience death beside the "painful passages" Michael has just described as the lot of most men, who die in a condition of "loathsome sickness." In a passage previously cited in part, Michael says that there is another way of dying,

> if thou well observe
> The rule of not too much, by temperance taught
> In what thou eat'st and drink'st, seeking from these
> Due nourishment, not gluttonous delight,
> Till many years over thy head return:
> So may'st thou live, till like ripe Fruit thou drop
> Into thy Mothers lap, or be with ease
> Gathered, not harshly plucked, for death mature . . .[86]

The advice, of course, is conventional. To be temperate, to eat only what one needs, not what one may allow oneself to desire, to eschew "gluttonous delight" in favor of nutrition — this we have heard again and again from early modern writers, as we have the benefits of practicing of temperance: long life. If there is anything original here, it is the irony of the image with which the poet chooses to represent longevity. By living temperately, the life of a man becomes like the life of a fruit; his lot will become among the "Fruits of Man's Disobedience" that the epic poem begins by citing; his lot will be to be gathered into death like an old plum fallen to the ground, rather than being snatched away while still vital, like that apparently "virtuous" apple that Eve had just unfortunately "plucked."

But the temperate life itself, as William Kerrigan, Michael Schoenfeldt, and Joshua Scodel have shown, was something of a struggle for writers like Milton.[87] It required militancy; to exercise it was a masculine virtue; to pursue it successfully was to pass a test worthy of a chivalric cavalier, or a knight of faith. Keeping gluttony at bay, provided one lived in circumstances where the supply and quality of one's food was not a problem, was a disciplinary act that might well require doing violence against the imagination's Bower of Bliss, or the temptations of the Comus within. In Milton's Paradise, however, the primitivist diet is easy and easily seductive, and the reader is inevitably left with something of a mixed message. On the one hand, along with Adam and Eve, the reader is duly chastised and forewarned. Do not give in to the greedy appetite. The greediness you experience, calling you to gluttonous delight, is itself an expression of the curse of the Fall. And if you give into it, you will not only sin; you will also do yourself harm. But on the other hand, the reader is duly delighted by the Paradise lost. Primitivism is attractive, and in *Paradise Lost* Milton concocts one of the most attractive primitivisms of all — a way of life followed before the corruptions of civilization that is not only to be regretted but desired. The poem affirms us in our *wish* for the food of a golden age; indeed, it arouses the wish in us and articulates its content. Is there not a utopian dimension to Milton's Paradise, then, a call to culinary and other sorts of corporeal redemption, as well as a recrimination in the face of the universal curse of original sin?

So many readers have thought, and it is not simply dismissive of their responses to point out the many ironies and difficulties implied in them. As Adam and Eve make love in Milton's Paradise — and make love in a way befitting both the conditions of irretrievable bliss and such a plausible scenario as to inspire the poet, looking toward present-day life as well as toward the irretrievable past, to exclaim to one and all: "Hail wedded love!" — so they also eat, and eat well, and discover that in eating well they are participating in the benign and holy order of the universe. They are vegetarians, of course, even fruitarians; but there is no loss in that. With "wholesome thirst and appetite," they fall to "nectarine fruits" whose "savory pulp they chew."[88] The fine repasts they partake of are even good enough for an angel, Archangel Raphael. And the angel himself, visiting them for a lunch that Eve labors playfully to prepare, confesses something all but original to Milton and what critics call his "monism," his philosophical insistence on the identity of matter and spirit: the universe itself — alive and material as well as eternal and spiritual — operates like a gigantic digestive organ. It is a sign of universal vitality that matter and spirit together are constantly feeding themselves, assimilating, and otherwise digesting other matter and spirit. "For know," says the archangel Raphael,

> whatever was created, needs
> To be sustained and fed; of Elements
> The grosser feeds the purer, Earth the Sea,
> Earth and Sea feed Air, the Air those Fires
> Ethereal, and as lowest first the Moon . . .

Eating is an expression of universal interdependence: everything depends on everything else, needs everything else, feeds on and processes everything else, up and down the scale of the great chain of being. In Raphael's universe, only God, the Uncreated, doesn't need to eat, and God Himself is thus the great Feeder. That feeding and digesting also require both refinement and excretion, the improvement of assimilated material and the rejection of the unimprovable, goes to show that this cosmos is not also democratic: it is hierarchical, marked by an infinity of gradations of high and low, the "grosser" and the "purer," nutrition and dross. But the archangel nevertheless paints a picture where digestion moves only in the direction of sublimation, of matter ascending ever higher toward rarity, purity, perfection; the human world above the animal world in this, the angelic world above the human, but all alike reaching — and digesting itself — toward God. He holds before Adam and Eve the possibility that their own corporeality, and hence their own digestive reality, may eventually sublimate toward the condition the good angels enjoy:

> time may come when men
> With Angels may participate, and find
> No inconvenient Diet, nor too light fare:
> And from these corporal nutriments perhaps
> Your bodies may at last turn all to Spirit,
> Improv'd by tract of time, and wing'd ascend
> Ethereal, as we, or may at choice
> Here or in Heav'nly Paradises dwell . . . [89]

Meanwhile, "Here," in the earthly Paradise, Adam and Eve live well indeed. The dinner we see Eve prepare for the angel is all about "delicacy." "Fruit of all kinds" she gathers, which she "heaps with unsparing hand." She makes must from grapes and a non-alcoholic mead from berries and "dulcet creams" "from sweet kernels pressed" to drink; the fruits and nuts she serves are not only delectable in themselves, but served, gourmet fashion (in words recalling the discourse of Montaigne's interlocutor, the Italian steward), in an order calculated to maximize pleasure, "so contriv'd as not to mix / Tastes, not well join'd, inelegant, but bring / Taste after taste upheld with kindliest change."[90]

Back to square one. Look again, as we did in chapter 1, at *Hamlet* and Hamlet's tragic vision of eating, and consider in that context how idealistic the angelic-paradisial vision of eating, unique to Milton, really is. Raphael's refining universe represents what amounts to a perfect contrast with the cannibal universe against which Hamlet so pointedly complained. And Eve and Adam's dinner with Raphael likewise represents a perfect contrast with that mundane, ceremonial feast as those at which Gertrude and Claudius are said to have dined over the leftover corpse of Hamlet's father. Not a morbid, disgusting, anthropophagic descent from royalty to worms and dust, but an ascent from vegetable and animal nature to participation in the divine is what eating represents in Raphael's cosmos. And not a cold and "thrift"-driven legitimation of incest, where the meats are both dead and corrupt, but a "kindly" fruitarian feast, elaborated for the sake of upholding "taste after taste," is what dinner at noon in Paradise presents us with. The Shakespearean tragedy requires us to descend to the ugliest consequences of humanity's contemptible corporeal, feeding-dependent condition since the Fall. Milton's epic invites us to ascend to glimpse the absolute alternative — eating and drinking as sublime communion with the cosmos.[91]

It is not only Shakespearean tragedy, however, that provides so stark a contrast with Milton's gustatory sublimity. Milton's own epic provides one too. When he explains this sublimity, the Archangel Raphael conveniently neglects to explain the other side of God's universe, where fallen angels dwell below an excremental Chaos, in the noxious, sulphurous pits of Hell.[92] Only when he recounts the War in Heaven between the apostate angels and the forces of God, and then later the Creation of the world out of the nothingness of Chaos, does he stumble upon the need to speak of this other part of existence. "Deep under ground, materials dark and crude, / Of spiritous fiery spume," provide the nutrients of natural growth in heaven, according to Satan; and when Satan invents a heavenly gunpowder, with which to attack the forces of the good angels, he has his workmen take "sulphurous and nitrous foam" out of the "celestial soil"; this is then "concocted and adusted" till it is "reduced / To blackest grain . . ." When the satanic cannons are discharged against the heavenly host, it is said that "those deep-throated engines belched, whose roar / Embowelled with outrageous noise the air, / And all her entrails tore, disgorging foul / Their devilish glut . . ." So there are matters and processes in the cosmos that cannot be assimilated into the general sublimation that Raphael extols. Even the Creation of the world requires the engagement of other processes. In the beginning, when the "Spirit of God" infuses "vital virtue" and "vital warmth" onto the dark and watery abyss, "downward purges / The black tartareous cold infernal dregs / Adverse to life." What is noteworthy is not only the existence of dark matters, which are apparently necessary to the created cosmos, but the corruptive digestion, the excretions and purgings of which they are a part— the concocting and adusting, the belching and emboweling and disgorging, the downward purging, leaving that "blackest grain," that "devilish glut," those "black tartareous cold infernal dregs." Nor should we neglect the existence of cannibalism in the Creation. Death, the offspring of incest between Satan and Sin, cannot restrain himself. He rapes his mother Sin, who gives birth to monsters who regularly return to Sin's womb, "and howl and gnaw / My bowels, their repast," as she puts it. Indeed, "me his parent," Sin continues, the Death her son "would full soon devour / For want of other prey, but that he knows / His end with mine involved."[93]

These alternative matters, digestive processes, and cannibalisms come before the Fall of man and woman, and even before the Creation of the world, of earth and its pendant universe within the general cosmos. But there is still more to come. At the time of the Fall, as Kerrigan puts it, earth suffers a "bellyache": in Milton's words, "Earth trembled from her entrails . . . in pangs"; and other digestive processes, again altogether un-sublime, are let loose. "At that tasted banquet"—that is, Eve and Adam's consumption of the forbidden fruit—"The sun, as from Thyestean banquet, turned / His course intended," and as a result the heavens produced "Vapor, and mist, and exhalation hot, / Corrupt and pestilent." The animals, till then in harmony with one another, "to graze the herb all leaving, / Devoured each other." Adam and Eve haven't made the transition from vegetarianism to carnivorousness; as we know, the tradition reserves that last transition to the age of Noah. But it is now, observing the prospect of the pestilent vapors and the carnivorous war among the animals, that Adam exclaims his lament: "All that I eat or drink, or shall beget, / Is propagated curse."[94]

So again: on the one side, Milton paints a utopian picture, where eating and drinking are a holy, alchemical communion of creation with the divine; on the other side, Milton forces non-utopian matters and processes into the Creation, which Raphael prefers not to think about or discuss. In addition, with the coming of the Fall, Milton depicts a disturbance of the innocence of eating even among the animals of the earth. The utopian picture is in part ironic: surely, when Milton has Eve produce a gastronomic feast, Italian-style, though with paradisial ingredients, he is making a comment about modern Epicureanism and what I have called the food of wishes. That kind of eating, with "taste after taste upheld," is proper to humanity only before the Fall. After the Fall, that kind of eating entails "gluttonous delight," and it is both sinful and pathological: it expresses a greedy appetite, and it makes people sick. That it is also carnivorous rather than innocently fruitarian only adds to the picture of depravity: like Shakespeare, Milton does not want to shy away from the idea that postlapsarian eating is at bottom murderous. However, even Milton's irony depends on the attractiveness of the image of the paradisial feast. If we are to regret the passing of a paradisial culinary order and find in it an ironic comment on our own depraved condition, we must also find that order desirable. There is something in us that wants, maybe even demands, the picture of eating and drinking as innocent and holy communion. But the story of the Fall as Milton handles it is a story with realist premises: it is a story that forces on our attention a representation of what life is really like; what life is really like given what we may wish — in the mode of primitivist nostalgia and in light of what we think we know about the inherent goodness of the Creation — life to have originally been. Whether or not the Fall is fortunate — that is, whether or not the epic argues that humanity is ultimately better off in its fallen condition — the realism of the story of the Fall requires us to come to terms, pragmatically, with what we have been left with since. We live, dine, and die on the leftovers from before the Fall. Or, as Milton puts it at the very opening of the epic, we live by "the Fruit [i.e., the "yield" as well as the "edible seed-bearing product"] / Of that Forbidden Tree."[95]

VIII

The forbidden fruit — in Milton and in the Genesis tradition generally — is many things. It is at once a polysemous token, a material object, and a medium of metamorphosis. As a token, it signifies obedience and all that "obedience" entails: the *noli me tangere* (or *noli me gustare*) that exacts prohibition; the practice of obedience, the observance of the prohibition to which Adam and Eve must keep; the two separate pledges that enforce obedience, one promising a reward for continued good behavior (God's original covenant with man), the other warning of punishment, which is to say death. From one point of view the forbidden fruit could thus have been anything; it did not have to be a fruit, or if a fruit, it could have been any of them that grew in the Garden. What was important was the prohibition — a prohibition that was not to be *questioned*. The actual token used to identify it was a matter of indifference. (And so interpreters of Milton have often thought.) Yet this token of obedience was also an object; both its identity as an object of a certain kind and its materiality as a object of nature were important, at once for biblical interpretation as a whole, which placed the Garden of Eden and the meaning of humanity's relation to it in a worldly and historical context, and for the Miltonic project of "monism," of identifying matter and spirit. The forbidden fruit was an "apple" or some such thing; it was an object of desire, of a corporeal appetite; it was of a nature that was both different from human nature and of a piece of it, since it represented a (fruitarian) source of nutrition; it was an object that could readily be plucked or gathered and eaten on the spot, so that eating it required a palpable act of the will. In addition, whether it was an apple or some other fruit, tasting it was metamorphic. The explanation for this metamorphosis was various, and many commentators even believed that the metamorphosis did not have to explained: it occurred because God willed it, for no other reason and by no other mechanical means than God's will. But the metamorphosis is there. It had a meaning, and it may well have had a means. The forbidden fruit could have had magical or scientifically efficacious properties — ordained by God, but efficacious all the same. And its properties would then have signified something. Frequently, the meaning had something to do with sensuality. A material bridge between the pre- and postlapsarian condition, a tool of both temptation and corruption, an object of nutrition the ingestion of which transformed both the body and the mind, not to mention the bodies and minds of generations to come, this token of obedience was also — given the nature of bodies and minds and innocence and guilt and temptation and corruption — a causative agent, growing in the midst of paradisial splendor. It was one hell of an apple.

I have elsewhere discussed the identity and nature of this fruit in some detail.[96] Here are some of the results, which I want to explore in terms of the theme of this chapter, the food of regrets. What matters here is where this apple brings us — brings us in view of the moral meaning of food in the early modern period, and in view of the guilty conscience that educated early moderns evidently brought to the table. If the food of wishes spoke to dreams of arousal, satiation, and justice in a world of insecure supplies, unequal distribution, and thwarted desires, the food of regrets, by contrast, spoke to the fear and discontent of an otherwise satisfactory gastronomy. Excess was feared, and the means of satisfying successfully satisfied needs provoked discontent. Perhaps there was a better way — the Horatian *vita parva,* or Senecan self-denial, or saintly anorexia, or mystical vegetarianism, or a sober diet of constant measure. But these were ways of repression, strenuous vigilance, or at best compensatory supplementation. However gratifying the results, they meant that a better way—an easier way, where no repression, vigilance, or supplement was required, and one could simply follow nature by doing what one pleased—had long since been lost to us. The Golden Age and the Garden of Eden alike signified both the perfection of the past and the insufficiency of the present. Our "nature" was corrupt; "following nature" therefore required unnatural effort. As we have seen, the story of the Golden Age failed to provide a causal connection between the ideal past and the depravity of the present. But the story of the Garden of Eden did. And it placed it, as Milton understood, both within the wills of God, Satan, and humanity and within a symbolic sport of nature, through which one thing became another. Moreover, this sport of nature, as Milton perhaps also knew, was as much a part of the human as the vegetable world. For to identify it, to represent it, was very likely to call attention to a product of horticulture, of human historical intervention, even if the object was in principle an invention of God alone.

So what results? In *Paradise Lost,* actually, two things. A long tradition of speculation, going back to rabbinic commentators, naturally enough imagined the fruit as a product of Middle Eastern provenance—figs or apricots or grapes, even wheat. All the Hebrew Bible says is that the forbidden fruit was a fruit—*tappuach;* so if it were a fruit with a specific identity, it was to be supposed that it was something native to the region where the Bible was first recorded, Palestine, or, similarly, to the area where the actual Garden of Eden had been located, most probably (given indications in the Bible that were difficult to interpret literally but that had literal associations all the same) in Persia. Coming into the Middle Ages, however, particularly in the northern reaches of Christendom, the forbidden fruit also begins to be imagined as an apple or a pear. These were the fruits, after all, that northerners were best familiar with, and they were encouraged by the Vulgate translation of the Bible (ca. 400 A.D.), which rendered *tappuach* as *malum.* A *malum* in Latin was any of three things: either it was any fleshy tree-born fruit, and thus close in meaning to *tappuach;* or it was the genus of a variety of fleshy tree-born fruits, including the *Pyrus malus* or *pomum* (the "apple" in the usual modern sense of the word, growing from the rosaceous tree), the *malum Punicum*—the "apple of Punic," or pomegranate—and the *malum Persicum,* that is, the "Persian apple," or peach; or, finally, the *malum* was simply the apple in our sense, the *Pyrus malus.* Jerome, the author of the authoritative Vulgate translation of the Bible, was writing at a time when the apple in our sense was being grown throughout the Roman Empire; but he perhaps chose *malum* because of an inherent the pun on *mălum* (with a short "a"), meaning "evil." In any case, by the time that Milton wrote *Paradise Lost,* writers and visual artists had been in-

Figure 5.2. Defendente Ferrari, *Eve Tempted by the Serpent* (1520–25). A solitary Eve expressing a solitary sensuality, plucking a fruit that resembles both an apple and an apricot. Reproduced by permission of the University of Michigan Museum of Art (Museum Purchase 1967/1.38).

terpreting the forbidden fruit in any of a number of ways, canny artists like Van Eyck, Tintoretto, Michelangelo, and Dürer in particular choosing to identify the fruit in ways that suggested not only botanical reality but richly various symbolic meanings.[97] And so it goes in Milton, though with a surprise in store. In *Paradise Lost* it turns out that the forbidden fruit has a double nature, and thus a double history. This doubleness is unique to Milton, so far as I know, and until recently it has escaped the attention of Milton scholars. The double nature of the forbidden fruit is Milton's private joke. But it is nevertheless indicative of Milton's reading of the nature of food and the significance of the culinary nostalgia and regret that early modern culture imposed upon people of means. For much of the epic, the forbidden fruit appears to be an apple, both in the generic sense of a "fleshy fruit" and in the familiar sense of a *Pyrus malus.* But eventually, and surprisingly, it turns out to be a peach, a *malum Persicum,* a "Persian apple," in connotation altogether a different sort of fruit.

As an "apple," this tree-born fruit is both generic and particular—for in early modern English, "apple" had both the same general meaning as *malum* and the specific meaning of *Pyrus malus.* When Milton's Satan tells the other fallen angels that he has seduced Adam "by fraud" and "the more to increase / Your wonder, with an Apple,"[98] he may be using the word in either of the two senses. What is crucial is that an apple in either sense is inherently trivial, even innocent. An "apple" either generically or particularly, is, in the scheme of nature and in the scheme even of culinary delights, not much upon which to throw away eternal life. Or so Satan here suggests.[99] But in terms of the drama of the Fall, the particular meaning of "apple" is often more important. Satan in the guise of the serpent begins to seduce Eve by telling her about "a goodly Tree . . . / Laden with fruit of fairest colors mixed, / Ruddy and gold," blowing a "savory odor . . . / Grateful to appetite . . ."[100] This is almost certainly an apple in the usual sense of the word, although neither Eve nor Adam calls it so. (They only call it "the Fruit.") If we keep in mind the tendency among northern European artists and writers when representing the forbidden fruit, as well as the fate in general of the "food of regret" in seventeenth-century England, we can only be confirmed in this suspicion. For what it is worth, the illustrator to the 1688 edition of *Paradise Lost* (coming out only a few years after Milton's death) makes the Tree of the Knowledge of Good and Evil a typical northern apple tree—though it grows in a southern garden among date palms and grape vines (see fig. 5.3). Meanwhile, English scientists were increasingly recommending the value of fruits to the diet and especially, indeed, the apple, England's "national fruit," so "good and healthful to the body, as well as pleasant to the taste," as Ralph Austen puts it, so "advantageous for health and long life," and, by the same token, for keeping the "spirits in a fine, pleasant, equal temper; yea some fruits have higher virtues ascribed to them then barely to nourish, some Apples are accounted Cordials. . . ."[101] Eve herself is attracted by the typical sensual qualities of this "ruddy and gold" fruit. "Fixed on the Fruit she gazed," the poem says, "which to behold / Might tempt alone." Indeed, as she stood before the Tree of the Knowledge of Good and Evil, with the serpent urging her on, "the hour of Noon drew on, and waked / An eager

Figure 5.3. Vignettes from the story of the Fall, illustration to John Milton, *Paradise Lost,* book 9 (1688). Although an earlier view of the Garden of Eden shows palm trees, here the Garden is decidedly northern, and the tree Eve plucks the fruit from is certainly an apple tree. Reproduced by permission of the British Library (1486.m3).

appetite, raised by the smell / So savory of that Fruit, which with desire, / Inclinable now grown to touch or taste, / Solicited her longing eye . . ." And again, as readers of Milton's time, we should have no suspicion but that what Eve is looking at, smelling, and desiring is a *Pyrus malus,* red and gold in color, sweet to look at and sweet to smell, innocently soliciting desire. Even the alleged "cordial" powers of the apple correspond to what we and Eve think of the forbidden fruit. For Eve has been beguiled by the serpent to believe that this appetite-soliciting apple is also "intellectual food"—it will make her wise, feeding "both body and mind"; and as we soon find out, among the first effects of ingesting the apple is a state of intoxication, making her "heightened as with wine, jocund and boon."[102] The sober, pro-vegetarian John Evelyn, in an appendix to the first book printed at the command of the Royal Society, similarly extols the "rare effects" of hard apple cider, the "most eminent" of all beverages, he says, "soberly to exhilarate the Spirits of us Hypochondriacal Islanders, and by a specific quality to chase away that unsociable Spleen."[103]

But once Eve has eaten the fruit and experienced her intoxication—wherewith she deludes herself into thinking that she has acquired godlike wisdom— the fruit itself seems to undergo a change. For the first time, looking at it from Eve's point of view, we encounter the noun "nectar," as well as the adjective "ambrosial" accompanied by "downy." Eve does "reverence" to the tree—an act of idolatry, among other things:

> as to the power
> That dwelt within, whose presence had infused
> Into the plant sciential sap, derived
> From nectar, drink of gods.

And as she brings a sample of it to Adam for him to taste, we are told that she has "in her hand / A bough of fairest fruit that downy smiled, / New gathered, and ambrosial smell diffused." The juice of an apple is never a "nectar," and the smell is never "ambrosial." Those are words, indeed, that mythology applies to the food and drink of the gods; and they are also words generally applied, in Milton's as in many other times, to the peach, the apple of Persia. And it is of course the peach (along with, to be sure, the apricot, although the apricot, unlike the peach, has little smell and is not usually considered "ambrosial") that is "downy" on the outside. Either the nature of the fruit has changed since Eve first ate and "Nature from her seat / Sighing through all her works gave signs of woe / That all was lost"; or else qualities of the fruit not previously perceived and hence not previously interpreted have now become obvious and demand recognition. And either

Milton is having a little joke at our expense, fooling us into thinking it is one thing while actually showing it to be another, or making a comment on the genuine duality of the forbidden fruit. Or else, most likely, Milton is doing a bit of both.[104]

Perspective, even a preternaturally postmodernist perspective avant la lettre, is what matters first of all, although an archaic historicism — Milton's — determines things as well.[105] Now, given the limits of the historical and geographical understanding that condition the poetics of the epic — now it's an apple. Now it is simply a "Fruit," or "that Fruit of this tree." Now it's a peach, depending on who is looking at it and how. Or it is a matter of which side of the Fall one is looking at it from, not only because being on one side or another of the Fall makes a difference, but because the Fall itself, in Milton's own account, causes a disturbance in the nature of the universe that humanity inhabits, making the sun tilt away from the earth (as from "Thyestean feast" — that is, a cannibal feast), creating bad weather, making the animals turn on one another, and, above all, making this universe — at least beneath the level of the moon, the sun, and the stars — into a temporal phenomenon, a world that knows death and that itself is bound to die. The apple is a peach — falsely thought to be ambrosial in the sense of "godlike." Or again, the fruit of the fruit — the yield of God's token of obedience and humanity's refusal to respect it — is . . . a peach. And one hell of a peach: for it is not only a fruit with somewhat more suspect connotations than the apple (neither England's "national fruit" nor an item to which connotations of simplicity and innocence were regularly attached, the peach was sometimes thought unhealthy and traditionally thought to be best when eaten with wine or when preserved in wine); and it is not only a fruit that in fact spoils far more quickly than the apple, so that it has a more intimate connection with natural corruption than the apple; and it is not only, alas, a fruit that when perfectly ripe is sweeter, more savory, and more succulent than the apple. This particular fruit of the tree of which we may not eat makes Adam and Eve drunk, "heightened as if with new wine." It immediately deranges Eve's appetite, her imagination, her will, and her self-possession as an eating, thinking, self-regulating being:

> For Eve
> Intent now wholly on her taste, naught else
> Regarded, such delight till then, as seemed,
> In Fruit she never tasted, whether true
> Or fancied so through expectation high
> Of Knowledge, nor was the God-head from her thought.
> Greedily she engorged without restraint . . .[106]

God has not only placed in the Garden a convenient symbol of the pledge; he has put in it a physically potent conductor of depravation. The modest Eve is suddenly a greedy glutton. She is not even the paradisial gourmet anymore, upholding "taste after taste . . .with kindliest change." No, for the moment she's on a binge: the doctors called this either bulimia, the "ravening appetite," or *pica malicia,* the "evil appetite." And all thanks to the *taste* of this object.

As I put it in my earlier article, the rest is history. History begins at this point for Milton and for the Genesis tradition generally. Milton's epic frequently emphasizes that Eve and Adam were "free" to fall or not to fall — which means that they were free to resist temptation and free to reject sin and death, given their endowment with reason. Milton criticism frequently emphasizes that Eve's plucking and eating follows upon a corruption of her understanding or imagination. And no doubt such a corruption of the mind is Satan's first accomplishment as he tempts Eve into plucking and eating. But Eve's engagement with the apple-fruit-peach on the level of sensuality and hunger precedes her actual decision to eat and her descent into depravity. The object "solicits" and the taste of it depraves, intoxicates the body and mind alike, sending Eve on a binge of grandiose self-delusion and ravenous consumption. In the context of the food of regret — the food we can no longer live by, although we ought to live by it still — here is one thing that the forbidden fruit means. However much we may idealize an innocent food and a suitably innocent appetite for consumption, however important this innocent food and appetite may be for understanding who we are and who we ought to be, food is a trigger. Food is intoxicating. Unless the gods or God keeps watch over us and day and night (and what kind of life is that, Eve once asks "thus to dwell / In narrow circuit"), eventually the trigger will be pulled. And all our eating, whatever "delight" it yields us, however much it takes us beyond the merest requirements of nature toward other, higher, more ravishing states, and regardless of how much we come to regret it — all our eating will be "propagated curse."

Chapter Six

BELCH'S HICCUP

I

TREMBLING ENTRAILS, disgorging cannons, the sulphurous belching of fallen angels and their fallen technologies and agents, all "propagated curse"— that is, the tragic, Christian, Miltonic version, which seems somewhat disappointingly compensated by the prospect of observing "the rule of not too much" and living till one drops like an overripe fruit. But there is another version, neither utopian nor tragic, but laughing at it all, considerations of which lead not to the Passion and the sins from which it should deliver us, but to the civilities and indiscretions of the secular self. And so we head from the dangerous and sulphurous pit of Chaos, throwing about the dregs of the universe, to . . . well, to Belch's hiccup, which has nothing to do with Sin and Death, nothing to do with the food of wishes, and nothing to do with cookbooks or medical texts or even baked meat and beef. Instead, it has something to do with herring, pickled herring, and thus with the geographical and historical placement of all of those things — Chaos, wishes, regrets, cookery, medicine, pies, and beef — in the context, surprisingly enough, of "progress" and "civilization." Or perhaps, by this point, not so surprisingly. For the civilities of civil society in the early modern period were understood in relation to the appetite, that bouncing belly of an instinct. Managing the appetite — not suppressing it, but guiding it along, using it wisely, but not overscrupulously either — was as fundamental to the conduct of civil society as putting food on the table, or for that matter managing its cousin, sexual desire.

The interjection appears in the fifth scene of the first act of *Twelfth Night,* somewhat after we have heard Sir Andrew Aguecheek stake his claim to being a great eater of beef, at a time when the main plot of the play — the marriage plot — is about to undergo a surprising but necessary complication. A "gentleman" is at the gate, we are told. The gentleman, in fact, is not a gentleman at all; it is the heroine Viola, dressed as a man, calling herself Cesario, and acting as messenger and suitor on behalf of Orsino, Count of Illyria. As this gentleman who is not a gentleman arrives on the scene, the story undergoes a classic reversal that eventually resolves the romantic intrigues of the play. "What is he at the gate, cousin?" Olivia asks her uncle, who, as another character has just told us, has been drinking this morning and is already "half drunk." "A gentleman," Sir Toby replies. "A gentleman? What gentleman?" "'Tis a gentleman here," Toby says. Period. And then: "A plague o' these pickled herring!"

What's that? A stage tradition at least as old as the first eighteenth-century editions of Shakespeare has it that Sir Toby makes some kind of noise of indigestion here. Nicholas Rowe and Alexander Pope suggest the placement of a period after the word "gentleman," so that the word "here" refers not to the gentleman but to something else, which Belch has difficulty naming. Rowe and Pope have Toby say, "'Tis a gentleman. Here — . . ." And then Toby apparently belches. An editor later in the century is bothered by the use of the word "here" in the text, spelled "heere," and presents a more elaborate set of stage directions, which continues to be used today. "This word, 'heere,'" he writes, "appears to be a corruption of some interjectory particle that directed a drunken *hiccuping;* followed, perhaps, by something for which the herrings are blamed."[1] In other words, first Toby hiccups out of drunkenness. And then he farts, blaming the herring he has eaten for his flatulence. Or perhaps he belches. In any case, he does what the eighteenth-century editor can only bring himself to call "something."

He is also doing something else. To put it in familiar structuralist terms, in interrupting the action with cries of indigestion, Sir Toby deflects the high, romantic comedy of the play with a lower order of comedy where not the lofty emotions of love and erotic interest but the base demands of the Rabelaisian "grotesque" body (Bakhtin) are given a chance, as it were, to speak. Toby is drunk. He hiccups or belches or some such thing. Perhaps he farts. And all this just at the moment when the crucial yet ambiguous question of "what is at the door" is being asked, and this "what" is leading the story into questions of "what" it is that Olivia ought to be expecting in her life and "what" it is that someone called a gentleman can provide her.[2] The deflection of the plot and the outburst of Toby's body, however, are not entirely unexpected. We've been waiting for more comedy from Toby; if nothing else, we've been waiting to get more laughter out of his dipsomania. Veterans of Shakespearean drama, we remember that other funny dipso, Sir John Falstaff, who claimed to have been representative of "all the world" and had a fondness for anchovies, herring's diminutive Mediterranean relative. And in the context of *Twelfth Night,* we've been led to understand that one of the problems of Olivia's household, in addition to her being a single woman bereaved of her father and brother and unwillingly pursued by the powerful count,[3] pertains precisely to the activities of eating and drinking and the revelries of the body in general. "What a plague means my niece to take the death of her brother thus?" Toby has earlier complained. "I am sure care's an enemy to life." And what is life? Well, it consists of the "four elements," Toby later states, as we have seen; and especially, as Sir Andrew Aguecheek adds, "it consists of eating and drinking." So that, as Sir Toby concludes, since life consists of eating and drinking, "let us therefore eat and drink."[4] Belching, hiccuping, and farting— however grotesque, offensive, or comic they may be — are corollaries to this "life" of eating and drinking that Sir Toby is committed to champion, and can only be threatened by that overweening "care" to which the excessively mourning Olivia seems to be devoted.

What kind of corollaries they are, however, and what kinds of interruptions they signify in the course of life and the cravings of romantic comedy are questions that warrant further scrutiny. Up to now the critical and editorial response to Sir Toby's noises, in fact, has been uncertain, indicating both its uneasiness with the subject matter and a will not to be uneasy; some more recent critics seem determined to positively embrace it. If the eighteenth-century editor has Sir Toby erupt in a "drunken *hiccuping;* followed, perhaps, by something for which the herrings are blamed," modern editors are more apt to follow A. L. Rowse, who drops the suggestion of farting, adopts a more sympathetic attitude toward Sir Toby, and ends up glossing the moment, somewhat gleefully, as "Sir Toby is blaming pickled herring for his drunken hiccoughing."[5] This, if I recall correctly, was my own response to the scene, long ago when I was reading the play for the first time, using the New Cambridge Shakespeare edition of 1971, where the editors also say nothing about a belch or a fart but have Sir Toby hiccup.[6] I thought the remark very funny, and I thought it entailed a wink by Shakespeare to me and the rest of his readers and auditors in support of the mischievous pleasures of drunkenness. Indeed, it was more than a wink. For readers like me, the noise of Sir Toby's indigestion was something of a heroic gesture, a gob of air and noise no less defiant of the niceties of courteously restrained, which is to say repressed, behavior than Sir Toby's challenge later on against the quasi-Puritan Malvolio, asserting the continued demand against the imperatives of virtue for indulgence in "cakes and ale." To the extent that one may find in *Twelfth Night* a celebration of festivity and revelry, and one may associate such carnivalesque activity with political opposition and social liberation, Sir Toby's indigestion may be interpreted as a classic gesture of rebellion—classic precisely in its going beyond speech, in its articulation—through a textual pause, through a hiccup or a belch or a fart—of a domain of bodily demands that can never be entirely arrested by the restraints of decorum and the intentional structures of language. That Sir Toby would then resort to subterfuge in order to excuse or dismiss this interruption of decorum and speech, blaming the pickled herring for something a quantity of alcohol has actually brought to pass, only illustrates the gap between systems of repression, on the one hand, and the insistence of the body, on the other. The body will speak, even if the mind will not acknowledge it, and even if the language the body has to speak is a language beyond words, a language that language itself can only jokingly dissimulate, dismiss, or curse: "A plague o' these pickled herring."

Or so it would seem. Behind the response of readers such as myself—and my response was somewhat typical of the critical literature on *Twelfth Night* after the Second World War—lies a whole system of psychology, physiology, gesture, and ethics, a whole morality of the body, which we cannot really apply to a product of the Elizabethan stage. I myself first realized this a few years ago, when, sitting at a crowded bar and distracted, I momentarily reflected on the text of *Twelfth Night*. Nobody in the bar, it occurred to me, was hiccuping; few ever do. "Drunken hiccoughing," when you think about it, is far more common on the stage and in the movies than in real life. Hiccuping is a conventional comic sign for drunken dissolution (going back, as we can see, at least to the early eighteenth century), but it is a rare real-life occurrence. And it seems unlikely that hiccuping was associated with drunkenness in the Tudor period. Medical writers of the early modern period seldom mention hiccups and never (to my knowledge) associate hiccuping with drinking, although they are often concerned with the "vapors," "fumosities," and "wind" generated by food. And for myself, one day after my epiphany at the bar, I made another discovery. I was living in a town where it was difficult to get fresh seafood, which for many years has been a staple of my diet. So I turned to preserved fish—not frozen fresh, which I don't usually enjoy, but things like gefilte fish in a jar and, yes, pickled herring, always a favorite. I was surprised to find that one day, having eaten a bit too much of the herring and brine, I was suffering from heartburn accompanied by a case of the hiccups.

II

In a world where the "eager" droppings of a poison can "posset and curd" a body unto death, and beef can make one stupid, what would a hiccup or other gastric interjection do? The answer is not self-evident. Between us and the hiccup, a language intervenes, a stage language that mediates our response to it. This language not only tells us what we have seen or heard or read about in our footnotes; it fills up a textual gap and a lapse in time; it provokes laughter; it provides a context in which that laughter is both comprehensible and sanctioned. We know *why* we are laughing even *while* we are laughing, and we know that our laughter — though it touches upon something that may otherwise be considered rude, embarrassing, or disturbing — is in this case sanctioned. It is *okay* to laugh (at this). And *okay,* I am laughing. (It would be rather different if when the actress playing Juliet rose from her deathlike sleep in the tomb, she should immediately let out a belch.) And yet we know all this, and do all this, merely on the basis of a stage convention, a familiar convention to which we remain the heirs.

Between the playgoer and the hiccup not only a language but an ideology intervenes; let us call it an ideology of laughter. As ideologies go, this one is perhaps not so pernicious. It enables what may be a socially valuable act. What in real life, in polite society, is not to be noted is here, in the context of the theater and comedy, allowed to be a raucous occasion of laughter. This is doubly valuable: it allows for the momentary release of otherwise repressed or shameful feelings about bodily functions, and it confirms the validity of the repression and shame in other situations. (I can be ashamed at the dinner table because I can laugh in the theater.) However, the ideology thus also serves, as is the way with ideologies, to mask the truth of the matter. We do not *see* the nature of our anxieties about bodily functions and the role they play in the social order — we only laugh at them; and today we do not even quite see what is going on in *Twelfth Night,* since although the continuity of the stage convention and its ideology puts us in a position to enjoy the humor, that continuity disguises major differences between what was seen, felt, and thought in the Shakespearean theater at the turn of the seventeenth century and what we may see, feel, and think today. (Of course, I include my self in this "we," and especially my younger self, when drinking was rebellion and what I took to be a sign of drinking — the drunken hiccup — was also a gesture of happy defiance against the moral order.)

But something more is at stake than a hiccup, a belch, a fart, a plaguey encounter with pickled herring, or the conditions of gusty laugher. Civilization hangs in the balance.[7] "Civility," a word originally designating the condition of citizenship — related to the word "city" and hence to the classical notion of participatory membership in the city-state — comes by the 1530s (in English) to denote the condition of good behavior or refined conduct appropriate to the citizen of a nation or the subject of a kingdom. The word "civilization" comes later; but already "civility" is associated with the framework of what we have come to call civilization, and if the civility of the good citizen can refer to such things as respect for the law, literacy, amiability, and cooperativeness, it can also refer to the management of bodily functions. The rule of good manners that Belch's eruption violates, and emphasizes by negation, is a rule of "civility," really; it is intimately connected with the other rules of civility, like respect for the law, and for a deep-thinking playwright like Shakespeare no less than a historical sociologist like Norbert Elias, it provides a key to conditions, good and bad, of social life as a whole.

The idea, originating with Elias, is that "civility" in the modern sense arose out of an earlier code of conduct, centered not on notions of "civil society" but on the court and courtly behavior. Out of one code of sociality, dominated by the notion of "courtesy," eventually arose a different code of sociality dominated by the notion of "civility." The first was centered on the medieval court — "courtesy" or "courtoisie" being a cognate of "court," and basically designated "court-like" behavior, which is to say behavior suitable to the ideals of life at court: behavior ruled by such qualities as deference to rank, liberality, obedience, service. The other was centered on modern "civil" society, related in part to the new urbanity of urban life and in part to the new nationalism of national life, and so governed by such qualities as respect, diffidence, cooperativeness, open-mindedness. Civil society emerged out of courtly society, triumphing in the eighteenth century: civility replaced courtesy; the city replaced the court; the nation-state replaced the kingdom; European "civilization" replaced Latin "Christendom." And the crucial period of transition is the sixteenth and seventeenth centuries. In fact, though the founding texts of this transitional stage are usually located in sixteenth-century humanism — above all, in Erasmus — the most interesting registration of the transition, and the conflicts and ambiguities attendant upon it, may well have been the English stage in the time of Shakespeare. For it was on the English stage, more than anywhere else, that Europeans allowed themselves the license to represent in detail the facts and values of everyday life.

Not to hiccup, belch, or fart in the company of others, not to eat too much or drink too much in the company of others, and not to do any of a number of other things that sixteenth- and seventeenth-century authorities thought reproachable with regard to eating and drinking, like dipping one's fingers or bread in the sauceboat — such prohibitions were part of a developing fabric of civility through which a new kind of sociopolitical entity, "civilization," emerged. Which is . . . what? The concept is notoriously complex and elusive. The new civility, writes Anna Bryson, had to do with "the demand for adaptability, the avoidance of offence, and the accommodation of the self to the needs of others."[8] These were operations that could be practiced on the tennis court or in a business meeting as well as at the table: one adapted to the situation (rather than demanding conformity to precedent); one avoided giving offense (rather than letting it all hang out or advertising one's rank); and one accommodated oneself to the needs of others. This was "polite" behavior, although the general guidelines for it also had to correspond to changes in fashion; and what it meant to fail to adapt, to give offense, or to disrespect the needs of others was subject to considerable variation. The most famous of these changes in fashion as courtly society gave way to polite society was the adoption of the fork — a thing almost unknown outside of Italy until the early seventeenth century, considered strange and affected and therefore rude when some people of the north first started using it (to the end of his days, Louis XIV continued to eat with his hands) and a requirement of all polite tables north and south by the early eighteenth century.[9] The particulars of civil behavior — to use or not to use a fork, or for that matter to fart or not to fart — could be just as important as the general principles Bryson describes: adaptation, fastidiousness, and accommodation. For these particulars add up to the "memory of the body."[10] And civility in this sense, written on the body, adds up to a much larger framework, whose significance can scarcely be understated. According to Elias, a "wide variety of facts" can be referred to by way of the concept of what we now call civilization, from technology and manners to scientific knowledge, religious ideas, home construction, and food preparation. "Strictly speaking, there is almost nothing which cannot be done in a 'civilized' or an 'uncivilized' way." So in a sense "civilization" refers to a universal principle. However, the concept entails a highly specific application. It "expresses the self-consciousness of the West." "By this term Western society seeks to describe what constitutes its special character and what it is proud of: the nature of *its* technology, the nature of *its* manners, the development of *its* scientific knowledge or view of the world, and much more."[11]

What we have seen so far in our examination of regimens of health, recipe collections, and the literature of dietary wishes and regrets underscores this march of the "civilizing process," and so we have had occasion again to allude to the idea: civility and its disciplines, its literatures, its science, its sociality, its aspirations. As the diet became more and more the subject of discourse, and thus more and more subjected to the surveillance of the printed word and the authorities who went about circulating it, and as dietary wishes shifted from overtly infantile and desperate demands to more socially responsible or philosophically ethereal desires, eating and drinking became more and more "civilized" in Elias's sense. From our own perspective today, any picture we draw of changes in the diet, in table manners, and in food preparation from the fourteenth to the eighteenth century will confirm us in the belief that eating and drinking became more "civilized." Trenchers of bread were replaced by fine porcelain plates, communal mugs by individual glasses, outstretched hands and wingings of the elbow by delicate operations of forks, spoons, and knives. The great ceremonies of power observed in great communal dining halls were replaced with more private, quiet rituals, where the old ostentatious rules of precedence — the great whole birds and quadrupeds brought out by a procession of liveried servants and presented with officious ceremony to the lord of the manor and his guests, in order of rank, thence to be ostentatiously carved by a high-ranking *trinciante* — were replaced by a glittering meritocracy of carefully set dishes of cut-up meats and vegetables, placed before everyone equally alike. In France by the middle of the seventeenth century, it was common to refer all manner of manners to the idea of "good taste," so that even an *honnête homme* might be first of all a man whose way of life was defined by its *délicatesse* and *bon goût*.[12] To us, too, all this is more "civil"—or at least, if someone should claim that such developments are more civil, we would know what the person meant. That educated individuals became more and more preoccupied with dietary health and well-being, that recipes became more and more systematic and often more refined, that intellectuals became more and more occupied with the problem of general (dietary) welfare and more and more aware of the moral complexities of eating, given the contradictions inherent to human nature and to the place of humanity in the universe, while in the meantime manners become more codified in the direction of generally observed law of fastidiousness about bodily functions and their role in "giving offense"—all those things, too, are signs of a world that has become more "civil." Yet it is not hard to find difficulties with the model, or sources of discontent with it.

III

Consider the various meanings with which "uncivilized" behavior might be associated, or against which the idea of "civility" might be opposed, from the sixteenth to the eighteenth century:

Courtesy (or "Courtoisie," the feudal ideal)
Rusticity
Barbarity
Savagery
Bestiality
Childishness

Rudeness
Crudeness
Buffoonery
Stupidity
Ignorance
Zealotry
Bigotry
Kultur

It has become fashionable to point out that the idea of civility was a powerful ideological weapon against the "savagery" of native peoples — the fourth term of our list — over whom early modern colonialists wished to assert their hegemony. Nor is this mistaken.[13] To be civilized for many thinkers of the sixteenth and seventeenth centuries was precisely not to be "savage," which is to say primitive in a negative sense. But the idea of civility had other uses, other kinds of practices and peoples against which it was opposed. Cervantes provides a wonderful model of several of these in the person of Sancho Panza, whose surname, of course, means "belly." "So long as I have plenty to eat," says Sancho, in the same scene where Don Quixote lauds the acorns of the Golden Age, "I can eat it as well, or better, standing by myself, as seated beside an Emperor. And, to tell you the truth, even if it's only bread and onion that I eat in my corner without bothering about table manners and ceremonies, it tastes to me a great deal better than turkey at other tables, where I have to chew slowly, drink little, and wipe my mouth often, and where I can't sneeze and cough when I want to. . . ."[14] Sancho's comic preference for uninhibited incivility is an expression of crude, rustic, lower-class, childish, bellyful buffoonery: it is funny on many different levels. It is also rather unfair — a cruel redaction of lower-class life encouraged by adherents of middle- and upper-class life.

But the idea of civility came to be an ideal against which the behavior of the upper classes could be disparaged as well. Civility was pitted not only against lower-class boorishness but also against older models of courtliness, hospitality, and the homespun virtues of modesty, chastity, and deference. The "new English and French fashion" championed by cookbook writer John Murrell in 1615 is an example of this newfangled civility, as is the logic of the ironically named Lady Frugal in Massinger's comedy *The City-Madam* (1632). This haughty lady, addicted to fashion and social climbing, tells her steward that she will only hire "Frenchmen and Italian" for cooks. The reason, she says, is that French and Italian chefs "wear satin, / And dish no meat but in silver."[15] (Lady Frugal eventually gets her comeuppance, as modesty, chastity, and deference ultimately triumph over fashion, but that's another story.) Civility is *cosmopolitan;* it is fashion-conscious: *à la mode.* And civility is *fastidious;* its cosmopolitan passions — satin and silver — are signs not only of wealth and power but of a certain scrupulousness with regard to personal and social habits; civility is *elegant* in this sense. What matters is the complex of traits, knowledgeably orchestrated, that the new civility demands: cosmopolitanism, fashionableness, fastidiousness, elegance, all at once, done with what would come to be known as "taste." The word we use today to denote this complex of traits that the eighteenth century called taste is "sophistication." If civilization is opposed to a presumably lower order of social life, it is also, in its "taste" or "sophistication," opposed to an older social system, which by current lights is distasteful and unsophisticated — provincial, passé, grungy, or crude, or even for that matter overly deferential and rigid. "One may know a Man that never conversed in the World" — that is, in the "World," *le monde,* of good society — "by his excess of Good Breeding," writes the civilized Joseph Addison in 1711. Never mind the problem of the Sancho Panzas of the world. "A polite Country Squire shall make you as many Bows in half, as would serve a Courtier in a Week." The problem isn't that the rustic isn't polite enough; it is that he is too polite, in an old-fashioned way. He is too *courteous.* He lacks what in more sophisticated circles is social ease. "I have known my Friend Sir Roger's Dinner almost cold," Addison goes on,

> before the Company could adjust the Ceremonial, and be prevailed upon to sit down; and have heartily pitied my old Friend, when I have seen him forced to pick and cull his Guests, as they sat at the several Parts of his Table, that he might drink their Healths according to their respective Ranks and Qualities.[16]

Civility is different from courtesy. It is less hierarchical, ceremonial, and formulaic; if it is more subject to the winds of fashion and the whims of status, it is also more subtle and democratic.

So if civility may be a counterpart of savagery, it may also be a counterpart of both lower-class buffoonery and upper-class courtesy. Nor was this all. Ignorance, stupidity, zealotry, and bigotry — these, too, were models of uncivil behavior and were the apt targets of spokesmen of civility. And they were not necessarily related to class or status. They were traits that could be found among the high and the low, the old and new alike: one could be an ignorant merchant, a stupid feudal lord, a zealous peasant, a bigoted cleric, and so forth. Such expressions of incivility were the best and most common targets of high humanist satire. There was nothing better for a master satirist — an Erasmus, a Jonson, a Molière, even a Pope or a Swift — to make fun of than individuals guilty of such uncivil failings.

But it is worthwhile to recall what for Elias is the most important antithesis to "civilization," a set of countervailing values that in German is termed *Kultur.* If civilization, a predominantly French and English idea according to Elias, represents the social, economic, and political progress of the modern nation-state, *Kultur* represents something that is thought to be more private, immaterial, and ahistorical. It has to do more with isolated artistic and intellectual achievements than with projects of a factional, national, or imperial scope. Civilization, from the point of view of *Kultur,* is superficial, technocratic, overly honorific, and fleeting; from its own point of view, *Kultur* is deep, creative, indifferent to outward rewards, and enduring. Civilization comes and goes; *Kultur* remains. Civilization behaves well; *Kultur is* well. If civilized behavior is polite, honorable, adaptable, and sociable, *Kultur* is moral, virtuous, and committed, and may even require unsociablity. Elias thus makes a good deal of the fact that its most serious expressions first came from an intellectual class in Germany that was far more alienated from centers of power than parallel classes in England and France. This *Kultur* is perhaps a value to be found in writers in French and English as well: certainly Jonathan Swift is as much a spokesman of the one as the other, as is Jean-Jacques Rousseau. In any case, in the context of the culture of eating and drinking, it is easy to see both how diametrically opposed the two could be to one another and yet how, in mutual opposition, they could be simultaneously attractive as well. Civilization prizes the fine meal, the sociable table, the sophisticated setting, the witty conversation. *Kultur* is suspicious of all that. From the point of *Kultur,* a taste for fine food, sophisticated surroundings, good manners, and sparkling wit is superficial; such a preference is not something that really *counts.* And who would disagree?

Yet the hiccup, the belch, or the fart, at least onstage, is nevertheless *funny.* As is, no less than Sir Andrew Aguecheek's beef, Sir Toby Belch's pickled herring.

IV

The herring, in northern Europe, was in fact one of the more semiotically interesting foodstuffs of the early modern period. It was a sign, by association, at once of wealth and poverty, of gluttony and abstinence, of internationalism and local pride, of exchange value and use value, and, in Lévi-Strauss's terms, of the raw, the cooked, and the rotten. One of the two most important products of the fisheries of England, the Low Countries, and Scandinavia — the other being cod — it was eaten both fresh (in the spring and fall) and in any of several preserved forms: salted, pickled, or smoked.[17] It was one of the most common commodities for fasting days and thus became an icon of Lent and Lenten fare. In Brueghel's famous painting *The War between Carnival and Lent,* it is a pair of measly herrings that the emaciated representative of Lent holds aloft. But in a Dutch portrait of 1616, now in the Carnegie Museum of Art in Pittsburgh, Frans Hals shows a prosperous merchant proudly displaying with an upraised hand a golden-hued smoked herring as if it were a gold medallion, signifying triumph. With his other hand he is clutching a bale of hay. That would be the hay in which he shipped his smoked herring; but the sly allusion seems to be folktales like the one we know as "Rumpelstiltskin": the merchant, Pieter Corneliesz, is boasting of his ability to turn straw into gold, herring into money.

Medical writers were not fond of the fish. "Herring is a fish most common and best cheap. Yet it is not very wholesome," Thomas Cogan writes. "As it is often proved by them who through eating of fresh herring, fall into fevers. . . ."[18] Where this idea of herring causing fever originated I have not been able to determine. But an erstwhile enemy of Shakespeare's, the writer Robert Greene, was infamously said to have died of a fever brought upon by a night of eating too much pickled herring. And the idea was common. Fish itself was often suspect, as we have already had occasion to see, because it was "cold and wet," or phlegmatic — eating it perhaps could give one a "cold" (as we say in English), one of whose symptoms (in reaction against the coldness and wetness) could be a fever. And yet preserved fish, with the phlegmatic elements of the fish reduced, could be even worse. Adding salt to fish — and salted, smoked, and pickled fish all have salt added as a preservative agent — made it harder to digest, harder to assimilate, according to the doctors: bad news especially for melancholics and choleric individuals, who were already too dried out, already too salty, but bad news for anyone really. At least, as Platina puts it, fresh fish might "moisten the stomach," if the stomach needed moistening. But herring, in any case — a fish of little interest to classical and Italian authors, who were accustomed to eating anchovies and sardines instead — had a bad reputation whether fresh or preserved, even though in northern Europe it was a very common dish. Herring could make you sick, and preserved herring could make you even sicker, bringing on fevers.

In England you could nevertheless eat it both because you liked it and because you had nothing else to eat. In *Doctor Faustus,* Marlowe has herring included in those foodstuffs identified with Gluttony: "I come of a Royall Pedigree," the figure of Gluttony says; "my father was a Gammon of Bacon, and my mother was a Hogshead of Claret Wine. My godfathers were these: Pickled-Herring, and Martin Martlemas-beef. . . ."[19] Like the fresh beef eaten on the occasion of the festival of Martinmas, herring was a commodity made available in quantities, and it was in a spirit of bingeing that one could then consume it. Yet writer after writer also dismisses herring as the food of the poor. Herring is "good

Figure 6.1. Frans Hals, *Pieter Cornelisz. van der Morsch (Man with a Herring)* (1616). Reproduced by permission of the Carnegie Museum of Art, Pittsburgh. Acquired through the generosity of Mrs. Alan M. Scaife.

for them that want better meat," writes Tobias Venner.[20] Herring "may not well be spared, of poor folks, who regard not so much the wholesomeness of meats, as that they fill up their hungry bellies," says Thomas Cogan.[21] The governing idea was that if the fish were "of poor nutrition," then if you had other choices, you ate it simply out of gluttony; and if you had no other choice, you ate it out of desperate hunger. In the first case, the gluttony was underscored by the fact that those who had choices often ate herring not as a part of a regular meal but as a snack, particularly at taverns, out of a large store of the commodity, where herring served as a "shoeing horn to pull on your wine." In the second case, the association of herring with poverty was underscored both by the fact that it was indeed "most common and best cheap" and by the fact that it was served on fast-ing days, as if eating it signified penitence. We are far away here from the whole-some yet enticing herring breakfast featured by Dutch painters, but we are, after all, speaking of England, whose food semiotics operated differently, and where the official discourse already betrayed an uneasiness with the pleasures of the table that would eventually become proverbial. And in this context, as one ob-server puts it, herring could be seen at one and the same time, paradoxically, as "an unusual" and a "common meat . . . coveted as much of the Nobility for vari-ety and wantonness, as used of poor men for want of other provision."[22]

But herring—at once unusual and common, associated with taverns and drunkards, with fevers and poor digestion, with the mischievous pleasures of the rich and the grudging hunger of the poor—was also, proverbially, the "majestical king of Fishes."[23] The herring could well serve, indeed, as a sign of civility in the broad sense, and the reservations of authors of the age of Shakespeare about it could well express reservations about the progress of civility over courtesy and its other counterparts. A contrast with beef—Aguecheek's beef—may illus-trate the point. Beef was domestic. Beef was the national dish of England. Beef, English dietary writers assure us, was of "high" nutrition, at least for English stomachs. It was a food fit—even necessary—for displays of generosity and hospitality. Beef was a food suited for fat days rather than lean, for feasting rather than fasting, for displaying a generously conceived prosperity rather than, on the one side, a selfishly delightful "wantonness" or, on the other side, a meager ab-stinence, imposed either by poverty or Lenten restrictions. In other words, beef was a food that could be associated with old-fashioned courtesy. We can quote the Puritan Phillip Stubbes in this connection again, where Stubbes complains that once upon a time "a good piece of beef was thought then good meat, and able for the best, but now it is thought too gross: for their tender stomachs are not able to digest such crude and harsh meats. . . ."[24] By contrast, herring was a dish not of domesticity, nationalism, hospitality, or homespun, courteous pros-perity, but of something at once suspicious and "majestical." A lot of that has to do with trade. For herring was harvested and processed for international dis-tribution; it traveled the world; it was a magical sort of commodity, turning straw into gold. And if this magical commodity also failed to conform to classic English notions of nutrition, hospitality, and good eating, it nevertheless made England a player on the international stage and served a major role in the prosperity of the nation.

Herring, in fact, had its own poet, Thomas Nashe, who may also be consid-ered among the most energetic spokesmen of civility of his day. (It will be re-called that Nashe wrote in praise of the lighter, beef-free Italian diet—as he wrote in praise of other Italian things, apart from religion. But Nashe was also a

champion of the national literature of England.)[25] Though he doesn't often use
the word, it is to something like civility, in opposition both to barbarity and old-
fashioned courtesy, that he continually addresses himself. His peculiar prose
tract *Lenten Stuffe; or, The Praise of the Red Herring* (1599) is a satiric and allegorical
exposition of the herring industry in Yarmouth, where Nashe was holing up
while in exile from London. It is not herring, or the red herring—a smoked,
salted fish that Yarmouth was famous for—that is the target of Nashe's satire,
however.[26] This ludic text may be an exercise in mock heroics and the mock en-
comium, but in the swirl of textual play, anti-Catholic rhetoric, recriminations
against London authorities for censoring his work, and an indirect defense of
literature and free speech, Yarmouth, its fisheries, and the red herring come to
stand for the values—and the valuing—of civilization: a sly sort of civilization,
perhaps, but a civilization in Elias's sense all the same. The town of Yarmouth—
"out of an hill or heap of sand reared and enforced from the sea most miracu-
lously, and by the singular policy and uncessant inestimable expense of the inhabitants, so firmly and rampiered against the fumish waves' battery"—is a
product of collective labor and "strict civil order." "Forth of the sands thus strug-
gling as it exalteth and lifts up its glittering head," it stands in contrast to inland
towns like the county seat Norfolk, where agricultural and landed wealth rule
the day. Yarmouth is a city of industry on the edge of the nation. Yet it is out-
standing for its "plentiful purveyance of sustenance." "Double beer, beef, fish,
and biscuit," among others, it has in abundance—not by way of the fantastic,
courtly hospitality of a place like Jonson's Penshurst, however, but by way of
the market, and in exchange for the produce of its own seagoing labors.[27] It provisions itself, and it provisions its many visitors—sailors from other countries,
naval personnel—by way of buying and selling, given the ready cash its fishing
industry brings in. It is even-handed in its distribution of wealth among its citizens; though neither a democracy nor a communist polity, it is managed with
an eye to the common good. And "this common good within itself is nothing to
the common good it communicates to the whole state." A "town of defense" to
the countryside, a proving ground for shipbuilding and the training of sailors as
well as fishermen, it is above all an icon of outward-looking but nation-building
trade. "All the realm it profiteth many ways, as by the free fare of herring chiefly,
maintained by the fishermen of Yarmouth themselves, by the great plenty of
salted fish there."[28]

This herring itself, for Nashe, is both a tool and a token of what we may now
call an early capitalist, monied exchange economy. "Behold, it is every man's
money," Nashe exclaims. It freely circulates. It is readily available. It generates a
profitable exchange of goods and it is itself a good. The fact, again, that it is both
food for the poor and food for the rich constitutes part of its value: "Every house-

holder . . . that keeps a family in pay, casts for it as one of his standing provisions. The poorer sort make it three parts of their sustenance; with it, for his denier, the patchedest leather *pilche labaratho* [leather-coated laborer] may dine like a Spanish duke." If this tool of exchange and token of consumption is also the "king of fishes," it is both because of the benefits it confers on those who worship it and because it is available to be worshipped by all. As an allegorical figure, the "king of fishes" may be a comical king of "uncrowning," of opposition and misrule, but he is also the king of kindness.[29] He is a king because he is humble; valued as one of a kind because he is so many; considered irreplaceable because he can be indefinitely resupplied; worshipped as regal because he is so anonymous; respected as powerful because he is so obliging. Like the golden herring in the Dutch painting, he brings wealth, security, and honor to Yarmouth and the nation: he does all the things a lordly king might do — and that was the main cluster of attributes associated with good monarchs at the time, that good monarchs conferred wealth, security, and prestige on their subjects — but by an inverted logic of commodities and exchange values where central power is never concentrated, but rather made to circulate and supply the nation freely. In every respect, herring, the herring trade, and the political economy of Yarmouth represent an alternative to — well, *landed* wealth, the wealth of inland England and what in 1599 could still be regarded as aristocratic privilege and the realm, indeed, of courtesy.

The most interesting part of *Lenten Stuff* pairs an anecdote about how red herring was invented with an anecdote about the selling of rotting red herring to the pope in Rome by a Yarmouth trader. The first anecdote, clearly a stock-in-trade item, tells how a rack of herring being salted and dried by a fisherman was accidentally caught in the smoke of a fire, and this smoking was found to enhance the herring's qualities, burnishing it a handsome gold. "A miracle! A miracle!" the fisherman and his wife exclaim. The second tells how this same fisherman took his wares to Rome and enticed the pope to pay three hundred pounds for a single smoked fish — a fish that was the last one he had left, and that by now was stinking to high heaven. This second anecdote contributes new allegorical dimensions to the praise of the red herring. Blasphemous though the suggestion may be, the miraculous herring, risen anew from its hanging by the fire, seems to become a kind of Christ figure. But the pope responds incorrectly to the miracle; he responds idolatrously. The pope overvalues the herring; he makes an idol of it; he over-corporealizes his relation to it. And if something like cannibalism is therefore suggested by the allegory, although that is really going too far, and itself something of red herring in a text that is filled with red herrings — false trails of meaning, as Nashe himself explains — so also is suggested, and this is not going too far, the deep semiotics of food and feeding.

The herring, for Nashe, is a vehicle for generating meaning along the symbolic axes of the raw, the cooked, and the rotten — axes of what Lévi-Strauss calls the "culinary triangle."[30] Lévi-Strauss has come into a good deal of criticism from subsequent sociologists of food, but partly, I think, because his work has been misread, and the heuristic and ethnographical uses of the culinary triangle or what Lévi-Strauss also playfully called the semiotic "grill" of food haven't been adequately appreciated.[31] In any case, the sixteenth-century satirist was already aware of something akin to Lévi-Strauss's semiotic "grill" and certainly appreciated the raw-cooked-rotten axes inherent in the production and consumption of herring. Nashe's understanding of these matters is not much different from the symbolic structures implied in the matter of Hamlet's baked meat. The red herring is smoked and salted but not exactly cooked. The herring is wrested from nature and won, by its processing, to the side of civilization. But the victory of civilization over nature is incomplete, inexact, and impermanent. Like the town of Yarmouth itself, which perennially struggles against the "battery" of sea and sand, the herring is a commodity that both symbolizes the "glittering head" of triumph against nature and the necessary transience of the triumph. Unlike the gold that it otherwise resembles, the herring is subject to rot. The preservation through smoking or other means is incomplete — corruption inevitably settles in. The preservation is even an incomplete enculturation of the fish. Nashe again and again emphasizes that though the red herring is preserved and capable of being eaten in its uncooked state, it is best served broiled. When the fisherman finally sells his last stinking fish to the pope's agent, he teaches the latter how to gut it, "sauce it, and dress it." When the fish is brought to the papal palace, "all the Pope's cooks in their white sleeves and linen aprons met him middle way, to entertain and receive the King of fishes, and together by the ears they went, who should first handle him or touch him. But the clerk of the kitchen would admit none but himself to have the scorching and carbonadoing of it. . . ." What the pope's cook has in mind is something like the refined dish that Sir Kenelm Digby would learn how to cook from a peer of the realm:

> My Lord d'Aubigny eats Red-herrings thus broiled. After they are opened and prepared for the Gridiron, soak them (both sides) in Oil and Vinegar beaten together in pretty quantity in a little Dish. Then broil them, till they are hot through, but not dry. Then soak them again in the same Liquor as before, and broil them a second time. You may soak them again a third time; but twice may serve. They will be then very short and crisp and savory. Lay them upon your Salad, and you may also put upon it, the Oil and Vinegar, you soaked the Herrings in.[32]

This was a rather strong-flavored and strong-smelling dish, even if the red herring was newly smoked. And when the pope's cook begins to cook his twelve-month-old herring, it "stunk so over the Pope's palace, that not a scullion but cried 'Foh!'" The raw, the cooked, the rotten, they all co-exist in the broiled red herring. (Notice that Lord d'Aubigny serves the hyper-prepared red herring with an uncooked green salad. Lévi-Strauss's qualification about these things should be kept in mind: "In any cuisine, nothing is simply cooked, but must be cooked in one fashion rather than another. Nor is there any notion of pure rawness: only certain foods can really be eaten raw, and then only if they have been selected, washed, pared or cut, or even seasoned. Rotting, too, is only allowed to take place in certain specific ways, either spontaneous or controlled.")[33] But if all three symbolic axes meet in the body of the red herring, only, comically, does the pope appreciate the fact. When told that the palace was stinking because of the "King of Fishes" he had ordered cooked, the pope says, "I conceited no less . . . for less than a king he could not be that had so strong a scent. And if his breath be strong, what is he himself? Like a great king, like a strong king, I will use him. Let him be carried back, I say, and my Cardinals shall fetch him in with dirge and processions under my canopy."[34]

Eating the fish turns out to be a lot like burying him. A funeral for the bones and head of the consumed king in fact soon follows. We are once more in a symbolic domain, warranted in part by the Catholic ceremony of the Eucharist, where eating is death and life mixed together. Yet Nashe also assures his readers that this unusual food is a "choleric parcel of food," a "hot stirring meat," that dries up the innards of the phlegmatic and makes normal men into brave soldiers: "enough to make the cravenest dastard proclaim fire and sword against Spain." If it is true that life "consists of eating and drinking," life also consists of a struggle against death and oblivion for which death and dying—in the form of the cooked and the rotten—have their elementary uses. And it is this death-defying, death-exploiting struggle that constitutes the civility that a proponent of civility like Nashe wants to encourage—even against the older stabilities of courtesy and *Kultur.*

V

But back to our belch, or hiccup, or fart. Sir Toby's expulsion of air is presumably funny because it violates, in an appropriate context, the sense of shame and the ideology of decorum that are inherent to the memories of our civilized bodies.

But what about his anger? "A plague o' these pickled herring!" We may now be in a position to see that, however we may want to respond to his expression of anger, whatever comic excuses and lies we may want to see in it, the pickled herring may well be what Sir Toby believes to be responsible for his indigestion. We are in a position to see this also: the expression of this indigestion may not even be entirely uncivil. The herring may be responsible for Sir Toby's gas because, as we have seen, herring was assumed to be difficult to digest. It may even be a cause of Sir Toby's anger. That is, if herring in its preserved state is a "choleric" food, Sir Toby may be angry because the herring has made him choleric. And in any case, whatever gas it is that Sir Toby expels, it would seem to be a result of the food he has eaten rather than the alcohol he has drunk.

The medical literature is not, unfortunately, greatly forthcoming on the subject. A statement by a non-medical writer, our friend Phillip Stubbes, may at least help orient us. Stubbes at one point observes that the drunken man may "froth and foam at the mouth like a bore" and "falter and stammer in his mouth" and, in words that closely anticipate the language of *Twelfth Night,* have "his wits and spirits as it were drowned" and "his understanding altogether decayed."[35] But it is the overeaters who have their "breath stink, their stomach belch forth filthy humors, and their memory decay" due to an excess of "impure vapors."[36] It is food, not drink, that generates wind — even that soundless wind or "vapor" that makes a man forgetful. Two medical treatises — one from the later Middle Ages, the other from the seventeenth century — both corroborate the point. Gilbertus Anglicus, in a Middle English text, provides discussions of both belching ("balking") and hiccups ("zosking"). Belching, Gilbertus writes, is either "smoky and hot" or "sour." "The first cometh of heat and of hot humors that be in the stomach. The second is of cold humors either or feeble heat of the stomach." Hiccuping, it is true, "cometh in many manners." An "excess of either eating or drinking that maketh the stomach too full" may be responsible. But it is the fullness, the surfeit, that causes the problem, and indeed the fullness of "humors," not drunkenness, on which the blame is laid.[37] The second treatise, from the Frenchmen Lazare Rivière — as translated by a team led by the physician and astrologer Nicholas Culpeper — includes comments on problems with the "retentive and expulsive faculties" of the stomach, grouping them at one point under the category of "dyspepsia." Belching (along with farting) is mentioned in the case of "Hypochondriacal Melancholy," in which case "much phlegm and fermentation of a black Humor [commonly] cause Crudities, Winds, Swelling, Rumblings, and sour Belchings." The only causes Rivière mentions have to do with food, which may "offend" the digestive system either in substance, quantity, quality, time, or order of being taken. Hiccuping, in Latin *singultus,* is character-

ized as "a depraved motion of the Stomach, by which it desires to expel something that is hurtful." On the authority of Hippocrates, Galen, and Avicenna,
Rivière explains the *singultus* as either an "Emptiness and Repletion, as of Con-
vulsion" or "a provocation by a sharp matter. . . . For what is more clear than that
the Singultus comes from the expulsive faculty provoked." It is caused by an
offending "Matter." This matter is "either gathered in the Stomach, or sent from
the Liver, Spleen, Guts, or other parts; or from the whole Body. So sharp Medicines, or sharp Humors, or gnawing worms contained in the Stomach, cause a
Singultus by propriety: but inflammation of the parts adjacent by water or vapors
sent to the Stomach, make it by consent. . . ." Rivière is a bit confusing here,
falling into the habit (here as elsewhere) that Molière would soon mock, of "explaining" physical causes by verbal constructions (though Galen, it is true, a good
Aristotelian, called such constructions "first principles")—"propriety," "consent." Rivière allows that hiccups can be caused, among other things, by "Meat,
Drink, or Cold," in which case the hiccuping "is not dangerous; as also that which
goes before a Crisis by Vomit. . . ."[38] But Aristotelian categories aside, what we
see here is that belching, farting, and hiccuping alike are fit into the intake-
discharge model of the body discussed in chapter 2, and that irritating agents like
harsh medicines and humors, as well as a quantitative overloading of the system,
are mainly to blame for the production of muscle spasms and gas.

If preserved herring causes fevers, just as it may for the same reason cause
anger, so it may also act as a provocative agent, inducing spasms. My own experience tells me that the brine of pickled herring may well cause dyspepsia, accompanied by hiccups, especially under conditions of what the early moderns called
a "surfeit." A couple of slices of pickled herring may do no harm, as an early modern writer might put it, but if you eat a whole jar of the stuff, though a jar is only
four ounces, you may have eaten too much and caused yourself some indigestion.
The "sharp matter" of preserved herring—it tastes sharp, it goes down sharp, it
is doused in salt and acid—can provoke the "expulsive faculty." Of course, so can
overindulgence in just about anything. But it is especially easy to surfeit on pickled herring—one can only eat *so much* of it. And consider again what this means
in moral terms. Poor people may well be condemned to surfeiting on such "unwholesome" and potentially offensive food because it is all they can afford: if they
could eat beef, they would eat beef, and they would eat more of it, and fatten up,
and still not suffer the discomfort of indigestion. Wealthy individuals will feed
themselves to the point of discomfort on products like pickled herring out of a
desire—irrational though this common desire, this intoxication with food may
be—to reach a state of discomfort, heedless of the dangers the discomfort may
warn them of. And one thing more: they are likely to be feeding themselves too

much herring because it helps and encourages them to drink more: eating herring, a classic bar food, is a spur to convivial dissipation. When Sir Toby curses the pickled herring and makes some sort of noise of indigestion, it is likely, in 1601, that the audience takes his anger seriously, and that it readily ascribes both his anger and his indigestion to a surfeit of pickled herring. But it will also understand that in eating too much pickled herring Sir Toby was in fact helping his consumption of alcohol along; the surfeit of pickled herring, as also the anger that the herring by itself may provoke, is itself a sign of dipsomania. Eating too much pickled herring is a sign of drinking too much wine — itself a provoker of anger and overeating, among other things.

As for belching, hiccuping, or farting, on the little evidence of attitudes toward them that one can find, it would seem that Sir Toby would most likely have belched, as his name implies, although it is not impossible that he hiccuped or farted or expressed some combination of two or all three of them. Yet it would also seem, given the peculiarities of the early modern regimen, that though whatever he did was meant for laughs, it was not quite so uncivilized as we may assume it to be. The demands of politeness and the demands of health are both demands of civility, even if they sometimes conflict with one another; and it often seems that early modern wits had less trouble with the conflict than people of a later age would have. A poem immortalized in a Dutch painting, *The Praise of Pickled Herring*, is a case in point.

A shiny pickled herring
stout, fat, and long,
Its head chopped off,
Its belly and back as a
whole nicely sliced,
the scales scraped off

The innards taken out
Raw or fried with fire
Then don't forget the onion
And before the evening sees
the sun set,
Devour with hunger.

It will make you piss,
And will not fail
(with pardon) to [make you] defecate
nor cease to release wind . . .[39]

Again, no doubt the references are played for laughs; but they also reveal a different understanding of the relation of foods to digestion and health, as well as a different attitude toward the natural processes. By the intake-discharge theory of the body, whatever the body expels, whenever the body expels it, is probably toxic; it is probably in excess of what the body can use, and may be in itself either useless — of "poor nutrition" — or else corrupt. So it is usually good to expel — whether by urine, by feces, by farting, by vomiting, by bloodletting, by belching, by sweating, or other means. Foodstuffs that provoke expulsion are generally good for you. Hippocrates, as Tudor author Thomas Paynel reminds his readers, even claimed that it was good to get roaring drunk once a month, "that of the drunkenness may come vomit: which thing preserveth us from ill diseases of long continuance."[40] If it is true that herring will make you piss, shit, and fart, so much the better: foods as diverse as pork and asparagus were praised for such qualities in the regimens of health. That pissing, shitting, farting, belching, and the like were considered shameful in Western culture, even well before the early modern period, is not in dispute: but they were also considered expressions of health. Not only was it the case that a healthy body would ordinarily expel urine, feces, and gas; it was also the case that the expulsion was a purgation of harmful matters and humors, the suppression of which was considered dangerous. "Great harms have grown, & maladies exceeding," says the School of Salerno,

> By keeping in a little blast of wind:
> So Cramps & Dropsies, Colics have their breeding,
> And Mazed Brains for want of vent behind . . .[41]

For this reason, when we look at early modern books on "civility," as Elias has shown, we encounter a somewhat more complex and tolerant response to expulsion than we might ordinarily expect. Thus, as far as belching and farting go, Erasmus, in the most influential conduct book of the sixteenth century, asserts that "to suppress a sound which is brought on by nature is characteristic of silly people who set more store by 'good manners' than good health." Or again: "There are some who lay down the rule that a boy should refrain from breaking wind by constricting his buttocks, but it is not a part of good manners to bring illness upon yourself while striving to appear 'polite.' If you may withdraw, do so in private. If not, then in the words of the old adage, 'let him cover the sound with a cough.'"[42] On the one hand, gas is embarrassing, indecent, something to be concealed; on the other hand, it is healthy and needs to be expressed. And a great and famous scholar, known for his critical analysis of the New Testament and his high humanist advice to princes, has no problem turning a public eye to the gassy emanations of a young boy's rectum. Still, as Elias would predict, attitudes slowly become less tolerant over the next two centuries. We are assured, in 1619, that

> To belch or bulch like *Clitipho*
>> whom *Terence* setteth forth
> Commendeth manners to be base,
>> most foul and nothing worth.

"Most foul" and "nothing worth," at least one of the natural functions no longer seems to serve a medical purpose. Still, even the author of these remarks, Richard West in *The Schoole of Vertue,* cautions his reader to

> Retain not urine nor the wind
>> which doth the body vex,
> So it be done with secrecy,
>> lest that not thee perplex.[43]

On the one hand, such natural functions are "base" as well as "foul"—the choice of words is significant—and therefore to be done in secret; on the other hand, they must not be repressed.

It is only when we come to the late seventeenth century that we come upon texts that are intolerant of the natural functions absolutely. Even then the necessity is acknowledged, as is, again, the non-alcoholic etiology of the hiccup we have just discussed; but the expression of bodily functions, especially at the dinner table, has become altogether taboo: "To blow your Nose publicly at the Table without holding your Hat or Napkin before your Face," writes the debonair Frenchman Nicholas Courtin in the popular *Rules of Civility;*

> to wipe off the Sweat from your Face with your handkerchief; to claw
> your Head, &c., to belch, hawk, and tear anything up from the bottom
> of your Stomach, are things so intolerably sordid, they are sufficient to
> make a Man vomit to behold them; you must forbear them therefore as
> much as you can, or at least conceal them. You must not be fantastical
> and affected in your eating, but eat soberly and deliberately, neither
> showing yourself insatiable, nor stuffing till you give your self the Hic-
> cup. . . ."[44]

By the time Courtin is writing—and this is a big part of Elias's thesis—the threshold of shame and disgust has been lowered. It is not just embarrassing or funny to fart or belch or hiccup in front of others; it is "intolerably sordid." It can "make a Man vomit." An uneasiness with bodily functions that were nevertheless considered signs of good health that ought not to be suppressed has become a disgust with processes that may easily go out of control and that therefore warrant vigilant policing. It is almost as if shame had transmuted into guilt. The functions must not only be concealed but, if possible, forborne. And what one does with one's body at the dinner table has become subject not only to a panoptic scrutiny — "you must not be fantastical and affected," lest anyone present *see* you in a certain way — but to internal repression as well. Note too: hiccuping can be repressed by suppressing one's appetite, nothing being said in this connection about alcohol. Food is found responsible for the problem. And even self-repression in advance of the onset of symptoms has become established as a "rule of civility."

Sir Toby and his indigestion need to be located somewhere within this continuum of changing attitudes toward the natural functions and rules of civility. On the one side, the belch or hiccup or fart would be shameful yet amusing; on the other side, it would be disgusting but outrageously funny. In either case, it would be a cause of laughter. But in the first case, it may nevertheless be associated with positive values — health and high spirits (even literally, as "fumosities" and vapors are kinds of spirits). In the second case, however, if belching or hiccuping or farting can be associated with positive values at all, the only one would be the inversely positive value of transgression and rebellion. My own response, fond laughter at what I took to be Sir Toby's mischievous drunkenness, was based on the second model. I was raised, in the twentieth century, as an heir to the spirit of Courtin's *Rules of Civility* and what has been called modernity's "tremulous private body."[45] But the response of Shakespeare's audience would have most probably fallen on the side of the first case, as heirs to the spirit of Erasmus and that early model of "civility" where that which was embarrassing was not yet disgusting and an excess of pickled herring had less to do with transgression than with a species of gluttony, of faulty but not disgusting consumption. And that brings us to a final topic raised by Belch's hiccup, the gluttony it entails, and the operations and regulations according to which gluttony may be expressed. For here the life that consists of eating and drinking is also a life of erotic attachments.

VI

The appetite — as concept and phenomenon alike — is key. "If music be the food of love," says Duke Orsino, at the very beginning of *Twelfth Night,* " play on, /

Give me excess of it, that surfeiting, / The appetite may sicken and so die." As a concept, appetite — from the Latin *appeto,* to make for or to grasp, and hence *appetitus,* an inclination toward or a longing to possess — had many applications among the early moderns. Appetite could be healthy or deranged, sensual or intellectual, natural or unnatural, temperate or "wanton," gustatory or carnal, or even experienced by the eye, the nose, or the ear. The philosophical and theological tradition allowed one to distinguish between appetites high and low, and it warranted an extremely important association, a metonymy of body parts, behaviors, and time frames, that connected hunger and desire, the cravings of the belly and the passions of the genitalia: food and sex, consumption and copulation. Beginning with Plato, the appetites for food and sex could be "bestial," a part of our "lower" nature, which we held in common with the beasts, and bestial inclinations required regulation by a higher order of nature — the heart, the will, the spirit, or the mind. Especially as codified by church fathers like Saint Augustine, all of Christendom would come to suffer the consequences of this doctrine. Nevertheless, the classical physicians looked on all this dispassionately and non-judgmentally. A healthy appetite for food was essential to health in general. One might well condone foodstuffs and beverages that could "procure appetite." The multicourse meal, which developed partly as a method of festivity and partly as an outcome of the technology of kitchens and dining rooms, was thus sanctioned by medical lore so far as it generated a healthy appetite, beginning with what in American English are still called "appetizers." We have seen on several occasions Italians taking pride in their ability to stimulate the appetite by feeding it, producing long drawn-out meals where one continues to want more and more. Similarly, a beverage could be preferred because of its appetite-enhancing properties. The early seventeenth-century writer Tobias Venner thus likes the red wine of Bordeaux because it "is very near of a temperate nature, and somewhat of an astringent faculty, as the savor of it doth plainly show: it breedeth good humors, greatly strengtheneth the stomach, quencheth thirst, stireth up the appetite, help concoction, and exhilirateth the heart."[46] So there are always two sides to the concept of appetite. It may be low, sensual, bestial, irrational, and corrupt; it may be healthy, sensual, vital, normal, and integral, and even — as we saw in the case of Francesco Colonna's *Hypnerotomachia Poliphili* (chapter 4) — assimilated into Neoplatonic longings for the divine.

We have come across these issues before, particularly with regard to regimens of health and the food of regret. But Belch's hiccup — not to mention Orsino's imaginary excess — encourages a look at the fundamentals. How in the early modern world were people to respond to the idea of the appetite? How to respond to the reality of it? Whether low or high, the appetite in Western discourse to this point was conceived of as something both internal and external —

internal to the self surely, since it was within the embodied self that appetite was experienced, but also external since it was, fundamentally, the other part of the self, that part of the self which was always *other*.[47] Subject therefore to regulation by the higher or more central and in any case more selfsame part of the self, the appetite was a phenomenon to be both nurtured and disciplined. If our bodies were our gardens, it was our rational and more selfsame selves that undertook the gardening. (This is yet another example of Foucault's "technology of the self.") If our appetite either made demands upon us or failed to respond to the demands that we placed upon it and needed suppression or encouragement or provocation, it operated in any case as that other function of the self—that part of me that was not *me*.

The varieties of the regulation of the appetite were endless. One could follow nature, control nature, repress nature, and even idolize it. In the Platonic tradition, one liked to think of the appetite for food, like the appetite for sex, as a kind of itch that needed scratching now and then. But that is not of course how the appetite for food (not to mention sex) actually works, and the attempt to regulate it had to deal with something more complex. The appetite can be aroused before it is needed, and needed before it is aroused. Doing something about it, attempting to satisfy it, may initially only stimulate it all the more. And the satisfaction of the need may arrive well before the well-stimulated appetite itself has been quelled. If we can say this today, when due to a dysfunction of the appetite overeating and obesity have become widespread social problems, the early moderns could say this too. Physicians, as we have seen, knew all about the "dog's appetite," about bingeing and "bulimia," just as they knew about the "woman's longing," cravings stimulated by pregnancy. And as they believed that overeating was a common cause of illness, since it led to an overproduction of humors, which would then be left to putrefy and obstruct the system, so they could find pathological dispositions in the "temperament" or "complexion" of the embodied self that inherently encouraged overeating. Thus Timothy Bright could mention that "melancholy persons" have an appetite for food that "for the most part exceeding, and far surpassing their digesture," the reason being a disposition toward sourness in the stomach caused by an excess of spleen, the spleen itself caused by an excess of black bile or melancholy in the system. Bright indeed called attention to the idea that "natural" functions like the appetite "are not at our beck, but are performed by a certain instinct of nature will we, nil we."[48] The appetite was quite the other, even if Bright wasn't passing judgment on it, and even if its otherness was internal to the structure of the individual. But more moralistically inclined medical writers would call attention to the deceitfulness of the appetite and would worry not just about pathological conditions but also about an activity to which a moral value was assigned, that is, gluttony. The Jesuit Leonardus Lessius thus deliberates on "why the Appetite is deceitful," when "its Longing is extended further, than is proportionable to any of the [healthy] Ends" of the desire for food. He gives both a medical and moral or social explanation: "this is either occasioned through some faulty, or evil Disposition of the Stomach, as it sometimes happens in that ravening Kind of Appetite, called *Bulimia;* or else by reason of the elaborate and ingenious Cooking of the Food itself; which by its luscious Variety, and exquisite Relish, tends not only to rouse a sickly Appetite to receive the unnatural Load, but at the same Time to render a natural good one incapable of knowing when it has enough."[49] In the middle of all this — a medical writer thinking only of the psychopharmacology of food, a humanist concerned with the truth of the appetite and the deceitfulness of gluttonous longings — one also encounters a characteristically French attitude from the seventeenth-century luminary Saint-Évremond, who puts it this way, in giving advice to a friend in exile:

> Let Nature incite you to eat and drink by a secret disposition, which is lightly perceived, and doth not press you to it through necessity. Without appetite, the most wholesome Food is capable of hurting, and the most agreeable of disgusting us. With hunger, the necessity of eating is a sort of Evil which causes another after the Meal is over, by making us eat more than we should. The Appetite (vulgarly called a *good stomach*) prepares, if I may so speak, an exercise for our heat in the digestion: whereas greediness prepares labor and pain for it. The way to keep us always in good temper, is to suffer neither too much emptiness, nor too much repletion: that so Nature may never be tempted to fill it self greedily with what it wants, not impatient to discharge its load.[50]

By this time the French had already acquired a reputation for culinary ascendancy, fine dining was a preoccupation of the French upper classes, and Saint-Évremond himself, an apostle of "good taste," was something of a gourmet. But it is not pleasure that Saint-Évremond extols — it is the appetite, the appetite as a natural force and "secret disposition," which is to be distinguished from mere "hunger": one encourages the appetite while avoiding the evils of hunger. One can see the defensive class struggle, the French *distinction,* inherent in this notion: the gentleman of good taste never eats out of hunger, which will of course differentiate him from members of lower classes who either do not have the option or do not have the good breeding to avoid eating out of hunger.[51] But one can also see the good sense, so far as eating is elevated to an art of pleasure. In

French today, one may still be said to do things before dinner like going for a long walk or drinking an aperitif in order to "open the appetite," *ouvrir l'appétit.* Hunger may be the best sauce, according to the proverbial wisdom, but according to an ethic of gastronomy that begins in the Italy of Platina and Messisbugo and the France of Montaigne and Saint-Évremond, the appetite, the "good stomach," is the faculty to cultivate.

Whatever attitude one took and however one conceptualized it, society itself was already structured as a system for regulating the appetite. It is always so, Lévi-Strauss encourages us to believe. But early moderns were in fact aware of the social mechanisms for accommodating the appetite as an expression of its own civility. Lessius, again, calls attention to it: "Now, if we shall consider the fittest time for [eating]," he writes, addressing a readership that thinks that it may in theory at least organize life according to rational principles,

> it will seem to be when the appetite doth demand it. And therefore *Diogenes* being asked when was the fittest time for food, answered; to him that hath it, when his stomach called for it; and to him that hath it not, when he can come by it. But all our civilist nations have accustomed themselves to some set times for their ordinary repasts. And because nature proceeds orderly in all her operations, therefore before we make a new meal we must see that the former be first concocted. . . .[52]

In other words, we eat according to a schedule of set meals because civility demands it, and we schedule the meals well apart from one another because apart from the demands of civility we need to eat one meal only after we have already digested the one before. All the conventions of dining of the early modern period, from the princely banquet to the homely *petit déjeuner,* could be seen as following a set schedule and form because of the demands of civility, placed by convention in relation to the medically conceived demands of the appetite. "Why, how have I done this forty years?" a sanguine, elderly merchant named Merrythought proclaims on the English stage only a few years after Sir Toby Belch first made his appearance there. "I never came into my dining room, but at eleven and six o'clock I found excellent meat and drink o'th'table . . . ; and without question it will be so ever."[53] The household—whose usual dominance by a woman and whose usual maintenance by a core of laborers is insufficiently appreciated by Elias and other theorists of the civilizing process, but whose "civility" when properly run was never in doubt—established a rhythm of production and consumption one of whose main purposes was to regulate the functioning of the appetite, to make it obey a social as well as a personal logic, to subordinate it to the spatiotemporal demands of a community. All efforts to come to terms with the idea and reality of the appetite in the early modern period had first of all to answer to the system already in place for regulating it. The system was subject to change — as, for example, the long-term trend among the prosperous was for later and later hours. It was sometimes challenged. When we see the dashing recusant Sir Kenelm Digby learning how to grill red herring from a peer of the realm, we are getting a glimpse of members of the nobility taking gustatory matters into their own hands, cooking their own food according to their own schedules and in their own locations, without the help of servants, using equipment suitable for a private chamber rather than the household kitchen. And when Sir Toby comes in before noon, already drunk and already bloated with pickled herring, or when we see him in a previous scene rabble-rousing with Sir Andrew after midnight, we observe yet another kind of challenge: a gentleman refusing to follow the rules, eating and drinking at the wrong hour, frequenting taverns where the usual household rules do not apply, and, when at home, disrupting the rhythms of others. "Is there no respect of place, persons, nor time in you?" Malvolio demands.[54] But still, such challenges to the system depended upon the system. All of European society — and we will see how peculiar this might have been, when we consider in the next chapter the eating habits of the "savage" Native Americans — was organized according to rules of set meals and set manners established and sustained by the rule of the household. Nor was this mainly a perquisite of the "better sort." The uneducated and the poor had set times for meals and a system of table manners too; it was only the myth of civility that said they didn't.

The appetite — this other part of the self that is "not at our beck" but that may nevertheless be regulated, cultivated, overindulged in, or suppressed — was not quite, so far as the early moderns were concerned, an expression of what Freud taught us to call the id. Nor was it quite a part of what Elias, inspired by Freud, called the "affect structure" of the individual. By both the Freudian and Eliasian model, the appetite can be conceived as an expression among other expressions of a primary, instinctual, systemic impulse. "The affect structure of man is a whole," says Elias.

> We may call particular instincts by different names according to their different directions and functions, we may speak of hunger and the need to spit, of the sexual drive and of aggressive impulses, but in life these different instincts are no more separable than the heart from the stomach or the blood in the brain from the blood in the genitalia. They complement and in part supercede each other, transform themselves

within certain limits and compensate for each other; a disturbance here manifests itself there. In short, they form a kind of circuit in the human being, a partial system within the total system of the organism.[55]

Elias may or may not be right about this: modern psychopathology still inclines toward confirming this model, though by other principles and according to different mechanisms than those that Freud and Elias took for granted. But if the appetite could be an "it" by early modern lights, it was not a primal unconscious subject, and it was not part of a "circuit" or a "partial system" within a "total system." How, in the universe of hydraulic and electrochemical metaphors that dominate Freud's and Elias's models, would we fit in an allegorical analogy like Edmund Spenser's, in *The Faerie Queene*, where a figure named Appetite is a "jolly yeoman," who acts as the "marshall" of the dining hall:

> he did bestow
> Both guests and meat, whenever in they came,
> And knew them how to order without blame,
> As him the Steward bade.[56]

The body, as we have had occasion to observe before, was not, for the early moderns, a machine. It was a microcosm, a little world. Sometimes, as we have seen, early moderns found it useful to think of the body as a castle, house, or town. In a long, belabored, but scientifically up-to-date didactic poem, Phineas Fletcher compared the human body to an island, indeed a "Purple Island."[57] The body in all such cases was an artifact of governmentality—something made, a little world, an architectural creation, an orderly territory (the Isle of Man, as Fletcher also calls it), that functioned the way a society functioned. When spitting, shitting, farting, or belching is not an "urge" of the electric tremulous mechanical body but a sloughing off of corruptible excesses that might otherwise obstruct the government of the self, and sex itself is a discharge of spirit, the appetite is not so much an affect as an intake device, a jolly "marshall," or a "porter," as Fletcher at one time calls it, which opens the way toward hospitality. A defective appetite in this case could be a "porter" corrupted by "evil" humors, obstructions, or the blandishments of the imagination. And an over-appreciation of the demands of the appetite could be a dereliction of duty, where the "sensible soul" as opposed to the intellectual faculty was allowed to call the shots, or where the bestial and sensual part of man was permitted to usurp the government of the higher faculties. But the appetite would not be a part of an "affect structure" of man as a whole—at least not in the inclusive sense that Elias concocts for this structure, and certainly not in terms of a mechanical model of the body, the idea of which would only first be introduced in the mid-seventeenth century by way of Descartes and his followers.

That meant that early modern science before the Cartesian revolution could not really *explain* the appetite for food or tie it into a system of instinctual drives. It could only recognize it as an instinct—perhaps as something identical to hunger, perhaps as an epiphenomenon in relation to hunger—which was also, by metonymy, contiguous with other instincts, including the sexual instinct. Early modern science was unable to consistently *locate* the appetite, even if both traditional Galenic science and the new science of the anatomy that begins to take off in the mid-sixteenth century say that the appetite ought to be *in* the body somehow; that it should be a function of the mouth or the stomach, above all, the stomach itself having the function of a desiring apparatus. If the appetite was *in* the stomach, or a passion or affection *of* the stomach—a kind of absorptive mechanism, a longing for the intake of materials into the stomach literally caused by its emptiness and the sensations thereof—what happened in the mouth, and why wasn't the mouth or the "palate" and the sense of taste the seat of the appetite? And what about the sense of smell? Or sight, for that matter? And of course, if the palate, the nose, and the eye were reckoned to play a role in the appetitive function, why was it so commonly reckoned to be a "lower" function, far below the brain and the mind, not to mention the heart and the will? The same fate was usually met by sexual desire, which is so often oral, and even oral first, yet which traditional science insisted on locating way down in the body and way down, by the same token, in the hierarchy of human nature. The predominant solution—not terribly satisfactory but a fixture of premodern thought—was to locate an appetitive function in a variety of organs and motions of the body: that is the Aristotelian solution, where the appetitive function of the stomach is merely the most obvious example of all the appetitive functions of the body and for that matter the soul.[58] "Propriety," "consent," and such like notions or first principles are qualifications of the general appetitive functioning of the organism and its organs.

Partly because of the influence of Aristotelianism, and partly for more diffuse reasons of language and custom, appetite was a word, again, that could be applied to a variety of inclinations and longings. It could refer to other senses besides taste and to other affections besides hunger. The tongue, the lips, the eyes, the ears, the nose, the hands, and all the erogenous zones could be involved in affections reckoned as the expression of an "appetite." All these starting points of an appetitive affection could thus be thought of as "low" or "high," as merely sensual or as a sensible longing for the transcendence of the senses. Plato's longing of the mortal for immortality and Aristotle's longing of the soul for knowledge are both cases of appetite in this last sense. So is the universal longing for nutrition and assimilation we saw depicted in Milton's vision of the cosmos. When appetite is a function of organs that are affected toward the things they need, or when appetite is a function of organisms as a whole that are in need of other organisms as a whole, up and down the great chain of being, all the human body, the "little world," is motivated by appetite, and all the universe, the "great world," is alive as an appetitive system. Most important in the present context would be the way the appetite of the senses, and most especially the appetite for food, could thus be associated with love, and love associated with the appetites of the senses, and hence, again, with both the high and the low, and indeed with both the productive and the destructive. The appetite in the sense of a function common to a variety of organs and instincts, the appetite as that which moves bodies and spirits toward one another, with the union, assimilation, or possession — this is a variety of love, of eros, that both moves the universe toward divine community and even mortal beings toward immortality. But it also moves things toward preying on one another and swallowing each other up. Without the check of order and deference, Ulysses complains in *Troilus and Cressida,*

> Then every thing includes itself in power,
> Power into will, will into appetite;
> And appetite, an universal wolf,
> So doubly seconded with will and power,
> Must make perforce an universal prey,
> And at last eat up himself.[59]

Simply as a matter of familiar metonymies — parts related to wholes, contiguities, and imperfect but compelling analogies — the appetites of the senses and the craving for love could be associated with one another. Lovemaking was *preceded* by eating, drinking, seeing, smelling, and so forth; the sexual organs were *contiguous* with the digestive organs and *dependent* for arousal on tasting, touching, seeing, smelling, and hearing. There were foods, as there were sights and smells and sounds, known to stimulate sexual desire. And the occasion of the banquet, large or small, was often represented, understandably enough, as the prelude to lovemaking. This happens in romances and stage plays all the time. In Pietro Aretino's *Dialogues,* the sumptuous banquet is the common preliminary not only to the services of courtesans and whores, but to the secret orgies of nuns and monks.[60] Galenic medicine even had a physiological explanation for the metonymy of eating and lovemaking: in the first place, they were analogous activities of intake and discharge; in the second place, they were sequential functions. The "spirit" of semen (male and female) was a product of digestion, no less than fecal matter. Alcohol could act as an aphrodisiac both because it lowered inhibitions, and because its fumes and spirits stimulated the production of the spumy yet spiritual substance of the semen. Food could act as an aphrodisiac not only because certain foods had the special vitalistic quality of stimulating erotic desire, but because an excess of food would generate an excess of excrement generally, and semen was one of the excrements.

But what of "music" being this "food," as Shakespeare's Orsino puts it, and what of this "love" being overstuffed, causing itself, as "appetite," to die? The metaphor doesn't quite parse, and it doesn't parse because, even if music can be a food, love cannot be an appetite. That is an idea with which not everyone in the early modern period would have agreed, but it is a consistent line of thought in Shakespeare. "O spirit of love! how quick and fresh art thou," Orsino soon adds, rejecting his initial analogy: ". . . thy capacity / Receiveth as the sea."[61] In all his plays and poems, Shakespeare uses what he makes into a sharp distinction between appetite and love in order to say something about each. He never uses the word "appetite" as a synonym for love (though other playwrights of his era would), and in fact he has speaker after speaker imply or even outright assert that something that may look like love is to be deplored because it is actually only an appetite. The reason is this: Shakespeare understands the appetite — a wolfish thing perhaps, and certainly an affection aimed at the consumption of the objects toward which it is affected — as something finite, fickle, and predatory. The appetite comes, it is satisfied, and it goes. It finds something to which it is attracted, it consumes it, and it is no longer attracted to it. It looks for something else to prey upon. Frequently, therefore, if appetite is to be compared to a part of romantic life, it is to lust. "Mark me with what violence she first loved the Moor," Iago says about Desdemona,

> but for bragging and telling her fantastical lies: and will she love him still for prating? — let not thy discreet heart think it. Her eye must be fed; and what delight shall she have to look on the devil? When the blood is made dull with the act of sport, there should be, again to inflame it, and to give satiety a fresh appetite, loveliness in favor, sympathy in years, manners and beauties. . . .[62]

Iago argues that Desdemona's love had been aroused, like an appetite for food, by a deceitful presentation. And now that this appetite-like desire has been satisfied, it can only be aroused by something that Othello doesn't have to give her. The eye must be fed, and her appetite will have to be inflamed by something new. Of course, Iago needs to think of Desdemona in this way. If her passion for Othello were really love, and not something like an appetite, she could not be diverted from it. But the point is clear. Real love, in Shakespeare, as opposed to mere sexual appetite or appetitive infatuation, is something larger, deeper, and livelier; it is neither momentary nor fickle; it is constant, and it is constant because it answers to a logic of desire, where desire is precisely that affection that can never be satiated, never filled up, never brought to a conclusion. It "receiveth as the sea." "Love surfeits not," the speaker intones in *Venus and Adonis;* and, by contrast, "Lust like a glutton dies."[63] Duke Orsino, in *Twelfth Night,* may be wrong, in the speech cited below, to claim that only men can thus experience love, and he may be even wrong about his own feelings, but he gives classic expression to the difference Shakespeare's language observes between the nature of love and desire, on the one hand, and lust or infatuation and appetite, on the other:

> There is no woman's sides
> Can bide the beating of so strong a passion
> As love doth give my heart; no woman's heart
> So big, to hold so much. They lack retention
> Alas, their love may be called appetite,
> No motion of the liver, but the palate,
> That suffer surfeit, cloyment and revolt.
> But mine is all as hungry as the sea,
> And can digest as much: make no compare
> Between that love a woman can bear me
> And that I owe Olivia.[64]

As far as I have been able to determine, there are no exceptions to this rule. Whenever Shakespeare allows a speaker to liken sexual or romantic feelings to an appetite, it is to indicate that there is something defective in the feelings. Not only does Shakespeare know the appetite to be subject to pathological derangement—an idea that Olivia refers to when she accuses Malvolio of being "sick of self-love" and "tasting" the remarks of others with a "distempered appetite," and that the speaker of Sonnet 147 refers to when he says, "My love is as a fever, longing still / For that which longer nurseth the disease . . . / Th'uncertain sickly appetite to please"—but he apparently believes that it is of itself, even when healthy, a less meaningful or valuable part of life. The closest Shakespeare comes to an exception may be the case of Cleopatra, whose charms are likened to a "fine Egyptian cookery," and who is said to attract all men because although "Other women cloy / The appetites they feed," Cleopatra "makes hungry / Where most she satisfies."[65] That is to say, although what Cleopatra trades in is lust and infatuation, she feeds them as if she were supplying the food of love. The need for her can never be satisfied, and thus it simulates boundless desire. But the idea underscores the sinister, bewitching side of Cleopatra's nature — the language itself is bewitching. It stimulates the "dog's appetite," or bingeing, and hence, no doubt, the paradoxically happy discomfort of a surfeit. A similar exception seems to arise in *Hamlet*, where Hamlet complains about his mother, whose love for Hamlet's father is likened to an insatiable appetite. There again, appetite operates paradoxically, like the boundless appetite for bingeing. But although the bingeing appetite may stand as an approximation to the insatiable cravings of love, the language itself already betrays uneasiness with the queen's desires, a disgust with them no matter who is the object she attaches them to. There may already have been something wrong with Gertrude's relation to her first husband, and with her relation to men generally, and indeed (as Hamlet gives way to a misogynistic outburst not unlike the comic Orsino's) with women and the relation of women to men generally.

> Why she would hang on him
> As if increase of appetite had grown
> By what it fed on . . .[66]

VII

Sir Toby and his hiccup, or whatever it was, were not signs of repression and de-repression, or of order and rebellion; but they were indicators of conflict all the same — conflict in the body and in its uses; conflict in the rules by which the body was to be managed; conflict in the materials by which the body was fed; conflict in the dreams of the body and the body's desires and pleasures. We only come closer to an understanding of the culture of food in the early modern period, I believe, by accounting for as many of these conflicts at once, even if they do not all parse, or fit together easily. Sir Toby's choice to drink and eat too much in the morning, and to eat and drink a dangerous combination of things, was in the first place a choice in favor of a certain sequence of bodily and mental states. That choice in turn implied others: the choice of one commodity, wine, that was available only by international trade;[67] the choice of another that was itself a sign of trade, as well as of both penitence and gluttony. Choosing wine and pickled her-

ring in the morning meant risking a "surfeit," along with inebriation and indigestion, and it meant risking an aggravation of what was actually Sir Toby's
most characteristic ill humor, anger. Certainly the choice was uncivil; for it
meant hazarding not just discomfort and disinhibition but disruptiveness, and it
was undertaken in violation of the regular rules of the household, with its set
schedule for consumption and recreation. When Malvolio and other members
of the household expressed impatience with Sir Toby's reckless habits, they were
speaking from the point of view of civility at its most basic level: the rules of the
day, the order of the clock and the household. Malvolio's complaints about Sir
Toby's behavior makes this unmistakable. Yet Sir Toby's choice was not, by the
standards of the day, wholly unredeemable. Sir Toby himself, who is after all a lovable character, defends his behavior by appealing to tradition. Like the squire
mocked by Joseph Addison, when he is drinking, he is "drinking healths"; when
he defends his dissolution after midnight, it is in terms of the traditional church-
sponsored "cakes and ale."[68] Sir Toby is all courtesy in these respects, like Falstaff
before him but more innocently, a defender of conventional gaiety. Many critics
have thus taken another step in the analysis, and thus seen Sir Toby as a representative of the carnivalesque. The conflict between Sir Toby and Malvolio on
this head is a conflict between Carnival and Lent, between ritual festivity and ritual abstinence.[69] When at the end of the play an unhappy Malvolio exclaims,
while storming offstage, "I will be avenged on you all," he is symbolically expressing the idea that in the rhythm of life in pre-capitalist Europe, Carnival and
Lent and indulgence and abstinence alternate by the cycle of the liturgical calendar, and if Carnival at one point triumphs, Lent will no doubt eventually return to triumph when its own day has come. If we cannot find an example of repression and de-repression in Belch's hiccup, since neither capitalism nor
Cartesianism has yet arrived and the "private body" is not yet so "tremulous" in
the face of its own organic needs, we can find in it the rhythm of revelry and discipline, of indulgence and denial. Yet Sir Toby's choice gestures in the direction
of progress and futurity as well, since it is a choice of proto-capitalist commodities, identified with civility; and if lovable Sir Toby reminds of us old merry courtesy, and indeed belongs to a line of English tradition that would come to include
both Addison's over-courteous country gentleman and Henry Fielding's Squire
Western, he also anticipates the figure of the libertine, which would play so large
a part in the seventeenth- and eighteenth-century literary scenes.

Libertinism, of course, was not a homegrown ethic; it was cosmopolitan and
adopted by English figures in emulation of the courtiers of France. And Sir Toby's
choice of drunkenness and indigestion at all hours is in that respect neither conventional nor domestic. One of the great spokesmen for libertinism, the French

Figure 6.2. Bacchic disorder. This is actually the inappropriate title page of a late (1643) edition of *Arte del cucinare*. Reproduced by permission of the Special Collections, Library of the University of Leeds.

poet Saint-Amant, for example, can be found taking pleasure in the idea that "Bacchus ayme le desordre": "Bacchus loves disorder."[70] And this, too, is part of what makes Belch hiccup. But we are getting ahead of ourselves.

Belch's hiccup is represented on the stage as an instance of lovable, laughable, interjectory indulgence, of appetite growing by what it feeds on until it can grow no more and something has to be expelled. That appetite has many limits in the world of Shakespeare, the physical limits of the body being only one of them. And if that appetite for excess leads us toward something grander, toward a desire waiting outside the gate — in other words, toward love — it can do so only in an outburst of ill health, derived from the ills of commodity consumption, sickened and so caused to die. That *strain* again, Orsino reports, it had a *dying* fall.

Chapter Seven

CANNIBALS AND MISSIONARIES

I

THIS CHAPTER WILL TELL A STORY of cannibals and missionaries, of visitors to America in the sixteenth and seventeenth centuries and their appetites for food, with particular reference to the Frenchman Jean de Léry, traveler to Brazil, and the Englishman Richard Ligon, an early visitor to the English colony of Barbados, both of whom were fine writers as well as witnesses to stunning developments. Fantasies, values, wonderful pleasures, and gritty realities all come together in the stories of cannibals and missionaries that they tell. So, too, comes another version of the march of civilization and its civilizing process, as these travelers sail the seas and report on circumstances both marvelous and awful: civilization as empire, and empire as an agent not of lofty ideals so much as the transplantation of social and religious conflict and the expansion of capitalist exploitation.

But let's begin with a sort of beginning and an earlier but abiding framework for the themes that come together in the writings of Léry and Ligon. It is 1494. Christopher Columbus has recently set sail on his second voyage to America, commanding a large flotilla, having advertised to the European world all its wonders. "It is a land to be desired," as one version of his "First Letter on America" puts it, "and seen, it is never to be left" ("Esta es para desear, é, vista, es para nunca dexar").[1] This is a new age, of course; all of humanity will be affected by the opening of the age of exploration. But at home, the first printed book to respond to Columbus's adventures is called, ironically perhaps, *The Ship of Fools.* It is dismissive of the significance of Columbus's discovery — the whole thing is only more foolishness, its author, Sebastian Brant, insists. Brant's enormously popular book, popular not just in Germany in 1494 but throughout western Europe for the next two centuries, responds to the new age the world is moving into with an attractively old-fashioned, one-sided moralism.

And Columbus aside, though the progeny of Columbus's adventures will be important throughout this chapter, let us look to what Brant has to say about a topic both old and new that is also crucial to the early modern period, but that has not been sufficiently dealt with yet — the topic of gluttony:

> He shoes a fool in every wise
> Who day and night forever hies
> From feast to feast to fill his paunch . . .
>
> Are wine and sumptuous food your itch?
> You'll not be happy, not get rich.
> Woe's to him and woe's his father too,
> He'll have misfortunes not a few
> Who always gorges like a beast
> Proposing toasts at every feast . . .[2]

Old-fashioned, indeed, this moralism. If anything is new about it, it is perhaps the fact that it now needs to be written about, published, and circulated so widely and in the vernacular, of course. The book addresses a middle-class readership for which it assumes such temptations as gluttony are readily available. And the book would be one among many publications expressing concern about what seems to be, in a medieval spirit but in a Renaissance mode, an early modern obsession, the problem of gluttony — gluttony the subject of countless condemnations, warnings, precepts, and morality tales.[3]

Before arriving at the Bower of Bliss, Spenser's Guyon, the Knight of Temperance, has to pass by the "Gulf of Greediness,"

> That deep engorgeth all this world's prey:
> Which having swallowed up excessively,
> He soon in vomit up again doth lay,
> And belcheth forth his superfluity,
> That all the seas for fear do seem away to fly.[4]

Gluttony to the early modern mind was offensive, disgusting. It was wasteful, unhealthful, and both spiritually and physically self-destructive. Dante may have been content to consign it, in an oddly colorless passage, to the third circle of hell, but there were many far more vehement censures. The *Kalendar of Shepherds* stuffs the mouths of gluttons in hell with rodents and toads, and makes them wash down the vile creatures with filthy water (see fig. 7.1). The seventeenth-century playwright Pierre Corneille roundly condemns it by forecasting its wages in the afterlife:

> L'ivrogne et le gourmand recevront leurs supplices
> du souvenir amer de leurs chères délices,
> et ces repas traînés jusques au lendemain
> mêleront leur idée aux rages de la faim.[5]

The drunk and the glutton would receive for a punishment the bitter memory of their dear delights. Subjected in hell to rages of hunger, they would so remember their long drawn-out meals on earth that their physical pain would only be aggravated by what for a seventeenth-century Frenchman is one of the worst of things possible: a malicious idea.

Why all this anger at the phenomenon of gluttony, even among men like Spenser and Corneille, who enjoyed the good life and lived well? It is true that Christianity said that gluttony was a sin, perhaps the first of sins. It is also true that classical culture said it was a shame, in addition to be being bad for one's health. But one suspects that apart from the many reasons that both Christianity and classical learning could muster against gluttony, something that was left unspoken was behind the contempt for overeating and over-drinking.[6] Clearly gluttony was a lot like lechery: there was something threatening about it, threatening to the order of things. But why? Some answers have been suggested by the preceding discussion of Belch's hiccup — most importantly, that overindulgence was potentially disruptive. ("Bacchus loves disorder," we heard the French poet say, who was thinking of bacchic food as well as bacchic drinking.) It could be disruptive to the peace of others, since it overwhelmed the customary rhythms of consumption, and it could be disruptive to the peace of the self, since it overburdened the digestive apparatus; and by the terms of moral thought in the premodern era, doing harm to either the one or the other was in fact harmful to both. Following medieval tradition, the *Kalendar of Shepherds* assigns the bough of gluttony, on the tree of sins, five separate branches of vicious development: delicacy, greediness, "delicious dressing," "eating without hour," and excess, all of which can be seen to harm the body, the soul, or the community at large.[7] But the calculus of harms and benefits, persuasive though it might be to any thinking person, could not by itself account for the vehemence of the responses to the

dzynkyng ꝗ eytyng cozꝛwmpys the body ꝛ engendzys fepznes and of the
q wych oftymys they ſhozt theyr ly we /ꝗ they q wych nozꝛyſhys weel theyr
bodys they grayth the meyt to wozmys. So the glowton ys kzuc to the woz
mys Đon mẽ of goog ſhoold ha we ſhã to be kzuc to ony lozd moꝛ thã they
ſhoolꝺ ſhaam to be kzut to the wozmys . Ꞇhey q wych ſe wys after the de /
ſyr of the fleßh ſe wys after the re wſof the ſwyn eyttys wyth owt howr
wyth owt meſ wr . So the ſow as theyr abot of the q wych they hold theyr
re wſq weyr foz they ar ſtreynzyt to hold them in the cloſter that ys in the
taweron and as the ſow q wych ys theyr abbot lyys ĩ the mowlz q wych ys
the infeccyon of glowtony .

Figure 7.1. The punishment of gluttons, from *The Kalendar of the Shyppars* (1503). Reproduced by permission of the British Library (g.132.i.2).

idea of gluttony, a vehemence suggesting that gluttony was not only a sin, a shame, a pathology, and a misdemeanor, but even a taboo.

A taboo — a metaphysical prohibition: for at the most basic level, the idea of gluttony identified the problem of consumption, the problem of living as a being in a world where all beings were subjects of consumption, and it drew a line between the moral subject, on the one side, and prohibited consumption, on the other. Given the law of necessity, of natural life and social life and the dependence of one on the other, what might be consumed and when and how much? In what state might it be consumed? How might it be consumed in view of the practices and needs of the self or of other people? How might it be consumed in view of the laws of God or the immanent sanctity of all things? Though usually defined in terms of the classical golden mean, according to which one should consume neither too much nor too little, the idea of gluttony really pressed against the problem of limits, of that beyond which one dare not go. In the absence of the dietary restrictions of Judaism, Hinduism, or other religions of dietary law, apart from an increasingly unimportant and secularized division between days of meat and days of fish, the idea of gluttony identified a dangerous frontier. Gluttony placed the individual outside a proper relation to his needs and, indeed, to the sanctity of his "nature." Moreover, it caused the glutton to tread past the principles of the common wealth that society had wrested from nature. A kind of "steady state" or "zero sum" economics prevailed in the period, so that under normal conditions of production, the store of consumables was thought to be more or less fixed in proportion to the needs of a population. For one person to consume too much meant that, except in the case of especially bountiful years, another person would be forced to consume too little.[8] (We have already seen how this notion operated in the context of utopian thought and the ideal that early utopias promoted of a commonality from which everybody was directed to share equally and private overindulgence was rendered moot. In *Utopia,* when population growth threatened to overwhelm the fixed productivity of the island, the obvious solution was colonialism — that is, the export of its citizens and their appetites elsewhere.) Gluttonous consumption engulfed or engorged, as Spenser's imagery expresses it; it ate up the "prey" of the world, removing it from the resources of the commonality and at most replacing it with waste. Acting against self and other and against nature and society all at once, gluttony was both a danger to everything and a sign of that danger. Adam and Eve themselves, according to one tradition, were thus guilty first of all of gluttony: they "obeyed their greedy appetite in eating the forbidden fruit," says the official Anglican book of sermons. "Even so, if we in eating and drinking exceed, when God of his large liberality sendeth plenty, he will soon change plenty into scarceness. And whereas we gloried in fullness, he will make us empty, and confound us with penury, yea, we shall soon change plenty into scarceness."⁹ When Milton's Eve was said to be guilty of taking "gluttonous delight" in the forbidden fruit, she was showing herself to belong, anachronistically, to a long line of Christian taboo-busters: the first of sinners, in this respect, she was also a contemporary of overeaters everywhere.

Sometimes the idea of gluttony was appropriated for metaphorical purposes, especially with regard to sexuality. "Pity the world, or else this glutton be," says the speaker of Shakespeare's sonnets to the young man, who won't procreate with women. "To eat the world's due, by the grave and thee." In Aretino, gluttony is a word for homosexuality. "Those big rascals and gluttons who run after nasty pleasures," says the nurse in *The Marescalco* about sodomites.¹⁰ To be a glutton in a sexual sense was to pursue a passion at the expense of others — the "world's due." But metaphorical sexual applications of the idea of gluttony paled beside the colorful vehemence of literal treatments of the subject. The best pages of Thomas Nashe's *Pierce Pennilesse* (1592) are devoted to gluttony and drunkenness. Nashe's treatment of lechery by contrast — and this from the author of the immortal comic pornographic poem "The Choice of Valentines" — is insipid. In *Les caractères* (1688) Jean de La Bruyère leaves us with two impressive portraits of gluttons. One, a person identified as Cliton — based on the Count of Broussin — is as much a gourmet as a glutton: "Cliton in all his life never had but two occupations, to dine in the morning and to sup at night." He is an expert on food, and not only preoccupies himself with eating but also always eats well. He would never be found "exposing himself to the horrible inconvenience of eating a bad ragoût or drinking a mediocre wine." The other glutton, Gnathon, based on the Abby Louis-Roger Danse, is more offensive:

Gnathon lives only for himself, and all men together are for his purposes as if nothing. Not content to take the first place at a table, all by himself he occupies two other places as well; he forgets that the meal is both for him and for all the company present; he makes himself the master of the platter, and makes each course all his own: he doesn't attach himself to any one of the dishes until he has tried them all; he would like to be able to savor all of them at the same time. He doesn't serve himself at the table but with his hands; he handles the meats, handles them again, dismembers them, tears them apart, and avails himself of them as if his fellow diners, if they want to eat at all, should only eat his leftovers.

There follows among other things a description of how he gets the sauces all over his beard.[11]

But La Bruyère's treatment alerts us to the idea that something was changing with regard to the discourse of gluttony, a splitting of the idea into two components: on the one side, the voracious antisocial pig, worthy perhaps of the contempt of the satirist or even fire and brimstone of a tragedian like Corneille and, on the other side, the selfish but harmless sociable epicure, the bon vivant, worthy at best of comic Horatian disapproval.[12] (Sir Toby Belch would seem to be halfway between the one and the other.) We have seen evidence of this development in other contexts. Cookbook writers in England and especially France attempt to make fine dining into a science as well as an art; Scarron and Saint-Amant wax poetic in praise of melons and hors d'oeuvres, Scarron happily identifying himself as a *glouton;* the Dutch make a fetish of the elegant table; Rubens imagines a seafood feast worthy of the gods. The change in sensibility that sets in during the early modern period, especially in Italy in the sixteenth century and in France in the seventeenth, has an impact in this respect as well. The glutton — reviled, anathematized, condemned to eternal punishment — may become the gourmet. Living self-indulgently at the expense of both oneself and others, he may become transformed, and transvalued, into living well for the sake of living well. "To eat is a necessity, but to eat intelligently is an art," as La Rochefoucauld puts it. This comedy of food is part of the serious business of consumption in the age of early capitalism. Gluttony may be hazardous to health and reprehensibly ill-mannered, but the gastronomy of the gourmet, devoted to the art of eating intelligently, is a reasonable if light-hearted response to the "world of goods" available in the new economic age.[13] All the discourse of taste in the seventeenth and eighteenth centuries depends on the idea of enlightened consumption, a terribly serious business in the case of such items as alexandrines and filigrees, and a little bit less serious but not ridiculous either in the case of fricassees and clarets.

One of the by-products of the development of gastronomy in this sense is the marginalization of gluttony as a moral category. Awareness of the problem that gluttony posed to health and well-being survived, but the terror before it as a taboo diminished, since eating well for the sake of eating well — that is to say, for the sake of intelligent pleasure — became more widely practiced and accepted. The early modern world was capable, however, of supplying new terrors in the place of the old deadly sin of gluttony. Two of them, whose prominence are indeed owing to the legacy of Christopher Columbus, are cannibalism and hunger.

II

Neither one nor the other was anything new, to be sure. Hunger was and is a feature of world history. Cannibalism, in legend if not in fact, was an idea that circulated in the West since ancient times. Indeed, appearing both in Homer and Herodotus, in the first case as a feature of life among the Cyclops and in the second as a feature of life among the savages living beyond the frontiers of Scythia, cannibalism can be said to have played an important role in the beginnings of Western myth, literature, and history. But something new happened in the early modern period with which the present study has yet to come to terms but that had an enormous impact on the culture of food and such ideas as cannibalism and hunger. The case of Sebastian Brant, *The Ship of Fools,* and its harsh response to the discovery of America may serve to remind us of that. For cannibalism became a new kind of reality with the opening of discovery, trade, conquest, and colonization. And so did hunger. Add that other cataclysmic shift in world history of the time, the Reformation, and the contours of the material and symbolic world of food have been transformed irrevocably. Forget gluttony—the passion of fools. Or if you will remember it, remember it in its new context: a new world, of which America and its "discovery" are only a part, albeit a large part. Two of the most interesting and important works about food in the early modern period—though they are seldom read in this light—are accounts of voyages to America, Jean de Léry's *Histoire d'un voyage fait en la terre du Brésil (History of a Voyage to the Land of Brazil),* published in 1578, and Richard Ligon's *A True and Exact History of the Island of Barbadoes,* first published in 1657. Léry's account, published in the aftermath of the French Wars of Religion and the St. Bartholomew's Day Massacre, is at once an ethnographic appreciation of the culture of the Tupinamba of Brazil, who practiced a form of ritual cannibalism, and a Protestant polemic against Catholics and Catholicism. Himself a Geneva-trained Calvinist minister, Léry accounts the doctrine of the Eucharist—of the presence of the body of Christ in the bread and wine of the Sacrament—as one of Catholicism's most fundamental errors, and so both the conflict between Catholics and Protestants and the encounter between Europeans and Americans turns out to be all about eating and its limits, and thus all about the taboo of cannibalism.[14] Ligon's account, by contrast, published in the waning days of the English Revolution, is not nearly so sensational. There are no cannibals in Ligon's world, although Ligon too, a High Church royalist, had cause to be alarmed at the wages of religious controversy. But if there are no cannibals in Ligon's world, there are slaves and the beginnings of the plantation revolution that would make Barbados one of the leading sugar factories of the world.[15] Ligon admires the sugar industry and writes in part to promote it among his readers, and so he also embraces the commodification of the food supply as well as the commodification of the labor that this new industry providing goods of mass consumption required. But Ligon is a gourmet and one of the first grand spokesmen for culinary hedonism in the English language. These two lively and engaging writings — on Brazil in the sixteenth century and Barbados in the seventeenth, charged from beginning to end with currents of unacknowledged contradiction — register essential shifts in the world of food, of foodways and food values. The problem of gluttony is as nothing given the nature of this shift. But the deeper problems of hunger and a taboo like cannibalism — the latter so central to the European mind-set, yet so quickly challenged in the face of the discovery of America, on the one hand, and the outbreak of the Reformation, on the other — came to prey upon European consciousness. As he triumphed in America, the European also discovered his vulnerability — not so much to sin, although there were temptations in that direction as well, but to something worse: his own hunger and the awfulness of what he could do in order to appease it.

Hunger, interestingly, has had something of a bad rap in traditional European thought. We have just seen a case of that in the discourse of Saint-Évremond: never eat out of "hunger," he says; instead, cultivate your "appetite." A term that we might take to be neutral, naming a biological function, a need or "instinct," is instead conventionally ominous. The primary meaning of the word in English, for example, according to the *Oxford English Dictionary,* is "the uneasy or painful sensation caused by want of food; craving appetite. Also, the exhausted condition caused by want of food." The dictionary has many examples to prove the point; and since the word is Anglo-Saxon in origin, its examples, which continue to the present day, begin in the ninth century. (One will find similar issues with Latinate/Romance terms, as in the French homology between *faim* and *famine.*) The moral implication is clear. Whatever the appetite may be in English usage, hunger can be dangerous. Though one proverb has it that "hunger is the best sauce" — the word "hunger" being at least sometimes equivalent to "appetite" — another equally common proverb says that "hunger pierces stone walls." Shakespeare himself has a character cite the proverb at one point, in *Coriolanus,* when a patrician complains that the food-rioting mob is making unwarranted demands on the state.

> They said they were an-hungry; sighed forth proverbs,
> That hunger broke stone walls, that dogs must eat,
> That meat was made for mouths, that the gods sent not
> Corn for the rich men only . . .[16]

In *As You like It,* Orlando calls attention to "two weak evils, age and hunger," and in *3 Henry VI* York tells us that soldiers retreating in the face of a superior army are "like lambs pursued by hunger-starved wolves."[17] Hunger may be a need, but awareness of hunger is often associated with pain, desperation, and aggression. However, as I will suggest in what follows, it need not be: this hunger that hurts, that leads one to despair and wolfish violence, is one cultural appropriation of biology among many, and choosing it has consequences.

As for cannibalism, there we have not only a concept with a bad reputation, but a phenomenon that has been the object of considerable controversy and that is surprisingly complex and resistant to analysis. Early modern cannibalism is controversial because we can seldom be sure that it actually happened; we always have to wonder about the adequacy of eyewitness reporting and the biases and symbolic associations implicit in accounts of the subject. It is complex because there are apparently so many different kinds of cannibalism that it may be unfair or inaccurate to group them all together, as if cannibalism were a single phenomenon, like the rosebush, with many varieties or species. William Arens, in an influential and controversial critique of the anthropology of cannibalism, pokes fun at the many categories that anthropologists have concocted (apparently) to differentiate the field: endocannibalism, exocannibalism, gustatory, survival, revenge, and ritual cannibalism.[18] The problem with these categories is that they create an illusion of scientific systematicity for a field of study whose empirical underpinnings and conceptual basis alike are subject to dispute. The categories themselves are a bit slippery. The distinction between endo- and exocannibalism, for example, is a distinction between eating a member within a social group or outside of the social group, but precisely how are these groups and their insides and outsides to be defined? What is inside in one sense may be outside in another, and vice versa. Ritual warfare in parts of the Americas, which may or may not have included an element of cannibalistic quarry (though usually it didn't), was waged between presumably distinct groups who were also nevertheless related to one another and even included in one another, sometimes by way of the instrumentality of the ritual of violence itself. Moreover, in most cases distinctions drawn between different types of cannibalism are as much a function of observation as the thing being observed. Writing some years after Arens's critique, the author of a book on "Cannibalism as a Cultural System," relying on the very terms Arens mocks, still includes in her body of data reports of cannibalism based on hearsay and still argues as if the terms of observation and analysis deployed by a Western comparative anthropologist are identical with such terms as the peoples under study would use to describe what they do.[19] Yet there are societies where "cannibalism"—that is, the eating of one human being by another—is another word for death.[20] As anthropologist Lawrence Goldman observes, before you can know what it means for a society to practice cannibalism, one first has to know what it means in that society to eat: eating is itself a metaphorical category, and to "eat" another or indeed to eat anything at all will not mean the same thing in all cultures.[21] Evidently, one also has to know what it means in a given society to die.

Given these issues, it becomes evident on analysis that European observations of cannibalism among early modern Americans were, if not all but entirely factitious, at least debased. The story is well known by now how the word "cannibal" derives from a corruption of the word "Carib," how Columbus and his men presumed to understand that the "Caribs" were man-eaters from conversations held with other Arawaks in a language the Europeans did not understand; how Columbus and many explorers to follow apparently observed cannibalism or at least were convinced by hearsay regarding what they took natives to be saying about cannibalism (again, in languages they could not really understand) because cannibalism was what they had learned from the ancients they ought to be looking for when traveling in unknown lands; and how, finally, European descriptions of cannibalism among Americans were expressions of European anxieties about their own civility in the face of a "savagery" that was otherwise both inexplicable and wonderful.[22] All this becomes clear from one of the best known of the early reports, in the *Decades* of the Italian Peter Martyr, as translated here in 1555 by the Englishman Richard Eden:

> The wild and mischievous people called *Canibales,* or *Caribes,* which were accustomed to eat man's flesh and called of old writers *Anthropophagi* molest [the rival Arawaks] exceedingly, invading their country, taking them captive, killing and eating them. . . . [The Arawaks] are no less vexed with the incursions of these manhunting *Canibales* when they go forth a voyage to seek their prey than are other tame beasts of Lions and Tigers. Such children as they take, they geld to make them fat as we do cock chickens and young hogs, and eat them when they are well fed: of such as they eat, they first eat the entrails and extreme parts, as hands, feet, arms, neck, and head. The other moist fleshy parts, they powder for store, as we do [bellies] of pork and gammons of bacon. Yet do they abstain from eating of women and count it vile. Therefore such young women as they take, they keep for increase, as we do hens to lay eggs.[23]

Most of this is nonsense, of course. It is meaningful only so far as it refers not to the natives of the Caribbean islands but to Europeans, busily trading in the idea of West Indian depravity.

More complex are the cases of the Iroquois in North America, with their ritual slaughters; the Aztecs in Mexico, with their human sacrifices; and the Tupinamba of Brazil. Here the European observers were responding to something that appeared to be going on before their eyes or to something they were hearing firsthand from presumably reliable informers.[24] It is never clear to me, however, that early observers really comprehended what they were seeing and hearing, or really had a language or method to explain it. How should they? The science of anthropology was several centuries in the future, and even today that science has its problems. Though early observers were aware of the symbolic density of culture — indeed, the most famous statements of cultural relativism in the early modern period, by Montaigne, were decisively influenced by his contact with the "cannibals" of America — they had little experience and no tried-and-true methodology for deciphering it. Nor, during the sixteenth and seventeenth centuries, were they meticulous about discriminating fact from legend, direct observation from hearsay, or original material from handed-down reports. Most of the observers were textual pirates — or plagiarists, if you prefer — constructing their accounts out of a bricolage of found, stolen, and stumbled-upon information. As Stephen Greenblatt once put it, one of the "key principles of the Renaissance geographical imagination" is that "eye-witness testimony, for all its vaunted importance, sits as a very small edifice on top of an enormous mountain of hearsay, rumor, convention and endlessly recycled fable."[25] Still, if European reports tell us little that is entirely trustworthy about Native Americans, they tell us *something* about them; and, again, they tell us a great deal about the Europeans themselves.

Americans, in any case, were not the only cannibals preying upon the European imagination. There was cannibalism at home as well. Homer's Cyclops, it should be remembered, were inhabitants of the Mediterranean. The ogre of folktales, similar to the Cyclops but with a particular appetite for stray children and adventurous adolescents and a predilection for inhabiting the European woodlands, remained a part of popular culture throughout the early modern period. Among the educated, a pair of high-culture literary legends circulated widely that had a strong impact on the imagination: Flavius Josephus's dramatic account (in Latin) of the siege of Jerusalem in *The Jewish War,* and Seneca's gory tragedy (also in Latin) of *Thyestes.* In the former, a people driven to starvation and despair find their penultimate humiliation — the ultimate humiliation would be the destruction of their temple — in the story of a mother who, driven to the point of madness by hunger, eats her child. "Poor little mite!" Josephus has her say to her child when she warms up to the act.

> "In war, famine, and civil strife why should I keep you alive? With the Romans there is only slavery, if we are alive when they come; but famine

is forestalling slavery, and the partisans are crueller than either. Come, you must be food for me, to the partisans an avenging spirit, and to the world a tale, the only thing left to fill up the measure of Jewish misery." As she spoke [Josephus continues] she killed her son, then roasted him and ate one half, concealing and saving up the rest.

Afterward, Josephus says, "the entire city could think of nothing but this abomination; everyone saw the tragedy before his own eyes and shuddered as if the crime was his."[26] It is no doubt significant that Josephus has the woman, Mary of Bethezub, recite a soliloquy before she commits the deed, and that Josephus refers to the story as a "tragedy." The added detail that later everyone "shuddered as if the crime was his" underscores both the dreadfulness of the act and the "tragic," which is to say theater-like pity and fear that Josephus requires such an event to evoke — the mixture of identification and revulsion that classical theory ascribes to tragic experience. Josephus was writing, of course, at about the same time as Seneca produced the play script for *Thyestes,* based on Greek mythology. There again, the story dwells not just on cannibalism or even "endocannibalism," but on a parri-endocannibalism, or even parri-infanti-endocannibalism. The motive for this dreadful event is revenge: one brother exacts revenge on another by surreptitiously murdering the second brother's sons and serving them up in a stew. The worst thing that could happen to a person, the story insists, is to eat one's own offspring, even if one does so inadvertently. As I have had occasion to remark before, when Shakespeare produced his own redaction of the story, in *Titus Andronicus,* he changed the dish served from a stew to a pasty, or baked meat, adding the imagery of burial and the dirt of the grave to the horror of eating one's offspring. (He also changed the child-eating father into a mother.) But Shakespeare, as far as I know, is the only playwright ever to have placed the victims into a pie. For most redactors of the myth — and there were quite a few in both England and France — revenge and horror, punctuated by the consumption of a boiled or roasted corpse, was quite enough. One hundred and ten years later, when the French playwright Crébillon produced his own *Atrée et Thyèste,* he followed the original Senecan story closer, among other things having his victims seethed in a stew; it is Crébillon's words about the parri-infanti-endocannibalism that Edgar Allan Poe quotes in "The Purloined Letter" and that Jacques Lacan quotes again in his famous seminar on the story: it is to parri-infanti-endocannibalism, forced upon a parent as an exaction of revenge for his criminal misdeeds to another, that Lacan obliquely refers when, as a metaphor for the return of the repressed, he presents the memorable expression "Eat your *Dasein.*"

In a major study of early modern accounts of cannibalism, Frank Lestringant divides the field roughly into reports of cannibalism as a form of revenge, and therefore as a form of ritual, and reports of cannibalism as a form of bestial or monstrous voraciousness.[27] Whatever the truth or source of these accounts, early moderns constructed them with these two different models in mind. Those in the first category could be worthy of respect; revenge cannibals might be thought to have something to say to the civilized, non-cannibalistic people of the West. It was to such revenge cannibals that Montaigne was drawn in his hallmark essay "Of Cannibals." But those in the second category could be worthy of nothing but contempt and disgust. Lestringant's point is that as Western man came to have less and less patience for the Other and imperialism came to be joined with racism, the "cannibals" of exotic places were placed in the category of bestial or monstrous voraciousness only. The truth of revenge and ritual and the density of cultural life was forgotten. The distinction is helpful. But there are probably still more nuances to consider: for in the first place, not all the cannibals were "Other," inhabiting exotic locales; in the second place, not all cannibals were actually cannibals (Lestringant rejects Arens and doesn't distinguish between fanciful accounts of cannibalism and possibly true ones); and in the third place, early modern writers themselves were capable of making finer distinctions than this and capable to boot of betraying deeper inconsistencies and contradictions in their responses.

In a footnote to his 1632 translation of Ovid's *Metamorphoses,* commenting on the Cyclops of Greek mythology, the traveler and colonialist George Sandys, writing perhaps with his own experience in Jamestown in mind, has this to say:

> Now the Cyclops (as formerly said) were a savage people given to spoil and robbery; unsociable amongst themselves, and inhumane to strangers: And no marvel; when lawless, and subject to no government, the bond of society; which gives to every man his own, suppressing vice, and advancing virtue, the two main columns of a Commonwealth, without which it can have no support. Besides man is a political and sociable creature: they therefore are to be numbered among beasts who renounce society, whereby they are destitute of laws, the ordination of civility. Hence it ensues, that man, in creation the best, when averse to justice, is the worst of all creatures. For injustice, armed with power, is most outrageous and bloody. Such is Polyphemus, who feasts himself with the flesh of his guests; more savage then are the West Indians at this day, who only eat their enemies, whom they have taken in wars; whose slighting of death and patient sufferance is remarkable; receiving the deadly blow, without distemper, or appearance of sorrow; their fellows looking on, and heartily feeding on the meat which is given them;

yet know how they are to supply the shambles perhaps the day following. The heads of men they account among their delicates, which are
only to be eaten by the great ones, boiling oft times so few as a dozen together, as hath been seen by our Countrymen. Injustice and cruelty are
ever accompanied with Atheism and a contempt of the Deity: which
Polyphemus himself thus professeth in Homer.

O fool! That hath com'st from far abroads,
To bid me fear or reverence the Gods.
We Cyclops care not for the Goat-nursed Jove;
More to be fear'd then those who sway above.
Nor will I, for Jove's wrath, forbear to kill
Thee or thy Mares: My God is my stern will. (Odyssey, l.9.272–278)

Like the Scythians who in their barbarous devotions accustomed to fix
a spear in the ground, and worship it, as they only God they acknowledged. But this contemner of Gods and men, this inhumane Monster,
is surprised in his drunkenness, and deprived of his only eye by despised
Ulysses; who would not kill him, the longer to protract his punishment.
In the person of Ulysses, that wisdom is prefigured, which undauntedly
and victoriously runs through all dangers: in Polyphemus, the folly of
barbarous strength, enfeebled with vices. He is also physically said to be
subdued by the other, in that wisdom discovers the secrets of nature;
which before they be known seem wonderful and formidable.[28]

The rest of this chapter could be devoted to a gloss of this one passage.[29]
Sandys himself adopts the distinction that Lestringant predicts between revenge cannibalism and voracious, bestial cannibalism. In words that echo Montaigne and perhaps such sources as Montaigne drew upon, including Jean de Léry,
the first are inherently noble in their courage, their patience, and their careful
observance of law and order. They can even distinguish between eating the heads
of the victims and eating the other parts, the heads — those noble crowns of the
microcosm — being reserved for the nobles among them. Meanwhile, the Cyclops, who are legendary or at least a part of history rather than contemporary
life, eat their victims out of hunger. And in eating out of hunger, though they
otherwise (apart from the single eye) betray human characteristics, the Cyclops
openly defy law and order: they are "contemner[s] of Gods and men"; "inhumane"; "unsociable." Gluttons in the worst sense of the word, instead of feasting their guests, they eat them. Sandys makes the purported cannibals of the
West Indies into figures who are "less savage" than the legendary Cyclops and

even admirable in a way because they obey the rules they have set for themselves and pause before the respect owed to the gods and their fellow men. They do not cannibalize out of hunger, and even in cannibalizing their enemies, they follow a rule of table manners and hospitality. Sandys, in other words, rejects the hysteria of an early writer like Peter Martyr and again, while adopting the categories predicted by Lestringant, even goes the latter one better by expressing a healthy skepticism regarding currently circulating accounts. But Sandys also adds a troubling qualification (just the kind of qualification that Léry and Montaigne call attention to in their attacks on the hypocrisy of Western society). All of the barbarism of the Cyclops can be summed up in the idea that the Cyclops are "averse to justice" and therefore the worst of creatures. And what is justice? It is among other things that value observed by Ulysses, that avatar of scientific reason, who mutilates his foe instead of killing him, "the longer to protract his punishment." As the West Indians are said to prosecute justice by cannibalizing their enemies, the European prosecute justice by torturing the criminal. And by the lights of George Sandys, the treasury secretary of Jamestown during the notorious "massacre" of 1622, both practices are admirable in their way — signs of culture, civility, and self-restraint. To be barbarous is to eat your guests. To be nobly savage is to eat your enemies. To be civil is to feast the former and, in the name of justice, torture the latter. If the barbarous cannibal is a monstrous glutton, eating the world's due, and the noble cannibal is something of a gourmet, Western man, visiting the shores of the savages and often being subject to less than hospitable treatment, has better things to do than eat.

III

When Jean de Léry published the account of his travels to Brazil, undertaken in 1557, nearly twenty years had passed, and he had already published another book, *L'histoire mémorable du siège et de la famine de Sancerre*, in 1573. The siege and the famine were brutal. In the midst of the religious wars in France, in the aftermath of the St. Bartholomew's Day Massacre, a Catholic army under royal authority surrounded the small Protestant citadel of Sancerre, cutting it off from the countryside and its food supplies; as many as five hundred died of starvation, and Léry, the Calvinist minister, was in the middle of it, charged with seeing that a certain civil order be maintained. He saw people trying to eat leather, rawhide, parchment, wild grasses, hay, nutshells, and candles. He had seen them picking through manure for undigested grains and other tidbits. In the midst of the alimentary despair, an elderly female lodger, a father, and a mother were found to have committed a terrible act of cannibalism on the corpse of a three-year-old girl. Then while traveling through France, after the surrender of the town and after having published his account of the siege, Léry came across a copy of the manuscript he had written many years before about Brazil. That manuscript formed the basis of his *Histoire d'un voyage fait en la terre du Brésil*. In this other "history," Léry wrote about the ten months he had spent in Brazil, in the area of what we now know as Rio de Janeiro, in the hope of helping to establish a reformed community in the land of the Tupinamba Indians. Like other travelers of the time who had written about the Tupi, notably Hans Staden and André Thevet, Léry claimed to have observed ritual cannibalism, regularly practiced, where Tupi captured enemies in battle, fattened them up, adopted them into the daily life of their villages, sometimes even married them to their own women, and eventually tortured, executed, slaughtered, and ate them.[30] Léry himself had been treated hospitably among the Tupi, who considered him one of their allies. But he quarreled with the nobleman Nicolas Durand de Villegagnon, the founder of the French colony, predominantly over religious matters—Villegagnon being sympathetic with Léry's reformed religion but not sympathetic enough. Villegagnon and Léry were especially piqued with another, according to the latter, over the matter of the Eucharist, which Villegagnon interpreted in a more traditional way than Calvinists like Léry. For Villegagnon some kind of real presence of Christ had to be realized in the bread and wine of the host. "Even as the earthly meat by the heat of the stomach is converted into blood and nourishment for the body," Léry reports Villegagnon praying in the midst of delivering a lay sermon, "grant so to nourish and sustain our souls with the flesh and blood of thy Son, so that he may be formed in us, and we in Him." Indeed, as Villegagnon later argues, "the words 'This is my Body; this is my Blood' cannot be taken other than to mean that the Body and the Blood of Jesus Christ are contained therein."[31] But for Léry the Eucharist was strictly a symbolic and spiritual affair, the commemoration of a real presence lost to history but recalled to men through the agency of the Holy Spirit. The cannibalistic overtones of a real substance or presence were obnoxious to him, even if he did not find the real cannibalism of the Tupi he had visited in all respects offensive. Eventually Léry and some of his companions were forced to leave the colony and return to France. On the way back, in a poorly fitted ship that drifted at sea for three months, Léry nearly starved to death. Some of the others on board actually did. And the survivors were beginning to consider committing cannibalism on the corpses of their shipmates when they suddenly found themselves off the coast of France and out of danger.

Léry himself does not seem to be entirely aware of the deep irony of his

Figure 7.2. The Tupinamba ritual of cannibalism, as observed (*center right,* the figure with the beard) by Hans Staden, from *Historia Americae sive Novi Orbis* (1634), compiled and illustrated by Theodor de Bry. Reproduced by the permission of the British Library (G.6627.(1.)).

writing: the preoccupation with food, starvation, and cannibalism that runs throughout. It may well be that Léry finds in food practices the "limits of civility," whether those limits pertain to Huguenots, Tupinamba, or Catholic loyalists;[32] but civility is not the only crucial idea in Léry's writing. Religious truth and the meaning of suffering are crucial as well. And Léry's preoccupation with food has other sources besides. One does not have to dwell too long in the dark caves of psychobiography to appreciate these other sources: for Léry was obviously traumatized by events at sea, in Brazil, and at Sancerre.[33] If he writes in the capacity of a polemicist, an adversary of Catholicism, and a defender of the Reformed faith, as well as a storyteller and ethnologist, his inspiration for both of the two books was his traumatization over matters of food, of eating and not eating, of eating the wrong things and eating nothing at all, at seeing people make mistakes about what they ought to eat and how and why, or otherwise at seeing people being forced to take crafty measures in the face of impossible choices: to dine on leather and grass or moldy ship's biscuit polluted with rat droppings and worms, to dine on one's enemy or, like Léry, to politely decline to dine on the enemy of one's friends, though in danger of giving offense to one's friends and being accused of treason as a result. Not all of what Léry has to say is reactive. For Léry can be said to have sought out some of the trouble he encountered. He was an adventurer, after all. Moreover, on the other side of Léry's tale of woe and transgression lies a love of good food. While he sometimes speaks dismissively of "finicky gentlemen" too refined to live on anything but the best and rarest of dishes, and by implication too complacent to seek after the kind of trouble he has found, Léry is himself an enthusiast. As he crosses the sea to Brazil, for example, what he seems to experience above all is the variety of foods he and his fellow travelers lived on; and if this sometimes means moldy ship's biscuit and bad water, it also often means the wonderful catches of fish the sailors take: bonito, "one of the best to eat that can be found"; albacore, "almost five feet long and as big as a man's body," "one of the best sea fish," which they cooked in slices with salt over coals and was "wonderfully good and flavorful cooked in this fashion"; the dorado, even better, for "neither in salt water nor in fresh water is there a more delicate one"; porpoises, which were not so good, though the fetuses of captured pregnant sows they "roasted like sucking pigs"; sharks; sea tortoises; flying fish.[34] There are a number of similar passages elsewhere in his writing. The deep irony, that the story of travels to exotic lands and the attempt to establish a self-sufficient community of true believers — like the story of being besieged in an ancient town for having likewise attempted to sustain a self-sufficient community of true believers — is fundamentally a story about food; this deep irony, which Léry may not have been fully aware of, is a creature of both trauma and desire. All Léry has wanted out of life, it appears, given his fundamental commitment to Calvinism and the community of the gathered church, was to be able to eat. But there lay the problem.

Léry was one among many colonialists who found themselves exposed in their travels to the awful logic, and awful appeal, of hunger. The reason for this was simple. Whatever the motives of exploration and settlement may have been, to venture onto the high seas for the sake of establishing a life elsewhere required first of all a change in one's relation to the need for food. "Upon arrival in that land in America," Léry learns unflinchingly before he sails, "one would have to be content to eat, instead of bread, a certain flour made from a root; and as for wine, not a trace, for no grapevines grow there. In short, just as in a New World . . . one would have to adopt ways of life and nourishment completely different from those of our Europe."[35] We have to imagine this prospect not simply as the substitution of one set of foods for another, everything else remaining the same, but the change from one whole regime or foodway to another—"ways of life and nourishment"—where everything else also changes. And we have to imagine the stakes involved, where the second foodway was of suspect reliability, comfort, taste, and healthfulness. The risk of exploration and colonization was the risk of uncertainty and death. At home, a man like Léry could always be sure of supply: reliably healthy and comforting foods, reliably provisioned, brought forth out of the unity of an ecology and a social world that was known to be secure and gratifying. On the high seas, or on an island in the Guanabara Bay, previous assumptions about food supplies and the comforts of life went for naught. One therefore had to regard food with a new rationality: as a quantified stock, planned in advance to provide for a quantifiable length of time, for the sake of the survival of a set number of bodies, regardless of the other considerations that usually went into the formation of a diet. This commodification of food supplies, though implicit in any sort of purveyance, attains a new level of abstraction in the age of exploration. Food, in the age of exploration, becomes a form of capital, and the survival of shipboard laborers becomes a kind of return on capital expenditure. Any other relation to food that seafarers might cherish becomes nugatory. "What do you say to that, my finicky gentlemen," Léry expostulates, after relating an interval of living on biscuits and worms and wormy water, "who . . . could not think of taking a meal unless the dishes are shining, the glasses polished, the napkins white as snow, the bread nicely cut, the meat, as delicate as you please, properly prepared and served, and the wine or other draught clear as emerald? Are you willing to board ship to live in such a fashion?"[36] Nor is there of course anything unique about Léry's experience and sentiments. The age of exploration brought about a revolution in the foodways of Europe and America alike. That revolution had many sides. The most famous of them was the introduction of new foodstuffs to the people on both sides of the Atlantic, cattle and wheat to America, potatoes and tomatoes to Europe. But there was also this other side of the food revolution: the new commodification of food supplies, and along with that the new relation of men to hunger.

Like Ligon and many others to follow, Léry both embraces that relation and resists it. Again and again, Léry insists upon the new relation as if it were a new kind of truth, as indeed it was. To experience alimentary desperation, to be forced to live on moldy biscuit or worse or on nothing at all, and to do so as the price of one's adventures in the world of colonialism and religious separatism, is to come into contact with a fundamental condition of life in the context of a quest for fundamentals. Alimentary despair is the material equivalent of spiritual alienation, the alienation Calvinists like Léry were in fact taught to seek out as a condition of salvation. "Our feeling of ignorance, vanity, want, weakness, in short depravity and corruption," Calvin once wrote, "reminds us that in the Lord, and none but He, dwell the true light and wisdom, solid virtue, exuberant goodness. We are accordingly urged by our own evil things to consider the good things of God; and, indeed, we cannot aspire to him in earnest until we have begun to be displeased with ourselves."[37] And so, on the one hand, Léry seeks out the condition of "want" and "weakness" that sailing to America entails and insists on it rhetorically to his reader. The fundamental truth of his experience in Brazil, as it would also be of his experience in Sancerre, is the truth of hunger, a truth he sought out, a truth he found, a truth he needs to remind himself and his readers of at every suitable occasion. Yet, on the other hand, even as Léry reaches toward the logic and awfulness of hunger, so he also, understandably, desires to overcome it, to achieve a condition of material, alimentary fulfillment. Arriving in Brazil, he takes pleasure both in learning to eat the way the native Brazilians do, on Brazilian food crops, seafood, and land animals, and in introducing European commodities there. He joys in eating cassava and maize in many forms. He learns to like the taste of armadillos and lizards — of course, according to Léry, they both taste like chicken — and to get drunk on the native brew, *caouin,* made from fermented manioc juice. He is especially enthusiastic about the "exquisite" fruit and seed crops in Brazil: pineapples, bananas, sweet potatoes, peanuts. Everywhere he goes the world is made of things to eat, often of wonderful things to eat. And everywhere he goes he finds opportunities for transplanting Old World foodways. If he likes the native fruit and the brew, he is also fond of the oranges, lemons, and sugarcane that the Portuguese have transplanted to Brazil, he is proud of his initial success in planting wheat and barley on the shores of the bay, and he is looking forward to the time when vines he has planted in Brazil will bear sweet crops of grapes, so that French settlers will be able to make their own wine.

The crosscurrents of gustatory motifs in Léry's *Voyage* are emblematic of the experience of early colonialism generally from a meta-semiotic point of view: the *commodification* of need and the goods required to satisfy it in the face of the logic of travel, colonization, and mercantilism; the *alienation* of the individual from material and spiritual comfort and therefore from customary selfhood; the *rediscovery* of the self through resistance to absorption in the alien world; the *hybridization* (or *creolization*) of cultural style through the conjunction of strange and familiar foodways; the *assertion of wonder* at the new horizons of possibility opening up before the subject. One can find these motifs as early as the journals and letters of Columbus. They are still operating as late as 1630, when the Great Migration is getting under way in Britain, and thousands of English subjects are preparing to sail away to start their lives anew in the West Indies, Virginia, and New

England.[38] *Cannibalism* in the face of these motifs obviously represents a limit. It is a practice beyond which commodification, alienation, self-discovery, hybridization, and wonder cannot go, but before which, in the hands of an observer-writer like Léry, the subject must pause.

In fact, Léry discovers many different kinds of cannibalism in the course of his life. Among the Brazilians there are already two or three. The Tupinamba, among whom he has lived, are the good cannibalists. Dignified in their own way, kind to their friends, intelligent and handsome, lively and warm, already inclined despite the darkness of their superstitions toward such beliefs and sentiments as would make them easy to convert to Christianity, the Tupi, Léry wants to suggest, are really inhumane in only this one practice, the brutal execution and cannibalizing of their enemies, and even in this there are things to admire. They do not eat their enemies for hunger, Léry insists, but as an expression of military virtue.[39] Nor are the victims of cannibalism saddened or humiliated, brutally executed and consumed though they are. "Although these barbarian nations have great fear of natural death," Léry writes, "nonetheless such prisoners consider themselves fortunate to die thus publicly, in the midst of their enemies and are utterly untroubled." Indeed, as other writers besides Léry confirm, the ritual victims die in noble, ritual defiance of their captors.[40] There is nothing shameful about Tupinamba cannibalism. This dignified practice contrasts, however, with the cannibalism of Brazilians whom Léry observes from a different angle. The Margaia — a tribe related by language and culture to the Tupi, who are nevertheless the prime enemy of the latter and allies of the Portuguese instead of the French — Léry observes only as a potential victim, and Léry sees dignity neither in the behavior of the Margaia nor in the prospect of being captured by them. The Margaia were "such enemies of the French," he notes, "that if they had us at their mercy, we would have paid no other ransom except being slain and cut to pieces, and serving as a meal for them." Though the pretext for belligerence associated with them is political enmity, the behavior itself is reduced to a species of gluttony — cannibalism for the sake of pleasurable nutrition. Nor are the Margaia the worst of the lot. Léry also encounters an unrelated tribe, the Outeca, who speak a different language. "These devilish Outeca remain invincible in this little region, and furthermore, like dogs and wolves, eat flesh raw, and because even their language is not understood by their neighbors, they are considered to be among the most barbarous, cruel, and dreaded nations that can be found in all the West Indies and the land of Brazil."[41]

And again, Brazilian cannibalism is not the only kind that Léry is aware of. First of all, there is the cannibalism of the Roman Catholics among whom he found himself in Brazil: "they wanted not only to eat the flesh of Jesus Christ grossly rather than spiritually, but what was worse, like the savages named *Outeca*, of whom I have already spoken, they wanted to chew and swallow it raw."[42] The charge of cannibalistic error was familiar in anti-Catholic rhetoric of the time. An especially striking example can be found in the pamphlet entitled *Satyres chrétiennes de la cuisine papale* (1560), which burlesques not only the Roman Catholic sacrament, but the worldly corruption of the church in general.[43] And yet the errors of the Catholics were mainly symbolic; certainly, they were victimless; and Léry was familiar with more pernicious cannibalisms at home. After accounting for cannibalism among the Tupinamba, he compares the practice favorably with atrocities familiar in European society, outrages that begin by appearing similar to the actual cannibalization of human flesh and eventually are identical to it. He complains about the criminal behavior of usurers, "sucking blood and marrow, and eating everyone alive — widows, orphans, and other poor people, whose throats it would be better to cut once and for all, than to make them linger in misery." He then notes cases of the mutilation of corpses during the religious wars in France, mutilations that were believed to have ended with the eating of the hearts and livers of the victims, as if Catholics had become Aztecs, sacrificing the innocent to a voracious God within.[44] When Léry makes comparisons like this, which would become a part of humanist rhetoric for years to come, the dignity of Tupinamba practices contrasts not only with voraciousness but cruelty.[45] The voraciousness of Outeca, of Catholics, and of usurers shows them to be gluttons, eating the world's due, obeying a "greedy appetite." But worse still is the cruelty practiced against victims. The usurers (another familiar target of Calvinist polemics, by whom are meant both Catholic bankers and Jews) eat their victims alive, prolonging their suffering; the perpetrators of the St. Bartholomew's Day Massacre devour their enemy's dignity, humiliating both victim and mourner by violating the sanctity of the dead body.

The cannibalism closest to home and self Léry saves for last. Aboard ship on his return journey, adrift at sea after several months and with all the ship's supplies having been exhausted, Léry finds hunger giving way to desperation, a desperation he would also experience during the siege of Sancerre. "I will speak here in passing of something I have not only observed in others, but felt myself during these two famines, as harsh as any that man has survived. When the bodies are weakened, and nature is failing, the senses are alienated and the wits dispersed; all this makes one ferocious, and engenders a wrath that can truly be called a kind of madness. The common expression we use for saying that someone lacks food is very accurate: we say that such and such a person is mad with hunger." The measures to which men in this condition had recourse were increasingly disgusting. "What would we not have eaten, or rather devoured, in such extremity?"

Léry asks. "For in truth, to appease our hunger we craved even the old bones and offal that the dogs drag off the dung heaps; without a doubt, if we had had green grasses, even hay, or leaves of trees such as one might have on land, we would have grazed on them like brute beasts." And then comes the idea of what would later be called the "custom of the sea": "I can testify that during our famine on the sea we were so despondent and irritable that although we were restrained by the fear of God, we could scarcely speak to each other without getting angry, and, what was worse (may God pardon us), glancing at each other sideways, harboring evil thoughts regarding that barbarous act." Almost dead with hunger—and indeed several had already died, and it would take months for Léry and the other survivors to recover from the effects—the travelers finally sight land, at which point the master of the ship makes a confession. "After we had thanked [God] for our approaching deliverance, the master of the ship said aloud that if we had remained in that state one more day, he had resolved for certain not to cast lots, as some have done in such distress, but, without saying a word, to kill one of us to serve as food for the others; which I feared the less for myself since (although there was not much fat on any of us) unless he had been willing to eat skin and bones, it would not have been me."[46]

So Léry writes about all these different varieties of cannibalism, using his own categories of response: the noble cannibalism of the Tupinamba; the vicious cannibalism of the Margaia; the uncivil, wolfish cannibalism of the Outeca; the erroneous cannibalism of the Catholics at Sacrament; the vicious, symbolic cannibalism of usurers; the blasphemous, heart-and-liver consuming cannibalism of Catholic rioters during the massacre; and finally, desperate survival cannibalism. Morality falls favorably on the side of the cannibal who eats his victims neither out of hunger nor out of viciousness. Though the act is in itself "cruel" and "barbarous," Léry never fails to remark, still, among the ritual cannibals, cannibalism can be practiced in a spirit of justice and sanctity, showing respect for the victims and proceeding according to the known laws of virtue, nature, and civility. This of course is another irony, intentional on Léry's part. The Tupinamba show themselves to live, indeed, within the "limits of civility," that is to say, to live within it except for one thing. To be brought wholly within the ken of civility, they would have to give up cannibalism, of course; but since they already display most of the prerequisites of civility, all they need is one thing more, which is the biggest thing of all, and perhaps the most difficult: they need to be converted to Christianity, the true Christianity of the Huguenot.[47] Meanwhile, those voracious savages, Roman Catholics and usurers whose cannibalism compares unfavorably with the Tupinamba, are probably outside the pale altogether. If, as it appears, they cannot be converted to the true religion, or even to the conditions of secular civility, then they can only be dismissed or reviled as enemies. As for survival cannibals, who would seem to have a strong moral claim as well, there Léry in fact pauses again. Survival cannibalism does not seem to be morally excusable either. It is "evil" and "barbarous." Though it might well correlate with common ethical ideas about the right of self-preservation, especially when the victim of the survival cannibalism was either a corpse or a victim fairly chosen by lots, Léry does not choose to represent it that way.

Survival cannibalism is absorbed, in Léry's writing as in many others', by what has been called "the hunger topos."[48] It arrives as the articulation of extremity, the reduction of that which is familiarly human to that which is strange, abhorrent, and finally inhuman. In the stories where it is encountered, this hunger topos with its conclusion in survival cannibalism follows from a sequence of deprivation and depravity: the hungry move down the scale of edibles, ending in the consumption of the most unpalatable things of all. We have seen the elements of the sequence already in the case of Shakespeare's Mark Antony with his "roughest berry," his staglike browsing of "the barks of trees," his "strange flesh."[49] Before reporting an instance of survival cannibalism, or even an instance of the temptation to survival cannibalism, the writer availing himself of the hunger topos will first document a sequence of gustatory depravity, from rough berries to bark to strange flesh and worse, and with it the descent into moral depravity. Thus Léry reports on the "old bones and offal" the seafarers would gladly have dined on had they the chance, as well the madness that eventually afflicted them. In his account of the siege of Sancerre, Léry goes considerably further. He painstakingly documents the scale of edibles down which the Sancerrois descended, even while also explaining the measures they took to make the unpalatable palatable. For meats he recounts the following sequence, given that no supplies of the usual livestock were any longer available: asses, mules, and horses, followed by cats, rats, moles, mice, and finally dogs. Among animal products apart from edible flesh, Léry gives the following sequence: hides of beef and mutton; followed by the hides of horses, dogs, and other unpalatable animals; then asses' ears, horses' hooves, horns and antlers, and finally leather. Among horticultural products, a descent is made from garden herbs and cabbage to vine twigs, wild herbs and roots, and finally hemlock root, the latter consumed by some to fatal effect. Among grains, a descent is made from wheat to linseed, wild grasses, hay, straw, and ground nutshells. Through all this Léry reports with a perverse, ironic relish the fine taste disgusting things acquired because of the hunger of the people and the ingenuity with which they prepared their provender: children were comforted with mice grilled over charcoal, "devouring" the rodents "with avidity"; "the thighs of greyhounds were found tender and eaten like saddles of hare." Leather was peeled into thin sheets, scraped, washed, parboiled, and then cooked in the fire or "roasted on a grill like tripes": "and if anyone had some fat, they made a fricassee with the leather, or a potted pâté; some also prepared it with a vinaigrette."[50] In the end, some were reduced to picking through excrement for their dinner, Léry asserts, or even eating the excrement itself. Or not quite the end: after detailing the consumption of excrement Léry describes cannibalism à la Sancerre.

Though the sequence seems to follow chronological developments, we cannot really be sure of that: for whatever the temporal order of the sequence from asses to excrement, it is first of all a moral order that Léry is following. This is a moral order, in fact, where the consumption of more and more abhorrent products is not even the most crucial of descents. Animals like rats and materials like leather can be treated as if they were normal foodstuffs — they can be broiled or fricasseed. Culture, in short, can be applied to them, and familiar scents and tastes associated with them. Still worse are two other alternatives: on the one hand, eating like "brute beasts," eating bark or twigs or (as did Léry's party aboard ship) dry wood, or picking through excrement like dogs; on the other hand, eating friendly creatures, pets and other companionable animals, who are already a part of human culture. Thus eating horses is worse than eating mules (though they taste better), and eating dogs is worse than eating rats (though dogs, too, taste better). During the famine aboard ship, Léry reminds his readers, while descending to leather and wood, the seafarers also regretfully descended to consuming the monkeys and parrots they had brought with them for sale in France. A pet parrot is the last thing Léry recounts eating before he moves on to relate the temptation of cannibalism aboard ship — the narrative slippage (from chronological to thematic sequence) in this is significant.[51] And in his story of the siege of Sancerre, when the episode of cannibalism comes — set up for the reader as a climax to the narrative, apparently temporal and ethical at once, the zenith of the plot and the nadir of the moral descent — it turns out to be the story of the eating not just of a human being, but a child. As in Josephus, whose story of the siege of Jerusalem Léry knew well, it is a case where parents consume their offspring, although murder is not also involved, since it is the corpse of a three-year-old girl that is cannibalized.

If ever Léry takes a perverse delight (and we along with him) in the grisly details of gustatory desperation, it is here. "But O God eternal!" he interjects. "Here again is the culmination of all misery and the judgment of God." A "crime prodigious, barbarous, and inhuman" ended up being committed, "perpetrated within the very walls" of the town. "A winemaker named Simon Potard, Eugene his wife, and an old woman who lived with them named Phillippes de la Feüille" (note the naming of names) were found to have eaten "the head, the brains, the liver, and viscera of their three-year-old daughter, who had just died of hunger and languor." Léry was an early witness on the scene and was so "shocked" and "dismayed" at what he saw that his "very entrails were moved": "the bone and top of the head of the poor girl, handled and gnawed"; "the tongue cooked, the thickness of a finger, which they had made ready to eat"; "the two thighs, legs, and feet in a pot with vinegar, spices, and salt, ready to cook and put on the fire; the two shoulders, arms and hands held together, with the breast broken and open, also dressed and ready to eat. . . ." Even in his ten months in Brazil, Léry notes, he had never seen anything like it.[52]

In the end, with Léry's blessing, the three perpetrators were executed as an example to others. "For if they had been allowed to get away with it, or to have been chastised with a light punishment, one might well have feared (and there were already enough signs of it coming) that, the famine growing, the soldiers and the people would not only have assuaged their hunger with corpses dead from natural causes, and those who had been killed in the war or otherwise, but would have begun killing one another for sustenance." Survival cannibalism was not an option in the long run, because it would have led to chaos, and it was not really an option in the short run either, because it was, simply, taboo — especially given its semiotic denouement in the mutilation and consumption by parents of their tender offspring. This was the limit against which the Huguenot experience simply could not be allowed to be pressed, whether aboard ship or holed up within the walls of Sancerre. In fact, the guilty husband and wife, Léry assures us, had not even quite arrived at the point where survival cannibalism was necessary, and therefore even a little bit excusable: it was found that at home they already had "a pot of vegetable soup, a supply of wine (though of bread no one spoke anymore) and that, in view of the necessity to which everyone was reduced, that would have been enough to live on for that day: so that in brief, not only the famine but a perverted appetite had caused them to commit this barbarous and worse than bestial cruelty: the husband and wife having for a long time been notorious as drunks and gluttons, as well as for being cruel toward their children." Drunks and gluttons! In fact, it comes as a relief to Léry to discover that this family of cannibals were already in bad standing with the Reformed Church and had been married in secret by a Catholic priest. As a punishment the wife was strangled to death, the man burned alive, and the wife's corpse (along with the disinterred corpse of the old woman, who had died by natural causes before the trial) thrown in the heap of the fire along with the burning man.[53] The cookers were cooked, the bodies mutilated, and the punishment prolonged past the limits of mortality.

IV

Nearly a hundred years after Léry's voyage to Brazil, and eighty years after the siege of Sancerre, the Englishman Richard Ligon set sail for the island of Barbados. Though little is known about Ligon apart from his *History,* it would appear that he was a victim of religious trouble as well, only in reverse. High Church and Royalist in the age of Puritan Parliamentarianism, he seems to have been on the losing side of the English Civil War. A business agent with failed land holdings in the East Anglian Fens, he writes that he had found himself, in 1647, "a stranger in my own Country," his money gone, his wealth indeed having been "stripped and rifled" from him, and most of his friends either in as bad a case as him, in exile, or dead.[54] The New World represented an opportunity to recoup his fortunes — nothing more or less — and he went there as an assistant to one Colonel Modiford, who was seeking to establish a trading post or estate in the islands. The ship he booked passage on was sent to trade in horses, cattle, and slaves, and to return from the West Indies laden with sugar.

Barbados at that time had only recently been settled by the English, the sugar trade was in its infancy, and the plantation revolution was just getting under way. By 1647 the native population of the island was already wiped out (Ligon claims — erroneously but understandably, given the evidence — that there had never been a permanent native settlement there, only temporary camps, set up by inhabitants of neighboring islands), and much of the land had already been divided up into large holdings; but labor was still provided by indentured servants from the British Isles as well as by African and Indian slaves, most of the latter brought over from the Spanish Main.[55] Ligon's sojourn to Barbados can be regarded as a kind of intervention in the process. A man of broad education, trained in the arts and sciences, a fine draftsman and amateur botanist as well as a gifted writer, bon vivant, and a bit of a wag — in every way what was then called a "virtuoso" — Ligon was as much a potential shaper of the colonial world as Léry had been. He was a kind of secular missionary, advancing the cause of the technology of empire. And this trader in slaves and sugar was also preoccupied with food. It is possible that he had once been employed as a professional chef, and certainly cooking was another one of his passions. As he traveled, everywhere he went Ligon saw commodities that could be eaten in one way or another. The delight he took in travel was above all the delight he took in the food he encountered, and though he had the standing of a gentleman, he was ready to pitch in and show the laborers on ship or on the island how to prepare a dish. He took pride in his knowledge of cooking fish. Yet it was part of Ligon's intervention in the affairs of the island to assess the situation abstractly, instrumentally. For the potential investor in Barbados, he thus lays out the mechanics and economics of the sugar trade with mathematic precision. Along with such help as a brilliant diagram showing how sugar processing on a large-scale works, he explains how the planter in Barbados may acquire, tend to, and manage his labor force, including the following information on providing for the laborers on average-sized estates, depending on whether they are indentured servants or slaves: "over and above the provisions which the Plantations bear," such as plantains and cassava, providing for them, Ligon assures the reader,

> will be no great matter. For they are not often fed with bone-meat. But we will allow to the Christian servants, (which are not above thirty in number) four barrels of Beef, and as much Pork yearly, with two barrels of salt Fish, and 500 poor-Johns, which we have from New England, four barrels of Turtle, and as many of pickled Mackerels, and two of Herrings, for the Negroes; all of which I have computed, and find they will amount unto £100 or thereabouts; besides the freight, which will be no great matter; for you must be sure to have a Factor, both at New England and Virginia, to provide you of all the Commodities those places afford, that are useful to your Plantation; or else your charge will be treble.[56]

It is something of a shock to see how readily Ligon, even as early as 1647, can distinguish between the nutritional needs of white servants and black slaves. (Such fans of herring as we encountered in the previous chapter might be disappointed to see that Ligon accounts it along with mackerel to be fit for the consumption of slaves only; but he later also recommends it as something for gentlemen to eat for recreation, while drinking.) Yet it is equally important to register the radical form Ligon can attribute to the enterprise as a whole. We are a long way away from the failed French colony in sixteenth-century Rio de Janeiro. The commodification of the diet, at least for the laboring force, has now been achieved. The idea has been both encoded in the language of business ventures — or "adventures" as they were still often called — and accommodated by an efficient system of international trade.[57] Already — and this would be true for the sugar island for some time — Barbados has been economically triangulated: capital and labor flow in from the British Isles and ships plying the Middle Passage, supplies flow in from New England and Virginia, and outward go the sugar and rum. And this means, among other things, that a new kind of gustatory alienation is institutionally in place. Sidney Mintz, ethnohistorian of the West Indian sugar industry, has spoken eloquently about this, with an eye toward developments in the eighteenth and nineteenth centuries, when the slaves and servants had been replaced by wage earners: "a newly emerging world in which working people produced less and less of what they themselves consumed; in which they filled most of their needs by selling their labor for wages and buying what they consumed in an impersonal market."[58] In Ligon's time the process is still in its infancy, and not wage earners but planters, servants, and slaves are producing "less and less of what they themselves consumed."[59] But the structure of trade and commodification is already securely in place, and the long-term consequences are already beginning to be felt. Beef and herring in, sugar and rum out: and not only did West Indian laborers end up as the unfortunate victims of the system, but whole classes of people in Britain as well, for whom sugar and rum would become major sources of nutrition in place of more wholesome commodities. For the record, briefly but discursively and persuasively, our English virtuoso and gourmet Richard Ligon stands at the center of the emergence of this new world.

We should not forget the absent natives, however—the Caribbean peoples all but missing from Ligon's Barbados.[60] Not much of an issue for the English settlers of Barbados, the Indian population being so small in comparison to the great numbers of white men and even greater numbers of African slaves laboring there, the Indians of this and neighboring islands in the Lesser Antilles were nevertheless a memory, important as much for their absence as for the presence of the few representatives among them still settled there, and they were, of course, among the original "Cannibals." Ligon's testimony to the present-absent Indian is the famous story of Yarico and Inkle, which Ligon is the first to record.[61] Yarico, a young Indian woman of the Spanish Main, protects an English adventurer from being captured by Indian warriors, having fallen in love with him "at first sight." But when the adventurer is finally rescued by his fellows, he sells the woman, "who was born as free as he," into slavery.[62] Ligon tells the tale as an example of European treachery, but he also tells it as an allegory of Indian femininity and desire in the face of European masculinity and ambition. The only Indians on Barbados that Ligon has any interest in are in fact the women, who are helpful in tending to the local crops and preparing food for the table. But the absent men— whom even Indian women no longer desire, apparently—are important too. In the triangulated world of early English colonialism, if settlers and traders had little contact with West Indians apart from a small number of feminized slaves, they were still involved in something of a struggle with the Indians of the eastern seaboard of North America—predominantly members of the Algonquian language group—as well as avoiding the Carib Indians still in possession of neighboring islands like Dominica. Ligon needn't mention them, but they are there, a part of English consciousness. The absence of hostile and masculine Indians in Barbados is one of its attractions for the English settler, making it easier for him to make of the island what he will; the few (feminized) Indians there, apparently, the English settler doesn't even have to worry about how to feed: they can take care of themselves. Meanwhile, the presence of hostile and masculine Indians elsewhere in the triangle of English colonialism is a complicating factor, inhibiting English ambition. When George Sandys, in his footnote to the *Metamorphoses,* favorably compares the West Indian cannibals with the mythological Cyclops, "averse to justice" and when "armed with power . . . most outrageous and bloody," the hostile North American Indian (if not the hostile remnant of Carib culture) is perhaps the missing term. Sandys, again, was one of the survivors of the 1622 "Massacre," sometimes (more accurately) called the 1622 Indian Uprising.

It is worth digressing, for a moment, to consider these masculine, potentially hostile Indians of North America, as they appear in English colonial writing, who are foils to the European masters, Christian servants, African slaves, and Indian women of Ligon's Barbados. For these other figures also had a noteworthy relation to food, rather unlike that of any of the other denizens of the colonial triangle.[63] (Peter Hulme even includes the native Virginians as being among the people of the extended Caribbean region.) Most of the Algonquian nations were agriculturally settled peoples, raising maize, beans, and other products while also hunting, fishing, and foraging in the woodlands. Many practiced what has been called a "seasonally mobile" system of subsistence.[64] Villages broke up, dispersed, and regathered according to the season, and thus according to where the readiest available resources were available, depending more on hunting or fishing some parts of the year and more on agricultural at other parts. They were probably not much different in many respects from the Tupinamba of Brazil — even many of the products, like maize, were the same — and like the Tupinamba, though they hunted and prized the consumption of animal flesh, they kept no livestock. But when English ethnographers observed Algonquian practices, they saw something inherently disorderly and uncivil. "They accustom themselves to no set Meals," Robert Beverley writes of the Indians of Virginia, "but eat night and day, when they have plenty of Provisions, or if they have got any thing that is a rarity." And conversely, "they are very patient of Hunger, when by any accident they happen to have nothing to eat; which they make more easy to them by girding up their Bellies, just as the wild Arabs are said to do, in their long marches; by which means they are less sensible of the impressions of Hunger."[65] The Indians are "very patient in fasting," Samuel Lee similarly reports of New England natives, "and will gird in their bellies till they meet with food; but then none more gluttons or drunk on occasion, they'll eat 10 times in 24 hours, when they have a bear or a deer." "At home," William Wood writes, also of Indians in the north, "they will eat till their bellies stand forth, ready to split with fullness; it being their fashion to eat all at sometimes, and sometimes nothing at all in two or three days, wise Providence being a stranger to their wilder ways."[66] I have cataloged these and other responses to eating customs among the Algonquians elsewhere and noted exceptions to these responses as well, as when Roger Williams writes that he "could never discern that excess of scandalous sins amongst them which Europe aboundeth with. Drunkenness and gluttony, generally they know not what sins they be. . . ."[67] But even the exceptions, as I have shown, subscribed to the same set of terms, the same language and values with regard to eating and drinking. Like Léry and other ethnographers before them, English ethnographers of North America took European habits as standards of measurement; and they took European worries and obsessions as sources, by way of inversion and projection, of their supposedly eyewitness knowledge of Indian habits.

In brief, English ethnographers examined North American Indian food practices as part of an inquiry into Indian voraciousness, and if they found no cannibalism to confirm their worst fears, they found something morally allied with cannibalism. The Indians were inclined, they maintained, to eat and drink too much when they had a chance; they were inclined to partake of their meals haphazardly, without a regular schedule, and they consistently failed to provide for themselves with systematic "providence" for the future. However, they were also strangely tolerant of hunger. Assertions to the contrary, as when Williams says that they were unfamiliar with gluttony but ate only as nature required them to eat, actually amount to the same thing. For in all cases the same categories of analysis shape the white man's observations and value judgments, and in all cases the Indian is found to have a relation to food that is defined in opposition to European customs of orderly, future-minded self-restraint. Even Jean de Léry's Tupinamba, when they weren't consuming their military prisoners, could be seen to behave along lines similar to the North Americans; or rather, to be subject to these same categories of analysis and judgment. After remarking on the Tupinamba fondness for drunkenness, he notes that "they do not observe particular hours for dinner, supper, or light repasts, as we do over here, and do not hesitate when they are hungry to eat as readily at midnight as at noon," adding only, to qualify the negative implications of the observation, that "since they never eat when they are not hungry, you could say that they are as sober in their eating as they are excessive in their drinking."[68]

So much for the missing term in Sandys's understanding of the Cyclops or Ligon's discussion of life in post-Indian Barbados. If there are no cannibals in the America of Sandys or the Barbados of Ligon, and if in fact there never had been (though there were certainly "Caribs" in ancient Barbados), there was at least a number of peoples whose foodways were less settled than the Europeans', and whose relative mobility could be taken as signs of an inherent voraciousness, a precivil or insufficiently civilized relation to eating and drinking. The existence of this class of voracious eaters as a product of European observation, again, provides less of a window on the Indians than on the Europeans. The Indians may have been more mobile than Europeans, and they may have had some different attitudes about eating and drinking, and even about hunger, but the wild habits of the wild Indian were actually a product of European and especially English preoccupations, stemming from their own long-established culinary traditions. *Sobriety* or *moderation,* we have seen again and again, was a preoccupation among early modern Europeans, as was suspicion of the alternatives, the *fasting* of medieval ascetics and the *gluttony* of intemperate contemporaries. "Particular hours," too, were important to the culinary identity of Europe. Snacking was frowned upon — it would appear that it was even difficult to practice snacking, since food supplies were controlled by purveyors who obeyed the rule and served out the food during "particular hours" — and so Europeans were accustomed to have few opportunities and few blessings for having something to munch on at midnight or midafternoon, regardless of whether they ever felt "hungry" at such times. Similarly, the idea of "providence," of planning for the future, was central to European foodways: it was a feature of the settled agricultural life of most inhabitants of Europe, and indeed, according to the practices and laws of private property, it was both an economic necessity and a moral imperative, internalized in both respects as if a law of nature, or even of God. As for tolerance or intolerance of hunger, given the regular schedule with which food was cultivated, prepared, and served, Europeans indeed needed to learn to *ouvrir l'appétit,* since one had to be hungry when one ate and one only had so many (scheduled) opportunities to eat. Or conversely: on the other side of European preoccupation with temperance, regularity, set schedules of eating, and the cultivation of the appetite, we might say, was a *fear of hunger,* a fear of that "painful sensation," capable of piercing stone walls.

Perhaps the fear was warranted; perhaps not. "Truly," an elder Tupi says to Léry, who is not unsympathetic, "I see now that you *Mairs* (that is, Frenchmen) are great fools; must you labor so hard to cross the sea, on which (as you told us) you endured so many hardships, just to amass riches for your children or for those who will survive you? Will not the earth that nourishes you suffice to nourish them? We have kinsmen and children, whom, as you see, we love and cherish; but because we are certain that after our death the earth which has nourished us will nourish them, we rest easy and do not trouble ourselves about it."[69] One way or another, this cavalier attitude toward material needs drove many Europeans crazy. This "idle, improvident, scattered people," Captain John Smith complains of the Indians of Virginia, who were from their own point of view nothing of the kind, "ignorant of the knowledge of gold or silver, or any commodities, and careless of any thing but from hand to mouth, except baubles of no worth; nothing to encourage us, but what accidentally we found Nature afforded. . . ." They not only had their own ways of seeing to survival, but appeared to do so both without the necessary, rational caution and without the necessary anxiety of Europeans.[70] When they ate, they either seemed to eat excessively, without restraint, or else, more nobly, to eat only according to a natural hunger that cultured Europeans had forgotten how to feel. When they didn't eat, they seemed all but indifferent to the problem. Patient or stoic in the face of it, they were free of anxieties about hunger: these peoples without stone walls also failed to experience the hungry desperation that could knock walls down. In other words, while cultured Europeans tried to see to it that they *never* experience the feeling, Algonquian Indians were *always* hungry: when they ate they ate out of hunger, and when they didn't eat they experienced hunger, though they weren't anxious about it.

Voraciousness was therefore both a result of the inadequate stage of development of civilization among native peoples — for surely a higher stage of development would entail an understanding of the civility of table manners, the economic importance of providence, and so forth — and an expression of something approaching a racial characteristic. The Indians were a people who were always hungry, who therefore hardly noticed it when the demands of nature beleaguered them, and who couldn't stop eating when the right kind of food was offered to them. Again, this charge of voracious precivility was unwarranted; it was mainly an attenuated expression of the voracious cannibalism that was associated with American Indians originally, before the evidence came in. And yet it had some important practical effects. English colonists adopted many of the Indian foodstuffs — corn, beans, squash, and manioc, most notably, and eventually products like potatoes, along with turkeys, deer, and other wild animals encouraged by Indian hunting practices — and they gathered a number of tips from the Indians about how best to raise them. But they adopted these products largely on their own terms: the hybridization of colonial foodways was asymmetrical or unbalanced. In the early stages of English colonialism, the condescension of the English toward Indian culture, in foodways as in other things, would be fatal. Coming over to America with poor advance planning, themselves betraying little "providence" with respect to the need to eat, the first colonists in Virginia ended up almost wholly dependent on the hospitality of the Indians, who were themselves going through a dearth because of poor weather and couldn't have accommodated all of the white men's needs even if they wanted to. Ideological verbiage and mercantilist greed aside, as many Indians soon discovered, what the English came over to America for was above all to eat. The colonists never said that. They didn't believe it. But the belly made its demands. And when the English first came over to North America, establishing the colony at Jamestown, the demands of the belly were soon the first and last order of business.

Not as many colonists at Jamestown died of hunger as was originally thought, though many of them — well over half of the original arrivers, for example — soon passed away, suffering pangs of hunger at the time of their death. Though infectious disease and poisoning from brackish water supplies is what probably caused most of the early fatalities, early settlers didn't really know this.[71] Hunger was what they ascribed the death of their fellows to, and it was the experience of hunger that provoked and filled them with horror. This horror not of disease or poisoned guts or even death but of hunger in and of itself determined the direction of subsequent colonial policy.[72] Disease was taken in stride: indeed, for a variety of reasons, including the fact that disease was often thought to be an outcome of nothing other than a poor diet, the problem of disease was often ignored. But the horror of hunger was the horror of a trauma that was not easy to forget. "WE ARE STARVED! WE ARE STARVED!" colony leader George Percy reports the men at Jamestown crying through the streets during the infamous Starving Time: "Many through extreme hunger have run out of their naked beds, being so lean that they looked anatomies."[73] In fact, the story of the Starving Time looks a lot like the famine in Sancerre, with its sequence of deprivation and despair, and the ghastliest of conclusions.

> Now all of us at James Town beginning to feel the sharp prick of hunger, which no man truly describe but he which hath tasted the bitterness thereof, a world of miseries ensued, as the sequel will express unto you, insomuch that some, to satisfy their hunger, have robbed the store, for the which I caused them to be executed. Then having fed upon horses and other beasts as long as they lasted, we were glad to make shift with vermin, as dogs, cats, rats, and mice. All was fish that came to net to satisfy cruel hunger, as to eat boots, shoes, or any other leather some could come by. And those being spent and devoured, some were enforced to search the woods and to feed upon serpents and snakes and to dig the earth for wild and unknown roots. . . .

The end of the sequence is almost predictable:

> And now famine beginning to look ghastly and pale in every face that nothing was spared to maintain life and to do those things which seem

incredible, as to dig up dead corpses out of graves and to eat them, and some have licked up the blood which hath fallen from their weak fellows. And amongst the rest, this was most lamentable that one of ours, Collines, murdered his wife, ripped the child out of her womb and threw it into the river, and after chopped the mother in pieces and salted her for his food.

Collines, too, was apprehended and eventually executed, a confession having been "enforced from him by torture, having hung by the thumbs with weights at his feet a quarter of an hour, before he would confess the same."[74] Perhaps he was to be commended for having the dignity of not eating his own unborn baby, but in addition to the murderousness and voraciousness of his behavior, he had the temerity of that other violation, similar to the couple in Sancerre, of salting his wife's dismembered body. The mutilation of the corpse, along with application of the culturally "cooked" process of salting the body parts — in other words, daring to act on barbarous impulses with all the Providence that civility demanded — is perhaps what most offended his executioners. The horror of cannibalism, at Jamestown as at Sancerre and even at the Jerusalem of Josephus, stemmed from the convergence of three separate horrors in addition to the act of eating in itself: the betrayal of a loved one committed to one's charge; the mutilation of the corpse; and the application of culture, culinary culture, to the body being eaten. The three together would seem capable of being associated only by way of a deranged appetite, a mad and monstrous voraciousness, a moral insanity, of which not even the Caribs or the Tupi were imagined to be capable.

V

But let us return to Richard Ligon, arriving in Barbados in 1647. By that time the alimentary despair of early colonists at Jamestown and elsewhere had become a memory. The next waves of colonists had learned how to avoid the conditions that might give rise to the horror. Even though the Indians of the eastern seaboard had never been assimilated into English life, and in pockets still resisted it, Virginians were making money raising tobacco, New Englanders were making money trading in fish — monoculture being the strategy by which the colonies learned to survive and the new economy of the Atlantic world took off — and the European ecosystem as a whole, albeit with such hybridized results as the adoption of maize and American beans into the local European diet, was already largely dominant. Indians were playing a smaller and smaller role even in the economy of English settlements, and English settlers up and down the coast of North America were prospering. On the small island of Barbados, already bereft of natives by the time the English got there, were thousands of fortune seekers, servants, and slaves. Ligon guesses the population to be as high as fifty thousand souls — an overestimate, no doubt, but not by much, and a fair indication of the busyness of the community as it played out before his eyes.[75] In fact, when Ligon's ship first arrived at the island's main port, the island population was being swept away by an epidemic of yellow fever: so that "before a month was expired after our Arrival, the living were hardly able to bury the dead." Nevertheless, "we found riding at anchor twenty-two good ships, with boats plying to and fro, with Sails and Oars, which carried commodities from place to place: so quick stirring, and numerous, as I have seen it below the bridge of London."[76]

It may be paradoxical, it may be accidental, and it may be symptomatic, but one way or another this first eloquent observer and participant in the emerging colonial economy of monoculture, commodification, and slaves was a consummate consumer. The wonder of the New World for Ligon is a wonder for its food. He is no less enthusiastic than Léry was for the local fruits, which were much the same in Barbados as in Brazil — plantains, guavas, pineapples. He is similarly pleased with the local fish, the fowl, the meat (he especially likes the local pork, "the sweetest flesh of that kind that ever I tasted, and the loveliest to look on in a dish"), along with the various beverages produced on the island: *mobbie,* a brew made from fermented potatoes; *perino,* the local version of what in Brazil was called *caouin,* made from fermented manioc pressings; *kill-devil,* that is rum, made from the local sugarcane, a dangerous drink in Ligon's view because of its high alcoholic content; punch made from water and sugar and perhaps a little rum or wine; plum juice; fermented plantain juice ("a very strong and pleasant drink, but it is to be drunk sparingly, for it is much stronger than Sack, and is apt to mount into the head"); molasses water; sweetened orange juice; pineapple juice, which he calls "the incomparable wine of the Pines" and even "the Nectar which the Gods drunk, for on earth there is none like it."[77] Life on the sugar island for the colonials is literally *sweeter* than it is back home, not to mention juicier, and Ligon is unreservedly enthusiastic for it. Yet it is not simply as a consumer, a devourer of good things, that Ligon appreciates the foodways of Barbados. He may more accurately be considered a consumer-producer: a true gourmet. He is an intelligent eater for whom eating is an art, and for whom part of that art is knowing how to provide for oneself, how to make good eating available to oneself. He does not simply tell his reader what is available on Barbados; he tells the reader how it is cultivated, gathered, and prepared. His "true and exact history" of Barbados is really less an account of the story of Barbados than an explication of the art of the colony — or better, of the colony as a work of art. Eating is one

The Queene Pine.

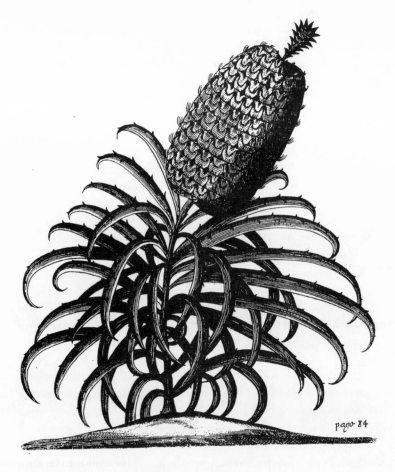

Figure 7.3. The incomparable pineapple, in its female form: The Queene Pine, from Richard Ligon, *A True and Exact History of the Island of Barbadoes* (1657). Private collection.

of the prime arts of life in Barbados, as well as the source of its revenue, and when Ligon expresses his wonder at the variety, healthfulness, and tastiness of the food of the island, he also expresses his admiration for the art with which he and his fellow colonials have produced it in such happy abundance.

It is in this spirit that Ligon alludes to his own prowess in the kitchen—a prowess that shows him adapting the products at hand to recipes and concepts that were already popular back home. His remarks about pork are characteristic. It is not enough to tell his reader that the pork on the island is sweet and lovely: it is sweet and lovely "either boiled, roasted, or baked." And that is not all. "With a little help of art, I will deceive a very good palate." Ligon's tastes are for baroque versions of centuries-old European traditions, where one of the chief marks of a good chef is his ability to make one thing seem like another. And if one reason for this is simply to stretch the palate with variety or to provide rare delicacies out of mundane ingredients—like Martino of Como, making a complicated delicacy out of the peasants' millet cake—another is to display the prowess of cookery itself, the better to encourage the art of eating.

> With a little help of art, I will deceive a good palate, with a shoulder of it for Mutton, or a leg for Veal, taking off the skin, with which there were wont to make minced Pies, seasoning it with salt, cloves, and mace, some sweet herbs minced. And being baked, and taken out of the Oven, opening the lid, put in a dram-cup of *kill-devil* [rum]; and being stirred together, set it on the Table; and that they called Calves foot pie; and till I knew what it was made of, I thought it very good meat. When I came first upon the Island, I found pork dressed the plain ways of boiling, roasting, and sometimes baking. But I gave them some tastes of my Cookery, in hashing and fricasseeing the flesh; and they all were much taken with it; and in a week, everyone was practicing the art of Cookery.[78]

If the colony is a work of art, if success in colonization is to be measured both by the art of producing wealth there and by the art of living itself, one of the triumphs of colonization should in fact be its cookery. Cookery is both expressive and constitutive in this respect: it *expresses* colonial hegemony and it *is* colonial hegemony. All the elements of the culture of colonial experiment—commodification, alienation, rediscovery, hybridization, and wonder—come together in colonial cookery. Ligon thus concludes his section on the foods of colonial Barbados by recounting a pair of feasts to which he was invited, one at an inland plantation, where it was unfeasible to provide seafood, the second at a seaside plantation, where seafood was to be had in surplus. The account of the inland feast is the more detailed, and it is worth looking at in full. It features beef, which is a rarity on the island but also of course a symbol of the aesthetic community of the England from which these colonials had emigrated. It includes a great deal of the "redundant profusion" familiar in early modern banquets generally,[79] and though it represents a triumph of the new capitalist economy and the commodification of goods and labor, it is also designed to express old-fashioned hospitality, the festive "liberality" of a lord of a manor. The colonial feast is first of all an expression of the power of its host's productive and distributive prowess. This capitalist apotheosis is after all a creature of the modern plantation system:

> First then (because beef being the greatest rarity in the Island, especially such as this is) I will begin with it, and of that sort there are these dishes at either mess,
>
> a Rump boiled,
> a Chine roasted,
> a large piece of breast roasted,
> the Cheeks baked, of which is a dish to either mess,
> the tongue and part of the tripes minced for Pies, seasoned with sweet Herbs finely minced, suet, Spice and Currants;
> the legs, pallets, and other ingredients for an Olio Podrido to either mess,
> a dish of Marrow bones:
> so here are fourteen dishes at the Table and all of beef: and this he intends as the great Regalio, to which he invites his fellow planters; who having well eaten of it, the dishes are taken away, and another Course brought in, which is
> a Potato pudding,
> a dish of Scots Collops of a leg of Pork, as good as any in the world,
> a fricassee of the same,
> a dish of boiled Chickens,
> a shoulder of young Goat dressed with his blood and thyme,
> a Kid with a pudding in his belly,
> a sucking pig, which is there the fattest whitest and sweetest in the world, with the poignant sauce of the brains, salt, sage, and Nutmeg done with Claret wine,
> a shoulder of mutton which is there a rare dish,
> a Pasty of a young Goat, and a side of a fat young Shot upon it, well seasoned with Pepper and salt, and with some Nutmeg,
> a loin of Veal, to which there wants no sauce being so well furnished with Oranges, Lemons, and Limes,

three young Turkeys in a dish,

two Capons, of which sort I have seen some extreme large and very fat,

two hens with eggs in a dish,

four Ducklings,

eight Turtle doves,

and three Rabbits;

and for cold baked meats, two Muscovey Ducks larded, and seasoned well
    with pepper and salt;

and these being taken off the Table, another course is set on, and that is of
Westphalia or Spanish bacon,

dried Neats Tongues,

Botargo,

pickled Oysters,

Caviar,

Anchovies,

Olives, and (intermixed with these)

Custards,

Creams, some alone, some with preserves with Plantains, Bananas, Guavas
    put in,

Cheese-cakes,

Puffs, which are to made with English flour, and bread, for the Cassava will
    not serve for this kind of cookery;

sometimes Tansies, sometimes Froizes or Amulets [kinds of dessert]

and for fruit Plantains, Bananas, Guavas, Melons, prickled Pear, Anchovy
    Pear, prickled Apple, Custard Apple, Watermelons, and Pineapples
    worth all that went before.

To this meat you will seldom fail of this drink, Mobbie, Beveridge, brandy,
    kill-Devil, Drink of the Plantain, Claret Wine, White wine, and Rhen-
    ish wine, Sherry, Canary, Red Sack, wine of Friuli, with all Spirits that
    come from England;

and with all this, you shall find as cheerful a look, and as hearty a welcome,
    as any man can give to his best friends.[80]

VI

Not every development in the history of food is entirely forward looking. What
anthropologists call a "foodway," as I suggested earlier, is inherently conserva-

tive.[81] That is to say, it marks out a pathway of nutrition whose value is that it can and will be repeated. The foodway enables *habit*. The reproduction of the foodway was largely what English colonialists meant when they referred to "Providence," and it was only their own blind commitment to the European foodway that prevented them from seeing that the "improvident" ways of Amerindians entailed a habitual foodway too. There are psychological reasons for alimentary habit as well as economic and biological ones, no doubt. Habit is central to security and sanity alike. But the foodway then, and the aesthetic community it creates, is first of all a pathway to the secure and sane repetition in the future of the actions of the past. Yesterday I ate bread, today I eat bread, tomorrow I will eat bread. If the bread is not available tomorrow, I may well feel deprived — biologically, economically, and psychologically. I may well feel "hungry" for bread, even if I have other food to eat in its place. The disruptions of travel and migration trouble both the mechanisms and rewards of habit, and the successful accommodation of habit in spite of disruption amounts to a kind of triumph of conservation, of going forward by going backward.

But travel, migration, and colonial life all but inevitably entail hybridization as well. The bread of the present is not exactly the bread of the past. It may even be made of cassava and be unfit, as Ligon complains, for many customary uses. To triumph, to recover old food habits, may require substitutions, amendments, additions. The Italian Americans of Philadelphia may be recalled, the ones who alternated "platter"-style American and "gravy"-style Italian food on their family dinner tables. Like the Philadelphians, Ligon's banqueters both repeat the past and creolize it. *Mobbie* is drunk along with claret, rum along canary and sack. Though no salad or artichokes or asparagus are on offer, the meat-heavy meal is modulated with plantains, bananas, pineapples, and guavas, as well as imported olives.

On the whole, to be sure, this colonial meal bespeaks a triumph of English culture over the land, people, and agricultural facts of the island. The hybridization is much less prominent than the imposition of English ingredients and cooking techniques on the foodway of this outpost of the empire. That *English* habit includes ingredients and dishes that had long since been imported and culturally assimilated in England: flavoring ingredients like nutmeg, currants, oranges, and claret; pungent staples like the Rabelaisian botargo, anchovies, and ham; complex dishes like the "poignant sauce" of brains, sage, and wine, clearly taken from French cuisine; as well as the Spanish "Olio Podrido," a mixed stew, here made out of different cuts of beef. (The author of the contemporary *The Compleat Cook*, one W.M., would have approved: "I am utterly against those confused Olios," he writes, "into which men put almost all kinds of meats and

Roots. . . .")[82] The menu here, like most such menus, as we saw earlier—if the reader will excuse this appeal to abstract categories of cultural analysis — is an exercise in commemoration, standardization, and synthesis. It features the form and matter of a redundant profusion, commemorated as an occasion worth remembering; it is constructed as a normative event, providing the model of a standard against which other dinners might be measured; and it synthesizes the whole as the picture of a society of producers and consumers gathered before the spectacle of the foodway they have established for themselves. The technicalities of the meal are both celebrated and subordinated to even higher values: the prestige of the host, the aesthetic aspirations of the guests, and the ratification of social distinctions. This is a dinner, Ligon specifies, given by the planters and for the planters, served up with a "cheerful look" and a "hearty welcome." Most likely a hierarchical order of seating was observed, a sharing of meats and other delicacies in descending order down the social scale was practiced, and many people were expressly excluded. Not only does Ligon say nothing about any servants attending the meal, he says nothing about slaves. But why should he? The point of the menu, like the point of the feast it commemorated, was to assert the aesthetics of hegemony and, by the same token, the hegemony of aesthetics. It no more took into account the exploited and the rejected who were also, dish by dish, involved in the making and observing the feast, than the great cathedrals of Europe documented the trials of the actual laborers who had erected them stone by stone. A gentle artist like Ligon might be included in the semiotics of festivity, but not a Simplicissimus, a Yarico, or, as Ligon elsewhere calls some of the slaves, a Pickaninny or a Sambo.

I will return to these exclusions in a moment. But let it first be recalled that this colonial feast, whatever its worth, was enjoyed at a critical moment in the history of food practices. It was promoted by men who, as Ligon puts it, were especially enthusiastic about the pursuit of "lawful recreations." The rise of the new planter class — and all that went along with it — may have been the single most important event in the development of the early English empire, changing as it did the economy of empire forever. That this new planter class came along at about the same time as the oft-noted revolution in cuisine in northern Europe may, again, be either paradoxical, accidental, or symptomatic, but there it is: the first great spokesman of the plantation revolution in the West Indies was a gourmet; the successful planters were more than a little inclined toward such lawful pleasures as the good eating of the gourmet entails; for better or for worse, the successful plantations transformed the economic logic as well as the ingredients and combinations of the American and European diets;[83] and meanwhile, in England and France (which was also involved in West Indian colonization at this time), an explosion of interest in food as a medium of both pleasure and civility takes place. The burgeoning publication of cookbooks in both countries is only the most obvious sign of this explosion.

Of course this convergence of hedonism, capitalism, and colonialism sits astride many older developments. We should not forget that a hundred years earlier the traumatized Léry is also a lover of good food, who can even document the advanced cooking techniques that the starving Sancerrois took for granted, fricasseeing the soles of their shoes. Hedonism was not invented in the age of colonial mercantilism; nor was complicated cookery. Prosperous colonials and their ilk could pursue a life way of "lawful recreations" because the recreations were already embedded in the framework of social life and the values and practices they entailed already obeyed a "lawful" logic. The sheer unleashing of culinary hedonism for its own sake — as in the case of the Clitons and Gnathons of the seventeenth century, and such real-life exemplars of gastronomy as Ligon appears to be — does gain ground in the bright new colonial period of England and France, but even so the energies of artful consumption were still usually associated with the moral and medical purposes of traditional European society. The old value of the hospitality of the great house was still central to the complicated feast, for example. Many of the new cookbooks of the mid-seventeenth century evoked the observance of traditional hospitality, La Varenne's *Le cuisinier françois* first among them in this respect. In England, Ligon's contemporary Robert May, author of the monumental recipe collection *The Accomplisht Cook* (1660), was ostentatious about it: like Ligon, he was even a victim of the civil wars, having served most of his life among Catholic Royalists; and he produced his cookbook in part as a celebration of a return with the Restoration of the old "hospitality," a word that appears as early as the dedicatory verse of the frontispiece and the heading to the dedicatory epistle on the first page of text.[84] May, indeed, is just one noteworthy example among many that could be cited: for all the rapid changes in styles of food and dining and in the attitudes toward them that can be found in the second half of the seventeenth century, including (as many historians have noted) a change in the *class system* of food — in France, for example, a "bourgeois" cuisine being developed, and here in Barbados, clearly, a plantation cuisine being invented — the whole apparatus of the meal was joined to earlier social formations and celebrated the new by ostensibly confirming the values of the old.

Yet even as it looked backward to European practices, such a menu and such a life as we thus see in Ligon's Barbados — creolized yet conservative, innovative yet old-fashioned, aristocratic yet operated by and for the nouveau riche — came with both suppression and oppression, the suppression of recent memories and the oppression of newly mobilized peoples. The Indian and his hunger and his cannibalistic or at least cannibal-like ferociousness are all *effaced*. The depredations of colonial struggle have all given way to wonder. Or not quite: for we know that the difficult world of managing slaves and servants and staving off hostile foreigners, insects, hunger, and disease is just outside the door and was entertained in the mind just a thought or two ago. Ligon himself is much too aware, astute, and honest to celebrate empire without reminding himself and his readers of its dangers and costs — especially, since like Léry, he is always preoccupied by it in terms of food. A case in point is that famous story of Yarico and her Englishman, which already served as a reminder of the treachery through which the European established hegemony and effaced the presence of the Amerindian in the Caribbean. Where later versions of the story emphasized erotic sentimentality, Ligon puts matters more elementally. When the English go to shore in Yarico's homeland, they are merely said to "try what victuals or water they could find." And when Yarico rescues the Englishman and shelters him, though later stories expand upon the love affair that develops between the two, culminating in pregnancy, Ligon simply says that the Indian maid "hid him close from here countrymen (the Indians) in a Cave, and there fed him."[85]

The colonial experience, from its origins in tales about the armed struggle between Europeans and Indians to its burgeoning into plantation society, is always first of all about eating and drinking, and what people have to do in order to accommodate the need. What the Indian does for the Englishman — the good Indian, that is — is she feeds him. Or so an advocate of empire like Ligon wishes to assure us. What the bad Indian does, from whom a Yarico protects the Englishman, Ligon leaves mostly unsaid, although the implication is clear enough; what the bad Englishman does is bad enough, for the Englishman bites the hand that has fed him, returning the "freedom" of the Indian cave with the slavery of English plantation.

But still more telling with regard to the problem of the costs and dangers of empire are perhaps two other passages in Ligon, with which this chapter may conclude. In the first we hear from many of those souls deliberately but quietly excluded from the colonial feast, African slaves; and what we hear both acknowledges the reality of hunger and ratifies the English attitude toward the phenomenon. The African slaves, it appears, are all in favor of the aristocratic code of hospitality through which English planters channeled their ideological energies. In terms that would become conventional in the discourse of slavery, the Africans thus show themselves to be considerably more pliable to the European way of life than the uncooperative, ferocious Indians ever would. Indeed, Ligon takes pain to assert, "there are as honest, faithful, and conscionable" among the Africans "as amongst those of Europe, or any part of the world," although to be sure the honesty, faithfulness, and conscience really only demonstrate how apt they are to be used as slaves. During "a time when Victuals were scarce," Ligon writes, "and Plantains were not then so frequently planted," some of the "high-spirited and turbulent" among the slaves "began to mutiny" and hatched a plot against their master.[86] However, some others among the slaves informed the master of the plot, who was then able to forestall the mutiny and punish the would-be offenders. To celebrate the thwarting of the plot, "the Master gave order to the overseer that the rest should have a day's liberty to themselves and their wives, to do what they would; and withal to allow them a double proportion of victual for three days." This, however, the African slaves refused. They said that "they would not accept any things as a recompense for doing that which became them in their duties to do, nor would they have him think, it was hope of reward, that made them to accuse their fellow servants, but an act of Justice. . . ." It would be fine, however, on some other occasion, "if it pleased their Master . . . to bestow a voluntary boon upon them, be it ever so slight, they would willingly and thankfully accept it."[87] The code of honor and the ethic of gift giving among those among the African slaves who prove themselves pliable to the wills of their masters are such that they willingly surrender to the ideology of what in Europe had once been called the freedom of the manorial household. The lord bestows; the bounty flows from the high to the low; and the circulation of goods and services is the award of freedom, expressed through unobligated generosity on the one side and voluntary gratitude on the other.

The sensitive Ligon wants us to read this story as an expression of the humanity of African slaves and of his own liberal attitude toward them. Again, it may or may not be symptomatic of deeper economic and social realities, but the consummate consumer-producer, the gourmet of colonialism, is a generous and tolerant and sympathetic man. He is even liberal in his attitude toward nature and the uses to which humanity is driven to put it. If Ligon's epicureanism is of a piece with other developments in European culture in the mid-seventeenth century, so is his solicitude for the goods of nature. No vegetarian, to be sure, Ligon is nevertheless representative of the movement toward a tender respect for nature that Keith Thomas documents in his *Man in the Natural World*.[88] His admiration for the flora and fauna of Barbados is neither patronizing nor clinical: for Ligon, the natural order of the Caribbean is what is most wonderful about it, even though with its predatory ants and mosquitoes and summer heat waves it is also often inconvenient. And what Ligon imagines is that Barbados will continue to develop into an artful colony that is in fundamental harmony with its ecology. That the harmony of a colony with its environment is one-sided, Ligon willingly acknowledges. The good colony exploits the resources at hand; it changes the

Diſſection du Coq-d'Inde.

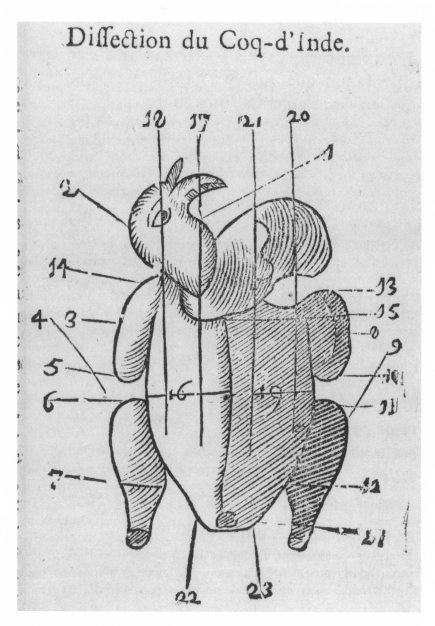

Figure 7.4. The dissection of a turkey, the "Indian Cock" or *Coq-d'Inde,* later to be called in French, more simply, *le dinde,* from *L'escole parfaite des officiers de bouche* (1662). Not quite a sea turtle, it illustrates how early moderns visualized the process of carving a creature. Reproduced by permission of the British Library (1037.c.21).

face of nature; it encourages what in human terms is successful in the terrain — pineapples, sugarcane, decorative palmettos — and it discourages what is not: forestland, fallow meadows, wild boar. But a man of sensibility, as the next century would call such a figure, admires what is natural in and of itself. Ligon sometimes sees human characteristics in the flora and fauna about him. The local thrush has a "melancholy look," the local wren is "as merry and jolly as the other is sad." The indigenous lizard "loves much to be where men are, and are delighted to stand and gaze in their faces, and hearken to their discourse." The palmetto, compared to which he thinks "there is not a more Royal or Magnificent tree growing on earth," he likens, so far as it can be an object of admiration, to a woman: "if you had ever seen her, you could not but have fallen in love with her."[89] So sensible Ligon is to the creatures of nature that even while seeing no reason for man not to exploit them to his own purposes, he shows himself capable, with a mixture of sadness, regret, irony, and resignation, to mourn the consequences. Ligon knows, in his own way, the terrible truth that "we fat all creatures to fat ourselves." If there are no cannibals on Ligon's Barbados, still there are men. And so, Ligon is both happy and regretful to report that among the goods of the island is the green turtle, "the best food the Sea affords."

The turtle is to the English colonist what the war captive is to the noble Brazilian cannibal, except that the turtle is more pathetic. "When you are to kill one of these Fishes," Ligon says, "the manner is, to lay him on his back on a table, and when he sees you come with a knife in your hand to kill him, he vapors out the grievousest sighs, that ever you heard any creature make, and sheds as large tears as a Stag, that has a far greater body, and larger eyes." Ever the artist, the cook in the kitchen as well as the gastronome at the table, Ligon pauses to explain how to slaughter and butcher the creature. "He has a joint or crevice, about an inch within the utmost edge of his shell, which goes round about his body, from his head to his tail, on his belly-side; into which joint or crevice, you put your knife, beginning at the head, and so rip up that side, and then do as much to the other; then lifting up his belly, which we call his *Calipee*, we lay open all his bowels, and taking them out, come next to the heart, which has three distinct points, but all meet above where the fat is; and if you take it out, and lay it in a dish, it will stir and pant ten hours after the fish is dead." Perhaps Ligon is unconsciously reminded here of the sacrificial practices of the Aztecs, ripping out the hearts of their victims and offering them to the gods. But in any case, the pathos of butchery for him is only equal to the pleasure of consumption. "Sure, there is no creature on the Earth, nor in the Seas, that enjoys life with so much sweetness and delight, as this poor fish the Turtle," Ligon concludes; "nor no more delicate in taste, and more nourishing than he."[90]

Conclusion

CRUSOE'S FRIDAY,
ROUSSEAU'S ÉMILE

I

SEVERAL YEARS ON, Robinson Crusoe is fully settled on his island. He has
established what he jestingly calls his "two plantations." Hard by the sea, near
where he was originally shipwrecked, Crusoe has set up his "castle": a fortifi-
cation jimmied against a rock, into which he has cut "several apartments, or
caves, one within another." There, in earthen pots, he stores the barley and rice
he has harvested from nearby fields as well as equipment and commodities like
rum and biscuits salvaged from his ship. Further inland Crusoe has his "country
seat." At this second plantation, he has built what he calls a "little bower," a tent
on poles set within a thicket of hedges and trees; he keeps an enclosure for his
"cattle," a herd of goats he has been raising, "a living magazine of flesh, milk, butter and cheese"; and he grows his grapes, which he originally found there wild,
and gathers them to make raisins of the sun, "the best and most agreeable dainty
of my whole diet; and indeed they were not agreeable only, but physical, wholesome, nourishing, and refreshing to the last degree."[1]

Two settlements, one military and agricultural, one pastoral and horticultural, one facing the elements, exposed to the ocean; the other protected, isolated, hidden. When he first discovered the opening in the woods he would make
into the latter, his "country seat," the whole of it appeared "so fresh, so green, so
flourishing, everything being in constant verdure, or flourish of spring, that it
looked like a planted garden." There he discovered not only grapes growing wild,
but lemons, oranges, coconuts, sugarcane, melons, tobacco. He would have re-
located there forthwith, he tells us, except that his settlement by the sea, in

287

harsher but secure conditions, had come to seem like home. And more important, the latter was a place of hope. Close to the beach where he had originally
foundered, "it was at least possible that something might happen to my advantage," allowing his escape; "though this was scarce probable, nevertheless, to
enclose myself among the hills and woods, in the center of the island, was to anticipate my bondage." It was better to chance his freedom at the edge of the sea
than to relax in comfort, in the womblike bower.[2]

Crusoe's island is not really a self-enclosed experiment in alternative living,
we discover. It is always a station on the way to something else, a stage for Crusoe's education and redemption and eventual liberation. But what a stage it is —
this island off the coast of Venezuela, modeled after Trinidad or Tobago, though
inaccurately so, since by the late seventeenth century, when the novel takes
place, Trinidad had long since been colonized by the Spanish, and Tobago was not
nearly so isolated from shipping lanes and European visitation as Crusoe makes
his island out to be. In spite of facts that Defoe has conveniently avoided, Crusoe finds himself on a "desert" island in that peculiarly early modern sense of
the term, a place uncultivated, even if fertile or lush, a place that has been ne-
glected or "deserted," emptied of use or wanting "improvement."[3] Crusoe will
need to find himself abandoned there, learn about who he is and why, learn not
only to survive but to thrive, acquire faith, become reconciled to the will of
God; he will have to act as the agent of salvation for other people — his man Friday, a Carib and cannibal whom he will also educate and convert to Christianity,
as well as the ship's captain, whom he will save from mutinous sailors and who
will then free Crusoe from his "bondage" by taking him aboard ship, so that he
may eventually return home. The island is the vehicle of Crusoe's manhood. The
bower of bliss he discovers in the center of the island, however much it may remind us and Crusoe himself of the original Garden of Eden, would never be sufficiently challenging for that. Nor would it be enough even when coupled with
the more challenging "plantation" by the sea. There on the island he was "King
and Lord of this country indefeasibly, and had a Right of Possession."[4] But Crusoe is not destined to be one of those colonists who becomes absorbed in his new
land, a stationary "planter," a giver of banquets, an extender of hospitality. For
Crusoe the point will be that he will have to take it all back home with him, and
what he will take is only partly wealth (ironically, it is mainly the wealth accumu-
lating on his plantation in Brazil during his absence that makes him rich); what
he will mainly take home is his self, his achieved, bettered, re-masculinized self.

Mere survival, in other words, is not really what *Robinson Crusoe* is about,
though the story of survival is what dominates the narrative. The novel is about
what it means to survive, and then go beyond survival and live life in full man-

hood. That at least was how one of its best early readers, Jean-Jacques Rousseau, responded to it, and the point is well taken. "Robinson Crusoe on his island, alone, deprived of the assistance of his kind and the instruments of all the arts, providing nevertheless for his subsistence, for his preservation, and even procuring for himself a kind of well-being"—that was the spectacle Rousseau recommended to the young reader, his fictional pupil Émile. And from this there were abstract lessons to learn: lessons about the nature of need, and the personal and social arrangements deployed to accommodate it. "There is an order no less natural and still more judicious" to the thinking person, "by which one considers the arts according to the relations of necessity which connect them."[5] For Rousseau what *Robinson Crusoe* provides, in the guise of an appealing adventure story, is an education in making one's way in the world. The far-off island is really a model of life in Europe, but stripped down, analyzed into its basic components, reduced to its basic laws, though accommodated by its indispensable technologies and disclosed as an environment where one can truly grow into an uncorrupted, godly, and virile adulthood.

It is important, then, that Defoe has taken care to falsify the circumstances of life on a Caribbean island in the late seventeenth century, when the story is said to have taken place. Defoe has not only occluded the actual social and political conditions of the Caribbean island—reducing it, perhaps, to what Peter Hulme suggests was its archetypal condition for the European mind, its status as a blank space for the plantation of European civility.[6] He has also greatly reduced the appeal of its *natural* conditions. Only the territory of his bower of bliss really lives up to what Defoe had to have known about the islands, and even there the bounty is depressed. There are no pineapples, guavas, cassavas, plantains, or avocados on Crusoe's island; if there are coconuts, Crusoe never mentions eating them, much less refreshing himself with their milk. The sugarcane is of poor quality; Crusoe never bothers to try to improve it or to eat it after his first taste. The grapes are mainly good as raisins. Crusoe believes that eating too many fresh grapes can lead to fever and diarrhea, and so he has the sun temper their dangerous coolness and moisture, just as he has his own participation in the process apply a measure of culture to their wildness, a measure of cooking to their rawness.[7] Crusoe's main means of sustenance comes from the wild goats he corrals, and the barley and rice he grows in his fields. Of course, there are no "wild goats" in the natural habitat of the Caribbean; any goats found in such a place would have to have been left there by previous European visitors (as probably also the oranges and lemons would have been).[8] And the barley and rice, which he grows from grains husbanded from his salvaging of the ship, were neither of them successful crops in the real Caribbean.[9] As much as possible, and indeed even more than possible, Crusoe lives as a non-creolized European in the West Indies, subsisting on European products, according to what the novel takes to be the "relations of necessity."

The rationale of necessity is not the only thing that prompts Crusoe's behavior, to be sure. As many critics have pointed out, there is a great deal of the irrational underlying Crusoe's responses to the world. It is especially to be remarked that throughout his story Crusoe betrays an irrational fear both of starvation and of being engulfed or devoured.[10] Crusoe goes overboard in his efforts to secure a steady supply of food, to practice that "providence" that Europeans felt to be so definitive about themselves when they came to the New World. He raises, herds, processes, and hoards far more food than he would ever need if he were to continue living alone; what he neglects is variety, not quantity. And the other side of the coin of Crusoe's overscrupulousness about feeding himself is Crusoe's fear that he will himself become food. With no little irony, the closest he actually comes to being devoured occurs when he has finally returned to Europe and is attacked by a pack of voracious wolves while crossing the Pyrenees. But he is afraid of being engulfed by the waves of the sea even before he experiences shipwreck, and he is afraid of being consumed by wild animals and voracious cannibals from the moment he sets foot on his island. His fear of being devoured dictates his behavior for most of his stay—dictates his living in fortifications, amid stores of plenty, as if he were living not on an uninhabited island paradise but in a sinister wilderness, where the law of the land is eat or be eaten.

II

"We go to dine in an opulent home," Rousseau imagines, in his role as tutor to the imaginary Émile.

> We find the preparation for a feast — many people, many lackeys, many dishes, an elegant and fine table service. All this apparatus of pleasure and festivity has something intoxicating about it which goes to the head when one is not accustomed to it. I have a presentiment of the effect of all this on my young pupil. While the meal continues, while the courses follow one another, while much boisterous conversation reigns at the table, I lean toward his ear and say, "Through how many hands would you estimate that all you see on this table has passed before getting here?"[11]

Rousseau is promoting what a late twentieth-century writer on food calls "mindfulness." Eating, according to author Deane Curtin, "is also a political act." The implications, if we live in a condition of mindfulness, are vast. "By being mindful of the ways food comes to our tables, we can become aware of the fact that to be healthy, to really care for oneself, one needs to care for others," including those "migrant workers" whose physical labor produces our food. This is not the way Rousseau would put it, but the sentiment is almost identical. "We should make the effort to know where our food comes from and decide whether to be part of that process," Curtin goes on to say.[12] Rousseau wants his Émile to learn pretty much the same thing. "While the philosophers, cheered by the wine, and perhaps by the ladies next to them, prate and act like children," Rousseau says, Émile "is all alone philosophizing for himself in his corner." Though the philosophers are taken in by the delights of civility, Émile is caused to reflect on his world in the antisocial, mindful spirit of *Kultur*.[13] "With a healthy judgment that nothing has been able to corrupt, what will [Émile] think of this luxury when he finds that every region of the world has been made to contribute; that perhaps twenty million hands have worked for a long time; that it has cost the lives of perhaps thousands of men, and all this to present to him with pomp at noon what he is going to deposit in his toilet at night?"[14]

The ideas originate in the discourse of the "food of regrets" discussed in chapter 5. The image of depositing the produce of civilization in the toilet comes perhaps from Seneca, the first-century Roman. But there is something new here as well. By the middle of the eighteenth century, a whole new regime of the culture of food has taken hold of the capitals of Europe and its colonial outposts. A certain doubleness in the realm of the wishful images of food remain the same, no doubt: on the one hand, visions of plentiful delight, now with the valence of the Enlightenment, the high civilization of bourgeois philosophers and their aristocratic patrons;[15] on the other hand, visions of nostalgia and regret, though now with the vision of "following nature" transformed by the experience of the New World and the idea, promoted by philosophers like Rousseau, that humankind had originated in an American-like state of nature that had been preferable to the current state of corrupt civility. The alternatives are both different from their classical and Renaissance forebears and pretty much the same: either civilization or *Kultur;* either the idea of living well and living intelligently, by way of the pursuit of "taste," of refinement, of dignified and opulent sociality, or else the idea of living philosophically, by way of the pursuit of "nature" and the dictates of reason, dwelling both within the social world and, spiritually, apart from it. In the fifteenth, sixteenth, and seventeenth centuries, the contrast was still exploratory, indefinite. The circulation of goods and the accumulation of capital that the Enlightenment could take for granted was imperfectly developed and inadequately understood. Conversely, in this earlier period, the opposition between wishes and regrets, or between opulence and austerity, could still be contained within a single dominant science of health, nutrition, and physicality. By the middle of the eighteenth century, however, that science had blown apart, and there was nothing really to take its place. So food, whether in the mode of hedonism or the mode of asceticism, had lost a good part of its meaning, its anchoring in the sensory wisdom of the human organism.[16]

At the end of the eighteenth century, indeed, a physician's publisher could boast, at least in the American edition of the author's collected lectures on the subject, that "before the present, no author had expressly undertaken to instruct mankind in the faculty of shunning disease by means so simple as the regulation of Diet."[17] Meanwhile, the lectures themselves, compared to the long tradition of Galenic regimens to which they claim only some little affinity, seem to involve, to use T. S. Eliot's term, a "dissociation of sensibility." There is little, in other words, that is "sensational" about the science of diet in the eighteenth century: the science has been dissociated from the knowledge and language of the senses.

In this quality of dissociation, the late eighteenth-century text in question, A. F. M. Willich's *Lectures on Diet and Regiment,* is similar to the few original, successful "regimens of health" that would see the light of day a generation or two earlier, like those of Dr. John Arbuthnot, friend to Pope and Swift, and Dr. George Cheyne, friend to the novelist Samuel Richardson.[18] These eighteenth-century texts—Willich's, Arbuthnot's, and Cheyne's—were no less rigorous than their classical and Renaissance precedents, and no less learned. Indeed, though they in fact have no more nor less to recommend themselves than the earlier regimens—for always the recommendation to practice moderation and evacuate regularly remains the same, even as the food products and means of responding to them change—the later texts originate in the perception that the older humoral physiology cannot be empirically validated. What constitutes empirical observation has changed. The classical observer could find "yellow bile" in the blood of an old man, produced by eating sweet yellow honey. The sixteenth-century nonagenarian Luigi Cornaro could determine simply on the basis of self-inspection that cold wine, melons, vegetable soups, and pork, though "agreeable" to his "taste," were "hurtful."[19] The eighteenth-century physician, by contrast, studied the salts, acids, oils, gases, and alkaline substances rendered from foodstuffs by chemical experiment. Cheyne could thus make the claim that "our Distempers generally arise from *Oils, Salts,* and *Spirits,* carried into the Habit by our Food"—whatever that might mean to a layman.[20] And Arbuthnot could call attention to the idea that "Vegetables differ from Fossils and Animals, in that, being burnt to Ashes, they yield a fixed alkaline Salt"—a salt, however, that is "in very small Quantity" in those vegetables of a "sharp Scent, as Mustard, Onions, &c."[21]

Regimens of health, if not so unknown as Willich's American publisher claimed them to be, were far less popular in the Age of Enlightenment than they once had been. Many fewer new texts were produced, and many fewer of the old texts were reprinted; fewer of either kind were sold, bought, or read. And the reason would seem to be that, however true or false their science, the regimens were less useful. The old texts spoke a language of the body that was no longer current. The newer texts, though they spoke a modern language, were no longer practical. Their language was too abstract, their concerns too analytical. They were too focused on illness rather than health. They were no longer holistic, that is; they were more inclined to treat the disease than the person, to recommend (possibly doubtful) cures for maladies instead of outlining the arts of a way of life. Cheyne thus found a readership among people who, like himself, suffered from obesity and depression — he recommended a milk and vegetable diet to the worse sufferers of the twin malady — but had little to say to the *homme moyen sensuel*. The best he could muster were empty precepts like this: "The great Rule of Eating and Drinking for Health, is to adjust the Quality and Quantity of our Food to our digestive Powers."[22] Nor was Arbuthnot any better, whose advice is a mixture (for us at least) of the sound and the foolish: "Fat People ought to avoid oily Nourishment; but Soaps, which consist of Oil and Salt, are proper, because they are resolvent [i.e., they dissolve fat]. Therefore Honey, Sugar, and ripe Garden-Fruits are useful."[23] The later writer Willich tries to adjust for the vacuousness of the new science and return to the holism of the ancients, but his empirical learning prevents him from making any progress. "It would be a fruitless and impracticable attempt, to lay down fixed rules, by which the respective salubrity or perniciousness of every species of aliment might be determined, in its application to the individual," he asserts. "Such rules do not exist in nature." However, it can be taken as a general rule that one should avoid "incongruous mixtures and compositions, for instance milk and vinegar or other acids. . . ." In addition: "Too little aliment debilitates the body, which thereby acquires less than it loses by respiration; it hastens the consumption of life; the blood becomes inert and rarefied; or is rendered acrid and liable to putrefaction." Nevertheless, when one eats enough, being careful to avoid debilitation, "the most simple dishes are the most nourishing." It is best, if possible, to eat "one kind of meat only" at a single sitting.[24] We are back to the advice and even many of the terms of the Anglophone Galenic regimenters; only, the advice is indefinite and the promised benefits are lacking in sensual specificity and emotional relevance, or for that matter presumed prognostic reliability.

All this has yet to be explained in full. The "long eighteenth century," as historians call it, extending from the late seventeenth to the early nineteenth century, gives us both a decline in Galenic medicine and its regimens of health and the birth of a consumer society, where pleasure and opulence — in "The Standard of Taste" David Hume calls it "splendor"—are promoted for their own sake. The cookery book, which began in the obscurity of the manor house and monastery, and only slowly emerged as an expression of the values of the palace and the bourgeois table, eventually becomes a staple of the literate household and circulates by the thousands. Seven, eight, nine, ten editions of even uncelebrated texts become common in England and France during the long period. A text like Eliza Smith's *The Compleat Housewife*, we have seen, can assimilate the art of cookery to the arts and sciences of the Enlightenment generally: the art of cookery is an expression of progress, and the ingenious, successful cook can aspire to contribute to the progress of the art in and of itself. Her contemporary Charles Carter was even more modernist in outlook, though in somewhat musty language:

> when 'tis considered, that *Variety* and *Novelty* are no small Parts of the *Cook's* Art, and that no Occupation in the World is more obliged to *Invention;* every Year, and every ingenious Artist constantly producing *New Experiments* to gratify the Taste of that Part of Mankind, whose splendid Circumstances make them emulous to excel in the Delicacies of this Mystery, especially when they exert their Wealth and their Magnificence to entertain their Friends with grand and sumptuous repasts, it will be allowed, that no Art can be said less to have reached Perfection than this, and that none is more capable of Improvement.[25]

In France an haute cuisine complete with celebrity chefs develops, and the whole culture of French cuisine becomes a standard for all of civilized Europe, as well as a commodity for export.[26] And of course the French were well aware of this: "The pleasures of the table are for all ages, all sexes, and all nations," writes the best-selling Frenchman François Massialot; "and there are none who do not want to dine in the French manner." The reason was that the French had mastered the rules of delicacy (*la délicatesse*) and etiquette (*la propreté*), which were good for both health and taste.[27] Rivalries over food in any case developed: the French against the English, the mobile professional male chef against the homebound housewife, the pursuit of novelty against the observance of time-tested, standardized tradition, local ingredients against imported exotica, nutrition against pleasure, sauces against gravies, salt against sugar. By the end of the long eighteenth century, a notion of "gastronomy" has been invented in France, and Jean Anthelme Brillat-Savarin would contribute his *Physiology of Taste* (1826), a book revered by food enthusiasts even today. It would appear that the collapse of the hegemony of Galenic medicine and its regimens of health provided a condition for the assertion, in a spirit not known since Roman times, of the culture of the foodie. But it also gives us conflict in the world of food — English or French, to start with — as well as dissociation. If Brillat-Savarin could say, "Show me what you eat and I will tell you who you are," he could not say, "Show me what you eat and I will tell you about your blood, your mood, your disposition; I will tell you about your soul." That kind of knowledge was no longer available. And if the joy of food in and of itself became a widespread feature of prosperous households, so did the degradation of the relation of humans to their land, their animals, and their fellow humans, the "twenty million hands," the thousands of lost lives. The standards of living in the eighteenth century were spectacularly uneven. Much of the European peasantry were poorer, and less well nourished, than they had been at any time in the previous four centuries. Many of the new Europeans — the Africans and Americans who had been absorbed into the European world system — were of course utterly debased.

The fissures in the new world of the long eighteenth century and its food are registered in many ways, and early. We know not only that something has been achieved for the autonomy of good cookery, but that something has gone amiss in the gustatory world when an anonymous satirist shrilly attacks the unexceptional household management of the good wife of the late Protector, Elizabeth Cromwell, reproducing what is purported to be her personal cookbook. We know not only that British cookery has become more capacious in its repertoire and exacting in its standards, but also that it has a guilty conscience when the master chef to Francophile, Catholic nobility, Robert May, newly restored to the glory of hospitality with the restoration of Charles II, has to complain that "the French by their Insinuations, not without enough of Ignorance, have bewitched some of the *Gallants of our Nation* with Epigram dishes, smoked rather than dressed, so strangely to captivate the *Gusto,* their *Mushroomed Experiences* for Sauce rather than *Diet,* for the generality howsoever called *A la Mode,* not being worthy of taken notice of."[28] We know that the inequitable divisions between male and female household workers, between workers of both sexes and their masters, and between the dignity of labor and the pleasures of the table are still very much a part of life when we encounter one of the first great boundary-crossers, Hannah Woolley, author of the first commercially successful books (cookbooks and household guides) ever written by a woman in England. Woolley promotes the art of cookery as a way for the servant to rise in station, whether male or female. She encourages young women especially to read and study and practice the arts, both to become better people and to become economically more self-sufficient. The cook's maid who learns the craft and the social niceties that go along with it "will not only make her Superiors happy in a good Servant, but she will make her self happy also; for by her Industry she may come one day to be Mistress over others."[29] All this seems to speak for a kind of progress. But what social goal is the career of the cook maid or the writer of cookbooks really serving? At whose pleasure is she serving, and for the sake of what pleasure? The idea that something is amiss, that the instrumentality of lower-class careerism is serving the ends of upper-class "splendor" is betrayed inadvertently in a dedicatory poem Woolley presents to her readers, a poem that asserts the happy autonomy of taste and good cheer, but also makes note of the sadness of the labor and subservience needed to cater to them:

Ladies, I do here present you
That which sure will well content you,
A Queen-like Closet rich and brave;
Such not many Ladies have:
Or Cabinet, in which doth set
Gems richer than in Karkanet;
They only Eyes and Fancies please,
These keep your bodies in good ease;
They please the Taste, also the Eye;
Would I might be a stander by,
Yet rather I would wish to eat,
Since 'bout them I my Brains do beat;
And 'tis but reason you may say,
If that I come within your way;
I sit here sad while you are merry,
Eating Dainties, drinking Perry,
But I'm content you should so feed,
So I may have to serve my need.[30]

Few students of early modern cuisine, who are by and large a wistful lot with great respect for the sensory life of the past, are ever really nostalgic for the lives of cook maids and butlers, or for that matter Spenser's "jolly yeoman." It is the food itself and the great occasions in which it was sometimes served that exert appeal. I myself would love to have been served at an outdoor banquet on the beautiful grounds of the Estes estate in Ferrara presided over by Cristoforo di Messisbugo, where cold and hot dishes, light dishes and heavy, vegetarian and meat, were alternated to the music played by M. Alphonso's chamber orchestra.

I would like to have seen for myself, and tasted for myself, during the age of Louis XIV, one of those intimate dinners for twelve people or so described by the author of *L'escole parfaite des officiers de bouche* or François Massialot, whose original bestseller was entitled *Cuisine royal et bourgeoise* and translated two years after as *The Court and Country Cook*. There, as a distinguished guest, one among twelve glittering diners, men and women of fashion, I would be seated at an oval table set with about twenty platters — for the first course alone — including potages and side dishes, "out-works" or hors d'oeuvres, and a "great dish" or *rôti* in the middle:

THE FIRST COURSE

Potages and Side-dishes

Two Potages, one middling Dish of a Bisque of Pigeons,
and the other of Capon with Roots.
Two other middling Dishes for Side-dishes; viz. one of a
Partridge pie hot.
The other of a large fat Pullet and Truffles garnished with Fricandeau.

The great Dish in the middle.

This shall consist of two Pieces of roast Beef, garnished with Cutlets of
marinated Veal fried, with good Sauce.

For the Out-Works

A Poupeton of Pigeons.
A Dish of Quails broiled upon the Coals.
One of farced Pullets, with Cullises or strained Liquor of Mushrooms.
One of Partridges, with Spanish Sauce.[31]

I simply cannot understand, nor has any scholar been able to explain to me, how this food, all arranged on a single table, was actually served to the diners seated along the circumference (see fig. 8.1). The arrangement is easy enough to appreciate, but how was the roast beef reached for and divvied out? How did one make a choice of an hors d'oeuvre between pigeon, quail, pullets, and partridge? How much did one, could one, actually eat this food, especially given that it was only served as the first of three courses? I would like to know this. And even more, I would like simply to have experienced such a meal, to sit around such a table with luminaries from the court of Louis XIV, all crinkling with linen and silk and sweating under the weight of their powdered wigs, consuming such prodigious yet "delicate" foods and wines, and no doubt engaging in the witty, *spirituel*

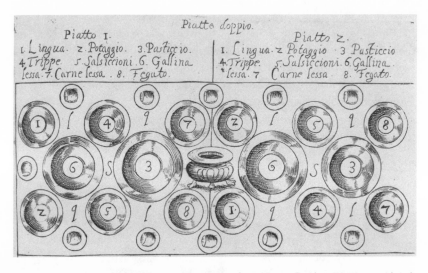

Figure 8.1. Seventeenth-century place setting, from Mattia Giegher, *Li tre trattati* (1639). The system, here in an early Italian version with a silver vessel in the center, was then adopted by the French. A "roast" (not always a roasted piece of meat, but a substantial meat dish in every case, a "great dish" as English translators called it) was placed in the center. The small plates were designated "hors d'oeuvres," literally "out-works," because they were placed outside the main dishes. Reproduced by permission of the British Library (1037.c.13.(1.)).

conversation that became increasingly rowdy as uptight propriety was overtaken by the fine champagnes and Bordeaux being poured out by the attentive waiters crowding about them.

Odds are, of course, that had I lived in such an age, I would not be one of the distinguished guests at the table, or even for that matter a resident of the Île-de-France. My own ancestors — so far as I know, since the records have been lost to the violence of time and ethnic cleansing — were peasants living on rye bread, onions, and beets on the cold plains of Belarus and Ukraine. And if any of them actually made it into one of Europe's cities and lived in relative comfort, they were far less likely to have been one of the great Parisian epicures, dining prodigiously on *potages, rôtis,* and hors d'oeuvres, than to be one of those ambitious "servant maids" to whom Hannah Woolley gives the following instructions:

> You must be at hand to help to lay out the cloth and to bring in Dinner; and if your mistress will give you leave to sit at the Table, you must give a good example to the rest, by being mannerly; eat not your meat greedily, nor be not too slow, for that is as bad. When any thing is given you,

be sure to bow to those who carve it to you; and if your Mistress doth you that favor, you must shew the more respect. Talk not at all at Table, for that is unseemly, unless it be to answer your Mistress when she asks you a question. Drink to no body that you think is better than your self.

Eat not in fear, for it is the best manners to eat one's meat. When you want bread or drink, call for it softly.

Fill not your mouth too full, nor drink before it be well emptied. Put not the whole piece of bread, which lies at your Plate or Trencher to your mouth at once; but break a bit of it.

Put not your Knife to your mouth unless it be to eat an Egg, or such like thing, which you cannot eat without it; nor hold your knife in your hand longer than while you are cutting, do not gnaw your bones, nor put both hands at once to your mouth.

Dip not your fingers in the dish for sauce, for that will render you saucy and liquorish.

If you meet with an hair or any thing unhandsome on your meat, or that any bit be unsavory, through the maids' neglect, lay it by privately, and do not discover it while you are at the Table, for such things will happen among the most careful people.

Leave no scraps on your trencher, but cut your meat handsomely, fat and lean together, cast nothing down under the table, but lay what cannot be eaten on one corner of your Trencher.

Let not your fingers be greasy, but wipe them often.

If you have liberty to carve for your self, be sure to cut the meat without mangling; not paring off the brown, nor all the fat, neither cut that which you think your Mistress, or any other person above your self doth like.

At your sitting down to the Table, be sure to make a reverent honor to your Mistress, and then to the rest of the company, casting your eye round on them all, and then sit down; at your rising do the same, and take your Plate or Trencher with you, having first taken up the crumbs round about it with your knife; if any rise from the Table before you, while they are making their honor to the whole company, be sure to bow, as you sit, to them.[32]

Such a meal may have been generously tasteful and nutritious, but I cannot imagine it as an occasion of joy. Certainly, it was no pretext for the bliss of dissipation. And certainly, though the long eighteenth century made progress in many areas — science, philosophy, democracy — the Age of Enlightenment did not progress in enhancing the equation, known well to such superstitious Renaissance writers as Francesco Colonna and François Rabelais, and even to some of the earlier period's clinical writers, according to which food is love, and love is food.

III

Any writer on food and culture today is apt to begin with the idea that food is more than itself, that over and above biology, food has meaning. This study has attempted to explain some of that meaning as it was articulated and experienced in the early modern period. One thing I hope to have underscored is that food in that period had not only more than one meaning but more than one *kind* of meaning. As different discourses articulated different kinds of relations between men, women, and the foodways in which they were involved, so food was made to generate different categories of signification. Though any attempt to characterize an aspect of the culture of another era must try as much as possible to synthesize, to show how all the evidence at hand was tied together in the coherencies of social, psychic, and material life, it is therefore also important to underscore the incommensurate natures of things and the disparities of the voices, strategies, and languages used to identify and discuss them. Such is the formal side of the ambivalence of culture. The early modern period believed that food had "powers" or "virtues," that an egg could "corroborate" and an arugula salad could "warm" and "provoke." An early modern cook might think about such things when putting together a recipe or a menu, and thus try to find an interesting way to make a meal both corroborating and provoking by combining arugula and eggs. But there is little evidence that cooks ever really tried to do something like that. Perhaps Platina and Martino were pioneering in that direction, but most cookbooks were silent about humoral physiology and the virtues of foods.[33] The discourse of cookery was different from the discourse of health; the practice it referred to, eating for state and pleasure, was different; the meaning of food for the discourse of cookery was different; it was *categorically* different.

Even as a medium of hopes and dreams, food could fall into disparate categories: the healthy plenitude of the utopian writer, the regretful asceticism of the polemicist in favor of vegetarianism, and other such disparate attitudes signified not only that food could be different things to different people, but that the way of putting food into language, of articulating it as a vehicle of meaning, could fall out according to incommensurate models of understanding. As the opening examples from Shakespeare may have demonstrated, disparate sensibilities could coexist within a single artistic mind: the buoyant eating and drinking of which life is happily said to consist may be contiguous with the appalling kind of eating and drinking where the living scandalously feed on the leftovers of the dead and must themselves remorsefully consider that they feed themselves only in order to be food for worms.

There is the matter of social conflict too. The lackey dines with a different agenda from the master, even if he is also, at the master's discretion, dining on the same food. And usually of course the lower orders of society—lackeys, laborers, peasant farmers—are not dining on the same food as the rich. They may belong to a single aesthetic community, yet they belong to it in a different way. The material available to them will likely be defined by the standards set by the rich, but it will not be the same material. It will be the food of the poor—food defined as that which is not the food that one eats if one is rich and able to eat anything one wants.

If one thing remained constant in the culture of food in the early modern period, it was perhaps the assumption that the meaning of food, for all the various ways by which it was articulated, must nevertheless be a *primary* meaning. It was something that must come first. The medical writers were of course committed to the idea. And so, in their own way, were all the others. When writers like Platina and Rabelais openly attacked the medieval convention that the pleasures of the table were evil and were by the holiest of people eschewed, they were calling attention to the idea that even when people eschewed such pleasures for the sake of spirituality, they also gave them a primacy in the meaning of human life: the ascetics were no less obsessed with food, and no less ideologically committed to its value, than the lowliest glutton. That was why Rabelais characterized them as "Gastrolaters." The primacy of food in the early modern period was the reason behind still other phenomena: it was why a new movement toward vegetarianism got under way in the seventeenth century, and why a new epicureanism took hold of the planters of Barbados along with the courtiers of Versailles. Food came first. It was the master of arts, the giver of wits. Indeed, the primacy of food was why a figure like Cornaro and his many followers weighed out their food every day of their lives, limiting themselves to a "sober" life measured out in ounces; and it was why a Counter-Reformation figure like Saint Teresa of Ávila made herself vomit every night by sticking feathers down her throat.

Perhaps in the return to basics, society stripped down to its essentials—evident in authors like Defoe and Rousseau—we discern a realization that food has somehow, over the years, become less primary to our values, that its meaning has become trivialized or marginalized.[34] Both Defoe and Rousseau make the claim, in other words, that modern man has lost touch with himself; he has become alienated from a primary fact of his existence. Rousseau's example of the glittering dinner table whose condition of gaiety is premised on a certain lack of consciousness — on an unmindful forgetting of what the food on the table represents, on where it comes from and how it got there — speaks to this alienation whose effects in his young Émile he is trying to subvert. Of course, Rousseau himself had known poverty and hunger and the humiliation of relying on the arbitrary kindness of strangers. And he had had plenty of occasions, as he reminds us in his *Confessions,* to observe what he took to be the great gulf between the honest, sensually satisfying lives of peasants, who dined simply on bread and wine and cheese, and the pretentious, never satisfied lives of the avatars of civilization, who dined on the most complicated of foods in the most complicated of circumstances, all for the sake of values of which they had forgotten how to take the measure.

In the mid-eighteenth century, Rousseau demands that the demands of *nature* — our nature — become primary to our consciousness and way of life. But what is this nature that is ours? Rousseau attempts to answer that question throughout his career, from the early publication of "Discourse on the Origin of Inequality," all the way to the end, in the *Confessions.* And again and again he comes up with the paradox, all too observable to the student of the culture of food, that *civilization* in *not* in our nature; and hence fine dining, by any name, is alien to our nature. On the one hand, we were made to eat, and that is our first nature. All children, Rousseau insists, are gluttons, and rightfully so.[35] But, on the other hand, civilization is both alienated and alienating, detaching us from our natural relations to food. Hence the child must be taught to think, to remember, to return in his mind to first conditions, where he will find both the nature of his appetite and the circumstances of artificial conventions — the relations of production — that might be deployed to accommodate it.

Mindfulness: or is it? As every reader of Rousseau can attest, there is something mythic, something unwarrantedly fictive and nostalgic, about Rousseau's recoiling from civilization. As he confesses early on, in "On the Origin of Inequality," Rousseau knows that any reconstruction of the primitive is speculative and therefore unreliable. Yet his speculation arrives at what necessarily must come first for us, in matters of food as in anything else. "The farther we are removed from the state of nature," Rousseau says, "the more we lose our natural tastes; or, rather, habit gives us a second nature that we substitute for the first to such an extent that none of us knows this first nature anymore." Mindfulness is the quality that Rousseau wants to inculcate in his pupil Émile; the faculty of reason should govern life in all things as much as it can. Yet what mindfulness wants to take cognizance of is something instinctual: an unmindful, primitive response to the world, a "first nature," whose inclinations and aversions stand for us as the lived embodiment of a norm. "The first time a savage drinks wine, he grimaces and throws it away." Even wine then is suspect. Almost everything is suspect, and should be rejected if it can. We should follow the example of the wine-disliking savage. "Let us preserve in the child his primary taste as much as possible. Let his nourishment be common and simple; let his palate get acquainted only with bland flavors and not be formed to an exclusive taste."[36]

Rousseau is seeking a philosophical way toward overcoming the disparities and incommensurabilities of social entities like food. He wants food to be one thing: an honest, wholesome, primitively gratifying source of nutrition. He wants the faculty of taste to be one thing: a guide to that which is primarily good for us, a window onto our "first nature." Rousseau knows perfectly well that one cannot achieve the ideal, that society is corrupt, and that to live in society one must learn how to deal with the corruption, sometimes making compromises with it. He is preparing his Émile not for a life in the woods but for a life in society. Still, again and again, it is mindfulness of the clash between our first nature and the seductions of civility that Rousseau wants to instill in his young pupil as the best guide to a life of dignified contentment. Émile needs to learn not to be taken in.

The desire is admirable, and many of the best attempts at establishing an ethics of food ever since have been similarly motivated. In the face of all the many things food can be, and all the many ways we have of making food accessible to us as a vehicle of meaning, the ethicist will often want it to be one thing only, and all of our languages of food amount to a single language. The medical book will be on the same plane as a cookbook; the dream of plenty will be on the same plane as the dream of equality and virtue; the comedy of food will be of the same import as the tragedy of food and of the romance of food; what the man of God will say about food will be the same thing, in effect, as what the man of worldly wisdom will profess. And all these things — the medical book, the cookbook, the fantastic fiction, the moral code, the religious homily, the practical conduct book—will speak the same language about an entity whose unity is assured. Some of the utopists of the Renaissance and later have imagined food in just this way. So have many health enthusiasts who have been also food enthusiasts, like Thomas Tryon in the seventeenth century, waxing poetic over turnips and butter, and even like the perennially obese, perennially dieting Dr. Cheyne in the eighteenth, all day consuming milk, cheese, and cabbage, along with bread and wine and the odd joint of red meat. With all due respect, the demand for mindfulness in all things, including food, so that what we put on our plate must also be what we want to accomplish for the benefit of humankind as a whole, admirable though it is, requires a unity of language and practice that the language and practice alike must always defy. We cannot always mean the same thing when we talk, from the context of our varied languages and practices, about food. My "health" may depend on the farmer's use of organic as opposed to pesticide-heavy farming techniques, but it does not—it cannot—depend on how much the farmer pays his laborers, unless what we are talking about is not the health of the body but the clear conscience of the soul. My pleasure in food may seem to be a sound guide to that which is good for me—as writers as early as Platina maintained—but really it is not, and cannot be, except unless I have learned to adapt my pleasure to my attitudes toward health, and I have conditioned myself to confound sensations with scientific knowledge. My fantasies about food may entail a moral order, worth designing a society around, but then again they may not: there is no necessary relation between the two, and there is no language of fantasy that is prima facie also a language of morality. More often than not, one would expect, the opposite is the case. Rabelais wasn't able to pull this off; nor was Tryon; nor was Willich; and when diet-book writers of today import such a necessary relation, telling us that we can eat what we really want and also lose weight or maintain an ideal physique, we know or ought to know that they are lying to us. What we really want—who can even say what this is? Who dares any longer even put this into language? Who dares even speak of free-floating fantasies anymore?

IV

The fault in the demand for a unified language concerning a unified phenomena, a single language concerning a single thing called food, shows up best when we consider the results of the demand in cases whose consequences are unacceptable to us. Let us conclude here with one such case, from *Robinson Crusoe,* a case that has the additional merit of summarizing many of the concerns touched upon in this book.

It comes in the narrative soon after Crusoe first rescues Friday from his tormenters, and Friday, in a stunning validation of European fantasies of paternalistic authority over its colonized peoples, makes signs to Crusoe of "Subjection, Servitude, and Submission." The first thing Crusoe does with this savage is to teach him to say "Master" and "Yes and No." The next thing is to "give him some Milk, in an earthen Pot, and let him see me Drink it before him, and sop my Bread in it." Friday is not just Crusoe's slave; he is Crusoe's child and Crusoe's Émile, and Crusoe sets about educating him by nourishing him—or perhaps, rather, he sets about establishing the relation of master to servant and tutor to pupil as a *relation of nutrition.* But the relation of nutrition turns out to entail a conflict between those first and second natures that an eighteenth-century educator might work upon. Crusoe's savage slave, it appears, is an avid practitioner of the art of cannibalism. He wants to eat the dead victims of Crusoe's rescue mission straightaway. And later on, even after Crusoe has discouraged his inclination in the strongest terms ("I had by some Means let him know, that I would kill him if he offered it"), "Friday had still a hankering Stomach after some of the Flesh, and was still a Cannibal in his Nature."[37] In his *Nature:* but which, the first or the second? It would seem that the educability of the savage native is at stake: if the first, then the civilization Crusoe represents is to provide the savage with a second, wresting him from the depravity of his native nature; if the second, if in other words cannibal society has depraved a natural non-cannibal appetite among its people, then the civilization Crusoe represents would aim instead toward returning the savage to his own natural innocence.

Both options may involve an attractive idea, perfectly in accord with eighteenth-century notions of civility, truth, and education. To be educated, which is to say to become civilized, is to learn how to eat: and either it is then to overcome an initial depravity, or else to return, as far as possible, to an initial innocence. In either case, reason intervenes: reason overcomes the first nature, or reason adjusts the will to the end of following nature. But though both alternatives would seem to be attractive, that is not how the civilizing process Crusoe imposes on his native ultimately succeeds. Perhaps it is because in this case the subject of civility is a Caribbean Indian and not thought fully capable of the exercise of reason that a white man must take for granted. But perhaps it is also because the fantasy of food and the unity of alimentary language that motivates *Robinson Crusoe* demand a more satisfying resolution: a resolution where reason is identical to taste, where a first nature can be made identical to a second, where pleasure can be identical to health, where desire can be identical to morality, where the body and its appetites can be identical to the mindfulness of a clear conscience and the exercise of charity, civility, and *Kultur.* All at once. All at once.

"In order to bring Friday off from his horrid way of feeding, and from the Relish of a Cannibal's Stomach," Crusoe decided that he "ought to let him taste other Flesh."[38] So he took his servant out hunting, where they killed a parrot, whose death they somewhat regretted, and a kid, whose death they did not. The parrot they apparently left alone, after marking its (or rather "her") pathetic agony;[39] the kid they carried "home." And Crusoe cooked it two ways. The first time he "stewed some of the Flesh, and made some very good broth." He showed Friday how to eat it, and Friday "seemed very glad of it, and liked it very well."

There was only one problem. Like the savage in Rousseau who objected, by way of a natural impulse, an impulse of his "first" nature, to the taste of wine, Friday objected to the use of salt. "He made a sign to me," Crusoe says, "that the Salt was not good to eat, and putting a little into his own Mouth, he seemed to nauseate it, and would spit and sputter at it."[40] Wine in the case of Rousseau and salt in the case of Defoe were both signs of Western civility, which to the American savages had previously been unknown. Our first nature, so far as the American represented a first nature, could apparently do without them, and the European thus stood rebuked for putting so much store in commodities so little essential to survival. But after the goat meat stew and the objectionable salt, Crusoe then cooked the flesh of the kid a second time. And the second time taste accomplished the impossible. It converted the cannibal to civility. It brought the whole order of Western practices and values into the empirical reality of gustatory sensation. It verified the unity of the languages of food and their investment in social life as such, marrying symbol and material product, mindfulness and pleasure, meaning and feeling. It did everything I have argued that the experience of food and our alimentary discourses cannot do, though so much energy, from the time of Platina to the present, has been expended insisting that they can and do and will.

The second time Crusoe roasted a "Piece of the Kid." As Hulme notes, Crusoe's cookery in this case was doubly and pathetically ironic. For in Defoe's fantasy, Crusoe assumed, apparently correctly, that Friday had never eaten animal flesh before, that the savage was exclusively cannibalistic. Yet the cookery Crusoe arranged and attributed to the civil life of English cooks was in fact an Indian custom too, the "barbecue" or "*boucan,*" observed by countless visitors to the New World, so that the native word "barbecue" and its variations quickly entered into many European languages. Crusoe cooked the flesh "by having it before the Fire, in a String, as I had seen many People do in England, setting two Poles up, one on each side the Fire [*sic*], and once cross the Top, and tying the String to the Cross-stick, letting the Meat turn continually." The narrative supposes that the savage had never seen the like before. "This Friday admired very much." But there is more. For all of Western civilization comes to hinge on the sensory experience, the sensational science, of a Caribbean dinner. When Friday "came to the Flesh, he took so many ways to tell me how well he liked it, that I could not but understand him; and at last he told me he would never eat Man's Flesh anymore. . . ." This, Crusoe writes, he "was very glad to hear."[41]

Notes

PREFACE

1. Fynes Moryson, *An Itinerary Containing His Ten Yeeres Travell,* 4 vols. (New York: Macmillan, 1907), 4:202.

2. Michel Foucault, *The Archaeology of Knowledge and the Discourse on Language,* trans. A. M. Sheridan Smith (New York: Pantheon, 1972).

CHAPTER ONE

1. William Shakespeare, *Twelfth Night,* in *The Norton Shakespeare,* ed. Stephen Greenblatt (New York: Norton, 1998), 1.3.81–83. All subsequent citations of Shakespeare will be taken from this edition.

2. Robert Appelbaum, "Aguecheek's Beef," *Textual Practice* 14, no. 2 (2000): 327–41.

3. Thomas Elyot, *The Castel of Helthe* (London, 1539), 19.

4. Raymond Klibansky, Erwin Panofsky, and Fritz Saxl, *Saturn and Melancholy: Studies in the History of Natural Science* (New York: Basic Books, 1964).

5. Gugliemo Grataroli, *A Direction for the Health of Magistrates and Studentes,* trans. Thomas Newton (London, 1574), H4–Hrv.

6. Andrew Boorde, *The Fyrst Boke of the Introduction of Knowledge. A Compendyous Regyment; or, A Dyetary of Helth* (London: Early English Text Society, 1870), 271.

7. Thomas Cogan, *The Haven of Health* (London, 1584), 130.

8. *The Good Huswifes Handmaide for the Kitchin* (London, 1594), n.p.

9. Thomas Nashe, *Works,* ed. R. B. McKerrow, 5 vols., rev. ed. (repr., New York: Barnes & Noble, 1966), 2:122.

10. Elyot, *Castel,* 200–201. On the general point of "geo-humoralism," see Mary Floyd-Wilson, *English Ethnicity and Race in Early Modern Drama* (Cambridge: Cambridge University Press, 2003). Also see Ken Albala, *Eating Right in the Renaissance* (Berkeley: University of California Press, 2001).

11. William Harrison, *The Description of England,* ed. Georges Edelen (Washington, DC: Folger Shakespeare Library; Ithaca, NY: Cornell University Press, 1968), 123.

12. Cogan, *Haven,* 129–30. On cattle raising in England, see C. Anne Wilson, *Food and*

Drink in Britain: From the Stone Age to Recent Times (Harmondsworth, UK: Penguin, 1973), chap. 3.

13. Nashe, *Works*, 1:200.

14. Fynes Moryson, *An Itinerary Containing His Ten Yeeres Travell*, 4 vols. (New York: Macmillan, 1907), 4:173.

15. On their habits generally, see Alberto Capatti and Massimo Montanari, *Italian Cuisine: A Cultural History*, trans. Aine O'Healy (New York: Columbia University Press, 2003).

16. Bartolomeo Platina, *On Right Pleasure and Good Health* (1470), critical ed. and trans. Mary Ella Milham (Tempe, AZ: Medieval and Renaissance Texts and Studies, 1998), 231.

17. Moryson, *Itinerary*, 4:83.

18. Giovanni de Roselli, *Epulario quale tratta del modo de cucinare ogni carne, ucelli, pesci de ogni sorte, et fare sapori, torte, et pastelli al modo de tutte le provincie* (Venice, 1518). The work was reprinted many times in Italy and translated into English in 1598: *Epulario; or, The Italian banquet: wherein is shewed the maner how to dresse and prepare all kind of flesh, foules or fishes. As also how to make sauces, tartes, pies, &c. After the maner of all countries. With an addition of many other profitable and necessary things. Translated out of Italian into English* (London, 1598).

19. Cicero, *On the Nature of the Gods*, 2.64; Varro, *On Farming*, 2.5.4. See Cristiano Grottanelli, "La viande et ses rites," in *L'histoire de l'alimentation*, ed. Jean-Louis Flandrin and Massimo Montanari (Paris: Fayard, 1996), 117–32; and Frederick J. Simoons, *Eat Not This Flesh: Food Avoidances from Prehistory to the Present*, 2nd ed. (Madison: University of Wisconsin Press, 1994), chap. 3.

20. Giacomo Castelvetro, *The Fruit, Herbs, and Vegetables of Italy*, trans. Gillian Riley (London: Viking, 1989), 99.

21. Platina, *Right Pleasure*, 231. For the record, Galen, having established that "of all foods, pork is the most nutritious," goes on to say the following about beef:

> Beef furnishes nourishment which is substantial and not easily digested, although it generates thicker blood than is suitable. If anyone more inclined by temperament to melancholy should eat their fill of this food, they will be overtaken by a melancholy disease. These diseases are cancer, elephantiasis, scabies, leprosy, quartan fever and whatever is detailed under the heading melancholia. With some people the spleen increases in volume through the action of this humor, as a result of which cachexy and dropsies ensue.

Galen, *On the Powers of Food*, in *Galen on Food and Diet*, trans. Mark Grant (London: Routledge, 2000), 154.

22. Marsilio Ficino, *Three Books on Life*, bilingual ed., trans. Carol V. Kaske and John R. Clark (Binghamton, NY: Renaissance Society of America, 1989), 1.7:125.

23. Keith Thomas, *Man and the Natural World: A History of the Modern Sensibility* (New York: Pantheon Books, 1983); Massimo Montanari, *The Culture of Food*, trans. Carl Ipsen (Oxford: Blackwell, 1994); Piero Camporesi, *The Juice of Life: The Symbolic and Magic Significance of Blood*, trans. Robert R. Barr (New York: Continuum, 1995).

24. Morris Palmer Tilley, *A Dictionary of the Proverbs of England in the Sixteenth and Seventeenth Centuries* (Ann Arbor: University of Michigan Press, 1951), B709–19, pp. 70–71.

25. The *Oxford English Dictionary* itself doesn't know what to make of this word. I suspect that it refers to the art of carving.

26. *Twelfth Night,* 1.4.101–15; 2.3.10.

27. Henri Bergson, *Laughter: An Essay on the Meaning of the Comic,* trans. Cloudesley Brereton and Fred Rothwell (1911) (Los Angeles: Green Integer, 1999).

28. See Louis Marin, *Food for Thought,* trans. Mette Hjort (Baltimore: Johns Hopkins University Press, 1989); and Catherine Gallagher and Stephen Greenblatt, "The Potato in the Materialist Imagination," in *Practicing New Historicism* (Chicago: University of Chicago Press, 2000), 110–35.

29. Claude Lévi-Strauss, *The Savage Mind* (Chicago: University of Chicago Press, 1966).

30. Primo Levi, *Survival in Auschwitz,* trans. Stuart Woolf (New York: Simon & Schuster, 1993), 76.

31. Claude Lévi-Strauss, "The Culinary Triangle," *Partisan Review* 33 (1966): 587. Also see Roland Barthes, "Toward a Psychosociology of Contemporary Food Consumption," in *Food and Drink in History,* ed. R. Foster and O. Ranum (Baltimore: Johns Hopkins University Press, 1979), 167.

32. Linda Keller Brown and Kay Mussell, eds., *Ethnic and Regional Foodways in the United States: The Performance of Group Identity* (Knoxville: University of Tennessee Press, 1984). But see, alternatively, Stephen Mennell, Anne Murcott, and Anneke H. van Otterloo, *The Sociology of Food: Eating, Diet, and Culture* (London: Sage, 1992); and Roy C. Wood, *The Sociology of the Meal* (Edinburgh: Edinburgh University Press, 1995).

33. Judith Goode, Janet Theophano, and Karen Curtis, "A Framework for the Analysis of Continuity and Change in Shared Sociocultural Rules for Food Use: The Italian-American Pattern," in *Ethnic and Regional Foodways in the United States,* ed. Brown and Mussell, 66–88.

34. See Wood, *Sociology of the Meal,* and Colleen Cotter, "Claiming a Piece of the Pie: How the Language of Recipes Defines Communities," in *Recipes for Reading: Community Cookbooks, Stories, Histories,* ed. Anne L. Bower (Amherst: University of Massachusetts Press, 1997), 51–72.

35. John Lanchester, *The Debt to Pleasure: A Novel* (New York: Picador, 1996), xv.

36. *A Relation, or Rather a True Account, of the Island of England; with Sundry Particulars of the Customs of these people and of the Royal Revenues under King Henry VII, about the Year 1500,* trans. Charlotte Augusta Sneyd (London: Camden Society, 1847), 20–21.

37. *Quo Vadis? A Censure of Travel, as It Is Commonly Undertaken by Gentlemen of Our Nation, The Works of the Right Reverend Joseph Hall, D.D.,* 10 vols., ed. Philip Wynter (Oxford: Oxford University Press, 1863), 9:558.

38. On the social theory of regionalism, see David Bell and Gill Valentine, *Consuming Geographies: Where Are Where We Eat* (London: Routledge, 1997).

39. Jean-Louis Flandrin, introduction to *Le cuisinier françois,* by Pierre de La Varenne,

ed. Philip and Mary Hyman (Paris: Montalba, 1983), 29. The English adoption of this French notion came in fits and starts.

40. Phillip Stubbes, *The Anatomie of Abuses* (1583; repr., New York: Garland, 1973), G3 v4.

41. Alison Sim, *Food and Feast in Tudor England* (New York: St. Martin's, 1997), 104–12.

42. Thomas Dawson, *The Good Huswifes Jewell* (London, 1587), 11–12.

43. Taillevent (Guillaume Tirel), *Le viandier,* ed. Jérôme Pichon and Georges Vicaire, 2 vols. (Paris, 1892).

44. The native British trend away from feudal artifice among the Tudors is traced, chauvinistically, in Colin Spencer, *British Food: An Extraordinary Thousand Years of History* (New York: Columbia University Press, 2002), 100–33; see esp. 122.

45. Sir Kenelm Digby, *The Closet of Sir Kenelm Digby Opened* (1669), ed. Jane Stevenson and Peter Davidson (London: Prospect Books, 1997), 174.

46. Digby's onion is significant not only because it is used along with aromatics, but because it is a newly acceptable vegetable among the wealthy. In earlier years onions were not thought fit to eat by people with status, and in Digby's time it was only beginning to be acceptable. His recipes frequently include the caveat that one may use an onion if one likes such things.

47. Harrison, *Description of England,* 126.

48. *Hamlet,* 1.2.172–80.

49. Catherine Gallagher and Stephen Greenblatt, "The Mousetrap," in *Practicing the New Historicism,* 155.

50. "But before the invention of canning, freezers or vacuum packs, pies were convenient and relatively durable portable food, easily packed and eaten without implements in lodgings. Gentlemen in chambers commonly kept a pie on the sideboard for anyone who cared to drop in and country people sent them as presents to friends or patrons in town." Hilary Spurling, ed., *Elinor Fettiplace's Receipt Book: Elizabethan Country House Cooking* (New York: Viking, 1986), 55.

51. Christopher Daniell, *Death and Burial in Medieval England, 1066–1550* (London: Routledge, 1997), 57.

52. David Cressy, *Birth, Marriage, and Death: Ritual, Religion, and the Life-Cycle in Tudor and Stuart England* (Oxford: Oxford University Press, 1997), 446.

53. John Partridge, *The Treasurie of Commodious Conceits, and Hidden Secrets, Commonly Called The Good Huswives Closet of Provision, for the Health of Hir Housholde* (London, 1584), A2v.

54. Carolyn Spurgeon, *Shakespeare's Imagery and What It Tells Us* (Cambridge: Cambridge University Press, 1935), 114, 121.

55. The serving of "Bake mete" is described in *The Boke of Nurture,* reproduced in *The Babees Book: Manners and Meals in Olden Times,* ed. F. J. Furnivall (London: Early English Text Society, 1868), 146–47. Also see Barbara Ketchum Wheaton, *Savoring the Past: The French Kitchen and Table from 1300 to 1789* (Philadelphia: University of Pennsylvania Press, 1983).

56. See the remarks of Francis Bacon on how "grievous beyond other matters" mur-

der by poisoning is in Andrew Amos, *The Great Oyer of Poisoning: The Trial of the Earl of Somerset for the Poisoning of Sir Thomas Overbury* (London, 1846), 70–71. Also see H. Brabant, *Médecins, malades et maladies de la Renaissance* (Paris: Renaissance du Livre, 1966), 99.

57. *Hamlet*, 1.5.59–73.

58. Annette Hope, *Londoners' Larder: English Cuisine from Chaucer to the Present* (Edinburgh: Mainstream, 1990), 70.

59. For example, in Orsino's opening speech: "O spirit of love, how quick and fresh art thou . . ." *Twelfth Night*, 1.1.9.

60. *Hamlet*, 3.4.142–44; 1.2.135–36; 5.1.156–57; 1.5.32–33.

61. Ibid., 3.4.67–68; 3.4.83–85. And see G. R. Hibbard, ed., *Hamlet* (Oxford: Clarendon Press, 1987), 281n68.

62. Wendy Wall develops the theme of playful triumphs over nature in *Staging Domesticity: Household Work and English Identity in Early Modern Drama* (Cambridge: Cambridge University Press, 2002), chap. 1.

63. Levinus Lemnius, *The Touchstone of Complexions,* trans. Thomas Newton (London, 1581), 10.

64. Thomas Paynel, *Regimen sanitatis Salerni* (London, 1541), Aiiv.

65. Faye Marie Getz, ed., *Healing and Society in Medieval England: A Middle English Translation of the Pharmaceutical Writings of Gilbertus Anglicus* (Madison: University of Wisconsin Press, 1991), 157.

66. Ficino, *Three Books on Life,* 173–75. Also see Lazare Rivière explaining how a pathological appetite may be produced when "the Stomach is filled with crude Excrements by reason of its evil Concoction and distribution," which causes these "excrements" to undergo "a peculiar kind of corruption" that "causes a desire of evil meats, and things not ordained for nourishment." Lazare Rivière, *The Practice of Physick, in Seventeen Several Books,* trans. Nicholas Culpeper, Abdiah Cole, and William Rowland (London, 1655), 401.

67. Timothy Bright, *A Treatise of Melancholie* (London, 1586), 2.

68. Some writers in English attempt to distinguish between cold "putrefaction" and hot "corruption," but the terminological distinction was not widespread. See chapter 2.

69. *As You Like It,* 1.3.36–38.

70. See Colin Spencer, *Heretic's Feast: A History of Vegetarianism* (Hanover, NH: University Press of New England, 1995); and below, chapter 5.

71. *Hamlet*, 4.3.22–27.

72. Ibid., 1.2.5.

73. See Janet Adelman, *Suffocating Mothers: Fantasies of Maternal Origin in Shakespeare's Plays, Hamlet to the Tempest* (New York: Routledge, 1992), where the corruptness of materiality is further associated with fears of the "maternal matrix."

74. *Titus Andronicus,* 5.2.175–80.

75. Ficino, *Three Books on Life,* 247.

76. *The Kalendar & Compost of Shepherds* (London: Peter Davies, 1931), 66.

77. *Hamlet*, 4.4.32–35.

CHAPTER TWO

1. John Archer, *Everyman His Own Doctor* (London, 1671), 40–41.

2. Ken Albala, *Eating Right in the Renaissance* (Berkeley: University of California Press, 2001).

3. See chapter 8.

4. Michel Foucault, *The Archaeology of Knowledge and the Discourse on Language,* trans. A. M. Sheridan Smith (New York: Pantheon, 1972), 64.

5. In a private communication, Ken Albala has informed me that the original title is *De literatorum et eorum qui magistratibus fugentur:* students and those who *flee* from public duties — that is, those who live in leisure.

6. Gugliemo Grataroli, *A Direction for the Health of Magistrates and Studentes,* trans. Thomas Newton (London, 1574), B4.

7. Ibid., B4v2. There is also a suggestion that magistrates and scholars are different because they live apart or at least dine apart from women.

8. Ibid., A1.

9. Ibid., A1v.

10. Ibid., B2v.

11. Luther H. Martin, Huck Gutman, and Patrick H. Hutton, eds., *Technologies of the Self; A Seminar with Michel Foucault* (Amherst: University of Massachusetts Press, 1988).

12. Galen, *On the Natural Faculties,* trans. Arthur John Brock (New York: G. P. Putnam's Sons, 1916), 197.

13. John Donne, *Devotions upon Emergent Occasions,* in *Selected Prose,* ed. Neil Rhodes (Harmondsworth, UK: Penguin, 1987), 99. On the metaphor, see Michael C. Schoenfeldt, *Bodies and Selves in Early Modern England* (Cambridge: Cambridge University Press, 1999).

14. Also see Margaret Healy, *Fictions of Disease in Early Modern England* (Houndmills, UK: Palgrave, 2001), which explores the political dimensions of regimens and the uses.

15. On the Greek and Latin revival, see the essays in *The Medical Renaissance of the Sixteenth Century,* ed. A. Wear, R. K. French, and I. M. Lonie (Cambridge: Cambridge University Press, 1985). On the politics of the profession, see Harold J. Cook, *The Decline of the Old Medical Regime in Stuart London* (Ithaca, NY: Cornell University Press, 1986).

16. Thomas Elyot, *The Castel of Helthe* (London, 1539).

17. Epicurus, letter to Menoeceus, in *The Philosophy of Epicurus: Letters, Doctrines, and Parallel Passages from Lucretius,* trans. George K. Strodach (Evanston, IL: Northwestern University Press, 1963), 181.

18. Andrew Boorde, *The Fyrst Boke of the Introduction of Knowledge. A Compendyous Regyment; or, A Dyetary of Helth* (London: Early English Text Society, 1870), 300.

19. Paul Slack, "Mirrors of Health and Treasures of Poor Men: The Uses of the Vernacular Medical Literature of Tudor England," in *Health, Medicine and Morality in the Sixteenth Century,* ed. Charles Webster (Cambridge: Cambridge University Press, 1979), 237–73.

20. Francis R. Packard, "History of the School of Salernum," in *The School of Salernum: Regimen sanitatis Salernitanum. The English Version by Sir John Harington* (New York: Paul Hoeber, 1920), 25.

21. Bartolomeo Platina, *On Right Pleasure and Good Health* (1470), critical ed. and trans. Mary Ella Milham (Tempe, AZ: Medieval and Renaissance Texts and Studies, 1998), 101.

22. Luigi Cornaro, *The Art of Living Long* (Milwaukee, WI: William F. Butler, 1903), 41. This modern translation may be compared with an earlier rendering based on a manuscript completed by the poet George Herbert: "O wretched, miserable *Italy!*" Cornaro writes. "Dost thou not plainly see, that Gluttony deprives thee of more Souls yearly, than either a War, or the Plague itself could have done? Thy true Scourges are thy continual Banquets, which are so intolerably extravagant and profuse, that there are not Tables large enough. . . ." Cornaro, *A Treatise of Health and Long Life, with the Sure Means of Attaining It, in Two Books,* trans. Timothy Smith (London, 1743), separate pagination, 5.

23. Elyot, *Castel of Helthe,* 43.

24. Thomas Paynel, *Regimen sanitatis Salerni* (London, 1541), Aii–Aiiv.

25. Phillip Stubbes, *The Anatomie of Abuses* (1583; repr., New York: Garland, 1973), G3v4.

26. Paynel, *Regimen sanitatis Salerni,* Aii.

27. Thomas Moulton, *This Is the Myrour or Glasse of Helthe* (London, 1540), n.p.

28. Archer, *Every Man,* A2–2v.

29. Norbert Elias, *The Civilizing Process,* trans. Edmund Jephcott (Oxford: Blackwell, 1994); Peter Stallybrass and Allon White, *The Politics and Poetics of Transgression* (Ithaca, NY: Cornell University Press, 1986); Gail Kern Paster, *The Body Embarrassed: Drama and the Disciplines of Shame in Early Modern England* (Ithaca, NY: Cornell University Press, 1993). For a recent reevaluation, see Anna Bryson, *From Courtesy to Civility: Changing Codes of Conduct in Early Modern England* (Oxford: Clarendon Press, 1998); and Jennifer Richards, introduction to *Early Modern Civil Discourses,* ed. Jennifer Richards (Houndmills, UK: Palgrave Macmillan, 2003), 1–18. The issue will be discussed throughout this study. See in particular chapter 6.

30. Michel de Montaigne, *The Complete Essays of Montaigne,* trans. Donald Frame (Stanford, CA: Stanford University Press, 1958), 832. Also see Albala, *Eating Right in the Renaissance,* chap. 5; and Alberto Capatti and Massimo Montanari, *Italian Cuisine: A Cultural History,* trans. Aine O'Healy (New York: Columbia University Press, 2003). Francis Bacon makes similar comments in his essay "Of Regimen," but Bacon's assessment is already moving in a more systematic direction. See below, chapter 5.

31. Platina, *On Right Pleasure,* 115–17.

32. Paynel, *Regimen sanitatis Salerni,* 17.

33. Anonymous, dedicatory poem, in Leonardus Lessius, *Hygiasticon; or, The Right Course of Preserving Life and Health unto Extream Old Age* (London, 1636), n.p.

34. Owsei Temkin, *Galenism: Rise and Decline of a Medical Philosophy* (Ithaca, NY: Cornell University Press, 1973), 89.

35. Hippocrates, *Of the Nature of Man,* in *Hippocrates,* trans. W. H. S. Jones, 4 vols. (London: William Heinemann, 1923), 4:11–13.

36. On the history of humoral theory, see Raymond Klibansky, Erwin Panofsky, and Fritz Saxl, *Saturn and Melancholy: Studies in the History of Natural Science* (New York: Basic Books, 1964). For an especially clear analysis of the theory, see J. B. Bamborough, *The Little*

World of Man (London: Longmans, 1951). Also see Nancy G. Siraisi, *Medieval and Early Renaissance Medicine* (Chicago: University of Chicago Press, 1990); and F. David Hoeniger, *Medicine and Shakespeare in the English Renaissance* (Newark: University of Delaware Press, 1992).

37. Sir John Harington, *The Englishmans Doctor; or, The School of Salernum ["Regimen sanitatis Salernitanum"]* (New York: Paul B. Hoeber, 1920), 132.

38. Ibid., 134, 136.

39. Levinus Lemnius, *The Touchstone of Complexions,* trans. Thomas Newton (London, 1581), 1.

40. Grataroli, *Direction,* F2v.

41. Boorde, *Compendyous Regyment,* 288–89.

42. *The Taming of the Shrew,* 4.1.151–56.

43. On the "natural faculties," see, for example, John Huarte, *The Examination of Mens Wits* (1594), facsimile (Gainesville, FL: Scholars' Facsimiles and Reprints, 1959), 322; Lemnius, *Touchstone of Complexions,* 9; and Bamborough, *Little World of Man,* 53. Although many writers use the term "concoction" to describe the whole of digestion, and even distinguish between first, second, and third stages of concoction (the first in the stomach, the second in the liver, the third in the heart), the identity of "concoction" and "digestion" is rejected by Gaspard Bachot, who argues that "digestion" properly refers only to the *distribution* of nutrients in the system, while "concoction" is "une mutation ou perfection de l'aliment en la propre qualité du corps qui doibt estre nourry, ou selon d'autres une perfections du mixte perfectible, procedant de la propre & naturelle chaleur qui cuit ou confit and converty en sang dans toutes les parties du corps." Gaspard Bachot, *Erreurs populaires touchant la médecine et régime de santé* (Lyon, 1626), 468.

44. Marsilio Ficino, *Three Books on Life,* bilingual ed., trans. Carol V. Kaske and John R. Clark (Binghamton, NY: Renaissance Society of America, 1989), 173.

45. Thomas Vicary, *The Anatomie of the Bodie of Man* (1548), ed. Frederick Furnivall (Oxford: Early English Text Society, 1888), 67.

46. Ibid., 56, 58.

47. Other parts of the gastrointestinal apparatus were understood to be conscious processes as well, but the stomach was the center to which all the other processes could be referred.

48. William Harvey, *The Anatomical Lectures,* ed. and trans. Gweneth Whitteridge (Edinburgh: E. & S. Livingstone, 1964).

49. Galen, *On the Natural Faculties,* 189.

50. Ibid., 193–95.

51. Hippocrates, *Of Ancient Medicine,* in *Hippocrates,* 1:72.

52. Boorde, *Compendyous Regyment,* 251.

53. Lemnius, *Touchstone of Complexions,* 10.

54. Harington, *The Englishmans Doctor,* 80.

55. Elyot, *Castel of Helthe,* 42.

56. James Hart, *Klinekeh; or, The Diet of the Diseased, Divided into Three Bookes* (London, 1633), 36.

57. Hippocrates, *Of Ancient Medicine*, in *Hippocrates*, 1:27.

58. Thomas Tryon, *Wisdome's Dictates; or, Aphorisms and Rules, Physical, Moral, and Divine; for Preserving the Health of the Body, and the Peace of the Mind* (London, 1691), 146. And see below, chapter 5.

59. Molière, *The Imaginary Invalid*, in *The Misanthrope and Other Plays*, trans. John Wood (Harmondsworth, UK: Penguin, 1959), 277–78.

60. Roy Porter, *The Greatest Benefit to Mankind: A Medical History of Humanity* (New York: Norton, 1997), 226–27.

61. *Le disciple de Pantagruel (Les navigation de Panurge)* (1538), ed. Guy Demerson and Christiane Lauvergnat-Gagnière (Paris: Nizet, 1982), 13.

62. Robert Burton, *The Anatomy of Melancholy*, ed. Thomas C. Faulkner, Nicolas K. Kiessling, and Rhonda L. Blair, 3 vols. (Oxford: Clarendon Press, 1989–2000), 1:416.

63. Lazare Rivière, *The Practice of Physick, in Seventeen Several Books*, trans. Nicholas Culpeper, Abdiah Cole, and William Rowland (London, 1655), 399.

64. Leonardus Lessius defines it as follows: "What we call Crudity, is the Imperfect Concoction of Food. For when the Stomach, either by taking down more in Quantity, or Things stronger in Nature, and of greater Resistance in Quality, than the Supplies of Action and Living require; finds that the active and concoctive Powers of the Solids are insufficient for them; then that Chyle or Juice, which is made of the Food so taken, is said to be crude, that is raw, or to have Crudity in it. . . ." *A Treatise of Health and Long Life with the Future Means of Attaining It: In Two Books*, trans. Timothy Smith (London, 1742), 47–48.

65. Rivière, *Practice of Physic*, 399.

66. Ibid., 402. The etiology was not original to the French physician. In Shakespeare's *2 Henry IV*, a similar problem, derived from drinking too much water (rather than wine), is said to be responsible for the chilly character of young men like Prince John, brother to the much warmer Prince Hal: "for thin [i.e., water] doth so overcool their blood, and making many fish meals, that they fall into a kind of male green-sickness; and then when they marry they get wenches" (4.2.88–91).

67. Rivière, *Practice of Physic*, 401–3.

68. John Symcotts, *Diary*, in *A Seventeenth Century Doctor and His Patients*, ed. F. N. L. Poynter and W. J. Bishop (Streatley near Luton, UK: The Society, 1951), 17–18.

69. Celsus, *De medicina*, trans. W. G. Spencer, 3 vols. (Cambridge, MA: Harvard University Press, 1935), 1:191–93.

70. On this, see especially Albala, *Eating Right in the Renaissance*, chap. 3.

71. Castor Durante, *Il tesoro della sanità* (Venice, 1586), 220.

72. Galen, *On the Power of Foods*, in *Galen on Food and Diet*, trans. Mark Grant (London: Routledge, 2000), 154.

73. This myth about pork and urine is behind much of the urinary comedy of Ben Jonson's *Bartholomew Fair*: a point missed in Paster, *The Body Embarrassed*.

74. Ficino, *Three Books on Life*, 137.

75. Grataroli, *Direction*, M2r1.

76. Hippocrates, *Of the Nature of Man*, 4:329.

77. Grataroli, *Direction*, O1.

78. Durante, *Il tesoro della sanità,* 127.

79. William Vaughan, *Naturall and Artificial Directions for Health* (London, 1600), 85.

80. Thomas Cogan, *The Haven of Health* (London, 1584), 152.

81. Ficino, *Three Books on Life,* 211-13.

82. Galen, *On the Power of Foods,* 173.

83. *Libro della cucina.* Quoted in Capatti and Montanari, *Italian Cuisine,* 77.

84. Gervase Markham, *The English Housewife,* ed. Michael R. Best (Kingston, ON: McGill-Queen's University Press, 1987), 67.

CHAPTER THREE

1. *Libellus de arte coquinaria,* ed. and trans. Rudolf Grewe and Constance B. Hieatt (Tempe: Arizona Center for Medieval and Renaissance Studies, 2001), 28-29. On the textual history of the book, see the introduction by Constance Hieatt, 1-20.

2. Hieatt notes that one does not in fact "hunt" a chicken but thinks this "irrelevant. . . . What such a name implies is things which can be cooked and eaten under simple outdoor conditions, as when one is hunting" (ibid., 89). But the reasoning is unconvincing. One would think that if one was hunting and needed to eat simply, it would be enough to spit-roast the chicken. Certainly, it would hardly be the most convenient thing for a hunter to do to have such ingredients as chicken broth — or for that matter chickens — brought along with him during the hunt. It would seem rather that "hunter style" will have to join the ranks of other oddly named famous dishes, like spaghetti carbonara, concerning which a variety of more or less likely myths of origins have arisen.

3. See Elizabeth Eisenstein, *The Printing Press as an Agent of Change: Communications and Cultural Transformations in Early Modern Europe* (Cambridge: Cambridge University Press, 1979); and Adrian Johns, *The Nature of the Book: Printing and Knowledge in the Making* (Chicago: University of Chicago Press, 1998). Eisenstein's main point — that "fixity" promotes communication, discussion, and innovation — is not entirely born out by the cookbook publication until the late seventeenth century. Amy B. Trubek, *Haute Cuisine: How the French Invented the Culinary Professions* (Philadelphia: University of Pennsylvania Press, 2000), 11-12, even argues the opposite position, claiming that the continuity of the cookbook tradition beginning in the seventeenth century made cookery "less permeable to change."

4. *Encyclopédie, ou Dictionnaire raisonné des sciences, des arts et des métiers, par une société de gens de lettres,* ed. Denis Diderot and Jean Le Rond d'Alembert (Paris: Briasson [etc.], 1751-65), vol. 4. Montaigne also cites this passage.

5. It has also been suggested that "recipe" derives from the term "to take," since so many recipes begin with the instruction to "take" something and do something with it. Stephen Mennell, *All Manners of Food: Eating and Taste in England and France from the Middle Ages to the Present,* 2nd ed. (Urbana: University of Illinois Press, 2000), 67.

6. For example, chicken baked in dough is sometimes a "koken" and sometimes a "pastel," the first word a Germanic term, the second Italian and French.

7. Jacques Derrida, "Freud and the Scene of Writing," in *Writing and Difference,* trans. Alan Bass (Chicago: University of Chicago Press, 1978), 196-231.

8. Allen J. Grieco, "From the Cookbook to the Table: A Florentine Table and Italian Recipes of the Fourteenth and Fifteenth Centuries," in *Du manuscrit à la table: Essais sur la cuisine au Moyen Age,* ed. Carole Lambert (Montréal: Les Presses de l'Université de Montréal, 1992), 33.

9. *The Viandier of Taillevent: An Edition of All Extant Manuscripts,* ed. Terence Scully (Ottawa: University of Ottawa Press, 1988), 71–72; *Curye on Inglisch,* in *English Culinary Manuscripts of the Fourteenth Century,* ed. Constance B. Hieatt and Sharon Butler (Oxford: Oxford University Press, 1985), 191; *The Sensible Cook: Dutch Foodways in the Old and New World,* trans. Peter G. Rose (Syracuse, NY: Syracuse University Press, 1989), 61–62.

10. Bruno Laurioux, *Les livres de cuisine médiévaux* (Turnhout, Belgium: Brepols, 1997).

11. On cookery as a "language" with a "grammar," see Florence Dupont, "Grammaire de l'alimentation et des repas romains," in *L'histoire de l'alimentation,* ed. Jean-Louis Flandrin and Massimo Montanari (Paris: Fayard, 1996), 198–214; Colleen Cotter, "Claiming a Piece of the Pie: How the Language of Recipes Defines Communities," in *Recipes for Reading: Community Cookbooks, Stories, Histories,* ed. Anne L. Bower (Amherst: University of Massachusetts Press, 1997), 51–72.

12. *Curye on Inglisch.*

13. Philip and Mary Hyman, "Imprimer la cuisine: Les livres de cuisine en France entre le XVe et le XIXe siècle," in *L'histoire de l'alimentation,* ed. Flandrin and Montanari, 644.

14. *Le menagier de Paris,* ed. Georgine E. Brereton and Janet M. Ferrier (Oxford: Clarendon Press, 1981).

15. See Alain Girard, "Le triomphe de *La Cuisiniere bourgeoise:* Livres culinaires, cuisine et society en France aux XVIIe et XVIIe siècles," *Revue d'Histoire Moderne et Contemporaine* 24 (1977): 497–523.

16. Robert Appelbaum, "Rhetoric and Epistemology in Early Printed Recipe Collections," *Journal of Early Modern Cultural Studies* 3, no. 2 (2003): 1–35.

17. See Louis Marin, *Food for Thought,* trans. Mette Hjort (Baltimore: Johns Hopkins University Press, 1989), 117–18ff.

18. Mary Ellen Milham, "Martino and His *De re coquinaria,*" in *Medieval Food and Drink* (Binghamton, NY: Center for Medieval and Renaissance Studies, 1995), 62–66.

19. On Platina, see Joseph Dommers Vehling, *Platina and the Rebirth of Man* (Chicago: Walter Hill, 1941); and Gillian Riley, "Platina, Martino, and Their Circle," in *Cooks and Other People,* ed. Harlan Walker (Devon, UK: Prospect Books, 1995).

20. Bartolomeo Platina, *On Right Pleasure and Good Health* (1470), critical ed. and trans. Mary Ella Milham (Tempe, AZ: Medieval and Renaissance Texts and Studies, 1998), 267.

21. Dennis Rhodes, "The Italian Banquet, 1598, and Its Origins," *Italian Studies* 27 (1972): 60–63.

22. Marsilio Ficino, *Three Books on Life,* bilingual ed., trans. Carol V. Kaske and John R. Clark (Binghamton, NY: Renaissance Society of America, 1989), 111.

23. Ibid., 135.

24. Platina, *Right Pleasure,* 101.

25. Ibid., 119.

26. Ibid., 265.

27. Ibid., 333.

28. Alberto Capatti and Massimo Montanari, *Italian Cuisine: A Cultural History*, trans. Aine O'Healy (New York: Columbia University Press, 2003).

29. See C. Anne Wilson, "Furniture and Setting of the Social Meal," in *The Appetite and the Eye": Visual Aspects of Food and Its Presentation within Their Historic Context*, ed. C. Anne Wilson (Edinburgh: Edinburgh University Press, 1991), 28–55.

30. Platina, *Right Pleasure*, 333.

31. Ibid., 293.

32. Michel Jeanneret discusses such occasions without documenting them: *A Feast of Words: Banquets and Table Talk in the Renaissance*, trans. Jeremy Whiteley and Emma Hughes (Chicago: University of Chicago Press, 1987), chap. 7.

33. Capatti and Montanari, *Italian Cuisine*, 98–100, 192–93. Bruno Laurioux, *La règne de Taillevent: Livres et pratiques culinaries à fin du Moyen Age* (Paris: Publications de la Sorbonne, 1997), 218.

34. Apicius, *The Roman Cookery Book, a Critical Translation of "The Art of Cooking,"* trans. Barbara Flower and Elizabeth Rosenbaum (London: Garrup, 1958), 69.

35. Ibid., 153.

36. Capatti and Montanari, *Italian Cuisine*, 98–99; Roy Strong, *Feast: A History of Grand Eating* (London: Jonathan Cape, 2002), 138–39, also claims a more practical effect: a renewal of interest in such items as truffles, oysters, sweetbreads, and a variety of vegetables, including "artichokes, cardoons, asparagus, and members of the cabbage and onion family."

37. Capatti and Montanari, *Italian Cuisine*, 192.

38. *The Court and Kitchen of Elizabeth Commonly Called Joan Cromwell, the Wife of the Late Usurper, Truly Described and Represented, and Now Made Public for General Satisfaction* (1664) (Cambridge: Cambridgeshire Libraries, 1983), 75.

39. Ibid., 17, 18.

40. Eliza Smith, *The Compleat Housewife*, 16th ed. (1758), facsimile reprint (London: Studio Editions, 1994), A2, 3r. Her remarks are to be compared with those of the encyclopedist, who writes that the fine art of cookery arose because "the habit of eating always the same things, and prepared in much the same manner, gave rise to disgust, disgust gave birth to curiosity, curiosity compelled experimentation, experimentation led to sensuality; man tasted, tried, diversified, chose, and succeeded in making for himself a simpler and more natural practical art." *Encyclopédie, ou Dictionnaire raisonné*, 4:537.

41. Timothy Morton, "Old Spice: William King, Culinary Antiquarianism, and National Boundaries," *Eighteenth-Century Life* 23, no. 2 (1999): 97–101, is the only other critical commentary on this poem I am aware of. Reading King's poem straight, however, Morton does not catch its satiric joy, even though it was openly published as a parody.

42. William King, *The Art of Cookery: In Imitation of Horace's Art of Poetry* (London, 1712), 2.

43. Ibid., A2v.

44. Ibid., 89.

45. A notable exception, though with an unusual slant on the subject, is C. Anne Wilson, "Ideal Meals and Their Menus from the Middle Ages to the Georgian Era," in *Appetite and the Eye,* ed. Wilson, 98–122. Also see the remarks in Ken Albala, *Eating Right in the Renaissance* (Berkeley: University of California Press, 2001), 213–16.

46. Barbara Ketchum Wheaton, *Savoring the Past: The French Kitchen and Table from 1300 to 1789* (Philadelphia: University of Pennsylvania Press, 1983), 6.

47. Thomas Dawson, *The Good Huswifes Jewell* (London, 1587), A2. The identical text may be found in *A Proper New Booke of Cokereye* (original ed., 1558), ed. Catherine Frances Frere (Cambridge: Heffer, 1913), 5–7, which itself is based on *This Is the Boke of Cokery* of 1500.

48. Michel de Montaigne, *The Complete Essays of Montaigne,* trans. Donald M. Frame (Stanford, CA: Stanford University Press, 1958), 222.

49. William Harrison, *The Description of England,* ed. Georges Edelen (Washington, DC: Folger Shakespeare Library; Ithaca, NY: Cornell University Press, 1968), 126.

50. The connection between individuality in a moral sense and one's characteristic choices of food is emphasized for an earlier period in Chaucer's *Canterbury Tales.* See Elizabeth M. Biebel, "Pilgrims to Table: Food Consumption in Chaucer's *Canterbury Tales,*" in *Food and Eating in Medieval Europe,* ed. Martha Carlin and Joel T. Rosenthal (London: Hambledon Press, 1998), 15–26.

51. Harrison, *Description of England,* 126. For a modern account of early modern English dining, see Peter Brears, "Decoration of the Tudor and Stuart Table," in *"Appetite and the Eye,"* ed. Wilson, 56–97, esp. 79.

52. Johann Jacob Grimmelshausen, *Simplicissimus,* trans. S. Goodrich (Sawtry, Cambs, UK: Dedalus, 1989), 64–65. A similar confrontation over a roasted dish is recorded in the sixteenth century by Hans Sachs in "The Cook and the Crane," in Hans Sachs, *Merry Tales and Three Shrovetide Plays,* trans. William Leighton (London: David Nutt, 1910), 79–81.

53. Giovanni Francesco Straparola, "Thirteenth Night, Third Fable," in *The Facetious Nights of Straparola,* 4 vols., trans. W. G. Waters (London: Society of Bibliophiles, n.d.), 4:147–48.

54. Dawson, *Good Huswifes Jewell,* A2–A3.

55. On Messisbugo's banquets, also see Albala, *Eating Right in the Renaissance,* 213–14.

56. Bartolomeo Scappi, *Opera* (Venice, 1570), 184–90.

57. For a theoretical account of the issue, see Gérard Genette, *Paratexts: Thresholds of Interpretation,* trans. Jane E. Lewin (Cambridge: Cambridge University Press, 1997).

58. On the genre, see Michael Best, introduction to Gervase Markham's *The English Housewife,* ed. Michael R. Best (Kingston, ON: McGill-Queen's University Press, 1987); Lynette Hunter, "'Sweet Secrets' from Occasional Receipt to Specialized Books: The Growth of a Genre," in *Banquetting Stuffe,* ed. C. Anne Wilson (Edinburgh: Edinburgh University Press, 1991), 36–59; and Wendy Wall, *Staging Domesticity: Household Work and English Identity in Early Modern Drama* (Cambridge: Cambridge University Press, 2002).

59. Hugh Plat, *Delightes for Ladies,* ed. Violet and Hal Trovillion (Herrin, IL: Trovillion Private Press, 1939), xviii.

60. Interestingly, the *Oxford English Dictionary* has little documentation of the language of early modern cookery, and three of the major terms here — "conceits," "secrets," and "closet"—are not documented in the senses here at all.

61. Chris Mead, *Banquets Set Forth: Banqueting in English Renaissance Drama* (Manchester: Manchester University Press, 2001).

62. John Marston, *Antonio's Revenge,* ed. W. Reaveley Gair (Manchester: Manchester University Press, 1978), 5.5.19–21.

63. John Partridge, *The Treasurie of Commodious Conceits, and Hidden Secrets, Commonly Called The Good Huswives Closet of Provision, for the Health of Hir Housholde* (London, 1584).

64. Ibid., A3.

65. Ibid., A2.

66. Markham, *The English Housewife,* 5–8.

67. John Murrell, *A New Booke of Cookerie* (London, 1615), A2v.

68. Ibid., t.p.

69. Ibid., 85–86.

70. The shift in the culinary fashions of Italy is documented in Capatti and Montanari, *Italian Cuisine;* the deeper meanings of this shift are explored in Piero Camporesi, *Exotic Brew: The Art of Living in the Age of Enlightenment,* trans. Christopher Woodall (Cambridge: Polity Press, 1994); and Piero Camporesi, *The Land of Hunger,* trans. Tania Croft-Murray and Claire Foley (Cambridge: Polity Press, 1996).

71. For an extended analysis, see Mennell, *All Manners of Food.*

72. Jean-Louis Flandrin, introduction to *Le cuisinier françois,* ed. Jean-Louis Flandrin, Philip Hyman, and Mary Hyman (Paris: Montalba, 1983), 14–34.

73. Wheaton, *Savoring the Past,* develops this point at length. Also see Mennell, *All Manners of Food,* 71.

74. Pierre de La Varenne, *The French Cook,* 3rd ed. (London, 1673), A5–A5v2.

75. L.S.R., *L'art de bien traiter* (Paris, 1674), 21.

76. Carol A. Déry, "The Art of Apicius," in *Cooks and Other People: Proceedings of the Oxford Symposium on Food and Cookery 1995,* ed. Harlan Walker (Devon, UK: Prospect Books, 1996), 116.

77. Leon Rappaport, *How We Eat: Appetite, Culture, and the Psychology of Food* (Toronto: ECW, 2003), is at least aware of the problem. The standard essays in Jane Ogden, ed., *The Psychology of Eating: From Healthy to Disordered Behavior* (Malden, MA: Blackwell 2003), are not. The experimental focus on eating disorders is partly to blame. Also see Elizabeth D. Capaldi and Terry L. Powley, eds., *Taste, Experience, and Feeding: Development and Learning* (Washington, DC: American Psychological Association, 1990).

78. L.S.R., *L'art de bien traiter,* 57.

79. Ibid., 63.

80. Silvano Serventi and Françoise Sabban, *Pasta: The Story of a Universal Food,* trans. Anthony Shugaar (New York: Columbia University Press, 2002), 264–47.

81. La Varenne, *Cuisinier,* ed. Flandrin, Hyman, and Hyman, 136.

82. Pierre de Lune, *Le Cuisinier,* in *L'art de la cuisine française au XVIIᵉ siècle* (Paris: Editions Payot & Rivages, 1995), 340–41.

83. L.S.R., *L'art de bien traiter,* 66.

CHAPTER FOUR

1. *Le disciple de Pantagruel (Les navigation de Panurge)* (1538), ed. Guy Demerson and Christiane Lauvergnat-Gagnière (Paris: Nizet, 1982), 51. The term "Coquards" is a double play on words, recalling Cockaigne as well as a characterizing (by way of poultry — *coqs*) how the people live.

2. Roland Barthes, "Lecture de Brillat-Savarin," in *Oeuvres complètes,* ed. Éric Marty (Paris: Éditions de Seuil, 2002), 821; Morris Palmer Tilley, *A Dictionary of the Proverbs of England in the Sixteenth and Seventeenth Centuries* (Ann Arbor: University of Michigan Press, 1951), A301.

3. Francesco Colonna, *Hypnerotomachia Poliphili: The Strife of Love in a Dream,* trans. Joscelyn Godwin (New York: Thames and Hudson, 1999), 111.

4. Desiderius Erasmus, *The Colloquies of Erasmus,* trans. Craig R. Thompson (Chicago: University of Chicago Press, 1965), 48–49.

5. See chapter 5. Roger Crab, *The English Hermit; or, Wonder of This Age* (London, 1655); reprinted in *Harleian Miscellany,* 6:391 (London: Robert Dutton, 1808–11).

6. Stephen Orgel, *The Illusion of Power* (Berkeley: University of California Press, 1975); Leonard Tennenhouse, *Power on Display: The Politics of Shakespeare's Genres* (New York: Methuen, 1986). But see Elisa Acanfora and Marcello Fantoni, "The Courtly Life," in *Italian Renaissance Courts,* ed. Sergio Bertelli, Franco Cardini, and Elivira Garbero Zorzi (London: Sidgwick & Jackson, 1986), 189–228; and Susan Weiss, "Medieval and Renaissance Weddings and Other Feasts," in *Food and Eating in Medieval Europe,* ed. Martha Carlin and Joel T. Rosenthal (London: Hambledon Press, 1998).

7. Paul Scarron, *Poésies diverses,* ed. Maurice Cauchie, 2 vols. (Paris: Marcel Didier, 1960–61), 2:130; Antoine Gérard de Saint-Amant, "Le Melon," in *Oeuvres poétiques,* ed. Léon Vérane (Paris: Garnier, 1930), 103–4.

8. Ernst Bloch, *The Principle of Hope,* 3 vols., trans. Neville Plaice, Stephen Plaice, and Paul Knight (Cambridge, MA: MIT Press, 1986). The expression "liberating laugh" is Herman Pleij's.

9. Giovanni Boccaccio, "Third Story, Eighth Day," *The Decameron,* trans. Frances Winwar (New York: Modern Library, 1955), 457–58.

10. Herman Pleij, *Dreaming of Cockaigne: Medieval Fantasies of the Perfect Life,* trans. Diane Webb (New York: Columbia University Press, 1997).

11. For overviews in addition to Pleij, see A. Huon, "Le Roy sainct Panigon dans l'imagerie populaire du XVIᵉ siècle," in *François Rabelais: Ouvrage publieé pour le quatrième centenaire de sa mort* (Geneva, 1953); G. Cocchiara, *Il paesse di Cuccagna e altri studi di folklore* (Turin: Einaudi, 1956); Veiko Väänänen, ed., "Le 'fabliau de Cocagne,'" *Bulletin de la Société Néophilogique de Helsinki* (1947): 3–36; Louise O. Vasvari, "The Geography of Escape and

322 : NOTES TO PAGES 124-128

Topsy-Turvy Literary Genres," in *Discovering New Worlds: Essays on Medieval Exploration and Imagination,* ed. Scott D. Westrem (New York: Garland, 1991), 178–92.

12. The French version has a framing story about a trip to Rome.

13. Mikhail Bakhtin, *Rabelais and His World,* trans. Hélène Iswolsky (Cambridge, MA: MIT Press, 1968); Piero Camporesi, *The Land of Hunger,* trans. Tania Croft-Murray and Claire Foley (Cambridge: Polity Press, 1996); Pleij, *Dreaming of Cockaigne.*

14. Gerrard Winstanley, *The True Leveller's Standard Advanced,* in *The Works of Gerrard Winstanley,* ed. George Sabine (repr., New York: Russell & Russell, 1965), 261.

15. See chapter 5.

16. "To eat one's fill, eat until the exhaustion of the appetite (*manger à sa faim*), was the principal pleasure that the peasants dangled before their imaginations, and one that they rarely realized in their lives." Robert Darnton, "Peasants Tell Tales: The Meaning of Mother Goose," in *The Great Cat Massacre and Other Episodes in French Cultural History* (New York: Vintage, 1985), 34. I am not sure that Darnton's characterization is correct— he may be inadvertently infantilizing the peasantry— but it has been the starting point for my own reflections on the matter. Meanwhile, for an understanding of hunger in the late Middle Ages, one can turn to William Chester Jordan, *The Great Famine: Northern Europe in the Early Fourteenth Century* (Princeton, NJ: Princeton University Press, 1996); and Christopher Dyer, "Did the Peasants Really Starve in Medieval England?" in *Food and Eating in Medieval Europe,* ed. Martha Carlin and Joel T. Rosenthal (London: Hambledon Press, 1998), 53–72.

17. For the "lying tale" see Vasvari, "The Geography of Escape." Mikhail Bakhtin, *Rabelais and His World,* trans. Hélène Iswolsky (Cambridge, MA: MIT Press, 1968), chaps. 5, 6.

18. Grégoire Lozinski, ed., *La bataille de caresme et de charnage* (Paris: H. Champion, 1933), 5, lines 101, 107. A summary of the story appears on page 26. Contemporary with Rabelais is a *Farce de Mardigras,* which tells the same story. See Alban Krailsheimer, "The Andouilles of the *Quatre Livre,*" in *François Rabelais: Ouvrage publié pour le quatrième centenaire de sa mort* (Geneva, 1953), 227–28; and Samuel Kinser, *Rabelais's Carnival: Text, Context, Metatext* (Berkeley: University of California Press, 1990).

19. The episode is the inspiration behind the whole of Kinser's *Rabelais's Carnival.*

20. I have not seen any analogues of "Hansel and Gretel" prior to the Grimms' that contain the feature of the gingerbread house: usually, the children enter a normal house where a married couple live, the husband being a cannibalistic ogre. Much of what I observe of the Grimms' version is nevertheless often true in the others— for example, "Le petit poucet" in French legend and "Molly Whuppie" and "Jack and the Beanstalk" in the English: the house may not be edible, but it is a place where the first attendant one meets, the wife, provides shelter and food alike, and the second one, the husband, turn out to a child-eating monster. The Grimms, incidentally, also recount a story that they call "The Tale of Cockaigne," but this is a short compilation of elements from lying tales that is of little interest here.

21. Giovanni Francesco Straparola, *The Facetious Nights of Straparola,* 4 vols., trans. W. G. Waters (London: Society of Bibliophiles, n.d.), 4:41–42.

22. Ibid., 4:44.

23. Hans Sachs, *The Grand Inquisitor in the Soup*, in *Nine Carnival Plays*, trans. Randall W. Listerman (Ottawa: Dovehouse Editions, 1990), 74–81.

24. Giambattista Basile, *The Pentamerone*, trans. Richard Burton (London: W. Kimber, 1952).

25. *Le disciple de Pantagruel*, 84–85.

26. "Familière description du très vinoporratimalvoise et très envitaillegoulmente royaume Panigonnois, mystiquement interprêté l'Isle de Crevepance," in Huon, "Le Roy sainct Panigon," 221–25.

27. Hans Sachs, "The Sluggard's Land," in *Merry Tales and Three Shrovetide Plays*, trans. William Leighton (London: David Nutt, 1910), 35–39.

28. Elfried Marie Ackermann, *"Das Schlaraffenland" in German Literature and Folksong* (Ph.D. diss., University of Chicago, 1944), 90–96.

29. Pleij, *Dreaming of Cockaigne*, 40–44.

30. Camporesi, *Land of Hunger*, 160–63.

31. Thomas Dekker, *The Shoemaker's Holiday*, in *Dramatic Works*, 4 vols., ed. Fredson Bowers (Cambridge: Cambridge University Press, 1953–61), vol. 1, 5.2.188–95.

32. Ben Jonson, *The Complete Poetry*, ed. William B. Hunter (New York: Norton, 1963), lines 29–38.

33. Thomas Carew, "To Saxham," in *The Poems of Thomas Carew, with His Masque Coelum Britannicum*, ed. Rhodes Dunlap (Oxford: Clarendon, 1949). And see Mary Ann C. McGuire, "The Cavalier Country-House Poem: Mutations on a Jonsonian Tradition," *Studies in English Literature* 19, no. 1 (1979): 93–109.

34. See Felicity Heal, *Hospitality in Early Modern England* (Oxford: Oxford University Press, 1990).

35. François Rabelais, *Gargantua and Pantagruel*, trans. Thomas Urquhart and Peter Le Motteux, 2 vols. (New York: AMS Press, 1967), 1:3. I cite by book and chapter, as is customary for Rabelais.

36. Ibid., 1:3.

37. Ibid., 1:6. And see M. A. Screech, "Eleven-Month Pregnancies," *Etudes Rabelaisiennes* (1969): 89–106.

38. Bakhtin, *Rabelais and His World*, 220–28; Michel Jeanneret, *A Feast of Words: Banquets and Table Talk in the Renaissance*, trans. Jeremy Whiteley and Emma Hughes (Chicago: University of Chicago Press, 1987), 24–25.

39. Bakhtin, *Rabelais and His World*, 285, 301–2.

40. See John Parkin, *Interpretations of Rabelais* (Lewiston, NY: Edward Mellen, 2002), 143–78. An extended discussion of this issue is also found in Peter Stallybrass and Allon White, *The Politics and Poetics of Transgression* (Ithaca, NY: Cornell University Press, 1986).

41. Rabelais, *Gargantua and Pantagruel*, 4:58.

42. Ibid., 4:59.

43. Ibid., 1:21.

44. Ibid., 1:57.

45. Bakhtin, *Rabelais and His World,* 138.

46. Relevant studies of utopia include the following: Bloch, *The Principle of Hope;* Frank E. and Fritzie P. Manuel, *Utopian Thought in the Western World* (Cambridge, MA: Harvard University Press, 1979); J. C. Davis, *Utopia and the Ideal Society 1516–1700* (Cambridge: Cambridge University Press, 1981); Louis Marin, *Utopics: The Semiological Play of Textual Space,* trans. Robert A. Vollrath (Atlantic Highlands, NJ: Humanities Press, 1984); James Holstun, *A Rational Millennium: Puritan Utopias of Seventeenth-Century England and America* (Oxford: Oxford University Press, 1987); Amy Boesky, *Founding Fictions: Utopias in Early Modern England* (Athens: University of Georgia Press, 1996); Marina Leslie, *Renaissance Utopias and the Problem of History* (Ithaca, NY: Cornell University Press, 1998); and my own, Robert Appelbaum, *Literature and Utopian Politics in Seventeenth-Century England* (Cambridge: Cambridge University Press, 2002).

47. Thomas More, *Utopia. Latin Text and Translation,* ed. George M. Logan, Robert M. Adams, and Clarence H. Miller (Cambridge: Cambridge University Press, 1995), 141.

48. Tommaso Campanella, *La città del sole: Dialogo poetico,* bilingual ed., trans. Daniel J. Donno (Berkeley: University of California Press, 1981), 159.

49. Johann Valentin Andreä, *Christianopolis: An Ideal State of the Seventeenth Century,* trans. Felix Emil Held (New York: Oxford University Press, 1916), 159–60.

50. Gerrard Winstanley, *A Watch-Word to the City of London and the Armie* (August 1649), in *Works of Gerrard Winstanley,* ed. Sabine, 315–16.

51. See Appelbaum, *Literature and Utopian Politics,* chap. 4.

52. Patricia Fumerton, *Cultural Aesthetics: Renaissance Literature and the Practice of Social Ornament* (Chicago: University of Chicago Press, 1991); also see Heal, *Hospitality.*

53. More, *Utopia,* 137–39.

54. Ibid., 167–79. See Edward Surtz, *The Praise of Pleasure: Philosophy, Education, and Communism in More's Utopia* (Cambridge, MA: Harvard University Press, 1957); Marin, *Utopics,* 171–74.

55. More, *Utopia,* 139.

56. Ibid., 229.

57. Gabriel de Foigny, *The Southern Land, Known,* trans. David Fausett (Syracuse, NY: Syracuse University Press, 1993), 78–79.

58. Thomas Lupton, *Siuqila. Too Good to Be True* (London, 1580), 28–29.

59. Ibid., 28.

60. Thomas Lupton, *The Second Part and Knitting Up of the Boke Entitled "Too Good to Be True"* (London, 1581), B3v2.

61. Colonna, *Hypnerotomachia Poliphili,* 106–7.

62. Ibid., 107–11.

63. Ibid., 111–12.

CHAPTER FIVE

1. John Milton, *Paradise Lost,* in *The Riverside Milton,* ed. Roy Flannagan (Boston: Houghton Mifflin, 1998), 10.560–70.

2. Ovid, *The XV. Bookes of P. Ovidius Naso, Entytuled Metamorphosis,* trans. Arthur Golding (London, 1567), 2.

3. Arthur O. Lovejoy and George Boas, *Primitivism and Related Ideas in Antiquity* (Baltimore: Johns Hopkins University Press, 1935); George Boas, *Primitivism and Related Ideas in the Middle Ages* (Baltimore: Johns Hopkins University Press, 1948); Harry Levin, *The Myth of the Golden Age in the Renaissance* (New York: Oxford University Press, 1969).

4. Ovid, *Ovid's Metamorphosis Englished, Mythologized, and Represented in Figures,* trans. George Sandys, ed. Karl K. Hulley and Stanley Vandersall (Lincoln: University of Nebraska Press, 1970), 28.

5. Lucretius, *On the Nature of Things,* trans. W. Hannaford Brown (New Brunswick, NJ: Rutgers University Press, 1950), 5.37, pp. 197–98.

6. Miguel de Cervantes Saavedra, *The Adventures of Don Quixote,* trans. J. M. Cohen (Harmondsworth, UK: Penguin, 1950), 85–86.

7. Eliza Smith, *The Compleat Housewife,* 16th ed. (1758); facsimile reprint (London: Studio Editions, 1994), A2 3r..

8. *Encyclopédie, ou Dictionnaire raisonné des sciences, des arts et des métiers, par une société de gens de lettres,* ed. Denis Diderot and Jean Le Rond d'Alembert (Paris: Briasson 1751–65), 4:537.

9. Ovid, *Ovid's Metamorphosis Englished,* , 59.

10. Torquato Tasso, *Aminta: A Pastoral Play,* trans. Charles Jernigan and Irene Marchegiani Jones (New York: Italica Press, 2000), 1.2.320–40.

11. John Donne, "Elegy 17," lines 38–39, 47–48, in *The Complete English Poems,* ed. A. J. Smith (Harmondsworth, UK: Penguin, 1971).

12. Shakespeare, *As You Like It,* 1.1.114–18.

13. Shakespeare, *The Tempest,* 2.1.138–64. This passage has been endlessly commented on, Harry Levin having first brought attention to its mytho-political dimensions, and Frank Kermode in his own edition of *The Tempest* (London: Methuen, 1964) being the first to suggest its colonialist dimensions. I recount some of these issues in chapter 7.

14. Shakespeare, *A Midsummer Night's Dream,* 3.1.148–49, 4.1.32–34, 3.2.332.

15. Guillaume de Salluste Du Bartas, *The Divine Weeks and Works,* 2 vols., trans. Joshua Sylvester, ed. Susan Snyder (Oxford: Clarendon Press, 1979), 1:176–78.

16. Torquato Tasso, *Creation of the World,* trans. Joseph Tusiani (Binghamton, NY: Center for Medieval and Early Renaissance Studies, 1982), lines 1270–83.

17. Ibid., lines 1810–30.

18. Martin Luther, *Works,* 54 vols. (St. Louis: Concordia, 1955–86), 1:36.

19. See, for example, the essays collected in David Armitage, Armand Himy, Quentin Skinner, eds., *Milton and Republicanism* (Cambridge: Cambridge University Press, 1995); and Stephen B. Dobranski and John P. Rumrich, eds., *Milton and Heresy* (Cambridge: Cambridge University Press, 1998).

20. Milton, *Paradise Lost,* 10.729.

21. Ovid, *Metamorphosis,* 1.145–48.

22. See, for example, Augustine, *Concerning the City of God against the Pagans,* trans. Henry Bettenson (Harmondsworth, UK: Penguin, 1984), 11.12.444.

23. For discussion of this in terms of utopia, see Ernest Lee Tuveson, *Millennium and Utopia* (Gloucester, MA: Smith, 1972).

24. Ovid, *Metamorphosis,* 15.96–98.

25. Christopher Columbus, *The Four Voyages,* 2 vols., ed. Cecil Jane (New York: Dover, 1988), 2:34–40.

26. Francis Godwin, *The Man in the Moone; or, A Discovrse of a Voyage thither by Domingo Gonsales: The speedy Messenger* (London, 1638), 75, 108.

27. Pierre de Ronsard, "La Salade," in *Poems of Pierre de Ronsard,* bilingual ed., trans. Nicholas Kilmer (Berkeley: University of California Press, 1979), 146. Kilmer's notes on the poem are also helpful but inaccurate to claim that Ronsard must be joking when he claims that eating salad will help cure his melancholy, since according to humoral physiology, salad after all is "cold." Castelvetro, for example, remarks that the "fresh greenery" of the spring "is a pleasure to the eye, a treat for the palate, and above all, a really important contribution to our health, purging us of all the unwholesome humors accumulated during winter months." Giacomo Castelvetro, *The Fruit, Herbs, and Vegetables of Italy,* trans. Gillian Riley (London: Viking, 1989), 62. Also see Barbara Ketchum Wheaton, *Savoring the Past: The French Kitchen and Table from 1300 to 1789* (Philadelphia: University of Pennsylvania Press, 1983), 63; and especially Leonard W. Johnson, "La Salade tourangelle de Pierre de Ronsard," in *Littérature et gastronomie: Huit études,* ed. Ronald W. Tobin (Paris: Biblio 17. Papers on French Seventeenth Century Literature, 1985), 149–74.

28. See chapter 1.

29. Francis Bacon, *History of Life and Death,* in *The Art of Living Long* (Milwaukee, WI: William F. Butler, 1903), 129.

30. Horace, Epode 16, lines 42–48, in *The Complete Odes and Epodes,* trans. David West (Oxford: Oxford University Press, 1997), 19.

31. Horace, Epode 2, lines 1–2, p. 4.

32. Horace, Odes 3.16, lines 43–44, 29–31, in *Complete Odes and Epodes,* 95.

33. Horace, Satires 2.2 and 2.8, in *Satires, Epistles, and Ars poetica,* bilingual ed., trans. H. Rushton Fairclough (Cambridge, MA: Harvard University Press, 1926). And see Niall Rudd, *The Satires of Horace* (Cambridge: Cambridge University Press, 1966), chap. 7.

34. Horace, Satire 2.4.12–13, 35–36, pp. 186–89.

35. Horace, Satire 2.2.19–20, 39, pp. 137–39.

36. Epicurus, letter to Menoeceus, in *The Philosophy of Epicurus: Letters, Doctrines, and Parallel Passages from Lucretius,* trans. George K. Strodach (Evanston, IL: Northwestern University Press, 1963), 181.

37. Seneca, letter 59, *Ad Lucilium epistulae morales,* 3 vols., ed. and trans. Richard Gummere (London: Heinemann, 1925), 2:409.

38. Seneca, letter 18, 1:23.

39. Seneca, letter 110, 2.273, 2.275–76.

40. Seneca, letters 90 and 34, X:000, 1:240–43.

41. Gaius Julius Caesar, *The Conquest of Gaul*, trans. S. A. Handford, rev. Jane Gardner (Harmondsworth, UK: Penguin, 1982), 2.15, p. 65; 5.15, p. 111; 6.22, p. 143.

42. Cornelius Tacitus, *Germania,* in *The Agricola and Germania,* trans. H. Mattingly, rev. S. A. Handford (Harmondsworth, UK: Penguin, 1970), 121.

43. Lovejoy and Boas, *Primitivism,* 215–344.

44. Dio Cassius, *Roman History,* bilingual ed., 9 vols., trans. Earnest Cary (Cambridge, MA: Harvard University Press, 1927), 3:263–65.

45. Plutarch, *Lives of the Noble Grecians and Romans,* 6 vols., trans. Sir Thomas North (London: David Nutt, 1896), 6:17.

46. Shakespeare, *Antony and Cleopatra,* 1.4.56–72.

47. Elaine H. Pagels, *Adam, Eve, and the Serpent* (New York: Random House, 1988).

48. John Milton, *In quintum novembris,* in *The Riverside Milton,* ed. Roy Flannagan (Boston: Houghton Mifflin, 1998), 209.

49. Desiderius Erasmus, *The Colloquies of Erasmus,* trans. Craig R. Thompson (Chicago: University of Chicago Press, 1965), 55.

50. Basil, *The Long Rules,* in *Ascetical Works,* trans. Monica Wagner, C.S.C. (Washington, DC: Catholic University of America Press, 1962), 270, 272.

51. *The Voyage of Saint Brendan: Journey to the Promised Land,* trans. John J. O'Meara (Atlantic Highlands, NJ: Humanities Press, 1976).

52. There is a good deal of important literature on this topic. See Caroline Walker Bynum, *Holy Feast and Holy Fast: The Religious Significance of Food to Medieval Women* (Berkeley: University of California Press, 1987); Rudolph Bell, *Holy Anorexia* (Chicago: University of Chicago Press, 1985); and Walter Vandereycken and Ron van Deth, *From Fasting Saints to Anorexic Girls: The History of Self-Starvation* (New York: New York University Press, 1994).

53. Vandereycken and van Deth, *Fasting Saints,* chap. 4.; Nancy A. Gutierrez, *'Shall She Famish Then?' Female Food Refusal in Early Modern England* (Aldershot, UK: Ashgate, 2003), chap. 5. A good example of the transformation of the hunger artist from a saint to a curiosity is Thomas Robin, *The Wonder of the World: Being a perfect Relation of a young Maid, about eighteen years of age, which hath not tasted of any Food this two and fifty weeks* (London, 1669). Gutierrez calls texts like these a "colonization" of the female body but provides little justification for the use of the term.

54. Nathalie Peyrebonne, "Le manger et le boire dans le *Libro de la vida* de Sainte Thérèse d'Ávila," *Annali Istituto Universitario Orientale, Napoli, Sezione Romanza* 41, no. 2 (1999): 581–87. Peyrebonne supplies the original Spanish that I comment on below.

55. Teresa of Ávila, *The Life of Saint Teresa of Ávila by Herself,* trans. J. M. Cohen (Harmondsworth, UK: Penguin, 1957), chap. 7, p. 55.

56. Ibid., chap. 40, p. 312.

57. Ibid., chap. 27, pp. 293–94.

58. See Michael C. Schoenfeldt, *Bodies and Selves in Early Modern England* (Cambridge: Cambridge University Press, 1999), 115–16.

59. Luigi Cornaro, *The Art of Living Long* (Milwaukee, WI: William F. Butler, 1903), 43–44.

60. Ibid., 45.

61. Bartolomeo Platina, *On Right Pleasure and Good Health* (1470), critical ed. and trans. Mary Ella Milham (Tempe, AZ: Medieval and Renaissance Texts and Studies, 1998), 295.

62. Cornaro, *Art of Living,* 46.

63. Ibid., 46–47.

64. Hillel Schwartz, *Never Satisfied: A Cultural History of Diets, Fantasies, and Fat* (New York: Free Press,1986), 11–12.

65. Peter D. Kramer, *Listening to Prozac* (New York: Viking, 1993).

66. Cornaro, *Art of Living,* 47–48.

67. Ibid., 47–48, 55.

68. Leonardus Lessius, *Hygiasticon; or, The Right Course of Preserving Life and Health unto Extream Old Age: together with soundness and integritie of the senses, judgement, and memorie.* Written in Latine by Leonard Lessius, and now done into English (Cambridge, 1634), 1–2.

69. Ibid., 10.

70. Bacon, *History of Life and Death,* 129.

71. Ibid., 127.

72. Ibid., 128.

73. Ibid., 129.

74. The only attempt at a comprehensive history of vegetarianism now available is Colin Spencer, *Heretic's Feast: A History of Vegetarianism* (Hanover, NH: University Press of New England, 1995), reprinted as *Vegetarianism: A History* (New York: Four Walls Eight Windows, 2000). The book provides an orientation for the subject, and I have taken some details in what follows from it, but it is often unreliable.

75. Bridget Ann Henisch, *Fast and Feast: Food in Medieval Society* (University Park: Pennsylvania State University Press, 1976); Michael D. Bristol, *Carnival and Theater: Plebeian Culture and the Structure of Authority in Renaissance England* (New York: Methuen, 1985).

76. Spencer, *Heretic's Feast,* 177–80. And see the most striking entry in the notebooks themselves: Leonardo da Vinci, *The Notebooks of Leonardo da Vinci,* ed. Edward MacCurdy, 2 vols. (New York: Reynal and Hitchcock, 1938), 1:90–91.

77. Jean-Louis Flandrin, "Les légumes dans les livres de cuisine français, du XIVᵉ au XVIIIᵉ siècle," in *Le monde végétale (XIIᵉ–XVIIᵉ siècles): Savoirs et usages sociaux,* ed. Allen J. Grieco, Odile Redon, and Lucia Tongiogi Tomasi (Saint-Denis: Presses Universitaires de Vincennes, 1993), 71–88; Joan Thirsk, "The Preparation of Food in the Kitchen, in Europe North of the Alps, 1500–1700," in *Alimentazione e nutrizione secc. XII–XVII,* ed. Somonetta Cavaciocchi (Florence: Le Monnier, 1997), 423–39.

78. See chapter 1. The English translation — an excellent work with an informative introduction — has been given a somewhat less accurate title: Giacomo Castelvetro, *The Fruit, Herbs, and Vegetables of Italy,* trans. Gillian Riley (London: Viking, 1989). See K. T. Butler, "An Italian's Message: Eat Your Vegetables," *Italian Studies II* (1938), 1–8; Massimo Montanari, *The Culture of Food,* trans. Carl Ipsen (Oxford: Blackwell, 1994), 113.

79. Castelvetro, *Fruit, Herbs, and Vegetables,* 62.

80. John Evelyn, *Acetaria: A Discourse of Sallets* (London, 1699), A4v4.

81. See Keith Thomas, *Man and the Natural World: A History of the Modern Sensibility* (New York: Pantheon Books, 1983), 288–300.

82. See Christopher Hill, "The Mad Hatter," in *Puritanism and Revolution* (London: Secker and Warburg, 1958), 314–22.

83. Publisher to the reader, in *The English Hermit; or, Wonder of This Age* (London, 1655), reprinted in *Harleian Miscellany* (London: Robert Dutton, 1808–11), 6:391.

84. Thomas Tryon, *The Way to Health and Long Life; or, A Discourse of Temperance* (London, 1726), 4.

85. Thomas Tryon, *Wisdom's Dictates; or, Aphorisms and Rules, Physical, Moral, and Divine; for Preserving the Health of the Body, and the Peace of the Mind* (London, 1691), 4–5, 41–42.

86. Milton, *Paradise Lost,* 11.525–37.

87. William Kerrigan, *The Sacred Complex: On the Psychogenesis of "Paradise Lost"* (Cambridge, MA: Harvard University Press, 1983); Schoenfeldt, *Bodies and Selves;* Joshua Scodel, *Excess and the Mean in Early Modern English Literature* (Princeton, NJ: Princeton University Press, 2002).

88. Milton, *Paradise Lost,* 4.333–35.

89. Ibid., 5.493–500.

90. Ibid., 5.333–47. And see Ann Torday Gulden, "Milton's Eve and Wisdom: The 'Dinner Party' Scene *in Paradise Lost,*" *Milton Quarterly* 32, no. 4 (1998): 137–43.

91. I follow Kerrigan in using "cosmos" to designate the whole created universe, of which the "universe" or "world" of earth and its heavenly spheres is only a small part.

92. The nature of this Chaos has been the subject of considerable controversy. I follow John Rumrich in seeing Chaos as a natural, divine source or home of creation whose use in Milton's work is troubling to orthodoxy; but I cannot agree that it is quite so benign or even anti-patriarchal as Rumrich wants to believe. See John Peter Rumrich, *Milton Unbound: Controversy and Reinterpretation* (Cambridge: Cambridge University Press, 1996).

93. Milton, *Paradise Lost,* 6.478–79, 6.510–15, 6.586–89, 7.234–39, 2.798–808.

94. Ibid., 9.1000–1001, 10.687–95, 10.711–12, 10.728–29.

95. Ibid., 1.1–2.

96. Robert Appelbaum, "Eve's and Adam's Apple: Horticulture, Taste, and the Flesh of the Forbidden Fruit in *Paradise Lost,*" *Milton Quarterly,* 36, no. 4 (2002): 221–39.

97. In the artworks I discuss in "Eve's and Adam's Apple," Van Eyck represents the fruit as a bitter citron; Tintoretto as a pomegranate, suggestive of the breast; Michelangelo as a phallic fig, inviting fellatio; and Dürer as a bland apple growing on the branches of a fig tree.

98. Milton, *Paradise Lost,* 10.486.

99. I should perhaps reemphasize here, as I did in my *Milton Quarterly* article, that in spite of suspicions often entertained about early English attitudes toward raw fruit, as in Jonathan Gil Harris's tendentious "Apples Beyond the Pale: The Irish Costermonger in the English Garden," in *Medieval Food and Drink,* ed. Mary-Jo Arn (Binghamton, NY:

Center for Medieval and Renaissance Studies, 1995), 127–37, apples were popular and plentiful throughout England at this time, eaten both raw and cooked, and proverbially benign.

100. Milton, *Paradise Lost,* 9.575–85.

101. Andre L. Simon, *The Star Chamber Dinner Accounts* (London: Wine and Food Society, 1959), 29; Ralph Austen, *A Treatise of Fruit Trees,* 2nd ed. (London, 1657), 36–37.

102. Milton, *Paradise Lost,* 9.735–43, 9.768, 9.793.

103. John Evelyn, *Pomona; or, An Appendix Concerning Fruit-Trees, in Relation to Cider,* in *Sylva; or, A Discourse of Forest-Trees, and the Propagation of Timber* (London, 1664), 3.

104. Milton, *Paradise Lost,* 9.835–38, 9.850–52, 9.781–74. On Eve's idolatry see John N. King, *Milton and Religious Controversy* (Cambridge: Cambridge University Press, 1999), 156–58; and Roy Flannagan, ed. *Paradise Lost,* in *Riverside Milton,* 608n224.

105. See Herman Rapaport, *Milton and the Postmodern* (Lincoln: University of Nebraska Press, 1983).

106. Milton, *Paradise Lost,* 9.785–92.

CHAPTER SIX

1. William Shakespeare, *Twelfth Night; or, What You Will,* New Variorum Edition, ed. Horace Howard Furness (Philadelphia: Lippincott, 1901), 1.5.113–16.

2. The concept of the grotesque body is first laid out in Mikhail Bakhtin, *Rabelais and His World,* trans. Hélène Iswolsky (Cambridge, MA: MIT Press, 1968), 317–23. Further developments of the concept will be found in Peter Stallybrass and Allon White, *The Politics and Poetics of Transgression* (Ithaca, NY: Cornell University Press, 1986); Thomas Laqueur, *Making Sex: Body and Gender from the Greeks to Freud* (Cambridge, MA: Harvard University Press, 1990); Gail Kern Paster, *The Body Embarrassed: Drama and the Disciplines of Shame in Early Modern England* (Ithaca, NY: Cornell University Press, 1993); and Bruce Thomas Boehrer, *The Fury in Men's Gullets: Ben Jonson and the Digestive Canal* (Philadelphia: University of Pennsylvania Press, 1997), 14–19.

3. See Stephen Greenblatt, "Fiction and Friction," in *Shakespearean Negotiations: The Circulation of Social Energy in Renaissance England* (Berkeley: University of California Press, 1988), 67–70; Lisa Hopkins, *The Shakespearean Marriage: Merry Wives and Heavy Husbands* (New York: St. Martin's, 1998), 35–36; and Cristina Malcolmson, "What You Will: Social Mobility and Gender in *Twelfth Night,*" in *New Casebooks "Twelfth Night,"* ed. R. S. White (New York: St. Martin's, 1996), 160–94.

4. William Shakespeare, *Twelfth Night,* in *Norton Shakespeare,* 1.3.1–2, 2.3.10–12.

5. A. L. Rowse, ed., *The Annotated Shakespeare,* 3 vols. (New York: Potter, 1978), 1:516.

6. *Twelfth Night; or, What You Will,* Cambridge New Shakespeare, ed. Arthur Quiller-Couch and John Dover Wilson (Cambridge: Cambridge University Press, 1971).

7. Norbert Elias, *The Civilizing Process,* trans. Edmund Jephcott (Oxford: Blackwell, 1994). Also see Jacques Revel, "The Uses of Civility," in *A History of Private Life,* ed. Roger Chartier, trans. Arthur Goldhammer, 6 vols., vol. 3, *Passions of the Renaissance* (Cambridge, MA: Belknap, 1989), 167–205.

8. Anna Bryson, *From Courtesy to Civility: Changing Codes of Conduct in Early Modern England* (Oxford: Clarendon Press, 1998), 71.

9. Alfred Franklin, *La vie privée d'autrefois; arts et métiers, modes, moeurs, usages des parisiens du XIIe au XVIIIe siècle d'après des documents originaux ou inédits,* 23 vols., vol. 6, *Les repas* (Paris: E. Plon-Nourrit et cie, 1887–1901); Giovanni Rebora, *Culture of the Fork: A Brief History of Food in Europe,* trans. Albert Sonnenfeld (New York: Columbia University Press, 2001).

10. Pierre Bourdieu, *Outline of a Theory of Practice,* trans. Richard Nice (Cambridge: Cambridge University Press, 1977), 94; Stallybrass and White, *Politics and Poetics,* 88.

11. Elias, *Civilizing Process,* 3.

12. Michael Moriarty, *Taste and Ideology in Seventeenth-Century France* (Cambridge: Cambridge University Press, 1988). Also see Jean-Louis Flandrin, "De la diététique à la gastronomie," in *L'histoire de l'alimentation,* ed. Jean-Louis Flandrin and Massimo Montanari (Paris: Fayard, 1996), 683–703.

13. See, for example, Michael Leroy Oberg, *Dominion and Civility: English Imperialism and Native America, 1585–1685* (Ithaca, NY: Cornell University Press, 1999).

14. Miguel de Cervantes Saavedra, *The Adventures of Don Quixote,* trans. J. M. Cohen (Harmondsworth, UK: Penguin, 1950), 85.

15. For Murrell, see chapter 3. Philip Massinger, *The City-Madam* (1632), ed. T. W. Craik (London: Ernst Benn, 1964), 1.155–56.

16. Joseph Addison, *Selections from the Tatler and the Spectator of Steele and Addison,* ed. Angus Ross (Harmondsworth, UK: Penguin, 1982), 277–78.

17. Georges and Germaine Blond, *Histoire pittoresque de notre alimentation,* 2 vols. (Ottawa: Fayard, 1961), 1:221–32; Maguelonne Toussaint-Samat, *History of Food,* trans. Anthea Bell (Cambridge: Blackwell, 1987), 317–19; Mark Kurlansky, *Cod: A Biography of the Fish that Changed the World* (New York: Walker, 1997); Mark Kurlansky, *Salt: A World History* (Harmondsworth, UK: Penguin, 2002), 129–43 and *passim.* Also useful, but not always reliable, is Mike Smylie, *Herring: A History of the Silver Darlings* (Stroud, UK: Tempus, 2004).

18. Thomas Cogan, *The Haven of Health* (London, 1584), 168.

19. Christopher Marlowe, *Doctor Faustus,* in *The Complete Plays of Christopher Marlowe,* ed. Irving Ribner (New York: Odyssey, 1963), 2.2.696–700.

20. Tobias Venner, *Via recta et viam longam* (London, 1620), 81.

21. Cogan, *Haven of Health,* 168.

22. Thomas Moffett, *Healths Improvement* (London, 1655); quoted in Sarah T. Peterson, *Acquired Taste: The French Origins of Modern Cooking* (Ithaca, NY: Cornell University Press, 1994), 146.

23. Morris Palmer Tilley, *A Dictionary of the Proverbs of England in the Sixteenth and Seventeenth Centuries* (Ann Arbor: University of Michigan Press, 1951), citing John Taylor, F320.

24. Phillip Stubbes, *The Anatomie of Abuses* (1583; repr., New York: Garland, 1973), G3 v4.

25. See chapter 1.

26. See Michael D. Bristol, *Carnival and Theater: Plebeian Culture and the Structure of*

332 : NOTES TO PAGES 215–219

Authority in Renaissance England (New York: Methuen, 1985), 95–103; Lorna Hutson, *Thomas Nashe in Context* (Oxford: Clarendon, 1989); and Henry S. Turner, "Nashe's Red Herring: Epistemologies of the Commodity in *Lenten Stuffe* (1599)," *ELH* 68 (2001): 529–61.

27. Thomas Nashe, *Lenten Stuffe; or, The Praise of the Red Herring,* in *Works,* ed. R. B. McKerrow, 4 vols. (Oxford: Basil Blackwell, 1958), 3:156–58.

28. Ibid., 3:169.

29. Hutson, *Thomas Nashe in Context,* 255.

30. Claude Lévi-Strauss, "The Culinary Triangle," *Partisan Review* 33 (1966): 586–95.

31. The main complaint, lodged by sociologists like Mennell, Goody, and Harris, is that Lévi-Strauss's approach was both too universalizing and too abstract, and proposed in willful dismissal of biological imperatives. See Roy C. Wood, *The Sociology of the Meal* (Edinburgh: Edinburgh University Press, 1995), 8–12. But it would seem that part of the problem was Lévi-Strauss's Gallic wit, which went over the head of more earthbound British sociologists. The culinary triangle as Lévi-Strauss explains it is not a universal structure but a possible structure for organizing a cuisine. All that Lévi-Strauss insists upon is that all cultures have some sort of "cuisine" (usually translated, misleadingly, as "cooking") so that all cultures have some sort of language (a triangle, a grill, or whatever) with which to organize the preparation and categorization of foodstuffs and processes, beginning with a determination of the distinction between processing and nonprocessing, or between (in some sense, depending on the culture) what is "raw" and what is "cooked." As for the complaint that Lévi-Strauss overlooks the concrete materiality and biological underpinnings of cuisines, one need only look at Lévi-Strauss's own remark that his system of analysis "demonstrates that the art of cooking is not located entirely on the side of culture. Adapting itself to the exigencies of the body, and determined in its modes by the way man's insertion in nature operates in different parts of the world, placed then between nature and culture, cooking rather represents their necessary articulation. It partakes of both domains, and projects this duality on each of its manifestations." Lévi-Strauss, "The Culinary Triangle," 593. Not surprisingly, the editors of *L'histoire de l'alimentation* invoke Lévi-Strauss as a guiding spirit for the contemporary cultural study of food (13).

32. Sir Kenelm Digby, *The Closet of Sir Kenelm Digby Opened* (London, 1669), 206.

33. Lévi-Strauss, "Culinary Triangle," 587.

34. Nashe, *Lenten Stuffe,* 3:206–8.

35. Stubbes, *Anatomie of Abuses,* F3r2. *Twelfth Night* (1.5.124–30) puts it this way:

OLIVIA: What's a drunken man like, fool?

FESTE: Like a drowned man, a fool, and a madman: one draught above heat makes him a fool, the second mads him, and a third drowns him.

OLIVIA: Go thou and seek the coroner, and let him sit o' my coz, for he's in the third degree of drink, he's drowned.

36. Stubbes, *Anatomie of Abuses,* F3v.

37. Faye Marie Getz, ed., *Healing and Society in Medieval England: A Middle English*

Translation of the Pharmaceutical Writings of Gilbertus Anglicus (Madison: University of Wisconsin Press, 1991), 162–63, 165.

38. Lazare Rivière, *The Practice of Physick, in Seventeen Several Books,* trans. Nicholas Culpeper, Abdiah Cole, and William Rowland (London, 1655), 262.

39. Alan Chong and Wouter Kloek, *Still-Life Paintings from the Netherlands 1550–1720* (Zwolle, Neth.: Waanders, 1999), 236.

40. Thomas Paynel, *Regimen sanitatis Salerni* (London, 1541), 35. An original owner of the volume in the copy found in the Huntington Library has added, in the margins, the following notation: "good advice."

41. *The Englishmans Doctor; or, The School of Salernum ["Regimen sanitatis Salernitanum"],* trans. Sir John Harington (New York: Paul B. Hoeber, 1920), 79.

42. Desiderius Erasmus, *On Good Manners for Boys,* in *Collected Works of Erasmus,* ed. J. K. Sowards, 85 vols. (Toronto: University of Toronto Press, 1978), 3:275, 277–78.

43. Richard West, *The Schoole of Vertue, the Second Part; or, The Young Schollers Paradice* (London, 1619), 10–11.

44. Nicholas Courtin, *The Rules of Civility* (London, 1685), 136–37.

45. Francis Barker, *The Tremulous Private Body: Essays on Subjection* (London: Methuen, 1984).

46. Venner, *Via recta,* 28.

47. Interesting remarks on how this works from a linguistic point of view will be found in George Lakoff, *Women, Fire, and Dangerous Things: What Categories Reveal about the Mind* (Chicago: University of Chicago Press, 1987).

48. Timothy Bright, *A Treatise of Melancholie* (London, 1586), 173–74.

49. Leonardus Lessius, *Hygiasticon; or, The Right Course of Preserving Life and Health unto Extream Old Age* (London, 1636), 89.

50. Charles de Marguetel de Saint-Denis, Seigneur de Saint-Évremond, *Letters of Saint Evremond,* ed. John Hayward (London: Routledge, 1930), 115–16.

51. See Moriarty, *Taste and Ideology,* esp. chap. 4.

52. Lessius, *Hygiasticon,* 36–37.

53. Francis Beaumont, *Knight of the Burning Pestle,* ed. Sheldon P. Zitner (Manchester: Manchester University Press, 1984), 1.1.362–66.

54. Shakespeare, *Twelfth Night,* 2.3.83–84.

55. Elias, *Civilizing Process,* 157.

56. Edmund Spenser, *The Faerie Queene,* ed. A. C. Hamilton (London: Longman, 1977), 2.9.28.

57. Phineas Fletcher, *The Purple Island; or, The Isle of Man Together with Piscatorie Eclogs and Other Poeticall Miscellanies* (Cambridge, 1633).

58. Aristotle, *Of the Soul,* 2.4.

59. Shakespeare, *Troilus and Cressida,* 1.3.119–24.

60. Pietro Aretino, *Dialogues,* trans. Raymond Rosenthal (New York: Marsilion, 1994).

61. Shakespeare, *Twelfth Night,* 1.1.9–12.

62. Shakespeare, *Othello,* 2.1.217–24.

63. Shakespeare, *Venus and Adonis,* stanza 137.

64. Shakespeare, *Twelfth Night,* 2.4.91–101.

65. Ibid., 1.5.90–91; Shakespeare, *Antony and Cleopatra,* 2.2.235–36, 2.6.63.

66. Shakespeare, *Hamlet,* 1.2.43–45.

67. One has to assume in these matters that Shakespeare's Illyria stands for or is at least on par with Britain.

68. See Leah S. Marcus, *The Politics of Mirth: Jonson, Herrick, Milton, Marvell, and the Defense of Old Holiday Pastimes* (Chicago: University of Chicago Press, 1986).

69. Michael Bristol's *Carnival and Theater* is in essence an extended meditation on this idea.

70. Antoine Gérard de Saint-Amant, "La crevaille," in *Oeuvres poétiques,* ed. Léon Vérane (Paris: Garnier, 1930), 132. In another poem, Saint-Amant makes the memorable statement, "Baille-moy donc de ce vin vermeil . . . / Bref, c'est mon feu, mon sang et mon soleil": "Pour me some of that red wine . . . / In brief, it is my fire, my blood, and my sun" (134).

CHAPTER SEVEN

1. Christopher Columbus, "First Voyage," in *The Four Voyages of Columbus,* ed. Cecil Jane, 2 vols. (New York: Dover, 1988), 1:12–13.

2. Sebastian Brant, *The Ship of Fools,* trans. Edwin Zeydel (New York: Columbia University Press, 1944), 96–98.

3. William Ian Miller, "Gluttony," *Representations* 60 (1997): 92–112.

4. Edmund Spenser, *The Faerie Queene,* ed. A. C. Hamilton (London: Longman, 1977), 2.12.3–7.

5. Pierre Corneille, *L'imitation de Jesus-Christ,* in *Oeuvres,* ed. Charles Marty-Laveaux, 12 vols. (Paris: Hachette, 1862–68), 8:156.

6. The period both distinguishes between drunkenness and gluttony and constantly elides the two, partly because eating and drinking went together and partly because drunkenness was not one of the official seven deadly sins.

7. *The Kalendar & Compost of Shepherds* (London: Peter Davies, 1931), 55–56. And see Barbara Ketchum Wheaton, *Savoring the Past: The French Kitchen and Table from 1300 to 1789* (Philadelphia: University of Pennsylvania Press, 1983), 67–68.

8. Paul A. Olson, *The Kingdom of Science: Literary Utopianism and British Education, 1612–1870* (Lincoln: University of Nebraska Press, 2003).

9. *Certain Sermons or Homilies Appointed to Be Read in Churches in the Time of Queene Elizabeth* (London, 1683), 178.

10. Pietro Aretino, *The Marescalco,* trans. Leonard G. Sbrocchi and J. Douglas Campbell (Ottawa: Dovehouse, 1986), scene 4, line 57.

11. Jean de La Bruyère, *Les caractères de Théophraste traduits du grec, avec Les caractères; ou, Les moeurs de ce siècle,* ed. Robert Garapon (Paris: Garnier, 1962), 335–37.

12. But see Jean-Louis Flandrin, "De la diététique à la gastronomie," in *L'histoire de l'alimentation,* ed. Jean-Louis Flandrin and Massimo Montanari (Paris: Fayard, 1996), 683–703; and Jean-Louis Flandrin, "Distinction Through Taste," in *A History of Private Life,* ed.

Roger Chartier, trans. Arthur Goldhammer, 6 vols., vol. 3, *Passions of the Renaissance* (Cambridge, MA: Belknap, 1989), 265–309. Flandrin adds a good deal of nuance to this account of the rise of gastronomy.

13. John Brewer and Roy Porter, eds., *Consumption and the World of Goods* (London: Routledge, 1993).

14. Frank Lestringant, "Calvinistes et cannibales: Les écrits protestants sure le Brésil français (1555–1560)," *Bulletins de la Société de l'Histoire du Protestantisme Français,* nos. 1–2 (1980): 9–26, 167–92; Janet Whatley, "Food and the Limits of Civility: The Testimony of Jean de Léry," *Sixteenth Century Journal* 15, no. 4 (1984): 387–400.

15. Richard S. Dunn, *Sugar and Slaves: The Rise of the Planter Class in the English West Indies, 1624–1713* (New York: Norton, 1973); Ira Berlin, *Many Thousands Gone: The First Two Centuries of Slavery in North America* (Cambridge, MA: Belknap, 1998).

16. William Shakespeare, *Coriolanus,* 1.1.204–8.

17. William Shakespeare, *As You Like It,* 2.7.132; *3 Henry VI,* 1.4.5.

18. William Arens, *The Man-Eating Myth: Anthropology and Anthropophagy* (New York: Oxford University Press, 1979).

19. Peggy Reeves Sanday, *Divine Hunger: Cannibalism as a Cultural System* (Cambridge: Cambridge University Press, 1986). See especially her remarks on the Iroquois, based on Jesuit accounts.

20. Joanna Overing, "Images of Cannibalisms, Death, and Domination in a 'Non-Violent' Society," in *The Anthropology of Violence,* ed. David Riches (Oxford: Basil Blackwell, 1986), 86–102.

21. Lawrence Goldman, "From Pot to Polemic: Uses and Abuses of Cannibalism," in *The Anthropology of Cannibalism,* ed. Lawrence Goldman (Westport, CT: Bergin and Garvey, 1999), 1–27.

22. In addition to Arens, see Peter Hulme, *Colonial Encounters: Europe and the Native Caribbean, 1492–1797* (London: Routledge, 1992); Tzvetan Todorov, *The Conquest of America: The Question of the Other,* trans. Richard Howard (New York: Harper & Row, 1984); and Frank Lestringant, *Cannibals: The Discovery and Representation of the Cannibal from Columbus to Jules Verne,* trans. Rosemary Morris (Berkeley: University of California Press, 1997).

23. Peter Martyr, *Decades,* trans. Richard Eden (London, 1555), 3.

24. Thomas S. Abler, "Iroquois Cannibalism: Fact Not Fiction," *Ethnohistory* 27, no. 4 (1980): 309–16; Donald W. Forsyth, "Three Cheers for Hans Staden: The Case for Brazilian Cannibalism," *Ethnohistory* 32, no. 1 (1985): 17–36; John M. Ingham, "Human Sacrifice at Tenochtitlán," *Comparative Studies in Society and History* 26, no. 3 (1984): 379–400.

25. Stephen Greenblatt, foreword to *Mapping the Renaissance World: The Geographical Imagination in the Age of Discovery,* by Frank Lestringant, trans. David Fausett (Berkeley: University of California Press, 1994), xi. Also see my "Anti-Geography," *Early Modern Literary Studies* 4, no. 2 / Special Issue 3 (September 1998): 12.1–17, http://purl.oclc.org/emls/04–2/appeanti.htm.

26. Flavius Josephus, *The Jewish War,* trans. G. A. Williamson (Harmondsworth, UK: Penguin, 1959), 341–42.

27. Lestringant, *Cannibals.*

28. Ovid, *Ovid's Metamorphosis Englished, Mythologized, and Represented in Figures,* trans. George Sandys, ed. Karl K. Hulley and Stanley Vandersall (Lincoln: University of Nebraska Press, 1970), 649–50. See John Wood Sweet, introduction to *Envisioning an English Empire: Jamestown and the Making of the North Atlantic World,* ed. Robert Appelbaum and John Wood Sweet (Philadelphia: University of Pennsylvania Press, 2005), 1–21.

29. See, for example, Hulme, *Colonial Encounters,* 153–55. For general background, see Deborah Rubin, *Ovid's Metamorphoses Englished: George Sandys as Translator and Mythographer* (New York: Garland, 1985).

30. Hans Staden, *The Captivity of Hans Stade of Hesse, in A.D. 1547–1555, among the Wild Tribes of Eastern Brazil,* trans. Albert Tootal, ed. Richard F. Burton (London: Hakluyt Society, 1874); André Thevet, *Les singularités de la France Antarctique: Le Brésil des cannibales au XVIe siècle,* ed. Frank Lestringant (Paris: Maspero, 1983).

31. Jean de Léry, *Histoire d'un voyage fait en la terre du Brésil* (Lausanne: Bibliothèque Rumande, 1972), 38, 41.

32. Whatley, "Food and the Limits of Civility."

33. Lestringant, *Cannibals,* 74–77, to whose account I am obliged, wittingly describes Léry's reversion to the Brazil story after the Sancerre experience as a case of the "return of the repressed."

34. Léry, *Voyage,* 15–19.

35. Ibid., 5.

36. Ibid., 21.

37. John Calvin, *Institutes of the Christian Religion,* trans. Henry Beveridge, 2 vols. (Grand Rapids, MI: Wm. B. Eerdmans, 1981), 1.1:38.

38. See Todorov, *Conquest of America;* Michel de Certeau, *The Writing of History,* trans. Tom Conley (New York: Columbia University Press, 1988), esp. chap. 5; Stephen Greenblatt, *Marvelous Possessions: The Wonder of the New World* (Chicago: University of Chicago Press, 1991); and Andrew Delbanco, *The Puritan Ordeal* (Cambridge, MA: Harvard University Press, 1989).

39. "For although all of them confess human flesh to be wonderfully good and delicate, nonetheless it is more out of vengeance than for the taste (except for what I said specifically of old women, who find it such a delicacy); their chief intention is that by pursuing the dead and gnawing them right down to the bone, they will strike fear and terror into the hearts of the living." Léry, *Voyage,* 127.

40. Ibid., 125. And see ibid., 244n5, the editor citing Thevet. Hans Staden makes a similar claim.

41. Ibid., 26, 29.

42. Ibid., 41.

43. See Yves Giraud, "Le comique engagé des *Satyres chrétiennes de la cuisine papale,*" *Studi di Letteratura Francese* 10 (1983): 52–72; and Lestringant, "Calvinistes et cannibales."

44. Léry, *Voyage,* 132.

45. A noteworthy example occurs in a regimen of health of the early seventeenth century, which includes a mention of voracious West Indian cannibalism and then goes on to

compare it with economic exploitation at home in Britain: "I doubt not but that the very reading of these things will strike a certain horror and amazement in the minds of many men, with an *horresco legens,* when they consider of the customs of these cruellest Cannibals of all others; and just so they may. But have we no such devouring *Cannibals* here at home among ourselves? . . . I could instance in many several sorts of extortioners, and daily grinders of the faces of the poor. . . . But there is one particular kind. . . . My meaning is of depopulating inclosures, whereby many wealthy townes, who before maintained a number of able people, and fit in time of need to doe their country good service, have now for the most part left only a shepherd and his dog." James Hart, *Klinekeh; or, The Diet of the Diseased, Divided into Three Bookes* (London, 1633), 87–88.

46. Léry, *Voyage,* 211–14. On the "custom of the sea" and related ideas, see Ted Motohashi, "The Discourse of Cannibalism in Early Modern Travel Writing," in *Travel Writing and Empire: Postcolonial Theory in Transit,* ed. Steve Clark (London: Zed Books, 1999), 83–99; and Gerald Porter, "'Eaten with Merriment and Sport': Cannibalism and the Colonial Subject," *Atlantic Literary Review* 3, no. 2 (2002): 21–32.

47. Léry, *Voyage,* 150–51.

48. Herman Pleij, *Dreaming of Cockaigne: Medieval Fantasies of the Perfect Life,* trans. Diane Webb (New York: Columbia University Press, 1997), 107–17.

49. See chapter 5.

50. Jean de Léry, *L'histoire mémorable du siège et de la famine de Sancerre* (1573), ed. Gérlade Nakamé (Genève: Slatkine Reprints, 2000), 283.

51. Bruce Thomas Boehrer, *Parrot Culture: Our 2,500-Year-Long Fascination with the World's Most Talkative Bird* (Philadelphia: University of Pennsylvania Press, 2004).

52. Léry, *Siège,* 290–91.

53. Ibid., 292–93.

54. Richard Ligon, *A True and Exact History of the Island of Barbadoes* (London, 1657), 1. On his life, see Karen Kupperman, *Oxford Dictionary of National Biography,* and Keith Sandiford, *The Cultural Politics of Sugar: Caribbean Slavery and Narratives of Colonialism* (Cambridge: Cambridge University Press, 1990), chap. 1.

55. See Hilary Beckles, *A History of Barbados: From Amerindian Settlement to Nation-State* (Cambridge: Cambridge University Press, 1990), 1–6; and Philip P. Boucher, *Cannibal Encounters: Europeans and Island Caribs, 1492–1763* (Baltimore: Johns Hopkins University Press, 1992), chaps. 1, 2. In fact, the absence of natives by the time they arrived on the scene was one of the factors prompting English colonialism in Barbados. Other islands, where Caribs still flourished and engaged in armed opposition to colonial interlopers, the English avoided. There is no ready explanation for why the Caribs were gone from Barbados by the time the English settled there — but Carib population throughout the area was in catastrophic decline from the time of Columbus's arrival, a victim of European disease, European predation, and the consequent social disorientation.

56. Ligon, *Barbadoes,* 113.

57. Hulme, *Colonial Encounters,* 182; and see, in general, Richard McKeon, *Origins of the English Novel* (Baltimore: Johns Hopkins University Press, 1986).

58. Sidney W. Mintz, "The Changing Roles of Food in the Study of Consumption," in *Consumption and the World of Goods*, ed. John Brewer and Roy Porter (London: Routledge, 1993), 261–73. And see his full-length study *Sweetness and Power: The Place of Sugar in Modern History* (New York: Viking, 1985).

59. Richard Dunn cites a letter of 1646 where a pair of colonists complained that food was getting scarce because of the lust for monocultural enterprise: men were "so intent upon planting sugar that they had rather buy food at very dear rates than produce it by labor, so infinite is the profit of sugar works after once accomplished." Dunn, *Sugar and Slaves*, 59. In my own "Hunger in Early Virginia: Indians and English Facing Off Over Excess, Want, and Need," in *Envisioning an English Empire*, 195–216, I report on an indentured servant whose master fed him almost nothing but venison for days and days on end—a supply of some eighty freshly slaughtered deer brought in by Indian traders in exchange for European commodities. "Before this Venison was brought to a period by eating," the servant wrote, "it so nauseated our appetites and stomachs, that plain bread was rather courted and desired than it." See Timothy Silver, *A New Face on the Countryside: Indians, Colonists, and Slaves in South Atlantic Forests, 1500–1800* (Cambridge: Cambridge University Press, 1990), 36.

60. Again, see Beckles, *History of Barbados*, and Boucher, *Cannibal Encounters*.

61. See Hulme, *Colonial Encounters*, chap. 6.

62. Ligon, *Barbadoes*, 55.

63. Much of the material in this section is borrowed from my "Hunger in Early Virginia."

64. William Cronon, *Changes in the Land: Indians, Colonists, and the Ecology of New England* (New York: Hill and Wang, 1983). Also see Silver, *New Face on the Countryside*.

65. Robert Beverley, *The History and Present State of Virginia* (1705), ed. Louis B. Wright (Chapel Hill: University of North Carolina Press, 1947), 181–82.

66. Cited in Cronon, *Changes*, 47.

67. Roger Williams, *Key into the Language of America* (1643), facsimile reprint (Menston, UK: Scolar Press, 1971), 135; see note 59 on Appelbaum, "Hunger in Early Virginia."

68. Léry, *Voyage*, 75.

69. Ibid., 102.

70. John Smith, *Complete Works*, ed. Philip L. Barbour, 3 vols. (Chapel Hill: University of North Carolina Press, 1986), 2:206–7.

71. Carville V. Earle, "Environment, Disease, and Mortality in Early Virginia," in *The Chesapeake in the Seventeenth Century: Essays on Anglo-American Society*, ed. Thad W. Tate and David L. Ammerman (Chapel Hill: University of North Carolina Press, 1979), 96–125.

72. Frederic W. Gleach, *Powhatan's World and Colonial Virginia: A Conflict of Cultures* (Lincoln: University of Nebraska Press, 1997), esp. 127, 265.

73. George Percy, *A True Relation of the Proceedings, 1609–1612*, in *Jamestown Narratives*, ed. Edward Wright Haile (Champlain, VA: Roundhouse, 1998), 507.

74. Ibid., 505.

75. Dunn, *Sugar and Slaves*, 55–56.

76. Ligon, *Barbadoes,* 21.

77. Ibid., 32–33.

78. Ibid., 34.

79. See chapter 3.

80. Ligon, *Barbadoes,* 38–39.

81. See chapter 1.

82. W.M., *The Compleat Cook* (London, 1659), 93.

83. Raymond A. Sokolov, *Why We Eat What We Eat: How the Encounter Between the New World and the Old Changed the Way Everyone on the Planet Eats* (New York: Summit Books, 1991).

84. Robert May, *The Accomplisht Cook, or, The Art and Mystery of Cookery: Wherein the Whole Art Is Revealed in a More Easie and Perfect Method than Hath Been Publisht in Any Language . . . / Approved by the Fifty Years Experience* (London, 1660). May's first recipe, by the way (pp. 1–3), is a "Royal" Olio Podrida that occupies three pages of text and uses over eighteen different kinds of meats, from rump roast, neat's tongue, and mutton to pheasant and plover; it also includes a large number of vegetables including carrots, turnips, and artichokes, and many kinds of herbs and other seasonings.

85. Ligon, *Barbadoes,* 55.

86. The terms "high-spirited" and "turbulent" were also often used by Royalists to describe Roundhead rebels.

87. Ligon, *Barbadoes,* 53–54.

88. Keith Thomas, *Man and the Natural World: A History of the Modern Sensibility* (New York: Pantheon, 1983).

89. Ligon, *Barbadoes,* 60, 62, 75.

90. Ibid., 36.

CONCLUSION

1. Daniel Defoe, *The Life and Strange Surprizing Adventures of Robinson Crusoe, of York, Mariner,* ed. J. Donald Crowley (Oxford: Oxford University Press, 1981), 152–53.

2. Ibid., 99, 101.

3. Jess Edwards, "Between 'Plain Wilderness' and 'Goodly Corn Fields': Representing Land Use in Early Virginia," in *Envisioning an English Empire: Jamestown and the Making of the North Atlantic World,* ed. Robert Appelbaum and John Wood Sweet (Philadelphia: University of Pennsylvania Press, 2005), 217–35.

4. Defoe, *Robinson Crusoe,* 100.

5. Jean-Jacques Rousseau, *Émile; or, On Education,* trans. Allan Bloom (New York: Basic, 1979), 184, 188.

6. Peter Hulme, *Colonial Encounters: Europe and the Native Caribbean, 1492–1797* (London: Routledge, 1992). I am indebted to Hulme's analysis of colonialism and *Robinson Crusoe* throughout this chapter.

7. Defoe's contemporary John Arbuthnot (of whom more below) states the case as follows: "Grapes, taken in moderate Quantities, help that Appetite and Digestion. In

great Quantities, they resolve the Bile too much, and produce Fluxes. Dried, they are pectoral." John Arbuthnot, *An Essay Concerning the Nature of Aliments, and the Choice of Them, According to the Different Constitutions of Human Bodies,* 2 vols. (London, 1731); 2:212–13. By "pectoral" Arbuthnot means that grapes are good for the lungs.

8. Crusoe's original, the Scottish sailor Andrew Selkirk, had been marooned on an island in the Pacific, off the coast of Chile. He had indeed found that island teeming with goats but was aware that earlier settlers were responsible for bringing them there. Woodes Rogers, *A Cruising Voyage Around the World; First to the South-Seas, thence to the East-Indies, and homewards by the Cape of Good Hope. Begun in 1708, and finish'd in 1711* (London, 1712), 127.

9. Richard Ligon, *A True and Exact History of the Island of Barbadoes* (London, 1657), 29–31; Charles-César de Rochefort, *The History of the Caribby-islands, viz, Barbados, St Christophers, St Vincents, Martinico, Dominico, Barbouthos, Monserrat, Mevis, Antego, &c,* trans. John Davies (London, 1666), 59–69, provides a detailed description of the ground plants that were thriving in the seventeenth century, including pulses and potatoes, but no grains.

10. See especially E. Pearlman, "Robinson Crusoe and the Cannibals," *Mosaic* 10 (1976); and Minaz Jooma, "Robinson Crusoe Inc(orporates): Domestic Economy, Incest, and the Trope of Cannibalism," in *Eating Their Words: Cannibalism and the Boundaries of Cultural Identity,* ed. Kristen Guest (Albany: State University Press of New York, 2001), 57–78.

11. Rousseau, *Émile,* 190.

12. Deane Curtin, "Food/Body/Person," in *Cooking, Eating, Thinking, Transformative Philosophies of Food,* ed. D. Curtin and L. Hedke (Indianapolis: Indiana University Press, 1992), 17.

13. On the distinction, adapted from Norbert Elias, see chapter 6.

14. Rousseau, *Émile,* 190.

15. See, above all, Piero Camporesi, *Exotic Brew: The Art of Living in the Age of Enlightenment,* trans. Christopher Woodall (Cambridge: Polity Press, 1994).

16. For accessible accounts of this development, see Owsei Temkin, *Galenism: Rise and Decline of a Medical Philosophy* (Ithaca, NY: Cornell University Press, 1973), chap. 4; and Roy Porter, *Flesh in the Age of Reason* (London: Allen Lane, 2003). More specialized accounts include Harold J. Cook, *The Decline of the Old Medical Regime in Stuart London* (Ithaca, NY: Cornell University Press, 1986); Harold J. Cook, *Trials of an Ordinary Doctor: Joannes Groenevelt in Seventeenth-Century London* (Baltimore: Johns Hopkins University Press, 1994); and the essays collected in *The Medical Revolution of the Seventeenth Century,* ed. Roger French and Andrew Wear (Cambridge: Cambridge University Press, 1989).

17. A. F. M. Willich, *Lectures on Diet and Regiment* (Boston, 1800), v. Willich was English, and the book is based on lectures delivered in Bath. The Boston edition is identical to the English except for the prefatory material.

18. On Cheyne, see Anita Guerrini, *Obesity and Depression in the Enlightenment: The Life and Times of George Cheyne* (Norman: University of Oklahoma Press, 2000).

19. Luigi Cornaro, *The Art of Living Long* (Milwaukee, WI: William F. Butler, 1903), 46–47.

20. George Cheyne, *An Essay of Health and Long Life* (London, 1724), 169.

21. Arbuthnot, *Essay,* 1:45.

22. Cheyne, *Essay,* 71.

23. Arbuthnot, *Essay,* 2:254.

24. Willich, *Lectures,* 17, 21, 23, 24.

25. Charles Carter, *The Complete Practical Cook; or, A New System of the Whole Art and Mystery of Cookery* (1730), facsimile (London: Prospect Books, 1984), n.p.

26. The best accounts of these developments, as I have had occasion to note before, are in Stephen Mennell, *All Manners of Food: Eating and Taste in England and France from the Middle Ages to the Present,* 2nd ed. (Urbana: University of Illinois Press, 2000); and Barbara Ketchum Wheaton, *Savoring the Past: The French Kitchen and Table from 1300 to 1789* (Philadelphia: University of Pennsylvania Press, 1983), whose work is usefully supplemented by T. Sarah Peterson, *Acquired Taste: The French Origins of Modern Cooking* (Ithaca, NY: Cornell University Press, 1994); Amy B. Trubek, *Haute Cuisine: How the French Invented the Culinary Professions* (Philadelphia: University of Pennsylvania Press, 2000); and Jean-Robert Pitte, *French Gastronomy: The History and Geography of a Passion,* trans. Jody Gladding (New York: Columbia University Press, 2002).

27. François Massialot, *Le nouveau cuisinier royal et bourgeois* (1724), 3 vols. (Paris, 1748–50), 1:1–2.

28. Robert May, *The Accomplisht Cook; or, The Art and Mystery of Cookery* (London, 1660), A4.

29. Hannah Woolley, *The Queen-like Closet; or, Rich Cabinet: Stored with all manner of Rare Receipts for Preserving, Candying, and Cookery. Very pleasant and beneficial to all Ingenious Persons of the Female Sex. To which is added A Supplement presented to all Ingenious Ladies and Gentlewomen.* 4th ed. (London, 1681), 335.

30. Ibid., n.p.

31. François Massialot, *The Court and Country Cook,* trans. J.K. (London, 1702), 47.

32. Hannah Woolley, *A Guide to Ladies, Gentlewomen and Maids* (London, 1668), 40–41.

33. A highly respected book in the field, Terence Scully, *The Art of Cookery in the Middle Ages* (Woodbridge, UK: Boydell Press, 1995), makes an extended case for such mingling of medicine and cookery up to the fifteenth century; but I find it unconvincing. Jean-Louis Flandrin, "De la diététique à la gastronomie," in *L'histoire de l'alimentation,* ed. Jean-Louis Flandrin and Massimo Montanari (Paris: Fayard, 1996), 683–703, tries to make a similar case, contrasting the medical cookery of the Middle Ages with the gastronomic cookery that came later. In fact, though there were no doubt many changes in attitudes and practices, the changes Scully and Flandrin note with regard to the adjustment of cookery to medical theory were chiefly linguistic. At one time the language of humoral physiology was readily applied to the domain of gustatory sensation and the practices undertaken to cater to it; at a later date this language was no longer dominant.

34. But see the nuanced account in Rebecca L. Spang, *The Invention of the Restaurant: Paris and Modern Gastronomic Culture* (Cambridge, MA: Harvard University Press, 2000).

35. Rousseau, *Émile,* 152.

36. Ibid., 151–52.

37. Defoe, *Robinson Crusoe,* 206, 208.

38. Ibid., 207.

39. The parrot would seem to serve a transitional role between human and beast: as in the case of Léry, this talking animal is not to be eaten except in cases of extremity. And Crusoe and Friday don't eat it. See Bruce Thomas Boehrer, *Parrot Culture: Our 2,500-Year-Long Fascination with the World's Most Talkative Bird* (Philadelphia: University of Pennsylvania Press, 2004).

40. Defoe, *Robinson Crusoe,* 212.

41. Ibid., 212, 213.

Select Bibliography

PRIMARY TEXTS

Addison, Joseph. *Selections from the Tatler and the Spectator of Steele and Addison.* Edited by Angus Ross. Harmondsworth, UK: Penguin, 1982.

Andreä, Johann Valentin. *Christianopolis: An Ideal State of the Seventeenth Century.* Translated by Felix Emil Held. New York: Oxford University Press, 1916.

Apicius. *Cookery and Dining in Imperial Rome.* Translated by Joseph D. Vehling. Chicago: Walter Hill, 1936.

———. *The Roman Cookery Book, a Critical Translation of "The Art of Cooking."* Translated by Barbara Flower and Elizabeth Rosenbaum. London: Garrup, 1958.

Arbuthnot, John. *An Essay Concerning the Nature of Aliments, and the Choice of Them, According to the Different Constitutions of Human Bodies.* 2 vols. London, 1731.

Archer, John. *Every Man His Own Doctor.* London, 1671.

Aretino, Pietro. *Dialogues.* Translated by Raymond Rosenthal. New York: Marsilion, 1994.

———. *The Marescalco.* Translated by Leonard G. Sbrocchi and J. Douglas Campbell. Ottawa: Dovehouse, 1986.

L'art de la cuisine française au XVIIᵉ siècle. Paris: Editions Payot & Rivages, 1995.

Audiger, *La maison réglée.* In *L'art de la cuisine française au XVIIᵉ siècle.* Paris: Editions Payot & Rivages, 1995.

Austen, Ralph. *A Treatise of Fruit Trees.* 2nd ed. London, 1657.

Avicenna. *Avicenna's Poem on Medicine.* Translated by Haven C. Krueger. Springfield, IL: Charles C. Thomas, 1963.

The Babees Book: Manners and Meals in Olden Times. Edited by F. J. Furnivall. London: Early English Text Society, 1868.

Bachot, Gaspard. *Erreurs populaires touchant la médecine et régime de santé.* Lyon, 1626.

Basil. *Ascetical Works.* Translated by Monica Wagner, C.S.C. Washington, DC: Catholic University of America Press, 1962.

Basile, Giambattista. *The Pentamerone.* Translated by Richard Burton. London: W. Kimber, 1952.

Beaumont, Francis. *The Knight of the Burning Pestle.* Edited by Sheldon P. Zitner. Manchester: Manchester University Press, 1984.

Benporat, Claudio, ed. *Cucina italiana del Quattrocento.* Florence: Leo S. Olshchki Editore, 1996.

Best, Henry. *The Farming and Memorandum Books of Henry Best of Elmswell, 1642.* Edited by Donald Woodward. London: Oxford University Press, 1984.

Beverley, Robert. *The History and Present State of Virginia.* 1705. Edited by Louis B. Wright. Chapel Hill: University of North Carolina Press, 1947.

The Bloody Banquet. 1639. Edited by Samuel Schoenbaum. Oxford: Malone Society, 1961.

A Bloudy Tenent Confuted; or, Bloud Forbidden: shewing the unlawfulness of eating blood, in what manner of thing soever. London, 1646.

Boorde, Andrew. *The Fyrst Boke of the Introduction of Knowledge. A Compendyous Regyment; or, A Dyetary of Helth.* London: Early English Text Society, 1870.

Brant, Sebastian. *The Ship of Fools.* Translated by Edwin Zeydel. New York: Columbia University Press, 1944.

Bright, Timothy. *A Treatise of Melancholie.* London, 1586.

Brillat-Savarin, Jean Anthelme. *The Physiology of Taste; or, Mediations on Transcendental Gastronomy.* New Haven, CT: Leete's Island Books, n.d.

Burton, Robert. *The Anatomy of Melancholy.* Edited by Thomas C. Faulkner, Nicolas K. Kiessling, and Rhonda L. Blair. 3 vols. Oxford: Clarendon Press, 1989–2000.

Butts, Henry. *Dyets Dry Dinner.* London, 1599.

Caesar, Gaius Julius. *The Conquest of Gaul.* Translated by S. A. Handford, rev. Jane Gardner. Harmondsworth, UK: Penguin, 1982.

Campanella, Tommaso. *La città del sole: Dialogo poetico.* Bilingual ed. Translated by Daniel J. Donno. Berkeley: University of California Press, 1981.

Carter, Charles. *The Complete Practical Cook; or, A New System of the Whole Art and Mystery of Cookery.* 1730. Facsimile. London: Prospect Books, 1984.

Castelvetro, Giacomo. *The Fruit, Herbs, and Vegetables of Italy.* Translated by Gillian Riley London: Viking, 1989.

Celsus. *De medicina.* Translated by W. G. Spencer. 3 vols. Cambridge, MA: Harvard University Press, 1935.

Certain Sermons or Homilies Appointed to be Read in Churches in the Time of Queene Elizabeth. London, 1683.

Cervantes Saavedra, Miguel de. *The Adventures of Don Quixote.* Translated by J. M. Cohen. Harmondsworth, UK: Penguin, 1950.

Cheyne, George. *An Essay of Health and Long Life.* London, 1724.

———. *An Essay of Regimen, Together with Five Discourses, Medical, Moral, and Philosophical.* London, 1740.

Cogan, Thomas. *The Haven of Health.* London, 1584.

Colonna, Francesco. *Hypnerotomachia Poliphili: The Strife of Love in a Dream.* Translated by Joscelyn Godwin. New York: Thames and Hudson, 1999.

Columbus, Christopher. *The Four Voyages.* Edited by Cecil Jane. 2 vols. New York: Dover, 1988.

Columella, Lucius Junius Moeratus. *On Agriculture (De re rustica).* Translated by Harrison Boyd. Cambridge, MA: Harvard University Press, 1948.

Cornaro, Luigi. *The Art of Living Long.* Translated by anonymous. Milwaukee: William F. Butler, 1903.

———. *A Treatise of Health and Long Life, with the Sure Means of Attaining It, in Two Books.* Translated by Timothy Smith. London, 1743.

Corneille, Pierre. *L'imitation de Jesus-Christ.* Vol. 8 of *Oeuvres,* edited by Charles Marty-Laveaux. 12 vols. Paris: Hachette, 1862–68.

The Court and Kitchen of Elizabeth Commonly Called Joan Cromwell, the Wife of the Late Usurper, Truly Described and Represented, and Now Made Public for General Satisfaction. London, 1664. Reprint, Cambridge: Cambridgeshire Libraries, 1983.

Courtin, Nicholas. *The Rules of Civility.* London, 1685.

Crab, Roger. *The English Hermit; or, Wonder of This Age.* London, 1655. Reprinted in *Harleian Miscellany,* 6:390–405. London: Robert Dutton, 1808–11.

Curye on Inglisch. In *English Culinary Manuscripts of the Fourteenth Century* [Includes the *Forme of Curye*]. Edited by Constance B. Hieatt and Sharon Butler. Oxford: Oxford University Press, 1985.

Dawson, Thomas. *The Good Huswifes Jewell.* London, 1587.

Defoe, Daniel. *The Life and Strange Surprizing Adventures of Robinson Crusoe, of York, Mariner.* Edited by J. Donald Crowley. Oxford: Oxford University Press, 1981.

Del Turco, Giovanni. *Epulario e segreti vari: Trattati di cucina toscana nella Firenze seicentesca.* Edited by Anna Evangelista. Bologna: Arnaldo Forni, 1992.

Digby, Sir Kenelm. *The Closet of Sir Kenelm Digby Opened.* London, 1669.

———. *The Closet of Sir Kenelm Digby Opened.* Edited by Jane Stevenson and Peter Davidson. London: Prospect Books, 1997.

Dio Cassius. *Roman History.* Bilingual ed. Translated by Earnest Cary. 9 vols. Cambridge, MA: Harvard University Press, 1927.

Le disciple de Pantagruel (Les navigation de Panurge). 1538. Edited by Guy Demerson and Christiane Lauvergnat-Gagnière. Paris: Nizet, 1982.

Du Bartas, Guillaume de Saluste. *The Divine Weeks and Works.* 2 vols. Translated by Joshua Sylvester. Edited by Susan Snyder. Oxford: Clarendon Press, 1979.

Durante, Castor. *Il tesoro della sanità.* Venice, 1586.

Elyot, Thomas. *The Castel of Helthe.* London, 1539.

Encyclopédie, ou Dictionnaire raisonné des sciences, des arts et des métiers, par une société de gens de letters. Edited by Denis Diderot and Jean Le Rond d'Alembert. Paris: Briasson, 1751–65.

Epicurus. *The Philosophy of Epicurus: Letters, Doctrines, and Parallel Passages from Lucretius.* Translated by George K. Strodach. Evanston, IL: Northwestern University Press, 1963.

Erasmus, Desiderius. *The Colloquies of Erasmus.* Translated by Craig R. Thompson. Chicago: University of Chicago Press, 1965.

———. *On Good Manners for Boys.* In *Collected Works of Erasmus.* Edited by J. K. Sowards, vol. 3. Toronto: University of Toronto Press, 1978.

L'escole parfaite des officiers du bouche. Paris, 1662.

Evelyn, John. *Acetaria: A Discourse of Sallets.* London, 1699.

———. *Pomona; or, An Appendix Concerning Fruit-Trees, in Relation to Cider.* In *Sylva; or, A Discourse of Forest-Trees, and the Propagation of Timber.* London, 1664.

Faccioli, Emilio, ed. *Arte della cucina: Libri di ricette testi sopra lo scalco il trinicante ei vini dal XIV al XIX secolo.* Milano: Edizioni Il Polifilo, 1966.

"Familière description du très vinoporratimalvoise et très envitaillegoulmente royaume Panigonnois, mystiquement interprêté l'Isle de Crevepance." In Antoinette Huon, "Le roy sainct panigon." In *François Rabelais: Ouvrage publieé pour le quatrième centenaire de sa mort,* 221–25. Geneva, 1953.

Ficino, Marsilio. *Three Books on Life.* Bilingual ed. Translated by Carol V. Kaske and John R. Clark. Binghamton, NY: Renaissance Society of America, 1989.

Foigny, Gabriel de. *The Southern Land, Known.* Translated by David Fausett. Syracuse, NY: Syracuse University Press, 1993.

Galen. *On the Natural Faculties.* Translated by Arthur John Brock. New York: G. P. Putnam's Sons, 1916.

———. *On the Powers of Food.* In *Galen on Food and Diet.* Translated by Mark Grant London: Routledge, 2000.

Getz, Faye Marie, ed. *Healing and Society in Medieval England: A Middle English Translation of the Pharmaceutical Writings of Gilbertus Anglicus.* Madison: University of Wisconsin Press, 1991.

Godwin, Francis. *The Man in the Moone; or, A Discovrse of a Voyage thither by Domingo Gonsales: The speedy Messenger.* London, 1638.

Grataroli, Gugliemo. *A Direction for the Health of Magistrates and Studentes.* Translated by Thomas Newton. London, 1574.

Grimmelshausen, Johann Jacob. *Simplicissimus.* Translated by S. Goodrich. Sawtry, Cambs, UK: Dedalus, 1989.

Harington, Sir John. *The Englishmans Doctor; or, The School of Salernum [*"Regimen sanitatis Salernitanum"*].* 1608. New York: Paul B. Hoeber, 1920.

Harrison, William. *The Description of England.* Edited by Georges Edelen. Washington, DC: Folger Shakespeare Library; Ithaca, NY: Cornell University Press, 1968.

Hart, James. *Klinekeh; or, The Diet of the Diseased, Divided into Three Bookes.* London, 1633.

Harvey, William. *The Anatomical Lectures.* Edited and translated by Gweneth Whitteridge. Edinburgh: E. & S. Livingstone, 1964.

Hippocrates. *Hippocrates.* Translated by W. H. S. Jones. 4 vols. London: William Heinemann, 1923.

Horace. *The Complete Odes and Epodes.* Translated by David West. Oxford: Oxford University Press, 1997.

———. *Satires, Epistles, and Ars poetica.* Bilingual ed. Translated by H. Rushton Fairclough. Cambridge, MA: Harvard University Press, 1926.

Huarte, John. *The Examination of Mens Wits.* 1594. Facsimile. Gainesville, FL: Scholars' Facsimiles and Reprints, 1959.

Jonson, Ben. *The Complete Poetry.* Edited by William B. Hunter. New York: Norton, 1963.

Josephus, Flavius. *The Jewish War.* Translated by G. A. Williamson. Harmondsworth, UK: Penguin, 1959.

The Kalendar & Compost of Shepherds. London: Peter Davies, 1931.

King, William. *The Art of Cookery: In Imitation of Horace's Art of Poetry.* London, 1712.

La Bruyère, Jean de. *Les caractères de Théophraste traduits du grec, avec Les caractères; ou, Les moeurs de ce siècle.* Edited by Robert Garapon. Paris: Garnier, 1962.

La Varenne, Pierre de. *Le cuisinier françois, Enseignant la maniere de bien apprester, & assaisoner toutes sortes de viandes, grasse & maigres, legumes, Patisseries, etc.* Paris, 1652.

———. *The French Cook. Prescribing the way of making all sorts of Meats, Fish, and Flesh, with the proper Sauces, either to procure Appetite, or to Advance the power of Digestion.* London, 1653.

Lemnius, Levinus. *An Herbal for the Bible.* Translated by Thomas Newton. London, 1587.

———. *The Touchstone of Complexions.* Translated by Thomas Newton. London, 1581.

Leonardo da Vinci. *The Notebooks of Leonardo da Vinci.* Edited by Edward MacCurdy. 2 vols. New York: Reynal and Hitchcock, 1938.

Léry, Jean de. *L'histoire mémorable du siège et de la famine de Sancerre.* 1573. Edited by Gérlade Nakamé. Genève: Slatkine Reprints, 2000.

———. *Histoire d'un voyage fait en la terre du Brésil.* Lausanne: Bibliothèque Rumande, 1972.

———. *History of a Voyage to the Land of Brazil.* Translated by Janet Whatley. Berkeley: University of California Press, 1992.

Lessius, Leonardus. *Hygiasticon; or, The Right Course of Preserving Life and Health unto Extream Old Age.* London, 1636.

Libellus de arte coquinaria. Edited and translated by Rudolf Grewe and Constance B. Hieatt. Tempe: Arizona Center for Medieval and Renaissance Studies, 2001.

Ligon, Richard. *A True and Exact History of the Island of Barbadoes.* London, 1657.

Lozinski, Grégoire, ed. *La bataille de caresme et de charnage.* Paris: H. Champion, 1933.

L.S.R. *L'art de bien traiter.* Paris, 1674. Reprinted in *L'art de la cuisine française au XVIIe siècle.* Paris: Editions Payot & Rivages, 1995.

Lucretius. *On the Nature of Things.* Translated by W. Hannaford Brown. New Brunswick, NJ: Rutgers University Press, 1950.

Lupton, Thomas. *The Second Part and Knitting Up of the Boke Entitled "Too Good to Be True."* London, 1581.

———. *Siuqila. Too Good to Be True.* London, 1580.

Lune, Pierre de. "*Le cuisinier.*" In *L'art de la cuisine française au XVIIe siècle.* Paris: Editions Payot & Rivages, 1995.

Luther, Martin. *Works.* 54 vols. St. Louis: Concordia, 1955–86.

Markham, Gervase. *The English Housewife.* Edited by Michael R. Best. Kingston, ON: McGill-Queen's University Press, 1987.

Marston, John. *Antonio's Revenge.* Edited by W. Reaveley Gair. Manchester: Manchester University Press, 1978.

Martino, Maestro. *Libro de arte coquinaria.* Edited by Emilio Montoforno. Milano: Terziaria, 1990.

Martyr, Peter. *Decades.* Translated by Richard Eden. London, 1555.

Massialot, François. *The Court and Country Cook.* Translated by J.K. London, 1702.

Massinger, Philip. *The City-Madam.* 1632. Edited by T. W. Craik. London: Ernst Benn, 1964.

May, Robert. *The Accomplisht Cook; or, The Art and Mystery of Cookery.* London, 1660.

Messisbugo, Cristoforo di. *Banchetti composizioni di vivande e apparecchio generale.* 1549. Edited by Fernando Bandini. Venice: Neri Pozza Editore, 1960.

Milton, John. *The Riverside Milton.* Edited by Roy Flannagan. Boston: Houghton Mifflin, 1998.

Misson, Maximilium. *Memoirs and Observations in His Travels Over England.* Translated by M. Ozell. London, 1719.

Moffet, Thomas. *Healths Improvement; Or, Rules Comprizing and Discovering the Nature, Method, and Manner of Preparing All Sorts of Food Used in This Nation.* London, 1655.

Montaigne, Michel de. *The Complete Essays of Montaigne.* Edited by Donald M. Frame. Stanford, CA: Stanford University Press, 1958.

More, Thomas. *Utopia. Latin Text and Translation.* Edited by George M. Logan, Robert M. Adams, and Clarence H. Miller. Cambridge: Cambridge University Press, 1995.

Moulton, Thomas. *This Is the Myrour or Glasse of Helthe.* London, 1540.

Murrell, John. *A Delightful Daily Exercise for Ladies and Gentlewomen.* London, 1614.

———. *A New Booke of Cookerie.* London, 1615.

———. *The Second Booke of Cookerie.* London, 1621.

Nashe, Thomas. *Works.* Edited by R. B. McKerrow. 4 vols. Reprinted and revised. New York: Barnes & Noble, 1966.

Ovid. *Ovid's Metamorphosis Englished, Mythologized, and Represented in Figures.* Translated by George Sandys. Edited by Karl K. Hulley and Stanley Vandersall. Lincoln: University of Nebraska Press, 1970.

———. *The XV. Bookes of P. Ovidius Naso, Entytuled Metamorphosis.* Translated by Arthur Golding. London, 1567.

Partridge, John. *The Treasurie of Commodious Conceits, and Hidden Secrets, Commonly Called The Good Huswives Closet of Provision, for the Health of Hir Housholde.* London, 1584.

Paynel, Thomas. *Regimen sanitatis Salerni.* London, 1541.

Peacham, Henry. *The Compleat Gentleman.* London, 1622.

Percy, George. *A True Relation of the Proceedings, 1609–1612.* In *Jamestown Narratives.* Edited by Edward Wright Haile, 497–519. Champlain, VA: Roundhouse, 1998.

Plat, Hugh. *Delightes for Ladies.* 1602–27. Edited by Violet and Hal Trovillion. Herrin, IL: Trovillion Private Press, 1939.

———. *Sundrie New and Artificall Remedies against Famine.* London, 1596.

Platina, Bartolomeo. *On Right Pleasure and Good Health.* 1470. Critical edition and translation by Mary Ella Milham. Tempe, AZ: Medieval and Renaissance Texts and Studies, 1998.

Price, Rebecca. *The Compleat Cook; or, The Secrets of a Seventeenth Century Housewife.* Edited by Madeleine Masson. London: Routledge and K. Paul, 1974.

A Proper New Booke of Cokereye. 1575. Edited by Catherine Frances Frere. Cambridge: Heffer, 1913.

Rabelais, François. *Gargantua and Pantagruel.* Translated by Thomas Urquhart and Peter Le Motteux. 2 vols. New York: AMS Press, 1967.

———. *Oeuvres Complètes.* Edited by Guy Demerson. Paris: Editions de Seuil, 1995.

Rabisha, William. *The Whole Body of Cookery, According to the Best Tradition of the English, French, Italian, Dutch, etc.* London, 1655.

A Relation, or Rather a True Account, of the Island of England; with Sundry Particulars of the Customs of these people and of the Royal Revenues under King Henry VII, about the Year 1500. Translated by Charlotte Augusta Sneyd. London: Camden Society, 1847.

Rivière, Lazare. *The Practice of Physick, in Seventeen Several Books.* Translated by Nicholas Culpeper, Abdiah Cole, and William Rowland. London, 1655.

Robin, Thomas. *The Wonder of the World: Being a perfect Relation of a young Maid, about eighteen years of age, which hath not tasted of any Food this two and fifty weeks.* London, 1669.

Rochefort, Charles-César. *The History of the Caribby-islands, viz, Barbados, St Christophers, St Vincents, Martinico, Dominico, Barbouthos, Monserrat, Mevis, Antego, &c.* Translated by John Davies. London, 1666.

Rogers, Woodes. *A Cruising Voyage Around the World; First to the South-Seas, thence to the East-Indies, and homewards by the Cape of Good Hope. Begun in 1708, and finish'd in 1711.* London, 1712.

Ronsard, Pierre de. *Poems of Pierre de Ronsard.* Bilingual ed. Translated by Nicholas Kilmer. Berkeley: University of California Press, 1979.

Rose, Peter G., trans. and ed. *The Sensible Cook: Dutch Foodways in the Old and New World.* Syracuse, NY: Syracuse University Press, 1989.

Rosselli, Giovanni de. *Opera nova chiamata Epulario, quale tracta il modo de cucinare, etc.* Venice, 1518.

Rousseau, Jean-Jacques. *Émile; or, On Education.* Translated by Allan Bloom. New York: Basic, 1979.

Sachs, Hans. *Merry Tales and Three Shrovetide Plays.* Translated by William Leighton. London: David Nutt, 1910.

———. *Nine Carnival Plays.* Translated by Randall W. Listerman. Ottawa: Dovehouse Editions, 1990.

Saint-Amant, Antoine Gérard de. *Oeuvres poétiques.* Edited by Léon Vérane. Paris: Garnier, 1930.

Saint-Évremond, Charles Marguetel de Saint Denis, Seigneur de. *Letters of Saint Evremond.* Edited by John Hayward. London: Routledge, 1930.

Satyres chrétiennes de la cuisine papale. 1560. Reprint, Geneva, 1857.

Scappi, Bartolomeo. *Opera.* Venice, 1570.

Scarron, Paul. *Poésies diverses,* edited by Maurice Cauchie. 2 vols. Paris: Marcel Didier, 1960–61.

Seneca. *Ad Lucilium epistulae morales.* Bilingual ed. Edited and translated by Richard Gummere. 3 vols. London: Heinemann, 1925.

Shakespeare, William. *The Norton Shakespeare.* Edited by Stephen Greenblatt. New York: Norton, 1996.

———. *Twelfth Night; or, What You Will.* New Variorum Edition. Vol. 13. Edited by Horace Howard Furness. Philadelphia: Lippincott, 1901.

Simon, Andre L. *The Star Chamber Dinner Accounts.* London: Wine and Food Society, 1959.

Smith, Eliza. *The Compleat Housewife.* 16th ed. 1758. Facsimile reprint. London: Studio Editions, 1994.

Smith, John. *Complete Works.* Edited by Philip L. Barbour. 3 vols. Chapel Hill: University of North Carolina Press, 1986.

Spenser, Edmund. *The Faerie Queene.* Edited by A. C. Hamilton. London: Longman, 1977.

Spurling, Hilary, ed. *Elinor Fettiplace's Receipt Book: Elizabethan Country House Cooking.* New York: Viking, 1986.

Staden, Hans. *The Captivity of Hans Stade of Hesse, in A.D. 1547–1555, among the Wild Tribes of Eastern Brazil.* Translated by Albert Tootal. Edited by Richard F. Burton. London: Hakluyt Society, 1874.

Straparola, Giovanni Francesco. *The Facetious Nights of Straparola.* 4 vols. Translated by W. G. Waters. London: Society of Bibliophiles, n.d.

Stubbes, Phillip. *The Anatomie of Abuses.* London, 1583. Reprint, New York: Garland, 1973.

Tacitus, Cornelius. *The Agricola and Germania.* Translated by H. Mattingly. Revised by S. A. Handford. Harmondsworth, UK: Penguin, 1970.

Taillevent (fl. 1392: Guillaume Tirel). *Le viandier.* Edited by Jérôme Pichon and Georges Vicaire. 2 vols. Paris, 1892.

———. *The Viandier of Taillevent: An Edition of All Extant Manuscripts.* Edited by Terence Scully. Ottawa: University of Ottawa Press, 1988.

Tasso, Torquato. *Aminta: A Pastoral Play.* Translated by Charles Jernigan and Irene Marchegiani Jones. New York: Italica Press, 2000.

———. *Creation of the World.* Translated by Joseph Tusiani. Binghamton, NY: Center for Medieval and Early Renaissance Studies, 1982.

Teresa of Ávila. *The Life of Saint Teresa of Ávila by Herself.* Translated by J. M. Cohen. Harmondsworth, UK: Penguin, 1957.

Thevet, André. *Les singularités de la France Antarctique: Le Brésil des cannibales au XVIᵉ siècle.* Edited by Frank Lestringant. Paris: Maspero, 1983.

Thorndike, Lynn. "Three Tracts on Food in Basel Manuscripts." *Bulletin of the History of Medicine* 8 (1940): 355–56.

Tryon, Thomas. *The Way to Health and Long Life; or, A Discourse of Temperance.* London, 1726.

———. *Wisdom's Dictates; or, Aphorisms and Rules, Physical, Moral, and Divine; for Preserving the Health of the Body, and the Peace of the Mind.* London, 1691.

Väänänen, Veiko, ed. "Le 'fabliau de Cocagne.'" *Bulletin de la Société Néophilogique de Helsinki* (1947): 3–36.

Venner, Tobias. *Via recta et viam longam.* London, 1620.

Vicary, Thomas. *The Anatomie of the Bodie of Man.* 1548. Edited by Frederick Furnivall. Oxford: Early English Text Society, 1888.

The Voyage of Saint Brendan: Journey to the Promised Land. Translated by John J. O'Meara. Atlantic Highlands, NJ: Humanities Press, 1976.

Warner, Richard, ed. *Antiquitates culinariae.* London, 1791.

West, Richard. *The Schoole of Vertue, the Second Part; or, The Young Schollers Paradice.* London, 1619.

Williams, Roger. *Key into the Language of America.* 1643. Facsimile reprint. Menston, UK: Scolar Press, 1971.

Willich, A. F. M. *Lectures on Diet and Regiment.* 2 vols. London, 1798.

———. *Lectures on Diet and Regiment.* 2 vols. Boston, 1800.

Winstanley, Gerrard. *The Works of Gerrard Winstanley.* Edited by George Sabine. Reprint, New York: Russell & Russell, 1965.

W.M., *The Compleat Cook: Expertly Prescribing the Most Ready Wayes, Whether, Italian, Spanish, or French, for Dressing of Flesh, and Fish, Ordering of Sauses, or Making of Pastry.* London, 1655.

Wood, William. *New-England's Prospect.* 2nd ed. 1635. Edited by Alden T. Vaughan. Amherst: University of Massachusetts Press, 1977.

Woolley, Hannah. *The Compleat Servant-Maid; or, The Young Maidens Tutor.* 3rd ed. London, 1683.

———. *The Cook's Guide.* London, 1664.

———. *A Guide to Ladies, Gentlewomen and Maids.* London, 1668.

———. *The Queen-like Closet, or Rich Cabinet: Stored with all manner of Rare Receipts for Preserving, Candying, and Cookery. Very pleasant and beneficial to all Ingenious Persons of the Female Sex. To which is added a Supplement presented to all Ingenious Ladies and Gentlewomen.* 4th ed. London, 1681.

SECONDARY TEXTS

Abler, Thomas S. "Iroquois Cannibalism: Fact Not Fiction." *Ethnohistory* 27, no. 4 (1980): 309–16.

Acanfora, Elisa, and Marcello Fantoni. "The Courtly Life." In *Italian Renaissance Courts,* edited by Sergio Bertelli, Franco Cardini, and Elivira Garbero Zorzi, 189–228. London: Sidgwick & Jackson, 1986.

Ackermann, Elfried Marie. *"Das Schlaraffenland" in German Literature and Folksong.* Ph.D. diss., University of Chicago, 1944.

Adamson, Melitta Weiss. *Medieval Dietetics: Food and Drink in Regimen Sanitatis Literature.* Frankfurt am Main: Peter Lang, 1995.

———, ed. *Regional Cuisines of Medieval Europe: A Book of Essays.* New York: Routledge, 2002.

Adelman, Janet. *Suffocating Mothers: Fantasies of Maternal Origin in Shakespeare's Plays, Hamlet to the Tempest.* New York: Routledge, 1992.

Albala, Ken. *Eating Right in the Renaissance.* Berkeley: University of California Press, 2001.

———. *Food in Early Modern Europe.* Westport, CT: Greenwood Press, 2003.

Appelbaum, Robert. "Aguecheek's Beef." *Textual Practice* 14, no. 2 (2000): 327–41.

———. "Belch's Hiccup: Disturbances of the Appetite in *Twelfth Night.*" *Textus* 13 (2000): 231–62.

———. "Eve's and Adam's Apple: Horticulture, Taste, and the Flesh of the Forbidden Fruit in *Paradise Lost.*" *Milton Quarterly* 36, no. 4 (2002): 221–39.

———. "Hunger in Early Virginia: Indians and English Facing Off Over Excess, Want, and Need." In *Envisioning an English Empire: Jamestown and the Making of the North Atlantic World,* edited by Robert Appelbaum and John Wood Sweet, 195–216. Philadelphia: University of Pennsylvania Press, 2005.

———. "Rhetoric and Epistemology in Early Printed Recipe Collections." *Journal of Early Modern Cultural Studies* 3, no. 2 (2003): 1–35.

Appelbaum, Robert, and John Wood Sweet, eds. *Envisioning an English Empire: Jamestown and the Making of the North Atlantic World.* Philadelphia: University of Pennsylvania Press, 2005.

Appleby, Andrew. *Famine in Tudor and Stuart England.* Stanford, CA: Stanford University Press, 1978.

Arens, William. *The Man-Eating Myth: Anthropology and Anthropophagy.* New York: Oxford University Press, 1979.

Arn, Mary-Jo, ed. *Medieval Food and Drink.* Binghamton, NY: Center for Medieval and Early Renaissance Studies, 1995.

Axtell, James. *The European and the Indian: Essays in the Ethnohistory of Colonial North America.* New York: Oxford University Press, 1981.

Bakhtin, Mikhail. *Rabelais and His World.* Translated by Hélène Iswolsky. Cambridge, MA: MIT Press, 1968.

Barker, Francis. *The Tremulous Private Body: Essays on Subjection.* London: Methuen, 1984.

Barthes, Roland. "Lecture de Brillat-Savarin." In *Oeuvres complètes,* edited by Éric Marty, 808–26. Paris: Éditions de Seuil, 2002.

———. "Toward a Psychosociology of Contemporary Food Consumption." In *Food and Drink in History,* edited by R. Foster and O. Ranum, 166–73. Baltimore: Johns Hopkins University Press, 1979.

Beardsworth, Alan, and Teresa Keil. *Sociology on the Menu: An Invitation to the Study of Food and Society.* London: Routledge, 1997.

Beckles, Hilary. *A History of Barbados: From Amerindian Settlement to Nation-State.* Cambridge: Cambridge University Press, 1990.

Bell, David, and Gill Valentine. *Consuming Geographies: Where Are Where We Eat.* London: Routledge, 1997.

Bell, Rudolph. *Holy Anorexia.* Chicago: University of Chicago Press, 1985.

Bloch, Ernst. *The Principle of Hope.* Translated by Neville Plaice, Stephen Plaice, and Paul Knight. 3 vols. Cambridge, MA: MIT Press, 1986.

Blond, Georges, and Germaine Blond. *Histoire pittoresque de notre alimentation*. 2 vols. Ottawa: Fayard, 1961.

Boas, George. *Primitivism and Related Ideas in the Middle Ages*. Baltimore: Johns Hopkins, University Press, 1948.

Boehrer, Bruce Thomas. *The Fury in Men's Gullets: Ben Jonson and the Digestive Canal*. Philadelphia: University of Pennsylvania Press, 1997.

Bourdieu, Pierre. *Distinction: A Social Critique of the Judgement of Taste*. Translated by Richard Nice. Cambridge, MA: Harvard University Press, 1984.

——. *Outline of a Theory of Practice*. Translated by Richard Nice. Cambridge: Cambridge University Press, 1977.

Braudel, Fernand. *Civilisation and Capitalism*. Vol. 1, *The Structures of Everyday Life*. Translated by Sian Reynolds. New York: Harper & Row, 1979.

Brears, Peter. "Decoration of the Tudor and Stuart Table." In *"The Appetite and the Eye": Visual Aspects of Food and Its Presentation within Their Historic Context*, edited by C. Anne Wilson, 56–97. Edinburgh: Edinburgh University Press, 1991.

Brewer, John, and Roy Porter, eds. *Consumption and the World of Goods*. London: Routledge, 1993.

Bristol, Michael D. *Carnival and Theater: Plebeian Culture and the Structure of Authority in Renaissance England*. New York: Methuen, 1985.

Bryson, Anna. *From Courtesy to Civility: Changing Codes of Conduct in Early Modern England*. Oxford: Clarendon Press, 1998.

Bynum, Caroline W. *Holy Feast and Holy Fast: The Religious Significance of Food to Medieval Women*. Berkeley: University of California Press, 1987.

Camporesi, Piero. *Bread of Dreams: Food and Fantasy in Early Modern Europe*. Translated by David Gentilcore. Cambridge: Polity Press, 1989.

——. *Exotic Brew: The Art of Living in the Age of Enlightenment*. Translated by Christopher Woodall. Cambridge: Polity Press, 1994.

——. *The Juice of Life: The Symbolic and Magic Significance of Blood*. Translated by Robert R. Barr. New York: Continuum, 1995.

——. *The Land of Hunger*. Translated by Tania Croft-Murray and Claire Foley. Cambridge: Polity Press, 1996.

——. *The Magic Harvest: Food, Folklore, and Society*. Trans. Joan Krakover Hall. Cambridge: Polity Press, 1989.

Capatti, Alberto, and Massimo Montanari. *Italian Cuisine: A Cultural History*. Translated by Aine O'Healy. New York: Columbia University Press, 2003.

Caton, Mary Ann, ed. *Fooles and Fricassees: Food in Shakespeare's England*. Washington, DC: Folger Shakespeare Library, 1999.

Cocchiara, G. *Il paese di Cuccagna e altri studi di folklore*. Turin: Einaudi, 1956.

Cook, Harold J. *The Decline of the Old Medical Regime in Stuart London*. Ithaca, NY: Cornell University Press, 1986.

——. *Trials of an Ordinary Doctor: Joannes Groenevelt in Seventeenth-Century London*. Baltimore: Johns Hopkins University Press, 1994.

Copeman, W. S. C. *Doctors and Diseases in Tudor Times*. London: Dawson, 1960.

Cotter, Colleen. "Claiming a Piece of the Pie: How the Language of Recipes Defines Communities." In *Recipes for Reading: Community Cookbooks, Stories, Histories,* edited by Anne L. Bower, 51–72. Amherst: University of Massachusetts Press, 1997.

Cronon, William. *Changes in the Land: Indians, Colonists, and the Ecology of New England.* New York: Hill and Wang, 1983.

Curtin, Deane, and L. Hedke, eds. *Cooking, Eating, Thinking: Transformative Philosophies of Food.* Indianapolis: Indiana University Press, 1992.

Darnton, Robert. *The Great Cat Massacre and Other Episodes in French Cultural History.* New York: Vintage, 1985.

Delumeau, Jean. *History of Paradise: The Garden of Eden in Myth and Tradition.* Translated by Matthew O'Connell. New York: Continuum, 1995.

Derrida, Jacques. *Writing and Difference.* Translated by Alan Bass. Chicago: University of Chicago Press, 1978.

Déry, Carol A. "The Art of Apicius." In *Cooks and Other People: Proceedings of the Oxford Symposium on Food and Cookery 1995,* edited by Harlan Walker, 111–17. Devon, UK: Prospect Books, 1996.

Douglas, Mary. "Deciphering a Meal." In *Implicit Meanings,* edited by Mary Douglas, 249–75. London: Routledge, 1977.

———. "Structures of Gastronomy." In *The Future and the Past: Annual Report of the Russell Sage Foundation,* 55–81. New York: Russell Sage Foundation.

Dunn, Richard S. *Sugar and Slaves: The Rise of the Planter Class in the English West Indies, 1624–1713.* New York: Norton, 1973.

Dyer, Christopher. "Did the Peasants Really Starve in Medieval England?" In *Food and Eating in Medieval Europe,* edited by Martha Carlin and Joel T. Rosenthal, 53–72. London: Hambledon Press, 1998.

Eisenstein, Elizabeth. *The Printing Press as an Agent of Change: Communications and Cultural Transformations in Early Modern Europe.* Cambridge: Cambridge University Press, 1979.

Elias, Norbert. *The Civilizing Process.* Translated by Edmund Jephcott. Blackwell: Oxford, 1994.

Evans, J. M. *"Paradise Lost" and the Genesis Tradition.* Oxford: Clarendon Press, 1968.

Fernandez-Armesto, Felipe. *Food: A History.* London: Macmillan, 1999.

Flandrin, Jean-Louis. "De la diététique à la gastronomie." In *L'histoire de l'alimentation,* edited by Jean-Louis Flandrin and Massimo Montanari, 683–703. Paris: Fayard, 1996.

———. "Distinction through Taste." In *Passions of the Renaissance.* Vol. 3 of *A History of Private Life.* 6 vols., edited by Roger Chartier, translated by Arthur Goldhammer, 265–309. Cambridge, MA: Belknap Press, 1989.

———. "Le Gout et la necessité: Reflexions sur l'usage des graisses dans les cusines de l'Europe occidentale. XIVe–XVIIIe siècles." *Annales ESC* 38 (1983): 369–401.

——— "Les légumes dans les livres de cuisine français, du XIVe au XVIIIe siècle." In *Le monde végétale. XIIe–XVIIe siècles: Savoirs et usages sociaux,* edited by Allen J. Grieco, Odile Redon, and Lucia Tongiogi Tomasi, 71–88. Saint-Denis: Presses Universitaires de Vincennes, 1993.

Flandrin, Jean-Louis, Philip Hyman, and Mary Hyman, eds. *Le cuisinier françois*, by Pierre La Varenne. Paris: Montalba, 1983.

Flandrin, Jean-Louis, and Massimo Montanari, eds. *Food: A Culinary History.* Translated by Albert Sonnenfield. New York: Columbia University Press, 1999.

————, eds. *L'histoire de l'alimentation.* Paris: Fayard, 1996.

Floyd-Wilson, Mary. *English Ethnicity and Race in Early Modern Drama.* Cambridge: Cambridge University Press, 2003.

Forster, Elburg, and Robert Forster, eds. *European Diet from Preindustrial to Modern Times.* New York: Harper & Row, 1975.

Forster, Robert, and Orest Ranum, eds. *Food and Drink in History: Selections from the Annales Économies, Sociétés, Civilisations.* Vol. 5. Baltimore: Johns Hopkins University Press, 1979.

Forsyth, Donald W. "Three Cheers for Hans Staden: The Case for Brazilian Cannibalism." *Ethnohistory* 32, no. 1 (1985): 17–36.

Foucault, Michel. *The Archaeology of Knowledge and the Discourse on Language.* Translated by A. M. Sheridan Smith. New York: Pantheon, 1972.

————. *Technologies of the Self; A Seminar with Michel Foucault.* Edited by Luther H. Martin, Huck Gutman, and Patrick H. Hutton. Amherst: University of Massachusetts Press, 1988.

————. *The Use of Pleasure.* Vol. 2 of *The History of Sexuality.* Translated by Robert Hurley. New York: Pantheon, 1985.

Franklin, Alfred. *La vie privée d'autrefois; arts et métiers, modes, moeurs, usages des parisiens du XIIᵉ au XVIIIᵉ siècle d'après des documents originaux ou inédits.* 23 vols. Paris: E. Plon-Nourrit, 1887–1901.

French, Roger, and Andrew Wear, eds. *The Medical Revolution of the Seventeenth Century.* Cambridge: Cambridge University Press, 1989.

Gallagher, Catherine, and Stephen Greenblatt, "The Potato in the Materialist Imagination." In *Practicing New Historicism,* 110–35. Chicago: University of Chicago Press, 2000.

Genette, Gérard. *Paratexts: Thresholds of Interpretation.* Translated by Jane E. Lewin. Cambridge: Cambridge University Press, 1997.

Girard, Alain. "Du manuscript à l'imprimé: Le livre de cuisine en Europe aux 15 et 16 siècles." In *Pratiques et discours alimentaires à la Renaissance,* edited by Jean-Claude Margolin and Robert Sauzet. Paris: G.-P. Maissonneuve et Larose, 1982.

————. "Le triomphe de *La Cuisiniere bourgeoise.* Livres culinaires, cuisine et societé en France aux XVIIᵉ et XVIIᵉ siècles." *Revue d'Histoire Moderne et Contemporain* 24 (1977): 497–523.

Giraud, Yves. "Le comique engagé des *Satyres chétiennes de la cuisine papale.*" *Studi di Letteratura Francese* 10 (1983): 52–72.

Gleach, Frederic W. *Powhatan's World and Colonial Virginia: A Conflict of Cultures.* Lincoln: University of Nebraska Press, 1997.

Goldman, Lawrence. "From Pot to Polemic: Uses and Abuses of Cannibalism." In *The Anthropology of Cannibalism,* edited by Lawrence Goldman, 1–27. Westport, CT: Bergin and Garvey, 1999.

Goode, Judith, Janet Theophano, and Karen Curtis. "A Framework for the Analysis of Continuity and Change in Shared Sociocultural Rules for Food Use: The Italian-American Pattern." In *Ethnic and Regional Foodways in the United States: The Performance of Group Identity,* edited by Judith Brown, Linda Keller, and Kay Mussell, 66–88. Knoxville: University of Tennessee Press, 1984.

Greenblatt, Stephen. "Fiction and Friction." In *Shakespearean Negotiations: The Circulation of Social Energy in Renaissance England.* Berkeley: University of California Press, 1988.

———. Foreword to *Mapping the Renaissance World: The Geographical Imagination in the Age of Discovery,* by Frank Lestringant. Translated by David Fausett. Berkeley: University of California Press, 1994.

———. *Marvelous Possessions: The Wonder of the New World.* Chicago: University of Chicago Press, 1991.

———. "The Mousetrap." In *Practicing New Historicism,* by Catherine Gallagher and Stephen Greenblatt, 136–62. Chicago: University of Chicago Press, 2000.

Guerrini, Anita. *Obesity and Depression in the Enlightenment: The Life and Times of George Cheyne.* Norman: University of Oklahoma Press, 2000.

Gulden, Ann Torday. "Milton's Eve and Wisdom: The 'Dinner Party' Scene *in Paradise Lost.*" *Milton Quarterly* 32, no. 4 (1998): 137–43.

Gutierrez, Nancy A. *'Shall She Famish Then?' Female Food Refusal in Early Modern England.* Aldershot, UK: Ashgate, 2003.

Harris, Marvin. *Good to Eat: Riddles of Food and Culture.* New York: Simon & Schuster, 1985.

Heal, Felicity. *Hospitality in Early Modern England.* Oxford: Oxford University Press, 1990.

Henisch, Bridget Ann. *Fast and Feast: Food in Medieval Society.* University Park: Pennsylvania State University Press, 1976.

Hess, John L., and Karen Hess. *The Taste of America.* 2nd ed. Urbana: University of Illinois Press, 2000.

Hobby, Elaine. "A Woman's Best Setting Out Is Silence: The Writings of Hannah Wolley." In *Culture and Society in the Stuart Restoration,* edited by Gerald Maclean, 179–200. Cambridge: Cambridge University Press, 1995.

Hoeniger, F. David. *Medicine and Shakespeare in the English Renaissance.* Newark: University of Delaware Press, 1992.

Hope, Annette. *Londoners' Larder: English Cuisine from Chaucer to the Present.* Edinburgh: Mainstream, 1990.

Horn, James. *Adapting to a New World: English Society in the Seventeenth-Century Chesapeake.* Chapel Hill: University of North Carolina Press, 1994.

Hulme, Peter. *Colonial Encounters: Europe and the Native Caribbean, 1492–1797.* London: Routledge, 1992.

Huon, Antoinette. "Le roy Sainct Panigon dans l'imagerie populaire du XVIᵉ siècle." In *François Rabelais: Ouvrage publiée pour le quatrième centenaire de sa mort.* Geneva, 1953.

Hutson, Lorna. *Thomas Nashe in Context.* Oxford: Clarendon Press, 1989.

Hyman, Philip, and Mary Hyman. "Imprimer la cuisine: Les livres de cuisine en France entre le XVᵉ et le XIXᵉ siècle." In *L'histoire de l'alimentation,* edited by Jean-Louis Flandrin and Massimo Montanari. Paris: Fayard, 1996.

Jeanneret, Michel. *A Feast of Words: Banquets and Table Talk in the Renaissance.* Translated by Jeremy Whiteley and Emma Hughes. Chicago: University of Chicago Press, 1987.

Johns, Adrian. *The Nature of the Book: Printing and Knowledge in the Making.* Chicago: University of Chicago Press, 1998.

Johnson, Leonard W. "La salade tourangelle de Pierre de Ronsard." In *Littérature et Gastronomie: Huit études,* edited by Ronald W. Tobin, 149–74. Paris: Biblio 17, 1985.

Kerrigan, William. *The Sacred Complex: On the Psychogenesis of "Paradise Lost."* Cambridge, MA: Harvard University Press, 1983.

Kinser, Samuel. *Rabelais's Carnival: Text, Context, Metatext.* Berkeley: University of California Press, 1990.

Klibansky, Raymond, Erwin Panofsky, and Fritz Saxl. *Saturn and Melancholy: Studies in the History of Natural Science.* New York: Basic Books, 1964.

Krailsheimer, Alban. "The Andouilles of the *Quatre Livre.*" In *François Rabelais: Ouvrage publieé pour le quatrième centenaire de sa mort.* Geneva, 1953.

Kurlansky, Mark. *Cod: A Biography of the Fish that Changed the World.* New York: Walker, 1997.

——. *Salt: A World History.* Harmondsworth, UK: Penguin, 2002.

Lambert, Carole, ed. *Du manuscrit à la table: Essais sur la cuisine au Moyen Age.* Montréal: Les Presses de l'Université de Montreal, 1992.

Laqueur, Thomas. *Making Sex: Body and Gender from the Greeks to Freud.* Cambridge, MA: Harvard University Press, 1990.

Laurioux, Bruno. "Cuisinier à l'antique: Apicius au Moyen Age." *Medievales* 26 (1994): 28–35.

——. *Les livres de cuisine médiévaux.* Turnhout, Belgium: Brepols, 1997.

——. *La règne de Taillevent: Livres et pratiques culinaries à fin du Moyen Age.* Paris: Publications de la Sorbonne, 1997.

Lestringant, Frank. "Calvinistes et cannibales: Les écrits protestants sure le Brésil français (1555–1560)." *Bulletins de la Société de l'Histoire du Protestantisme Français,* nos. 1–2 (1980): 9–26, 167–92.

——. *Cannibals: The Discovery and Representation of the Cannibal from Columbus to Jules Verne.* Translated by Rosemary Morris. Berkeley: University of California Press, 1997.

Levenstein, Harvey. *Revolution at the Table: The Transformation of the American Diet.* New York: Oxford University Press, 1988.

Lévi-Strauss, Claude. "The Culinary Triangle." *Partisan Review* 33 (1966): 586–95.

——. *Tristes Tropiques.* Translated by John Weightman and Doreen Weightman. New York: Atheneum, 1984.

Lovejoy, Arthur O., and George Boas. *Primitivism and Related Ideas in Antiquity.* Baltimore: Johns Hopkins University Press, 1935.

Marin, Louis. *Food for Thought.* Translated by Mette Hjort. Baltimore: Johns Hopkins University Press, 1989.

——. *Utopics: The Semiological Play of Textual Space.* Translated by Robert A. Vollrath. Atlantic Highlands, NJ: Humanities Press, 1984.

McGuire, Mary Ann C. "The Cavalier Country-House Poem: Mutations on a Jonsonian Tradition." *Studies in English Literature* 19, no. 1 (1979): 93–109.

Mead, Chris. *Banquets Set Forth: Banqueting in English Renaissance Drama.* Manchester: Manchester University Press, 2001.

Mennell, Stephen. *All Manners of Food: Eating and Taste in England and France from the Middle Ages to the Present.* 2nd ed. Urbana: University of Illinois Press, 2000.

Mennell, Stephen, Anne Murcott, and Anneke H. van Otterloo. *The Sociology of Food: Eating, Diet, and Culture.* London: Sage, 1992.

Milham, Mary Ellen. "Martino and His *De re coquinaria.*" In *Medieval Food and Drink,* 62–66. Binghamton, NY: Center for Medieval and Renaissance Studies, 1995.

Miller, William Ian. "Gluttony." *Representations* 60 (1997): 92–112.

Mintz, Sidney W. "The Changing Roles of Food in the Study of Consumption." In *Consumption and the World of Goods,* edited by John Brewer and Roy Porter, 261–73. London: Routledge, 1993.

———. *Sweetness and Power: The Place of Sugar in Modern History.* New York: Viking, 1985.

Moriarty, Michael. *Taste and Ideology in Seventeenth-Century France.* Cambridge: Cambridge University Press, 1988.

Morton, Timothy. "Old Spice: William King, Culinary Antiquarianism, and National Boundaries." *Eighteenth-Century Life* 23, no. 2 (1999): 97–101.

Motohashi, Ted. "The Discourse of Cannibalism in Early Modern Travel Writing." In *Travel Writing and Empire: Postcolonial Theory in Transit,* edited by Steve Clark, 83–99. London: Zed Books, 1999.

Overing, Joanna. "Images of Cannibalisms, Death, and Domination in a 'Non-Violent' Society." In *The Anthropology of Violence,* edited by David Riches, 86–102. Oxford: Basil Blackwell, 1986.

Pagels, Elaine H. *Adam, Eve, and the Serpent.* New York: Random House, 1988.

Paster, Gail Kern. *The Body Embarrassed: Drama and the Disciplines of Shame in Early Modern England.* Ithaca, NY: Cornell University Press, 1993.

Peterson, T. Sarah. *Acquired Taste: The French Origins of Modern Cooking.* Ithaca, NY: Cornell University Press, 1994.

Peyrebonne, Nathalie. "Le manger et le boire dans le *Libro de la Vida* de Sainte Thérèse d'Ávila." *Annali Istituto Universitario Orientale, Napoli, Sezione Romanza* 41, no. 2 (1999): 581–87.

Phillips, F. Taverner. *A History of the Worshipful Company of Cooks, London.* London, 1932.

Pitte, Jean-Robert. *French Gastronomy: The History and Geography of a Passion.* Translated by Jody Gladding. New York: Columbia University Press, 2002.

Plard, Henri. "La critique théologique et morale des voyages de découverte dans *Das Narren Schyff* de Sebastian Brant, 1494." In *La satire humaniste,* edited by Rudolf de Smet, 223–38. Brussels: Peeters Press, 1994.

Pleij, Herman. *Dreaming of Cockaigne: Medieval Fantasies of the Perfect Life.* Translated by Diane Webb. New York: Columbia University Press, 1997.

Porter, Roy. *Flesh in the Age of Reason.* London: Allen Lane, 2003.

———. *The Greatest Benefit to Mankind: A Medical History of Humanity.* New York: Norton, 1997.

Pullar, Philippa. *Consuming Passions: A History of English Food and Appetite.* London: Hamish Hamilton, 1970.

Rappoport, Leon. *How We Eat: Appetite, Culture, and the Psychology of Food.* Toronto: ECW, 2003.

Rebora, Giovanni. *Culture of the Fork: A Brief History of Food in Europe.* Translated by Albert Sonnenfeld. New York: Columbia University Press, 2001.

Revel, Jacques. "The Uses of Civility." In *Passions of the Renaissance.* Vol. 3 of *A History of Private Life.* 6 vols., edited by Roger Chartier, translated by Arthur Goldhammer, 167–205. Cambridge, MA: Belknap Press, 1989..

Rhodes, Dennis. "The Italian Banquet, 1598, and Its Origins." *Italian Studies* 27 (1972): 60–63.

Riley, Gillian. "Platina, Martino, and Their Circle." In *Cooks and Other People,* edited by Harlan Walker. Devon, UK: Prospect Books, 1995.

Rudd, Niall. *The Satires of Horace.* Cambridge: Cambridge University Press, 1966.

Sanday, Peggy Reeves. *Divine Hunger: Cannibalism as a Cultural System.* Cambridge: Cambridge University Press, 1986.

Sandiford, Keith. *The Cultural Politics of Sugar: Caribbean Slavery and Narratives of Colonialism.* Cambridge: Cambridge University Press, 1990.

Schama, Simon. *The Embarrassment of Riches: An Interpretation of Dutch Culture in the Golden Age.* New York: Knopf, 1987.

Schoenfeldt, Michael C. *Bodies and Selves in Early Modern England.* Cambridge: Cambridge University Press, 1999.

Schwartz, Hillel. *Never Satisfied: A Cultural History of Diets, Fantasies, and Fat.* New York: Free Press, 1986.

Scodel, Joshua. *Excess and the Mean in Early Modern English Literature.* Princeton, NJ: Princeton University Press, 2002.

Screech, M. A. "Eleven-Month Pregnancies." *Etudes Rabelaisiennes* (1969): 89–106.

Scully, Terence. *The Art of Cookery in the Middle Ages.* Woodbridge, UK: Boydell Press, 1995.

Silver, Timothy. *A New Face on the Countryside: Indians, Colonists, and Slaves in South Atlantic Forests, 1500–1800.* Cambridge: Cambridge University Press, 1990.

Sim, Alison. *Food and Feast in Tudor England.* New York: St. Martin's, 1997.

Simon, Andre L. *The Star Chamber Dinner Accounts.* London: Wine and Food Society, 1959.

Simoons, Frederick J. *Eat Not This Flesh: Food Avoidances from Prehistory to the Present.* 2nd ed. Madison: University of Wisconsin Press, 1994.

Siraisi, Nancy G. *Medieval and Early Renaissance Medicine.* Chicago: University of Chicago Press, 1990.

Slack, Paul. "Mirrors of Health and Treasures of Poor Men: The Uses of the Vernacular Medical Literature of Tudor England." In *Health, Medicine and Morality in the Sixteenth Century,* edited by Charles Webster, 237–73. Cambridge: Cambridge University Press, 1979.

——— . *Poverty and Policy in Tudor and Stuart England.* London: Longman, 1988.

Smith, Nigel. "Enthusiasm and Enlightenment: Of Food, Filth, and Slavery." In *The Coun-*

try and the City Revisited 1550–1850, edited by Gerald Maclean, Donna Landry, and Joseph P. Ward, 106–18. Cambridge: Cambridge University Press, 1999.

Smylie, Mike. *Herring: A History of the Silver Darlings.* Stroud, UK: Tempus, 2004.

Spang, Rebecca L. *The Invention of the Restaurant: Paris and Modern Gastronomic Culture.* Cambridge, MA: Harvard University Press, 2000.

Spencer, Colin. *Heretic's Feast: A History of Vegetarianism.* Hanover, NH: University Press of New England, 1995.

Spurgeon, Carolyn. *Shakespeare's Imagery and What It Tells Us.* Cambridge: Cambridge University Press, 1935.

Stallybrass, Peter, and Allon White. *The Politics and Poetics of Transgression.* Ithaca, NY: Cornell University Press, 1986.

Strong, Roy. *Feast: A History of Grand Eating.* London: Jonathan Cape, 2002.

Sweet, John Wood. Introduction to *Envisioning an English Empire: Jamestown and the Making of the North Atlantic World,* edited by Robert Appelbaum and John Wood Sweet, 1–21. Philadelphia: University of Pennsylvania Press, 2005.

Temkin, Owsei. *Galenism: Rise and Decline of a Medical Philosophy.* Ithaca, NY: Cornell University Press, 1973.

Thirsk, Joan. "Food in Shakespeare's England." In *Fooles and Fricassees: Food in Shakespeare's England,* edited by Mary Ann Caton, 13–26. Washington, DC: Folger Shakespeare Library, 1999.

———. "The Preparation of Food in the Kitchen, in Europe North of the Alps, 1500–1700." In *Alimentazione e nutrizione secc. XII–XVII,* edited by Somonetta Cavaciocchi, 423–39. Florence: Le Monnier, 1997.

Thomas, Keith. *Man and the Natural World: A History of the Modern Sensibility.* New York: Pantheon, 1983.

Tilley, Morris Palmer. *A Dictionary of the Proverbs of England in the Sixteenth and Seventeenth Centuries.* Ann Arbor: University of Michigan Press, 1951.

Tobin, Ronald W. *"Tarte à la crème": Comedy and Gastronomy in Molière's Theater.* Columbus: Ohio State University Press, 1990.

———, ed. *Littérature et gastronomie: Huit études.* Paris: Biblio 17, 1985.

Todorov, Tzvetan. *The Conquest of America: The Question of the Other.* Translated by Richard Howard. New York: Harper & Row, 1984.

Toussaint-Samat, Maguelonne. *History of Food.* Translated by Anthea Bell. Cambridge: Blackwell, 1987.

Trubek, Amy B. *Haute Cuisine: How the French Invented the Culinary Professions.* Philadelphia: University of Pennsylvania Press, 2000.

Turner, Henry S. "Nashe's Red Herring: Epistemologies of the Commodity in *Lenten Stuffe.* 1599." ELH 68 (2001): 529–61.

Väänänen, Veiko. "Le 'fabliau de Cocagne.'" *Bulletin de la Société Néophilologique de Helsinki* (1947): 3–36.

Vandereycken, Walter, and Ron van Deth. *From Fasting Saints to Anorexic Girls: The History of Self-Starvation.* New York: New York University Press, 1994.

Vasvari, Louise O. "The Geography of Escape and Topsy-Turvy Literary Genres." In *Discovering New Worlds: Essays on Medieval Exploration and Imagination,* edited by Scott D. Westrem, 178–92. New York: Garland, 1991.

Vehling, Joseph Dommers. *Platina and the Rebirth of Man.* Chicago: Walter Hill, 1941.

Walker, Harlan, ed. *Cooks and Other People: Proceedings of the Oxford Symposium on Food and Cookery 1995.* Devon, UK: Prospect Books, 1996.

Wall, Wendy. *Staging Domesticity: Household Work and English Identity in Early Modern Drama.* Cambridge: Cambridge University Press, 2002.

Walter, John. "The Social Economy of Dearth in Early Modern England." In *Famine, Disease, and the Social Order,* edited by John Walter and Roger Schofield, 75–128. Cambridge: Cambridge University Press, 1989.

Webster, Charles, ed. *Health, Medicine, and Mortality in the Sixteenth Century.* Cambridge: Cambridge University Press, 1979.

Weiss, Susan. "Medieval and Renaissance Weddings and Other Feasts." In *Food and Eating in Medieval Europe,* edited by Martha Carlin and Joel T. Rosenthal. London: Hambledon Press, 1998.

Whatley, Janet. "Food and the Limits of Civility: The Testimony of Jean de Léry." *Sixteenth Century Journal* 15, no. 4 (1984): 387–400.

Wheaton, Barbara Ketchum. *Savoring the Past: The French Kitchen and Table from 1300 to 1789.* Philadelphia: University of Pennsylvania Press, 1983.

Wilson, C. Anne. *"The Appetite and the Eye": Visual Aspects of Food and Its Presentation within Their Historic Context.* Edinburgh: Edinburgh University Press, 1991.

———. *Food and Drink in Britain: From the Stone Age to Recent Times.* Harmondsworth, UK: Penguin, 1973.

———. "From Medieval Great Hall to Country-house Dining-room: The Furniture and Setting of the Social Meal." In *"The Appetite and the Eye,"* 28–55.

———. "Ideal Meals and Their Menus from the Middle Ages to the Georgian Era." In *"The Appetite and the Eye,"* 98–122.

———. "Ritual, Form, and Color in the Medieval Food Tradition." In *"The Appetite and the Eye,"* 5–27.

Wood, Roy C. *The Sociology of the Meal.* Edinburgh: Edinburgh University Press, 1995.

Index

Émile (Rousseau), 289–90, 302–3
Encyclopédie, 68, 158, 318n40
enemas, 55
England, 41; cattle of, 5–6; culinary iden-
    tity of, 110; English stomachs, 4–5,
    7; food practices of, 4, 7, 12–13, 95,
    99–109, 214–15; press of, 86
English Hermit, The (Crab), 185
English Hus-wife, The (Markham), 64, 107
Enlightenment, 293, 299
Epicurus, 40, 54, 169–70; Epicureanism,
    168
Epulario, 6, 74, 76, 80
Erasmus, Desiderius, 119–20, 140, 206;
    The Godly Feast, 119, 129, 169, 174,
    210; *On Good Manners for Boys*,
    222–23
Escole parfaite des officiers de bouche, L', 74,
    94, 297
essen: human eating as opposed to *fressen*,
    animal feeding, 10, 26
Estes, of Ferrara, 96, 296
Eucharist, 218, 255
eucrasia (the good temper of health), 39,
    50, 79, 147, 183
Eve, 32, 164, 173–74, 188–92, 195f, 196–
    200, 243–44
Evelyn, John, 185, 198
excretion: and excrement, 39, 51, 54, 56–
    57, 60, 136–37, 190–91, 221–22, 264;
    in the *Terre Australe connue*, 149. *See
    also* digestion; dyspepsia; intake
    and discharge, theory of
exercise, 37

fabliau, 126–27
Facetious Nights, The (Straparola), 93–94,
    127–28
Faerie Queene, The (Spenser), 230, 240, 243
Fall, the, 164–65, 174, 187, 190–200
"Familière description du très vinoporra-
    timalvoise . . . ," 59, 129–30, 132, 137

fantasy, 118–19, 304
fasting, 170, 174, 175–77, 184, 214, 271. *See
    also* fish days
Feast of Archeloüs, The (Rubens and
    Brueghel), 120–21
feasts and feasting, 120–21, 133–34, 138–
    39, 150, 169, 214; the colonial feast
    in Barbados, 278–79. *See also* ban-
    quets; menus
feminism, 173–74
Ferrara, 96, 296
Fettiplace, Elinor, 310n50
Ficino, Marsilio, xii, xv, 7, 31, 40, 54, 62–
    63, 77–78
Fielding, Henry, 236
fish, 24–25, 27, 143, 179, 204, 212, 257, 266.
    See also fish days; herring; Lent;
    salt fish
fish days, xi, 95, 184, 211
Flandrin, Jean-Louis, 341n33
flatulence, 202–5, 211–24
Fletcher, Phineas, 230
Florence, 70
Flower, Barbara, 114
Foigny, Gabriel de, 148–49
folktales, 127–28
fond, 110–11
"food of the poor," 79–81, 212–14
foodways, 10–11, 247, 258, 272, 279–81
Forbidden Fruit (in Garden of Eden),
    188, 192–200
forks, 15, 207
formal realism, xii
Forme of Curye, 72
Fortunate Isles, 168
Foucault, Michel, xiii, 36, 39, 70, 226
France, xvi; cookbooks of, 110–13; cui-
    sine and eating practices of, xii,
    227–28, 245, 282, 294; press of, 86
Freud, Sigmund, 9, 13, 27, 229–30
Friday (character in *Robinson Crusoe*), 32,
    288, 304–6